War of the Black Heavens

WAR
of the
BLACK
HEAVENS

▲ ▲ ▲

THE BATTLES OF WESTERN
BROADCASTING IN THE COLD WAR

Michael Nelson

WITH A FOREWORD BY LECH WAŁĘSA

SYRACUSE UNIVERSITY PRESS

First Edition 1997

97 98 99 00 01 02   6 5 4 3 2 1

The paper used in this publication meets the minimum requirements of American National Standard for Information Sciences—Permanence of Paper for Printed Library Materials, ANSI Z39.48-1984. ♾

Permission to reprint brief extracts from documents of the BBC Written Archives Centre and the UK Public Record Office is gratefully acknowledged. Crown copyright is reproduced with the permission of the Controller of Her Majesty's Stationery Office. Also, gratitude is extended to The Master, Fellows, and Scholars of Churchill College for permission to examine the papers of Sir Alexander Cadogen and Sir Ian Jacob.

Library of Congress Cataloging-in-Publication Data

Nelson, Michael.
    War of the black heavens : the battles of Western broadcasting in
  the cold war / Michael Nelson. — 1st ed.; with a foreword by Lech Wałęsa
       p.   cm.
    Includes bibliographical references and index.
    ISBN 0-8156-0479-3 (cloth : alk. paper)
    1. Radio in propaganda—History—20th century. 2. International
  broadcasting—History—20th century. 3. Cold War—History.
  4. British Broadcasting Corporation—History. 5. Radio Free Europe—
  America (Organization)—History. I. Title.
  HE8697.N45 1997
  384.54'09171'3—dc21   97-13789

Manufactured in the United States of America

They are jointly known as the "black heavens" . . . historians have still to elucidate fully the vile role played by these Western radio stations

—Karl Nepomnyashchi
Correspondent of Novosti News Agency,
Izvestia, 21 August 1968,
the day of the invasion of Czechoslovakia.

MICHAEL NELSON spent most of his working life in Reuters, the international news organization. He studied modern history at Magdalen College, Oxford, joined Reuters as a trainee journalist, and traveled widely in Eastern Europe during his career. He became one of the principal architects of the massive development of Reuters in the last quarter of the twentieth century. At the time he retired from Reuters in 1989 he held the positions of General Manager, Chairman of the Reuter Foundation, and Chairman of Visnews, now Reuters TV.

CONTENTS

ILLUSTRATIONS

FOREWORD

LECH WAŁĘSA

IF IT WERE NOT for independent broadcasting, the world would look quite different today. Without Western broadcasting, totalitarian regimes would have survived much longer. The struggle for freedom would have been more arduous and the road to democracy much longer.

In Poland, as in other communist countries, we listened to Radio Free Europe and other Western broadcasting stations despite the continual interference. From these broadcasting stations we gleaned our lessons of independent thinking and solidarity action.

When it came to radio waves, the iron curtain was helpless. Nothing could stop the news from coming through—neither sputniks nor mine fields, high walls nor barbed wire. The frontiers could be closed; words could not.

The bloodless war on air ended with the defeat of the regimes that tried so hard to suppress the truth. And although today we know well how this recent cold war ended, the study of its course is truly exciting. And so Michael Nelson's book is worth reading. It is not only a significant contribution to contemporary history but it also makes for a revealing and first-class read.

INTRODUCTION

THE COMMUNISTS CONCLUDED the story of Western broadcasting to the Soviet Union and its satellites with an elegance that history's muse, Clio, has rarely demonstrated. No historian could have asked for a neater denouement: the Soviet president, Mikhail Gorbachev, the target of the failed coup that finally toppled communism, depended on Western Radios, so long attacked by the Communists, for the information on which he staged his comeback.

Why did the West win the cold war? Not by use of arms. Weapons did not breach the Iron Curtain. The Western invasion was by radio, which was mightier than the sword. Those skilled in war subdue the enemy's army without battle, wrote Sun Tzu, the author of the first known book on warfare.

The frequently accepted reason for the collapse of communism, the failure of the economy because of the burden of the arms race and because of the intrinsic weakness of the system, is quantifiable. Before the revolution, Russia was seventh in the global league table of per capita consumption. In 1989 it was seventy-seventh. The impact of propaganda is not quantifiable. But the communist targets had no doubt about its efficacy against their creed in the cold war. Gorbachev told Margaret Thatcher that it was not the Strategic Defense Initiative that was the decisive factor. The first impulses for reform were in the Soviet Union itself, in a society that could no longer tolerate the lack of freedom, he told her. Whence came the knowledge of freedom? It came from the Radios.

The Polish government believed that if the Americans closed Radio Free Europe, the underground would completely cease to exist. Another Pole, Zbigniew Brzezinski, director of the U.S. National Security Council under President Carter, believed the loss of communist monopoly over mass communications was the key to the breakdown of communist totalitarianism. Aleksandr Solzhenitsyn felt that the Western imagination could not grasp the nonmilitary power of the broadcasts. The cost of the defenses set up against "the Voices," as the Russians called them, which was principally incurred by jamming, shows to what ends the Communists would go to stop the messages from getting through. The British Broadcasting Corporation (BBC) estimated that jamming cost as much as $918 million (£626 million) each year. In 1990 Eduard Shevardnadze, Gorbachev's foreign minister, told the Twenty-eighth Party Congress that the cost of ideological confrontation with the West over the previous two decades had been 700 billion roubles.

Research for this book in the archives of the Central Committee of the Communist Party of the Soviet Union confirmed that the Communists believed that Western radio propaganda was the strongest and most effective weapon that existed for ideological intervention in the Soviet Union.

The Communists were so frightened by the Western Radios that they even resorted to assassination of their staffs and bombing of their stations. The Bulgarians had broadcaster Georgi Markov murdered because they felt that his broadcasts were undermining the very foundations of the regime.

The weapons used in the propaganda war were the same on both sides, with one difference. Both sides broadcast to the world, but the Communists had few listeners. The difference was the weapon of defense: the Russians used jamming; the West used free communication.

The principal broadcasters were the British Broadcasting Corporation (BBC), the Voice of America (VOA), and Radio Free Europe (RFE) and Radio Liberty (RL), which were eventually merged as Radio Free Europe/Radio Liberty (RFE/RL). The characters of the main broadcasters were very different. RFE and RL were founded by the Central Intelligence Agency (CIA) as surrogate domestic broadcasters, designed to be like local radio stations of the target countries, and to deliver lots of local news. The BBC and the VOA did not pretend to be local radio stations. They were national broadcasters, speaking for their home countries but with strong international content. The international services of the BBC were provided by the independent corporation but were paid for by the British government. The Voice of America was part of a department of the American government.

Western broadcasting might not have succeeded. Militating against success, on the one hand, was a combination of the Russians' traditional distrust of foreigners and the need of the Communists to control people's minds. On the other, was the Americans' traditional distrust of propaganda. Let the Radios take their rightful place in the graveyard of cold war relics, Senator Fulbright told the U.S. Senate when he tried to shut them down. But Cord Meyer, one of the CIA architects of the Radios, was proud of what they did because the Radios did continue despite the opposition, and it was one of the few cases in which the American government and people managed to stick to something over a long period.

From the end of the Second World War farsighted Americans and Britons who believed that the West had to talk to the people of the communist East had to contend in the West with widespread disillusionment with the past. It is easy to forget that background today. The historian A. J. P. Taylor in 1945 held that nobody in Europe believed in the American way of life, that is, in private enterprise. Orwell dismissed capitalism as a failed system that manifestly had no future. Even as late as 1975 Daniel P. Moynihan, the U.S. senator, wrote that liberal democracy on the American model had no relevance to the future. The intellectuals with whom the Radios had to battle after the war were not in the Soviet Union because almost all had died in the gulags; they were in the West, and it was they who were legitimizing the communist regimes.

Their view of the Soviet Union was formed because they either did not know, or did not want to know, the communist attitude toward truth—that Lenin believed that socialist realism meant reporting "not what is, but what should be."[1] He was convinced that a true Bolshevik would be ready to believe that black was white and white was black if the Party required it. Four decades of Western broadcasting exposed those lies.

In Orwell's *Nineteen Eighty-Four* the telescreen behind Winston Smith's back babbles away about pig iron and the overfulfillment of the Ninth Three-Year Plan. That, and the like, encouraged the view that the technology available to governments precluded revolution. If revolution would never again be possible, why bother with propaganda? Ironically, it was technology that undermined totalitarian power through terrestrial and satellite television, the copying machine, the tape recorder, the telephone, and the fax and the radio. As President Reagan said, "The biggest of Big Brothers is increasingly helpless against communications technology."[2] And in one of the most bizarre examples of incompetence in the history of the Soviet Union, despite the billions of dollars spent on jamming, the Soviet state itself saw to it that its citizens had cheap shortwave radios, which they used to listen to Western propaganda through that jamming.

For most of the cold war Western propaganda was subtle. The Americans soon learned that the brash frontal attack was less effective than the low-key approach of the British. The message was to convey not just a social system or politics or economics but a total culture. Russian Communists saw the dangers for them in the Radios' techniques of inspiring confidence by admission of the faults of the West and the development of a tolerant and neutral reaction toward gentle criticism of socialism. Pop music and talk about consumer goods conveyed the message that life abroad was better and, thus, spread discontent and insecurity.

How different would history have been if there had been no Western broadcasting? Since the end of the cold war I have posed this question to many Russians and East Europeans for this book. "The revolutions would have come later." "The Soviet Union would today be like North Korea." These were typical responses. But perhaps the most interesting one was this: "The revolutions would have been bloodier because from 1956 the Western Radios always counseled restraint."

Communism wanted to make everything and everyone the same. But the Radios always emphasized individuality, variety, difference. They developed the critical faculties of their listeners. The Radios did not only convey information. They helped convey the concept of a civil society and of basic human values; they preserved a sense of national identity and made the connection with the broader cultural movement of Europe.

As Milan Kundera, the Czech writer and dissident, said, "The struggle of man against power is the struggle of memory against forgetting."[3]

ABBREVIATIONS

ACPIC	American Council on Private International Communications
ADN	Allgemeiner Deutscher Nachrichtendienst (East German news agency)
ADPC	Assistant director for policy coordination (U.S.)
AEJ	Association for Education in Journalism (U.S.)
AIDS	Acquired immunodeficiency syndrome
Amcomblib	American Committee for Freedom for the Peoples of the USSR, Inc.
AP	Associated Press (U.S.)
ARD	Arbeitsgemeinschaft der oeffentlich-rechtlichen Rundfunkanstalten der Bundesrepublik Deutschland (a grouping of West German public broadcasters)
ASNE	American Society of Newspaper Editors
BBC	British Broadcasting Corporation
BIB	Board for International Broadcasting (U.S.)
CBC	Canadian Broadcasting Corporation
CIA	Central Intelligence Agency (U.S.)
CIPC	Colonial Information Policy Committee (U.K.)
Cmd.	Command (for the identification of U.K. government White Papers)
CNET	Centre National des Etudes des Télécommunications (French National Center for Telecommunications Studies)
CNN	Cable News Network
CPA	Communist Party Archives (Soviet Union)
CPSU	Communist Party of the Soviet Union
CRS	Congressional Research Service
CSCE	Conference on Security and Cooperation in Europe

CW	Lenin, *Collected Works*
DDEL	Dwight D. Eisenhower Library, Abilene, Kans.
DLF	Deutschlandfunk (West German national and international radio)
DIAS	Drahtfunk im Amerikanischen Sektor (cable radio in the American sector of Berlin)
DW	Deutsche Welle (West German international radio)
EEAOR	East European Audience and Opinion Research Division of RFE/RL, Munich
EVE	Emissions vers l'Etranger (French government international broadcasting administration)
FCO	Foreign and Commonwealth Office (U.K.)
FDJ	Freie Demokratische Jugend (East German Communist youth organisation)
FDP	Freie Demokratische Partei (Free Democratic Party, West Germany)
FO	Foreign Office (U.K.)
FOIA	Freedom of Information Act (U.S.)
FRUS	Foreign Relations of the United States
GAO	General Accounting Office (U.S.)
GCHQ	Government Communications Headquarters (U.K. international radio monitoring facility)
GDR	German Democratic Republic—East Germany
HMSO	His or Her Majesty's Stationery Office (U.K.)
HSTL	Harry S. Truman Library, Independence, Mo.
IFRB	International Frequency Registration Board
IIA	International Information Administration (U.S.)
INRA	International Research Associates (U.S.)
INS	International News Service (U.S.)
IPI	International Press Institute
IRD	Information Research Department (U.K.)
ITU	International Telecommunications Union
KAL	Korean Airlines
KGB	Komitet Gosudarstvennoy Bezopasnosti (Soviet Committee for State Security)
MGB	Ministerstvo Gosudarstvennoy Bezopasnosti (Ministry of State Security)
MIT	Massachusetts Institute of Technology

MOR	Media and Opinion Research (set up in RFE/RL in Munich in 1990 to combine EEAOR and SAAOR)
MTI	Magyar Tavirati Iroda (Hungarian news agency)
NARA	National Archives and Records Administration (U.S.)
NATO	North Atlantic Treaty Organization
NSA	National Students Association (U.S.)
NSC	National Security Council (U.S.)
NSDD	National Security Decision Directive (U.S.)
OIC	Office of Information and Cultural Affairs (U.S.)
OIE	Office of International Information and Educational Exchange (U.S.)
OII	Office of International Information (U.S.)
OPC	Office of Policy Coordination (U.S.)
OSI	Office of Scientific Intelligence (U.S.)
OSS	Office of Strategic Services (U.S.)
OWI	Office of War Information (U.S.)
PCIAA	President's Committee on Information Activities Abroad
POQ	*Public Opinion Quarterly* (U.S.)
PRO	Public Record Office (U.K.)
PSB	Psychological Strategy Board (U.S.)
PSS	Polnoe sobranie sochinenii (Lenin, Complete Works)
RCI	Radio Canada International
RFE	Radio Free Europe
RFE/RL	Radio Free Europe/Radio Liberty
RFI	Radio France Internationale
RIAS	Radio in the American Sector of Berlin
RIIA	Royal Institute of International Affairs (U.K.)
RIO	Regional intelligence officer (U.K.)
RL	Radio Liberty or Radio Liberation
SAAOR	Soviet Area Audience and Opinion Research Division of RFE/RL, Paris
SAPMO-BArch	Stiftung "Archiv der Parteien und Massenorganisationen der ehemaligen DDR" im Bundesarchiv (Foundation "Archive of the Party and Mass Organizations of the Former GDR" in the German Federal Archive)
SED	Sozialistische Einheitspartei Deutschlands (Socialist Unity Party of East Germany)

SIS	Secret Intelligence Service (U.K.)
SPD	Sozialdemokratische Partei Deutschlands (West German Social Democratic Party)
SPGPD	Special Planning Group on Public Diplomacy (U.S.)
StB	Statni Bezpecnost (Czechoslovak secret service)
TASS	Soviet news agency
UNESCO	United Nations Educational Scientific and Cultural Organization
UP	United Press (U.S.)
UPI	United Press International (U.S.)
USIA	U.S. Information Agency
USIE	U.S. International Information and Educational Exchange Program
USSR	Union of Soviet Socialist Republics
VFH	Voice of Free Hungary of RFE
VOA	Voice of America
WAC	Written Archives Centre, BBC
WEAC	West European Advisory Committee of RFE
ZDF	Zweites Deutsches Fernsehen (West German commercial television station)

War of the Black Heavens

1

PROLOGUE

The Russians Started It

The irony of international broadcasting is that what had been started by the Soviet Union ultimately became a significant factor in the regime's own downfall. Further, to reach its citizens across its great land mass the Soviet Union used shortwave radio, and the same shortwave receivers it made so freely available were eventually also tuned in to the anticommunist broadcasts of the Western powers.

The Bolsheviks' broadcasting began at two o'clock in the morning of November 7, 1917, when the cruiser *Aurora* broadcast from St. Petersburg a message to the citizens of Russia written by Lenin.[1] That message was in Morse code although some writers have erroneously believed it was a transmission of Lenin's voice.[2] Not until December 8, 1922, was Lenin's voice heard on radio.[3]

Lenin recognized the importance of radio in reaching the largely illiterate population of Russia. On July 19, 1918, he took the first step in organizing the radio propaganda machine by transferring radio stations from military to civil administration. At the same time he established a radio laboratory in Nizhni Novgorod under an engineer named M. A. Bonch-Bruevich. Astounded radio hams, used to hearing only the stuttering of Morse code, at the end of 1919 reported that they had heard a human voice over the airwaves. "Please explain," they pleaded. Lenin's vision, as he described it on February 5, 1920, in a note to Bonch-Bruevich, was of a newspaper without paper and "without distances."[4] Lenin elaborated on this idea on January 26, 1921, when he wrote: "The matter is of gigantic importance. (A newspaper without paper and without wires, for with a loudspeaker and with the receiver which Bonch-Bruevich has developed in such a way that we will easily get hundreds of receivers, all Russia will hear a newspaper being read in Moscow)."[5]

1

The gramophone was important, and Lenin recorded sixteen speeches between 1919 and 1921, which were widely distributed. On June 7, 1921, the first radio loudspeakers were set up in six of Moscow's major squares. News bulletins from the Russian news agency ROSTA were broadcast for two hours every evening.[6] Domestic broadcasting was formally inaugurated on November 7, 1922, and the signals of the Comintern Radio Station, the most powerful in the world, were received as far away as Yugoslavia.[7]

From the start of the revolution the Bolsheviks used radio telegraphy addressed internationally to present their point of view. On November 12, 1917, under the call sign "To everyone . . . to everyone . . . to everyone," the Council of the People's Commissars' Radio transmitted Lenin's historic message: "The all-Russian Congress of Soviets has formed a new Soviet Government. The Government of Kerensky has been overthrown and arrested. Kerensky himself has fled. All official institutions are in the hands of the Soviet Government."[8]

Lenin reported to the all-Russian Central Executive Committee that "our wireless message about the victory over Kerensky was picked up by the Austrian wireless telegraph and relayed" while "the Germans, on the other hand, sent out jamming signals to block it." He considered the fact that "we can contact Paris by wireless" extremely important for notifying the French people about a European armistice and peace treaty.[9] On February 4, 1918, Lenin addressed a radio report "to everyone" in which he rejected what he claimed was false information disseminated by foreign newspapers and in which he gave information about conditions in the Soviet Union and about decrees of the government.[10] On November 23, 1918, the Russians sent a radiogram addressed to the executive of the council of workers' and peasants' deputies in Berlin and to all the Soviets of Germany. It said that from the next day they would transmit a radio newspaper to Germany in German. They proposed that the Germans should broadcast similarly to Moscow.[11]

The nineteenth-century liberal writer, Herzen, was prescient enough to see the dangers of telegraphy. What he most feared for the future, he said, was "Genghis Khan with the telegraph."[12]

Radio telegraphy had been used for propaganda since 1915 when Germany transmitted regular news bulletins to neutral countries from a transmitter at Nauen near Berlin, a wireless substitute for cable that was largely in the hands of the Allies. The signal reached Persia in the east Mexico in the west. German representatives picked up the messages and relayed them by radio to farther points. At each reception point representatives translated the service into the local language and offered it to local editors free. Western news agency services were costly, so the free service got wide publication. It was even used in the United States.[13]

But it was the Soviet Union in 1924 that started international radio broadcasting as it is known today, in voice and intended for listeners with their own radio sets.[14] It was initially only spasmodic. In 1925 a commentary on the funeral of the minister of defense in Red Square was broadcast abroad in French, English, and German. In August of the same year the world's first station using shortwaves, on which the Russians had been working since 1920, went into operation in Moscow.[15] In 1926 the Russians used radio to attack Romania over a dispute about Bessarabia.[16] The Soviet Union broadcast in English to the striking British miners in 1926 for a short period. "Moscow Reds Now Use Radio to Address British Miners" was the headline on the front page of the *New York Times* on October 21, 1926. "The enemies of Bolshevist propaganda are now confronted with the need for a barrier in the ether," the newspaper's London correspondent reported. Regular broadcasts began in October–November 1929, and the first language used was German. A few days later broadcasts in French and English started. At the beginning each broadcast lasted only one hour. Broadcasts began daily in January 1930; the governing principle was a "great and holy hatred of capitalism."[17]

The Lonely Listener in the Bush

Pope Pius XI inaugurated Vatican Radio on February 12, 1931. His speech in Latin was heard across the globe and generated great excitement and press comment.[18] It is significant that the word *propaganda* came from the Catholic Church, and it is not surprising that when the new medium of communication arrived, the church was among the first to exploit it. As early as July 25, 1925, a Jesuit priest, Fr. Giuseppe Gianfranceschi, president of the Papal Academy of Science and an associate of Guglielmo Marconi, the Italian inventor of radio, proposed the establishment of a Vatican radio station.[19] On June 11, 1929, four days after the ratification of the Lateran treaty between Italy and the papacy that established Vatican City as a sovereign state, the pope received Marconi in audience and charged him with setting up a radio station. At Marconi's suggestion Pius XI appointed Gianfranceschi as the first director of Radio Vatican.[20] As a consequence, control of Vatican broadcasting was secured for the Jesuit Order.

"Cock-a-doodle-do" or, because it was a French chicken, "Cocorico, Cocorico," not the "Marseillaise," was what French colonials in the African jungle heard when they tuned in to the first international broadcast of the French government on May 6, 1931. It preceded the speech of Marshal Lyautey as he inaugurated the Paris Colonial Exhibition. The broadcasts were in the evening because colonials liked to listen while sipping their aperitifs.[21]

The BBC started an empire service in English only in 1932, with the needs of the Briton overseas very much in mind. The broadcasts, which started on December 19, were aimed toward "the lonely listener in the bush." One writer at the time imagined "the men in the heart of an African desert hearing the frantic applause at a vaudeville item in the Palladium."[22]

Like the Netherlands beforehand in 1927 and Germany in 1929, the countries of Western Europe initially started international broadcasting to serve their colonists.[23]

For Germany the objective soon became different. Hitler's belief in propaganda was behind the expansion of German broadcasting abroad in 1935. Goebbels believed that what the press was in the nineteenth century, radio would be in the twentieth. He said that whereas Napoleon was said to have claimed that the press was the seventh power, he considered radio the eighth power.[24] The chief of German radio, Eugene Hadamowski, waxed lyrical about radio's powers: "We spell radio with three exclamation marks because we are possessed in it of a miraculous power—the strongest weapon ever given to the spirit—that opens hearts and does not stop at the borders of cities and does not turn back before closed doors; that jumps rivers, mountains, and seas; that is able to force peoples under the spell of one powerful spirit."[25] Mussolini followed Hitler, and by 1937 Rome was broadcasting in sixteen languages, Berlin in six, and Moscow in seven.[26]

The Communists and Fascists spent a lot of their radio time attacking each other. Radio Center Moscow rejoiced in covering the extramarital activities of such Nazi leaders as Goebbels. In response the Third Reich started jamming.[27]

To counter Italy's service to the Middle East and Germany's to Latin America, in 1938 the BBC started its first foreign language transmissions in Arabic and Spanish and Portuguese.[28]

Gone was the luxury of twenty years earlier. The Foreign Office had then been forbidden to become involved in any form of cultural propaganda.[29] As diplomat Harold Nicolson wrote: "If foreigners failed to appreciate, or even to notice, our gifts of invention or our splendid adaptability, then there was nothing that we could or should do to miti-

gate their obtuseness. The genius of England, unlike that of lesser countries, spoke for itself."[30]

Two days before the Munich conference of September 1938 the BBC
made its first broadcasts in French, German, and Italian. The circumstances would have done credit to an Ealing Studios comedy film. On
September 27 the British Foreign Office asked the BBC to make arrangements to broadcast in German, French, and Italian a speech to the British
people that Prime Minister Neville Chamberlain was to make at 8:00
P.M. The Foreign Office said it would provide both the speakers and the
translations but later in the day realized that it had no one who could do
the French and German. As if that were not enough, at 6:00 P.M. the
Whitehall mandarins asked the BBC to provide news bulletins as well.

The BBC frantically searched for translators and announcers. At a
cocktail party, the director of overseas services tracked down G. Walter
Goetz, the German artist, who drew cartoons for the *Daily Express.* He
rushed to the BBC to do the German version. A BBC announcer read the
French version. The translators got the speech page by page from 8:15
P.M. to 8:30 P.M. and translated page by page as it was broadcast.

A BBC report afterward said that "there had been inevitable delays
and stumblings by the announcers, which caused unfavourable comment in many quarters and spoilt the effectiveness of Mr Chamberlain's
speech. But in view of the difficulties under which the work was carried
out this was excusable."[31]

It was unfortunate that in the BBC's first broadcast to the European
Continent the British prime minister should have spoken of the Czechoslovak crisis as "a quarrel in a far-away country between people of
whom we know nothing."[32]

One British broadcaster had a curious idea about propaganda. F. W.
Ogilvie, the director-general of the BBC, believed on the eve of the war
that it would be a good idea to relay to Germany the song of a night-
ingale in an English wood as a token of Britain's peace-loving intentions.[33]

In the United States three attempts to get the government into international broadcasting were aborted. In 1936, 1937, and 1938 bills were
drafted, but they were dropped in the face of opposition from the radio
industry. NBC and CBS experimented with shortwave broadcasting as
early as 1929 and later began regular broadcasting, but at a loss.[34]

In 1815 Thomas Jefferson expressed the hope that the American government would see that its ministers at foreign courts kept Europe truly
informed of occurrences in the United States to counteract the slanders
and falsehoods disseminated by English papers.[35] One hundred and

twenty years later the American people had forgotten Jefferson's injunction to keep Europe informed. The bills before Congress in the 1930s had also to contend with the American phobia against the word *propaganda*. It was, as a report for the Psychological Strategy Board put it later, "a horrid, sinister word, a really un-American word and activity."[36]

An Instrument of War

Radio became an instrument of war in 1939, and both the Axis powers and the Allies used it to full advantage. The British and Americans largely told the truth, the Axis many lies. As the war progressed, the British and Americans were able to expose the German falsehoods.

The British massively increased their international broadcasting when war came. On the eve of the war the British were broadcasting in ten languages, but by the end of 1943 in forty-five. Comparable German figures were thirty-six and fifty-two.[37] By the end of the war the BBC was broadcasting 850 hours each week in forty-five languages.

The U.S. radio industry became convinced of the need for some cooperation with government as the possibility of war loomed. In 1941 a coordinator of information and a coordinator of inter-American affairs were appointed to work with private broadcasters and to encourage and direct the expansion of their shortwave services. When war broke out, the government established the Office of War Information (OWI) and took over the thirteen privately owned shortwave transmitters then operating.[38]

The U.S. government founded the Voice of America in 1942, and it went on the air seventy-nine days after the attack on Pearl Harbor. The first broadcast on February 24, 1942, was in German, and English and French followed shortly afterward. That first broadcaster said: "Daily at this time we shall speak to you about America and the war. The news may be good or bad. We shall tell you the truth."[39]

Totalitarian regimes had three ways of countering foreign broadcasts: jamming the radio signals, restricting the receiving equipment, and intimidating the listeners. The Germans and Russians jammed, the British and Americans did not. A typical restriction on receiving equipment required that it be manufactured to receive only domestic frequencies. The extreme intimidation was in Germany where some listeners were executed.

The Germans banned listening to overseas radios the day war broke out although some people had been punished even earlier. Some offenders who passed on what they had heard were executed.

The *Strassburger Neueste Nachrichten* carried this report under a Wuerzburg dateline on March 15, 1941, with the headline, "He Got His Deserts; Radio Criminal Condemned to Death":

The Nuremberg Special Court has sentenced the traitor Johann Wild of Nuremberg to death for two serious radio crimes. Both before and after the coming into effect of the radio decree he behaved as an enemy of state and people by continually listening to hostile broadcasts from abroad. Not content with that, he composed insulting tirades whose source was the enemy station. In these tirades he revealed his treachery to the people by vulgar abuse of the Leader.

On April 5, 1941, the *Hamburger Fremdenblatt* reported:

Emil Kasper, aged sixty-six and fifty-year-old Heinrich Kerkhof, both from Cuxhaven, were two lost members of the community. They stood before the special court at Hannover on a charge of being radio criminals. In spite of the penalties imposed for radio crimes they had been unable to resist listening regularly to the lying news of the English broadcasts. . . . The special court sentenced Kasper to three years' penal servitude and loss of civil rights for five years. . . . Kerkhof had to pay for his crime against the community with one and one-half years' penal servitude and loss of civil rights for three years.

According to the *Muenchner Nueste Nachrichten* of August 4, 1940, there were 225 convictions for listening between April 1939 and March 1940. Sentences were inflicted as early as 1937 for listening specifically to Moscow.

Howard K. Smith, the Columbia Broadcasting representative in Berlin, reported in November that all Germans received with their ration cards a little red card with a hole punched in the middle of it so that it could be hung on the dial of a radio set. It carried the legend: "Racial Comrades! You are Germans! It is your duty not to listen to foreign stations. Those who do will be mercilessly punished." Local Nazi chiefs visited houses and checked whether the cards had been affixed. As a result, many who had been afraid to listen became so curious that they converted to regular listening.

The Propaganda Ministry's justification for the punishments was put thus in the *National Zeitung* on May 14, 1941, "Their listening lowers their powers of resistance and brings about a spiritual self-mutilation no less criminal than self-mutilation by an army conscript."[40]

The punishments gave BBC editors a particularly good line with which to castigate journalists who had submitted poor copy. "Would you risk your life to listen to *this?*" Noel Newsome, the European news editor, a man of rather Churchillian mien, would bark at his underlings.[41]

On June 24, 1924, the Russians passed a law on the freedom of the radio waves that allowed private citizens to use radio receivers. They had the right to listen to foreign broadcasts.[42] Although it was not illegal to listen to foreign broadcasts, Articles 70 and 190 of the criminal code, concerning the distribution of critical information and propaganda, were sometimes interpreted to include repeating information from foreign broadcasts.[43]

There was nothing to stop the British from listening to German radio, and millions did so. The BBC calculated in late 1940 that six million listened regularly to Reichsrundfunk. One of the reasons was that Germany had the greatest international broadcasting star of all time—Lord Haw Haw. The minutiae of his information about British life, including which village clocks were stopped, made people think there was a vast fifth column in Britain. He doubtless damaged morale and was hanged for his pains.[44]

The outstanding broadcasting gimmick of the War was the "V" for victory sign. It worried Goebbels, who complained about "the intellectual invasion of the continent by British radio." The Germans cleverly ran off with the Allies' clothes and appropriated the "V" sign for themselves. The German home service even broadcast a concert conducted by Furtwaengler, which included the whole of Beethoven's Fifth Symphony, whose opening bars corresponded to the Morse code for *V*.[45] Nevertheless, it made a lasting mark on the popular imagination.

The most important contribution by radio to the Allied war effort was in broadcasting to the occupied territories. This was particularly marked in France where London radio played a key role in persuading the French to turn their backs on the despair that came from defeat and to resume the fight. General de Gaulle believed that broadcasting had provided him with "a powerful means of war."[46]

Both the Germans and the British engaged in "black broadcasting"—pretending to be a domestic broadcaster. Goebbels conceded that one of the British stations did "a very clever job of propaganda."[47]

Both sides clearly believed that international broadcasting played an important role in the war. That experience persuaded the British and Americans to continue international broadcasting after the war. The respect that the BBC had gained in Europe meant that there was an audience well used to listening to London when they changed their Nazi masters for communist rulers. This was particularly noticeable in Poland. Lord Asa Briggs points out in his history of broadcasting in the United Kingdom that "the feeling of generalized 'resistance' in Europe, a movement with some kind of 'solidarity,' owed much to BBC reports of what was happening, often spontaneously, in scattered countries."[48] East Europeans listening to the British and Americans during the cold war had the same experience, particularly during the revolutions of 1989.

2

THE START OF
THE COLD WAR
(1945–1947)

One-Two to the Jaw

THE RUSSIAN AMBASSADOR, Ivan Maisky, "shied like a young colt," as British Foreign Secretary Anthony Eden raised the possibility of the British broadcasting to the Soviet Union in Russian. The ambassador then remarked darkly that it was an extremely delicate question. The meeting took place on June 23, 1941, the day after the Germans had invaded the Soviet Union. The Foreign Office decided against upsetting the Russians by launching a service because it would not have served much purpose; radios had been confiscated in the Soviet Union when war came.[1]

On March 24, 1946, the BBC did start broadcasting in Russian to the Soviet Union.[2] Almost one year later the Americans did likewise; on February 17, 1947, the Voice of America (VOA) inaugurated its broadcasts in Russian.[3]

The start of these two transmissions showed how bad relations with the Soviet Union had become. They were two important new weapons in the cold war although that term had then only recently been invented by George Orwell.[4]

Theories on the origins of the cold war range from the changing power structure in the Far East at the turn of the twentieth century through the Nazi-Soviet Pact of August 1939 and the difficulties in negotiating the Anglo-Soviet Treaty of May 1942.[5] Another view is that disputes over Poland in 1944 and 1945 caused a breakdown of trust between the Allies.[6]

Russian historians claimed in 1984 that the cold war began with the Bolshevik revolution in November 1917 because this was when the capitalist world started to try to undermine the world's first socialist state.[7] Some Americans thought it started about April 1945 when William J. Donovan, director of the Office of Strategic Services (OSS), put out his first directive, which changed OSS intelligence targets from strictly German and Middle Eastern to Russian intentions in the Balkans.[8] A number of historians also put the start in April 1945—April 23, when President Truman lectured Soviet Foreign Minister Molotov on Stalin's failure to carry out the Yalta agreement. "I gave it to him straight, one-two to the jaw," Truman claimed.[9]

The cold war was a propaganda war, and in its early years many Americans believed they were losing it.

BBC: Programs in the National Interest

Against the background of "a rising flood of provocative attacks on British policy in the Russian press and radio" the British Embassy in Moscow had urged before the end of 1945 that the BBC should start a service in Russian.[10] Although wireless sets had been impounded during the war, they had then been returned to their owners. Manufacture of sets, including sets able to receive foreign stations, was to be resumed on a large scale.[11] On February 21, 1946, Sir Ivone Kirkpatrick, the deputy under secretary at the Foreign Office, wrote to Sir William Haley, director-general of the BBC, to tell him that "the Secretary of State has now instructed me to approach you with a firm request for the initiation of Russian broadcasts."[12] They started one month later on March 24.

The service began with three daily transmissions totaling one and one-quarter hours. Reactions were mixed. The *Daily Telegraph* on March 25, 1946, reported that "they like the talking but not the music. The two marches played might have come from anywhere. . . . They prefer English dance music." The British Embassy in Moscow reported that listeners did not like the accents of the announcers, which were described as the equivalent of "exaggerated Oxford." The speakers were émigrés, who had no knowledge of current spoken Russian. But the situation improved; there were claims of a substantial following for the broadcasts.[13] A *Daily Express* correspondent reported on group listening and said there was no evidence that people were seeking to conceal the fact that they were listening. In some blocks of flats the block guardian joined in. The listeners passed on to their neighbors what they had heard.[14] Members of the Supreme Soviet visited London in 1947 and were present at a studio transmission. But the honeymoon was not to last.

The BBC viewed its role as less violent than did the Russians. Major General Sir Ian Jacob, the controller of the BBC European service, told his staff that "Britain has to struggle against calumny and insidious propaganda poured out by upholders of a different way of thinking. Our part in counteracting this is not by refuting it but by seizing and retaining the initiative."[15]

The dichotomy between the attitudes of the British and the Russians toward broadcasting is evident in this extract from an article in *Komsomol'skaya Pravda*:

> The foundation of BBC propaganda is the latest news, broadcast with emphatic objectivity. It should be noted that in selecting material for broadcasting to the USSR the BBC does not draw any conclusions of its own but leaves this to its listeners, who sometimes, through lack of experience or lack of knowledge, are hooked by those who for years have made it their practice to fish in troubled waters. . . . "White" propaganda is straightforward propaganda. It is waged by enemies of communism quite openly, even though under the mantle of "impartiality" and "objectivity." But this does not lessen its hostile nature.[16]

On the day that the BBC started broadcasting to the Soviet Union the cabinet rejected government control of the corporation, and Ernest Bevin, the foreign secretary, stated that "he was anxious to establish the independent status of the BBC."[17] The relationship of the BBC External Services and the government was set out in a White Paper of July 2, 1946, which said that the government intended the corporation to remain independent in the preparation of programs for overseas audiences.[18] The Licence and Agreement said that the BBC had to send overseas programs to prescribed countries. It had to consult and collaborate with government departments and should "obtain and accept from them such information regarding conditions in, and the policies of His Majesty's Government towards, those countries so prescribed and other countries as will enable the Corporation to plan and prepare its overseas programmes in the national interest." The wording was not changed materially in subsequent Licences and Agreements.[19]

In the parliamentary debate that followed the publication of the White Paper Lord President of the Council Herbert Morrison, said it would be unthinkable for the BBC to broadcast to Europe at the taxpayer's expense doctrines hopelessly at variance with the foreign policy of the government. But it would be equally undesirable that the Foreign

Office should itself become responsible for the foreign services. He explained that the government had come to an arrangement with the BBC whereby the BBC would accept the guidance of the Foreign Office on the "nature and scope" of its foreign language services and the relationship between the two of them would be very close. "But once the general character and scope of the service has been laid down, the BBC will have complete discretion as to the content of the services themselves."[20]

The case in the White Paper for broadcasting to Europe was "The European Service retains a large audience and friends of this country on the continent are anxious that it shall continue. Moreover there are clear indications, at present, that other powers intend to continue to use the broadcasting medium to put their point of view before the European audience and we cannot let the British viewpoint go by default."[21]

One example of the impact of the BBC in Europe came in Czechoslovakia. Six months before the 1948 communist coup the Czech Ministry of Information determined that one in five Czechs listened to the BBC. After the coup, one in two owners of wireless sets in Czechoslovakia were listening to the BBC, and the audience was far greater than that of the Czechoslovakian Broadcasting System.[22]

A few months after the debate on the White Paper William Haley gave the BBC board of governors a note on the principles and purpose of the BBC's External Services. He believed the news service made the truth available in places where it might not otherwise be known. By its presence it forced newspapers and broadcasters in authoritarian countries themselves to approximate closer and closer to the truth. He did not believe news bulletins should seek to persuade. Nor did he think it was a function of the BBC to interfere in the domestic affairs of other countries. "The services do not exist to throw out Governments or to change regimes," he said. His interpretation of Herbert Morrison's reference to Foreign Office guidance on the "nature and scope" of the services (which he changed without explanation to "character and scope") was, slightly oddly, that it was understood that this meant the time and money devoted to the different language transmissions. Not surprisingly, the board chairman annotated his copy with question marks against this section. Haley told the board that there had been occasions when it had been necessary for the BBC to take a firm line with the Foreign Office to distinguish "information" or "guidance" from "directives."[23]

One month before Britain started broadcasting to Russia, Bevin told the cabinet that "the best means of preventing the countries of Southeastern Europe from being absorbed into an exclusive Soviet sphere of influence was to provide a steady stream of information about British life and culture."[24] But Foreign Office officials wanted to go further than that. On April 2, 1946, the under secretaries formed the Russia Committee, which would hold weekly meetings to assess Soviet action and to define policy.[25] In a paper, "The Soviet Campaign Against This Country and Our Response to It," the committee proposed to direct the campaign against communism as such, rather than against the policy of the Soviet Government.[26] Bevin and Prime Minister Clement Attlee endorsed the general principle of the paper, and Ivone Kirkpatrick put forward a program.[27] It was not implemented because of the government's hesitancy about openly breaking with the Soviet Union while still trying to negotiate deals with them on Europe. Also the government did not want to risk a split in the Labour Party with a change in foreign policy.[28] One of the proposals was to enlist the cooperation of the BBC foreign services, which were much more amenable than the home service.

In September Jacob approached the Foreign Office for guidance on the attitude to be adopted toward Russia and communism. The response was an invitation to attend the Russia Committee in his personal capacity, and the committee changed its meetings from Tuesday to Thursday to fit Jacob's schedule. The Russia Committee minutes noted: "General Jacob had raised the question of the general line on our relations with the Soviet Union which was being taken in the European Service of the BBC. He had enquired whether we were not being too indulgent, and whether we should not make a more vigorous reply in our broadcasts to Russian propaganda against us, by carrying more anticommunist material."[29] In the following year the Foreign Office told the British ambassador in Moscow that the BBC was over the whole foreign field extremely helpful and cooperative.[30]

Jacob had special experience with Russia. He had been at Yalta with Churchill. When he left the army at the end of the war, he was offered the position of head of MI6, but declined it.[31] Ivone Kirkpatrick, who had been seconded from the Foreign Office to become controller of European services at the BBC during the war, proposed Jacob for the BBC job. (Jacob's closeness to the government is indicated by the fact that when Churchill became prime minister again, he returned to government service from the BBC for six months in 1952 as chief staff officer to the minister of defence. A few months before Jacob took over as director-general of the BBC on December 1, 1952, the BBC–Foreign Office links were further strengthened by the appointment of Sir Alexander Cadogan, the recently retired head of the Foreign Office, as Chairman of the Board of Governors.)[32]

VOA: The Illegitimate Child at a Family Reunion

Well before the end of the war, President Roosevelt said that he thought it important that proper foundations should be laid then for an effective system of international broadcasting for the future.[33] On February 19, 1945, an interdepartmental Special Committee on Communications approved the following statement prepared by the Department of State:

> 1. Direct short wave broadcasts originating in the United States should be continued after the war on a daily basis.
> 2. Facilities, both as to quantity and quality should in general be as good as those of any other country.[34]

Those pious words did not stop Congress from slashing the budget of the Office of War Information (OWI) for fiscal 1946. The executive branch had knives out too. In August President Truman ordered the abolition of the OWI and a residual organization by the end of 1945. The rump was handed over to the State Department to do with as they wished.[35] Nevertheless, the president directed Secretary of State James Byrnes to investigate the establishment of an overseas information program because, he said, it was essential for the United States to maintain informational activities abroad as an integral part of the conduct of foreign affairs.[36]

In 1944 the State Department commissioned Arthur MacMahon, a consultant on administration, to prepare a report on the postwar international information program. It was published in December 1945. It is a curious document in that the section on international broadcasting contains only one reference to the Voice of America and that in a note.[37] It is short on recommendations, other than one calling for the establishment of an intergovernmental working group under the chairmanship of the Federal Communications Commission to submit recommendations to the president for the attention of Congress concerning postwar ownership and operation of a shortwave broadcasting entity. Its boldest statement is that the continuation of shortwave broadcasting seemed justified. It sets out the pros and cons of private and government ownership and operation and mixtures of the two, but does not come down on one side or the other.[38]

The VOA continued but was cut back. From 168 program hours daily at the height of the war, by the end of December 1945 it was transmitting a daily average of only 64 hours. That was more than Radio Moscow with about 48 hours, but less than the BBC with 90 hours.[39] At the end of 1945 Byrnes told the president he planned a modest program of international broadcasting compared with that of wartime, and he would not try to outdo the efforts of foreign governments in this field.[40] The Office of Information and Cultural Affairs (OIC) took over the Voice—the International Broadcasting Division.[41]

The American distaste for propaganda might have caused the closure of the Voice, had the Russians not started to blast the Americans with their propaganda weapons.

Some years later, Theodore Streibert, director of the United States Information Agency (USIA), summed up the dilemma:

> This has to be accepted as a useful and necessary instrument of national policy. We don't like it. It is repugnant to us. It is not in the American tradition. Propaganda methods are associated with dictatorships. We are running an information program overseas, without reference to the U.S., and it is forced on us by our enemies just as our immense armaments are forced on us. I think it is not only just as necessary but perhaps more so in an effort to keep down these tensions and have our policies understood and keep our friends with us.
>
> Congenitally I think most Americans don't want any part of it, but they must face it intellectually, that it is a necessary instrument even though emotionally we might not want to have anything to do with it, any more than we want anything to do with the atomic bomb.[42]

The attitude toward propaganda was similar to the view of Henry L. Stimson, the American secretary of state and later of war, who objected to code cracking because gentlemen do not read each other's mail.[43] Code cracking and propaganda were acceptable in time of war but not of peace.

In November 1945 Averell Harriman, the United States ambassador to the Soviet Union, suggested that the United States should establish a powerful radio transmitter in Europe to broadcast the truth to the Soviet Union in a number of languages. In one of his last communications to Washington before he left Moscow in January 1946 he said Soviet rulers had consistently sought to represent to the Soviet people a distorted and unfavorable picture of the United States. The Russians had been told that three million women in the United States had been discharged from war work to become housemaids, prostitutes, or live mannequins in shop windows. The ambassador wanted a "vigorous and intelligent American information programme." The medium should be radio.[44]

Despite the Russian vitriol the broadcasts of the Voice of America followed a policy that was called "the full and fair picture." The programs contained criticism of the United States society but there was no criticism of the Soviet Union and no attacks on it, nor was propaganda directed toward Russia. Charles Thayer, a diplomat who was the first chief of the Russian desk and later was chief of the VOA, says it was a consequence of the influence of fellow travelers, unwillingness by wartime broadcasters to change, and indifference by the State Department.[45] The international information service was in the traditional role of "the illegitimate child at a family reunion," according to one official. Only a minority of key State Department officials recognized its value or saw any use for it.[46]

Assaults on the VOA came not only from outside the country but from within. The man who carried the principal burden of parrying the attacks was William Benton, who was appointed assistant secretary of state for public affairs on September 14, 1945. He had his own advertising agency, Benton and Bowles, and owned Encyclopaedia Britannica and Muzak.[47] The principal attacks were twofold: in Congress on the budget front and from the news agencies.

The attack by the news agencies, Associated Press (AP) and United Press (UP), is important because it encapsulated the great American tradition of freedom of information but, paradoxically, hindered the attempts of government to impart the principles of that freedom of information to the totalitarian states of the world.

In January 1946 the AP and UP told Benton they were going to stop supplying their news services to the VOA. That move would leave the VOA with only the International News Service (INS), which had a thin U.S. domestic service (it was eventually taken over by UP to form United Press International [UPI]) and Reuters, which at that time supplied only international news in the United States. AP and UP said that by selling their services to the U.S. government overseas information service they ran the risk of accusations that they were controlled by the U.S. government, which might damage overseas sales. Benton "let out a blast against AP and UP," as he claimed, pointing out that the Soviet government news agency, TASS, and the BBC received U.S. news from the AP and that had not affected AP's reputation for objectivity. So why would supplying the VOA do so? The AP and UP then tried to persuade editors to present a resolution at the convention of the American Society of Newspaper Editors (ASNE) in Washington, D.C., in April 1946 that would condemn the VOA and demand the end of the State Department's international information services.

An ASNE committee investigated and concluded that the State Department's information was in the national interest. So the attempt by the AP and the UP to shut down the VOA failed, but the AP still refused to let the VOA use its service except as a check on other news services, and for that they did not charge.[48]

The AP did not give up the battle against the VOA. "Legalisation of peacetime news propaganda and annual multimillion dollar appropriations were finally gained as a result of a hasty European visit of junketing congressmen, who, in the fall of 1947, went to Europe for a look-see," wrote Kent Cooper, chief executive of the AP.[49]

The bizarre attitude of many in the media toward the VOA is exemplified by the fact that for years TASS had a seat in the press gallery of the Senate, but the VOA did not. The same prohibition applied to Radio Free Europe (RFE) and Radio Liberation, later Radio Liberty (RL). The Senate arranged for a group of media representatives to set up a committee to decide who should be accredited to the Senate press gallery. They accredited TASS, *Pravda*, *Izvestia*, and Radio Moscow, among other communist government organizations, but refused to accredit U.S. government "propaganda" organizations. Only when in 1983 the VOA, the Board for International Broadcasting (BIB), and RFE/RL persuaded the chairman of the Rules Committee to hold hearings on the ban were the VOA and RFE/RL accredited. Organizations speaking against the VOA and RFE/RL were CBS, *U.S. News and World Report*, and the AP.[50]

When the Voice started broadcasting in Russian on February 17, 1947, the casts lasted one hour each day.[51] The American ambassador, General Walter Bedell Smith, ("Beetle" Smith) had written to *Pravda* and *Izvestia* asking them to publish the date, time, and wavelength of the first program. Not suprisingly, the newspapers ignored the request. The ambassador was pleased with the language and voices and handling of the news. "Reception, however, was poor; subject matter was not sufficiently light and entertaining; much of the music was bad for short-wave; and the pacing of the various parts of the programme (news, technical features, light features, dance music and serious music) was off," he later wrote. Bedell Smith was happy with the impact:

> We received a report that Soviet engineers working on the Dnieper dam were "amazed" at the President's speech (about aid for Greece and Turkey) and that they had asked an American to make a check at the Embassy to find whether the President really made such as speech or if they had heard an underground station. They said they had not heard such things for thirty years. From bits of conversation here and there, members of the Embassy staff were able to piece together extensive indications that "Voice of America" programmes were being heard not

only in Moscow but also in a number of provincial areas. A Soviet executive from an industrial city near Moscow stated that he and many of his acquaintances listened regularly; a traveller in Byelorussia found that half of the persons he talked to on the train knew of the broadcasts; a farmer from the Caucasus discussed the programme content in some detail with an American army officer whom he met in the street; a United States naval representative at Odessa reported that in Odessa "our broadcasts are apparently now receivable and are being listened to by most Russians having seven-tube sets or better"; visitors returning from Leningrad reported that the programme was being listened to there just "as in Moscow."[52]

But some citizens were not that eager to be known as listeners. A senior Soviet Army officer, who could overhear his neighbors' radio receiving VOA, asked them to stop listening. "If it were known that I was exposing myself to the 'Voice of America,' my career would be completely ruined," he said.[53]

The radio receiver–owning population who could listen to the VOA in the Soviet Union was small with about 1.3 million sets.[54] It was nearly two months before the Russian media mentioned the existence of the broadcasts. The first attack came in an article by Ilya Ehrenburg in *Culture and Life*, the organ of the Department of Propaganda and Agitation of the Central Committee, under the title "False Voice." The attacks on the VOA concentrated particularly on its role as a tool of Wall Street, which the media likened to that of Goebbels, who, although dead, continued to dictate the propaganda apparatus of the State Department from his grave.[55] The magazine *Ogonyok* later described a supposed editorial conference at the VOA.[56] Present were Zaburdaev, a former Cossack officer, "scraggy, with bulging eyes and a scar on his right cheek"; Funtikov, former leader of the Russian Mensheviks, "bald, with an eternally wet hanging lip"; and Kozel-Ragovsky, a former capitalist and owner of estates," who had "a triple chin and a purplish blue nose." Their pulchritudinous deficiencies were, no doubt, the result of the vile green liquid dope, which, according to *Ogonyok*, they took for their nerves. They prepared for their broadcasts by making up "eye-witness accounts" and writing diaries "uncovered" in slave labor camps.

3

THE BEGINNING OF
THE AGE OF JAMMING
(1947–1950)

Jamming: The Deprived Volga Boatman

On FEBRUARY 3, 1948, the Soviet Union started deliberate jamming of VOA transmitters. The Americans had had but one year of freedom to broadcast unfettered to the Soviets. On April 13, 1948, the Russians started partial jamming of the BBC.

The first jamming of radio telecommunications seems to have been during World War I when the Germans used a five-kilowatt transmitter to try to black out telegram traffic between Paris and St. Petersburg.[1] But the first jamming in broadcasting seems to have been after the revolution when Lenin said the Germans were sending "counter waves" to stop Soviet news from getting through.[2] Ironically, the first recorded official protest against radio broadcasts was against the Soviet Union by Germany.[3]

The Romanians had tried to jam Soviet propaganda in 1932 but were technically unsuccessful. In 1934 the Dollfuss government of Austria jammed German radio to try to stop Nazi propaganda for the incorporation of Austria into the Reich and the development of the Austrian Nazi party. By the end of the thirties jamming was common. During World War II the Axis powers jammed British broadcasts to the Continent. The BBC declined to jam the enemy's broadcasts. In a statement issued in 1940 it said: "Jamming is really an admission of a bad cause. The jammer has a bad conscience. . . . He is afraid of the influence of the truth. . . . In our country we have no such fears and to jam broadcasts in English by the enemy might even be bad propaganda."[4]

It was unfortunate that the British did not heed these sentiments in

1956 when they jammed Greek broadcasts at the height of the Cyprus crisis. The moral authority of the Western governments' protests against Soviet jamming suffered a serious, if only temporary, setback.[5]

Jamming nearly ceased after the end of the war, but Spain started it again in 1946 by jamming the Soviet-controlled broadcasts of "Independent Spain" and began retaliatory broadcasts in Russian. These the Russians promptly jammed.

Jamming is done in two ways: skywave and groundwave. Skywave jamming is long distance. The high-powered jammer sends up a short-wave signal to the ionosphere where it is reflected back to earth and hits the signal to be jammed. The jammers are about the same distance from the target as the transmitters that are jammed, usually about fifteen hundred to two thousand miles. Groundwave jamming is local. It is very effective, and little gets through it. Smaller lower-powered short-range transmitters transmit noise locally from tall buildings. *Twilight immunity* is a period of two or three hours a day when sky-wave jamming does not work in Eastern Europe. When it is still light where the transmitters are in Western Europe, but dark where the jammers are in Eastern Europe, the jamming signals penetrate the ionosphere and are not bounced back to earth.

Some frequencies were not jammed because the jamming governments needed to hear what was being broadcast. Monitoring was important for both sides. Propaganda could not be conducted without good intelligence, which was partly provided by the other side's radios, both domestic and foreign. So the paradox was that without the other side's radio transmission it would have been very difficult to conduct international radio.

The jamming that had started early in 1948 soon increased, and on May 26 instructions were issued for VOA transmitters to take evasive action. These instructions were implemented a few days later with some success.[6]

On August 12, 1948, a Russian school teacher, Anna Kasenkina, jumped out of a window in the Soviet Consultate in New York to escape. The Kremlin suppressed the news within both the Soviet Union and the satellites. The Voice of America, of course, carried it, and within a few hours diplomats in Moscow found it being talked about all over the city. Twenty-four hours later the Soviet media admitted the episode, but the distorted versions caused plenty of muted horse laughs. General "Beetle" Smith said, "It may have been the Kasenkina affair that caused the Kremlin to decide to eliminate this source of truthfulness."[7]

On April 24, 1949, when TASS announced discussions on lifting the

Berlin blockade, the Russians stepped up all-out jamming. Beeps, howls, and squawks tore across every frequency used by the VOA from the United States, the Far East, and Europe. (In 1980 the Russians began "Mayak" jamming, which consisted of distorted versions of normal Soviet programs.) The Russians were now using at least 100 long-distance skywave and 250 local groundwave jammers. By early 1950 the local jammers had increased to 500. This jamming was totally different from that of the Germans during World War II, which had just distorted transmissions and made listening difficult. The Russians jammed to blot out completely the target station.[8] Again, the Americans fought back, and on April 27, 1949, the entire Russian language service of the VOA began twenty-four-hour operation, repeating programs around the clock.[9] April 24, 1949, also marked a new phase in the intensity of Russian jamming of the BBC.

Jamming success was considerable. The American Embassy in Moscow reported in May 1949 that the VOA was getting through only for rare intervals of a few minutes.[10] According to Edward W. Barrett, the assistant secretary of state from 1950 to 1952, research indicated that in early 1950 only about 5 percent of VOA Russian language transmissions were getting through to Moscow.[11] This estimate was more pessimistic than evidence presented in Senate hearings in 1949 that one hundred long-distance jammers were interfering with BBC and VOA Russian broadcasts up to 88 percent of the time.[12] Evidence given to the Senate may not have included local jammers.

The British government took a more sanguine view in public. In response to a question in the House of Commons in October 1949 the postmaster general said that "adequate reception should be obtained at nearly all times in most parts of Russia on one or more wavelengths."[13] British Minister of State Hector McNeil told the United Nations on November 16, 1949, that BBC programs were breaking through Soviet jamming and could be heard regularly in the Moscow area mornings, afternoons, and evenings.[14] The BBC view was, no doubt, different. Their spot check on June 18 had showed that 67 percent of their transmissions had been obliterated. Some representatives of the BBC felt by September, according to the CIA, that they had nearly exhausted their ideas on combating Russian jamming.[15] And by early 1950 the British Embassy in Moscow reckoned that the BBC was broadcasting to "a mere handful of people in the Soviet Union." They thought the effective audience was confined to members of the Soviet armed forces outside the Soviet Union.[16]

The difference between the American and British public views of the impact of jamming did not stop them from collaborating in transmitting. In this effort they had been joined by the Italians, the Greeks, and the Canadians. Transmissions were reorganized so that the same broadcast would be carried at the same time on the maximum possible number of frequencies. VOA and BBC transmitters were also linked.[17] (When in 1955 the VOA wanted to change the times of the twinned transmissions, the BBC refused partly because it would have seriously disturbed the empirewide broadcast of the queen's Christmas Day message.)[18] Technical ploys included overmodulating a transmitter or speech clipping, which increased the average power in the modulation envelope.

Programming was enhanced by improving the quality of articulation, by using very short sentences, and by repeating the same message several times interspersed with long pauses.[19]

Reports from the Soviet Union on the effects of jamming varied greatly. The CIA quoted a Latvian interviewed July 8, 1949, in Moscow who said reception of VOA was somewhat better than in the early weeks of intensive jamming.[20] A person living in Noginsk, about seventy kilometers from Moscow, told the British Embassy in the autumn of 1950 that he could usually hear the BBC at 5:15 P.M. Moscow time. "It appears that local inhabitants, including engineers from a nearby factory, frequently come in to listen although they make no comment and keep their visits as inconspicuous as possible," the embassy reported.[21] British travelers, however, said a man from Dnepropetrovsk told them he used to listen to the BBC in his hometown but could no longer hear it. A Volga boatman, a radio operator, said he used to listen frequently to the VOA, but could no longer hear it.[22]

Some in the USIA consoled themselves that jammed radio had its positive aspects compared with easy listening wall-to-wall radio. One report said: "Listening-through-jamming is a particularly attentive form of listening. Those who, for whatever reasons, are patient and persistent in searching for an intelligible foreign broadcast, and finally succeed, are not likely to throw away their hard-won prize by giving it less than their full attention."[23]

The American Embassy believed Soviet jamming was not a tactical but a strategic operation directed at mastery of the air that would not merely rest on the present victory but seek to keep constantly ahead in the radio race. "Drive for air mastery is vital part of drive for world mastery," its telegram said. It recommended that the resources of the best U.S. and British brains should be pooled to counter jamming as was done in the development of the A-bomb. It said the army, navy, and airforce supported the idea of a joint project with the armed services.[24]

The British Foreign Office felt the Americans tended to exaggerate the importance of broadcasting as a weapon in the cold war but agreed with the stress laid on joint planning.[25]

The CIA was concerned about jamming not just because of its impact on international broadcasting but also because it disrupted telecommunications. In a January 20, 1950, report for President Truman on the jamming of the VOA by the Soviet Union the CIA said that if jamming were carried to its logical conclusion, it could result in "virtual annihilation of international radio communication, not only for the United States, but for the whole world."[26]

In the report the CIA debated the pros and cons of continuing VOA broadcasts to the Soviet Union without coming to a conclusion other than to recommend further study. They summarized the position: "The situation at present is nearly static, with the VOA effectiveness on a level estimated at 15 to 20 percent and with the U.S. and USSR each occasionally obtaining slight, temporary advantages."[27]

The VOA looked at alternative means of sending news. They considered but rejected the use of migratory birds or seals.[28]

No English language broadcasts of either the VOA or the BBC were jammed.[29] Jamming of the VOA broadcasts to Czechoslovakia and Hungary started in August 1949 and soon spread to other bloc countries.[30] The Russians also jammed broadcasts to bordering countries such as Finland, Iran, and Turkey. The Russians continued to jam services in Polish when the Poles stopped jamming in 1956.[31]

It is not clear when jamming of RFE started. The Board for International Broadcasting report for 1987 said RFE was jammed from its inception on July 4, 1950.[32] Yet on August 15, 1950, Frank Altschul, first head of the RFE division of the National Committee for a Free Europe, wrote, "The possibility of jamming must be given due weight."[33]

The costs of jamming were colossal. When the Poles stopped jamming in 1956, the government spokesman said that the annual cost of the jamming operation in Poland was 83 million zlotys, or the equivalent of $1,400,000. The expenditure of money and skilled effort, he said, was enough to supply electric power for a medium-sized town.[34] The cost was about one-third of the total annual cost of domestic Polish broadcasting.[35] In 1981 the BBC estimated that just four days of jamming cost the Russians as much as the BBC's Russian Service cost for a whole year.[36]

The West claimed that jamming was illegal. This assertion was based on Article 44 of the Atlantic City Regulations of 1947, signed by the Soviet Union, which stated: "All stations, whatever their purpose, must be established and operated in such a manner as not to cause harmful interference to the radio service or communications of other members or associate members."[37]

American efforts to avoid provoking the Soviets are evident in two notes delivered to the Soviet government in March and April 1948 in which they protested about radio interference but did not refer to jamming or intentional interference. The Soviet minister of foreign affairs denied to the U.S. ambassador that the frequencies in question had been used for any Soviet transmissions. Diplomatic niceties had disappeared into the ether one year later when at his first meeting with Stalin on August 15, 1949, U.S. Ambassador Kirk pressed for a solution to the jamming problem. The CIA note for the president does not record Stalin's reaction.[38]

The United States lodged a protest to the secretary-general of the International Telecommunications Union on April 29, 1949, noting the Soviet violation. The Soviet Union did not reply.[39]

On December 14, 1950, the United Nations General Assembly passed a resolution condemning jamming by forty-nine votes to five. Although it urged all governments to refrain from radio broadcasts that represented "unfair attacks and slanders against other peoples anywhere," it plainly stated that some countries were "deliberately interfering with the reception by the peoples of those countries of certain radio signals originating beyond their territories" and condemned "measures of this nature as the denial of the rights of all persons to be fully informed."[40]

The resolution followed a study on jamming by the Subcommission on Freedom of Information and the Press, established by the U.N. Commission on Human Rights, which presented the Economic and Social Council with a draft resolution, which they revised and submitted to the General Assembly. The opponents argued that countries had the same right to defend themselves against hostile propaganda as against opium smuggling or the entry of pornographic literature. The Soviet position was that unless a state was permitted to bar the inflow of news and opinions it considered subversive, the free flow of information was an infringement of sovereignty. Most countries argued against such barriers and said the listener had the right to judge the value of the program.[41]

The Soviet foreign minister, Andrei Vyshinsky, had said in the United Nations one year earlier that the Soviet government jammed the BBC because the broadcasts were full of untruths about his country. The government was afraid that the Russian people would react so violently that cooperation between the two countries would suffer.[42] The Russian people had to be prevented in the name of world peace from rising up in wrath to attack the United States as they assuredly would if they were to hear the American broadcasts, he declared.[43]

BBC: Mad Agitators and Disruptionists

When Christopher Mayhew, a junior British Foreign Office minister, attended the General Assembly of the United Nations in New York in the autumn of 1947, he was appalled that there was no organized response to the flood of Russian propaganda.[44] As he luxuriated in the pleasures of the Queen Mary liner on his way back across the Atlantic, he wrote a classified top secret paper for Ernest Bevin of the way he proposed to create a "Communist Information Department in order to concoct the special material required for our publicity." The link that is often present between propaganda and intelligence work existed in Mayhew too. He had been involved in intelligence in the Special Operations Executive during the war.[45] The worker's paradise of the Soviet Union was to be presented as a "gigantic hoax." He sent the note to Bevin on December 6.[46]

Prime Minister Clement Attlee invited Mayhew down to Chequers, his country house, to discuss the paper. He was in favor of the proposal but was concerned about the opposition it would arouse in the left wing of the Labour Party. "I don't think Nye Bevan needs to be troubled with this paper," he told Mayhew.[47] The project was kept secret. The American government followed the same policy of secrecy when it later started activities with similar objectives through the CIA. Thus, two of the most important organs in combating communism, Mayhew's Foreign Office section and Radio Free Europe and Radio Liberty, had to keep their true characters secret because of likely opposition in the legislatures of the United Kingdom and the United States. The timing of the establishment of the department is important. It was a British socialist government, not an American administration, that led the way in setting up a propaganda organization to attack communism. Mayhew did not involve the Americans, as he later recalled, because "I thought we would be rather better at it."[48]

On January 8, 1948, the cabinet adopted proposals by Bevin that included the future form of British propaganda and the setting up by the Foreign Office of a section "to oppose the inroads of communism, by taking the offensive against it."[49] The fullest cooperation of the BBC overseas services would be desirable. The propaganda line was to be different from that of the Americans:

In general we should emphasise the weakness of Communism rather than its strength. Contemporary American propaganda, which stresses the strength and aggressiveness of Communism, tends to scare and un-balance the anti-communists, while heartening the fellow-travellers, and encouraging the Communists to bluff more extravagantly. Our pro-paganda, by dwelling on Russia's poverty and backwardness, could be expected to relax rather than to raise the international tension.[50]

The propaganda section was established with the innocuous name of the Information Research Department (IRD) and was to be funded by a secret vote in the same way as the security and intelligence services, MI5 and MI6 were.[51] The spy, Guy Burgess, was a member of it briefly, so it was not a secret to the Russians for long. Mayhew had Burgess sacked for being "dirty, drunk and idle."[52] When the Russia Committee was informed of the cabinet decision on January 15, Jacob, who had just been promoted to head all the BBC's overseas services, said a speech Attlee had made on January 3 on British foreign policy must be followed by other ministerial speeches on which the BBC could base its publicity.[53]

The Foreign Office telegram of January 23, 1948, which outlined the new policy to British embassies, carried the rubric that it was "of partic-ular secrecy."[54] It said: "His Majesty's Government have decided that the developing Communist threat to the whole fabric of Western civilisation compels us to adopt a new publicity policy designed primarily to give a lead and support the truly democratic elements in Western Europe, which are anti-Communist and, at the same time, genuinely progressive and reformist in withstanding the inroads of Communism."

The main target was the broad masses of workers and peasants in Europe and the Middle East. Only in later years would some commis-sions investigating broadcasting say the target had to be the elite.

By April Bevin had hardened up on the desirability of the fullest cooperation with the BBC and in a top-secret memorandum stated cate-gorically that the views of the British government should be made clear in the Iron Curtain countries principally through the BBC and pro-nouncements made in London.[55] But there was unease about how much the BBC could be relied on:

General Jacob is taken fully into the confidence of the Foreign Office. Doubts are, however, fairly frequently expressed by those who follow the broadcasts to foreign countries closely as to whether the B.B.C.'s cherished tradition of independence from government control (of which Sir William Haley is a strong exponent) and their fear of incurring accusations of bias, coupled with the personal views of some of the personnel concerned with foreign broadcasts, does not prevent their broadcasts from being effective instruments of the Government's present publicity policy. The view has been expressed to me that the situation will not be satisfactory unless we alter the present relationship with the B.B.C. so far as overseas broadcasts are concerned, and insist that they accept definite official direction as to their contents. But I should not be in favour of this. It would raise very serious issues here and might well diminish the influence and reputation in foreign countries of the B.B.C.'s broadcasts.[56]

Bevin said he was going to have the BBC output checked and if it was not in line with present policy would take it up with the BBC. The Foreign Office produced the results of the checks on July 15.[57] The conclusion was that the BBC services to Eastern Europe suffered from "false objectivity."[58] Jacob agreed with this conclusion. By giving the news "straight," they gave a false impression, which needed correcting by commentary. Christopher Warner, the assistant under secretary in charge of Information Services, proposed to Jacob in a meeting about the survey that the embassies should provide material that they would like used by the BBC. Jacob welcomed it. The Foreign Office established a special series of telegrams from embassies behind the Iron Curtain to be passed on to the BBC with the rather curious prefix of "ASIDE."[59] The relationship in 1948 seems a far cry from that described by Herbert Morrison in 1946, whereby once the general character and scope of the service had been laid down, the BBC would have had complete discretion as to the content.

Organizations concerned with external communication are not, of course, usually any better in dealing with problems of internal communication than others. So it is, perhaps, not surprising that, despite the eagerness of Jacob to collaborate with the Foreign Office, the report concluded that one of the reasons the new publicity policy had not been reflected more thoroughly in the BBC's broadcasts was that some of the BBC officials were either not aware of the existence of the policy or had not received directions to follow it. Ralph Murray, the head of IRD, believed that arrangements were being made with the BBC for them to adopt "an editorial line" to reflect the policy, particularly in the overseas service.[60] The Foreign Office regarded the BBC as by far the most important propaganda weapon it had in Eastern Europe.[61]

The new policy was associated with the Third Force. The British government did not want to create the impression that the Foreign Office was organizing an anticommunist campaign. The Foreign Office was anxious that the people—journalists and others—to whom they were passing documents should not be embarrassed by being open to the charge of "receiving anti-Communist briefs from some sinister body in the Foreign Office engaged in fabrication of propaganda directed against the Soviet Union."[62] The only government that was advised of what the British were doing was that of the United States.

Jacob had changed his position from his 1946 statement of policy when he had said the BBC was not waging an ideological war with anyone.[63] He had no doubt that he was engaged in propaganda. "It is evident that any country deciding to embark on a service of broadcasts to foreign audiences does so because it wants to influence those audiences in its favour. All such broadcasting is therefore propaganda," he wrote.[64] He was anxious to work with the IRD and took the initiative in proposing that Tangye Lean, editor, European services, should be put in direct touch with Murray. Jacob said that the essence of the matter was to be sure that the material it would be getting from the IRD was accurate. But he went beyond that and wanted the BBC to make suggestions on the IRD's projects.[65] One month later Jacob told Warner that he would tell R. McCall, controller of overseas services, to keep in touch with Murray with a view to making suggestions about his output.[66] The BBC, therefore, took upon itself the role of adviser on British government propaganda. Surprisingly, the Foreign Office dragged its feet on Jacob's suggestion of contacts—Jacob had to make the proposal twice before anything happened—but on June 9 Murray, Tangye Lean, and McCall had their first meeting over lunch in the red-plush luxury of the Café Royal.[67]

Jacob himself was no passive participant at meetings of the Russia Committee but gave his views on how the British Government should conduct its propaganda. The minutes recorded:

[General Jacob stressed] the importance from a propaganda point of view of taking the initiative at the United Nations meetings. He said that the Soviet delegation with their simple proposal for disarmament had got the initiative leaving us on the defensive. We had now by the speeches of U.K. delegates, wrested it back to some extent but it was important that in future we should on such occasions be ready with a simple proposition which would capture public opinion. General Jacob also said that in his opinion it was more important to emphasize the advantage of living under a democratic regime than to try to explode the "myth" of the Soviet Union.[68]

By July 1948 Mayhew was reporting that the new Information Research Department was turning out a fairly steady stream of anti-Communist propaganda material. In the same month the Colonial Information Policy Committee (CIPC) was established to coordinate programs in Britain's colonies. In addition to senior government officials it included Jacob of the BBC.[69] Its existence was kept secret even from other Whitehall departments.[70]

The communist vituperation against the BBC continued. On March 12, 1949, the Russians, in their German service, had called the BBC's broadcasters "mad agitators and disruptionists" and on March 27, 1949, in their Polish service, described the BBC as a "crying radio crocodile." All this was part of the heightened tension of the cold war evidenced by the coup in Czechoslovakia and the Berlin blockade of 1948.[71]

Although listening was still not forbidden in Russia, by March 1949 the BBC claimed to have evidence that members of the party had been expelled for listening to London. In these circumstances the BBC believed listening was evidence of doubt and the first faint sign of opposition.[72]

Shortwave sets were fairly freely available, although expensive. A medium-priced set cost 850 roubles, which was about two months' pay for an artisan.[73] A dealer could only sell a set when the set's card with the potential buyer's name and particulars on it had been signed and stamped by the Ministry of State Security (MGB). If the buyer was not already under suspicion there was no difficulty.[74] Russians do not appear to have suffered in the same way as Bulgarian peasants, who were offered a free overhaul of their radios. When they got them back, they could only receive Radio Sofia.[75]

By 1949 the idea of a Third Force was no longer a viable option for British foreign policy, and the government went fully on the offensive. In December 1949 the ad hoc ministerial committee on anticommunist propaganda decided that all restrictions on subversive propaganda should be removed.[76] The Foreign Office had in July circulated a paper to ministers in which it concluded that every opportunity had to be taken to weaken Russian control over the satellite states, although actions involving serious risk of war or likely to encourage fatal resistance had to be avoided.

The IRD wanted to plant stories to draw the Soviets out on subjects to which the IRD would like to know the answers. They had no doubt the BBC would agree to broadcast them because Jacob had said the BBC would temper its broadcasts to accord with the national interest. It is not surprising he said that because the BBC had always had that obligation since the 1946 Licence. The BBC considered the IRD's idea of planting stories but decided it should be put in cold storage because of jamming.[77] The Foreign Office and the BBC were later to make the remarkable admission that "much of the material and a great deal of the background for the BBC's broadcasts to the Soviet Union, the satellites and China reaches the BBC from this department. The liaison in this respect is both close and constant."[78] So close was the relationship that in 1953 when the Czech service wanted Eden to give them a message to commemorate the fifth anniversary of the coup, the head of the Central European service first approached the IRD to get it. Anatol Goldberg, chief commentator for the Eastern European services, considered his contacts with the IRD personal, and he maintained very good relations with various IRD representatives.[79] By the mid-fifties the IRD had sixty staff, permanent and contract, in the Soviet section.

During the Suez crisis of 1956 the IRD was converted into the Information Coordinating Executive under military command. Two years later the IRD was split into two sections, one for the Soviet bloc and the other for areas outside Europe.[80]

The BBC had no qualms about accepting the specific advice of the Foreign Office on handling particular aspects of anticommunist propaganda. In a letter marked secret of June 20, 1950, Murray pointed out to Jacob that it would be very helpful if his editors could pay special attention to the evidence the British planned to raise at a forthcoming meeting of the United Nations Economic and Social Council about forced labor in the Soviet Union and the satellites. The letter carries the annotation, "all services alerted."[81] Shortly afterward the BBC agreed to a suggestion by Murray that it set up a quarterly meeting under Foreign Office chairmanship to plan output on communism.[82] But for the BBC there was a lot of difference between accepting advice and accepting instructions. Some notes the BBC had received from the southern department of the Foreign Office "give one the impression that they are trying to get into a position to direct our broadcasts," Jacob had warned two years earlier.[83]

A Foreign Office official replied to an inquiry into BBC policy that the BBC never persistently broadcast a line that was inconsistent with the policy of the British government although the Foreign Office had never claimed that they had the right to stop them from doing it.[84] Some years later the cabinet itself reviewed policy about propaganda and publicity toward the Soviet Union and satellites. It concluded that the general line should be unchanged, but, in the case of Russia, particular attention should be given to encouraging Russian interest in and knowledge of the outside world. The BBC agreed to implement the policy.[85]

There were BBC connections with British intelligence. The BBC European service liaison officer in Berlin, A. Earley, in a memorandum on June 21, 1949, included the following:

> Captain Robert, who is on the Staff of R.I.O.[regional intelligence officer] Berlin (and who, I believe, is known to Chris Rhodes [Earley's predecessor]) has asked me to bear in mind that Eastern Zone visitors to this office may give assistance to his organization in passing their knowledge of the Russian occupation army or of the Volkspolizei and its various organizations to the right quarter. I promised to pass on suitable visitors to him but only such visitors who will not "take fright" and not come to see us again as a result.[86]

The BBC European service representative was also in touch with the British Political Division at this time about some lists the BBC had had from the Sozialdemokratische Partei Deutschlands (SPD) (German Social Democratic Party) in Hanover of purported agents and informers of the Sozialistische Einheitspartei Deutschlands (SED) (Socialist Unity Party) in the Eastern Zone. The SPD wanted the BBC to use the names in its broadcasts to warn off their East German listeners. The Political Division passed the lists to the Intelligence organization at Herford. The BBC representative showed a certain schadenfreude in reporting that Radio in the American Sector (RIAS), Berlin, had broadcast some of the lists, but "two of the names mentioned were quite definitely incorrect, one of them being that of a man long since dead and the other being that of a man who, as a long-standing resident of Western Berlin, is now somewhat displeased."[87] The Intelligence division could not guarantee any part of the list. The Political Division agreed with the head of the BBC German service that to be able to warn Eastern Zone inhabitants against people of this sort would be of very great value but questioned the advisability of doing so on the very slim evidence available.

The correspondent of the BBC External Services in Berlin was an important channel for IRD material. His relationship with the British government representatives was, in any case, special. The post had been established with the title BBC European service liaison officer at the request of the U.K. high commissioner. He paid no rent for his office in Lancaster House, the headquarters of the British military government in Berlin, nor for his private accommodation. His telephone calls, except those to London, which were paid for in London, were borne by the British military government.[88] In the early fifties the BBC European service man, together with other British correspondents, had moved out of Lancaster House, but even in the sixties he still lived in a British army major's house. Eventually, the BBC combined the posts of the correspondents in Berlin so that one person covered for both External and Domestic Services. Part of the costs were carried by the German government as occupation costs into the eighties.[89]

Charles Wheeler was assigned to the BBC liaison post in Berlin in 1953. He recounts how one of the two IRD men in Berlin would visit him in his office armed with cyclostyled sheets of information. He was not allowed to look at them, but the IRD man paraphrased the contents. They were gossipy news items about East Germany, which Wheeler sent to London for use in German service programs. The IRD had access to the clandestine British intercepts of domestic East German communications, so it was not too difficult to find items that put the regime in a bad light or stories that made it look foolish. Those items in the latter category were particularly valuable for the satirical program *Zwei Genossen* (Two comrades) about two party officials.

On June 16, 1953, Wheeler was walking along the street when a car drew up beside him. In it was Peter Seckelmann of the IRD. "Get over to East Berlin," he told him. The tip-off enabled Wheeler to steal a march on his colleagues with his story of the outbreak of the Berlin riots. Wheeler believes Seckelmann had learned of the riots from the intercepts.[90]

From the end of 1954 the BBC passed letters from East European countries to a secret department of the Foreign Office. In a letter dated December 18, 1954, R. O'Rorke, head of the German service of the BBC said to R. A. Harrison, its representative in Berlin:

> It has been decided here on a high level that the European Services should make available to an unspecified but secret department of the Foreign Office all mail originating from East European countries. Wherever possible, letters to be provided with the original envelopes. After scrutiny letters will be returned to us. At the meeting on this subject I pointed out to the Controller that a) we had already done this once in the past and been told that the letters were of no interest and that b) in any case you made immediately available to intelligence sources in Berlin any material which you considered of interest. These two points were noted, but it was decided nonetheless that we must cooperate in the scheme, at least experimentally.[91]

"The postcard from Czechoslovakia . . . was of great interest and we shall be grateful if you will let us see in future any mail coming from this and other satellite countries in East Europe apart from East Germany," a Foreign Office official wrote to the BBC one month later.[92] The official was one Dennis Ambler, but his name did not appear in the

Foreign Office staff lists. Wheeler received eight or ten visitors a day who would give him information. Sometimes he would persuade them to sit down in the office and write a letter to the BBC.

Wheeler says the only time he knowingly gave information to MI6 was at the request of an informant, a young West German engineer who had been put in touch with Wheeler by a BBC engineer. He gave Wheeler information and wanted Wheeler to put him in touch with MI6. Wheeler discouraged this idea but agreed to pass on to British Intelligence what the engineer told him. Wheeler's successor, R. A. Harrison, gave MI6 the man's name when things began to become dangerous, and the British got him out of East Germany.

Not so fortunate was a defector who was an officer in the People's Police. The British authorities told Harrison the location of the safe house where they had hidden him. Harrison went there once a week and taped what the defector wanted broadcast to his former colleagues in the police in East Germany. One night the police officer was invited to a party, kidnapped, taken to East Berlin, and never heard of again.[93]

In 1957 the BBC German service administration reported an intensified campaign by the local authorities to discourage inhabitants of the Soviet Zone from writing letters to it. Emil Tauber, an assistant taxation officer, was sentenced to four years hard labor on the charge of having sent inflammatory and libellous letters about conditions in the Soviet Zone to the BBC, the report said.[94]

When the Berlin Wall went up in 1961, the BBC received few visitors from East Germany and letters came via cover addresses.

As soon as the Second World War ended, BBC services to Europe were reduced, but no single service was eliminated and there were almost no reductions to services to the rest of the world. At the end of the war the BBC broadcast more hours than did any two nations in the world added together.[95] It was a two-power standard, similar to the two-power naval standard that Britain had to abandon in 1909 when the two next largest navies combined, the German and the American, became larger than the Royal Navy. Britain lost the two-power standard in broadcasting in 1950. In 1949 the BBC broadcast 687 hours a week, the Soviet Union 434, and the United States 214; in 1950 the BBC was down to 643, the Soviet Union up to 533, and the United States up to 497.[96] It is not surprising that, despite the importance the government attached to propaganda, as Britain tried to find its role in the postwar world, the size of the broadcasting effort was often challenged and was frequently cut back.

VOA: Keeping the Soviet Bear Busy

Domestic attacks on the VOA continued. Such was the opposition to VOA in some quarters that when considering 1948 appropriations the House Appropriations Committee eliminated the entire OIC appropriation. The committee thought the government should not be in the news business and suggested as alternatives the United Nations Educational, Scientific and Cultural Organization (UNESCO) and private enterprise.[97] The president and secretary of state intervened, and the Senate subcommittee restored about one-third of the funds. Meanwhile, the State Department abolished the OIC and created the Office of International Information and Educational Exchange (OIE) in its place.[98]

Not until January 27, 1948, after much debate and the congressional tour referred to by Kent Cooper, was the VOA given a firm legislative foundation through the Smith-Mundt Act, P.L. 402, the United States Information and Educational Exchange Act of 1948. In recommending the bill, the Senate Committee on Foreign Relations felt that the communist propaganda campaigns against the United States called for urgent, forthright, and dynamic measures to disseminate truth. They believed that the bill would constitute an important step in the right direction toward adequate dissemination of the truth about America, its ideals, and its people.[99] The act set the task of providing for the preparation and dissemination abroad of information about the United States, its people, and its policies through press, publications, radio, motion pictures, and other information media. It created a United States Advisory Commission on Information to formulate and recommend policies and programs. Significant, in light of later developments, was the provision for maximum use of private agencies.[100]

As a result of the assaults on the VOA, despite the cold war the hours broadcast to Eastern Europe in December 1947 were, at 4 hours 15 minutes a day, less than at the end of 1945 when they were 5 hours 9 minutes a day.[101]

George V. Allen, a diplomat and former newspaperman, succeeded Benton as assistant secretary of state for public affairs on February 25, 1948, and out went the Madison Avenue advertising style. Another diplomat, Charles Thayer, the chief of the Russian desk, had just become the chief (later to be called director) of the VOA. The OIE was abolished, and the Office of International Information (OII) became responsible in the State Department for international broadcasting.[102] Thayer had no doubt that the VOA had to change its Madison Avenue style and to learn from the Communists, "who despatch to foreign areas not super-salesmen but fanatical believers in the students of the Communist religion whose emphasis is not on the techniques of persuasion but on the persuasivenesss of the theory they are propagating."[103]

Between 70 percent and 75 percent of the VOA's output was handled by private broadcasters. The continuation of that policy was laid down in the Smith-Mundt Act. Fortunately for the VOA, a program series produced by NBC put an end to it. Representative John Tabor, chairman of the House Appropriations Committee, asked to see one day's VOA output. It contained a program in a series *Know North America*. And, as Representative Tabor read out to the House, the section on Wyoming carried the stunning assertion that "our Indian maidens run in races dressed in nothing but feathers." The House erupted, and so later did the Senate. Senator John Connelly of Texas got hold of the program on Texas. The script, he told the Senate, provided for a Latin American to ask, "Don't you have a saying that Texas was born in sin but New England was born in hypocrisy?" The programs had been produced by a Cuban author and a Venezuelan supervisor employed by NBC. The programs had neither been seen nor heard by any one else at NBC.[104]

The House and the Senate opened investigations into the Voice's activities. They criticized the lack of supervision and checking of program content.[105] It was a god-given gift to Thayer, who had been trying to get more VOA control over output. The NBC and CBS programing contracts with the VOA ended.[106]

The start of jamming in February 1948 and the increased intensity of the cold war caused the VOA gradually to take a more aggressive stance in its broadcasts. Congress encouraged the VOA and instructed it to refute Soviet misstatements and lies more quickly. Surprisingly in an arm of the U.S. government, Congress specifically wanted the VOA to discomfort local governments and encourage resistance of people in totalitarian and satellite countries by broadcasting suppressed news.[107] The tone of VOA broadcasts varied through the early years of the cold war. John Albert, then chief of the German section, summed it up well: "As the official statements of the United States leaders took up polemics and attacks on the USSR, so too, did the VOA. . . . And with McCarthy, if you weren't hard hitting, you ran the risk of being soft on communism."[108] All this was in contrast to the "calm" BBC.

A summary of how the main international broadcasters operated on content is contained in a study on broadcasting to Germany by a team from the Committee on Communication of the University of Chicago begun in July 1949 under contract with the Department of State.

> The Voice talked mainly about the United States, its people and its poli-cies; the USSR paid primary attention to German conditions; while the BBC held to a middle position. The VOA always described America and its policies in favorable terms—American shortcomings were ex-plained away or ignored. Only occasionally did the VOA admit that the United States had some economic and social problems which were not completely solved. The BBC gave a cross-section in national self-pro-jection; there was no attempt to paint a rosy picture. Moscow's self-projection was the best of the three.[109]

In late 1949 the State Department saw to it that the VOA moved away from the old theory of the "fair and full" picture of America. VOA programs discrediting the Russians were also developed.[110]

By September 1949 VOA transmission time had been increased to 2 hours 30 minutes, plus another 30 minutes to Siberia. In 1949 the State Department claimed that eight to ten million people in the Soviet Union listened to the Voice.[111] There had been a big drive to increase production of radio receivers, and some estimates put the population of radio re-ceivers at the end of 1950 at four million plus.[112]

Four years later a study of the English language services said that Radio Moscow sounded like a propaganda agency using news to illus-trate themes, whereas the BBC sounded like a news service almost self-consciously trying to make everything come out 50 percent on each side. The VOA sounded like the news service of one of the great protagonists of the cold war. It was neither as neutral as the BBC nor as carefully propagandistic as Radio Moscow.[113]

Edward W. Barrett, who succeeded Allen as assistant secretary of state on February 16, 1950, said one of his objectives in the job was "keeping the Soviet bear so busy scratching his own fleas that he has little time for molesting others."[114] He had been editorial director of *Newsweek* magazine, had founded the *Colombia Journalism Review,* and had worked in the OSS in propaganda during the war. Foy D. Kohler, a career foreign service officer, had succeeded Thayer as chief of the VOA toward the end of 1949. The task of Barrett and Kohler was to imple-ment the "Campaign of Truth," which the Eighty-first Congress autho-rized and which saw the most spectacular increase in the activities of the VOA since its founding.

President Truman laid out the aims in his "Campaign of Truth" speech on April 20, 1950:

> The cause of freedom is being challenged throughout the world today by the forces of imperialistic Communism. This is a struggle, above all else, for the minds of men. Propaganda is one of the most powerful weapons the Communists have in this struggle. Deceit, distortion and lies are systematically used by them as matter of deliberate policy. This propaganda can be overcome by truth—plain, simple, unvarnished truth—presented by newspapers, radio, newsreels, and other sources that the people trust. . . . We know how false these Communist promises are. But it is not enough for us to know this. Unless we get the real story across to people in other countries, we will lose the battle for men's minds by pure default. . . . We must make ourselves known as we really are—not as Communist propaganda pictures us. We must pool our efforts with those of other free peoples in a sustained, intensified program to promote the cause of freedom against the propaganda of slavery. We must make ourselves heard around the world in a great campaign of truth.[115]

The objectives of the campaign were first, to establish a healthy international community; second, to present America fairly; third, to deter the Soviets from further encroachments; fourth, to help to roll back Soviet influence by all means short of force.[116]

The Campaign of Truth was the beginning of pyschological planning in the State Department. It then moved on to draw up a plan to counterbalance jamming by setting up a ring of powerful transmitters along the Iron Curtain.[117]

Barrett had started to campaign in Congress to get more money for the information program, which he complained was less than General Motors alone was spending on its public relations and its advertising. The outlook was gloomy. Senator Pat McCarran of Nevada almost succeeded in getting the program abolished in early 1950. Barrett said, "No one could prove that last year's funds had been well spent by producing a cage filled with 7,000 Russians who had deserted communism."[118] But all was to change when, as Barrett put it, on June 25 Joseph Stalin pulled the trigger for the Korean invasion and flooded the world with propaganda to the effect that the United States had started it all.[119]

By September 1950 President Truman issued a classified message to the State Department laying down a new tough propaganda line. It was to combat communism and communist media output "by exposing its lies . . . and subjecting it to ridicule."[120]

CIA: And the Truth Shall Make You Free

Why did the U.S. government decide that the VOA was inadequate and that they had to establish another international radio network? General Lucius Clay, former commanding general of the U.S. occupation forces in Europe, tried to explain: "When I left Germany, I came home with a very firm conviction that we needed in addition to the Voice of America a different, broader voice—a voice of the free people—a radio which would speak to each country behind the Iron Curtain in its own language, and from the throats of its own leaders who fled for their lives because of their beliefs in freedom."[121]

But Frank Altschul made it plain that when the Free Europe Committee had been set up, a no less important objective was "to provide a channel over which American citizens, not subject to the restrictions which hamper a government agency, could say things on their own responsibility which it was considered desirable to have said, but which the Voice of America, as an agency of government, was not in a position to say."[122] The CIA later coyly explained that because private funding would not be enough, "non-attributable government funds would have to be provided."[123]

There were other reasons for the structure, too. Washington was inundated with East European exiles, many former cabinet ministers and intellectuals of standing. They were an embarrassment to the government and time consuming, taking up hours of the time of senior government officials with their complaints and pet schemes and ideas. Thomas Braden, a CIA man much concerned with them, likened them to refugees described in Macaulay's *History of England from the Accession of James II*.[124] One comment of Macaulay's inspired by the English refugees in Holland in the seventeenth century would ring true: "A politician driven into banishment by a hostile faction generally sees the society which he has quitted through a false medium. Every object is distorted and discoloured by his regrets, his longings and his resentments. Every little discontent appears to him to portend a revolution. Every riot is a rebellion."[125] The refugees in the United States had no money. Ways of employing them had to be found. "There had to be some way of keeping them in a blue suit," Braden said. The CIA wanted them for intelligence gathering although Braden said that after a while the intelligence they were giving was nothing but gossip. Shades of Macaulay! And there was also the thought that they would represent a cadre to return to their homelands if the Soviet grip loosened.

The more immediate international political background lay in three

events of 1948: the communist coup in Czechoslovakia, the start of the
Berlin blockade, and the success of the CIA in manipulating the Italian
elections so that they were won by the Christian Democrats and not by
the Communists.

The story of the founding of Radio Free Europe has an overt and a
covert version. Robert T. Holt published *Radio Free Europe,* the first history of the organization, in 1958. His book starts: "Radio Free Europe
was established by a group of private citizens in December 1949, for the
purpose of conducting a propaganda campaign against six Communist-
dominated satellites in central and Eastern Europe."[126] After an eighteen-
month study of RFE he came to the conclusion that "RFE has no formal
relationship with the State Department or other governmental agency,"[127]
although he also said, "Some people might object to referring to RFE as
a 'private' or 'non-official' undertaking because it is commonly believed
that it has received funds from the United States government. Obviously
any financial relationships that might exist between Washington and
RFE cannot be discussed in this volume."[128] One wonders why not.

His overt version was that George F. Kennan, the director of the
policy planning staff of the State Department, had informal discussions
about the exiles problem with a number of people in and out of government. "They came to the conclusion that the proper place for help and
comfort lay not in the official chambers of the United States government
but in the hearts of the American people." In February 1949 Kennan
discussed it with Joseph C. Grew, a distinguished former diplomat. He
was an old Moscow hand with an implacable hatred of the Soviet Union
and communism.[129] In 1919 he had strongly opposed recognition of the
Bolshevik regime.[130] On April 19, 1949, Kennan wrote to Dean Acheson,
the secretary of state, that a planned national committee to deal with the
émigré problem had been designed "to become one of the principal in-
strumentalities for accomplishing a number of our most important policy objectives."[131] Acheson agreed with Kennan's ideas, and shortly
Grew received a message from Acheson asking if he would establish a
private group to deal with certain aspects of the refugee problem. Grew
contacted DeWitt C. Poole, a former colleague. DeWitt Poole, who had
been chargé d'affaires in Moscow in 1917 and had been a State Department expert in anticommunist propaganda, had founded the *Public
Opinion Quarterly (POQ)* at Princeton University before the war. He had
been chief of the Foreign Nationalities Branch of the OSS.[132]

After the war the *POQ* frequently published articles advocating expanded U.S. psychological warfare programs. They were representative
of the views of an important group of academics.[133] Grew and Poole met

in May 1949 and agreed to form a committee broadly representative of the major religious, economic, and political groups. Among those who joined were Frank Altschul, a New York banker; Adolf A. Berle, a lawyer and former assistant secretary of state; James B. Carey, a labor leader; Henry R. Luce, editor-in-chief of Time, Inc.; and Dwight D. Eisenhower.[134] On the list also, but not mentioned in Holt's main text and relegated to a note at the back of the book, was Allen W. Dulles, lawyer, OSS representative in Switzerland during the war. Holt's coyness about Dulles is the more curious because Dulles was briefly the first president of the Free Europe Committee and by the time Holt published in 1958 had already been director of the CIA for five years. On June 1, 1949, the Committee for a Free Europe, Inc., was formed.

Grew, elected chairman two weeks later, held a press conference during which he announced the formation and listed three objectives:

> 1. To find suitable occupations for those democratic exiles who had come from Eastern Europe.
> 2. To put the voices of the exiled leaders on the air, addressed to their own peoples back in Europe, "in their own languages, in the familiar tones." They would also be helped, if possible, to get their messages back by printed word.
> 3. To enable the exiled leaders to see democracy at work and to experience democracy in action so that they could "testify to what the trial of freedom and democracy in the United States has brought."[135]

On June 2 the name of the committee was changed to the National Committee for a Free Europe. It was chopped back again in 1955 to the Free Europe Committee, Inc., because the organization moved into new offices at 110 West 57th Street in New York, and the old name would not fit over the door.[136]

Three committees were formed to implement Grew's three objectives. Frank Altschul was the driving force behind the idea of using radio.[137] He was appointed chairman of the committee on radio and the press. Poole succeeded Dulles as president, and Dulles became chairman of an executive committee.[138] They also established national committees of the émigrés.

The origins of the covert RFE story lay in the inaugural meeting of the National Security Council (NSC) on December 19, 1947. At that meeting Directive NSC 4, requiring the secretary of state to coordinate anticommunist propaganda activity, was issued.[139] Minutes later it approved the top secret NSC 4A, directing that the newly approved overt programs be supplemented by covert psychological operations.[140] On June 18, 1948, the NSC issued NSC 10/2, which replaced NSC 4A, authorizing the creation of a covert action organization, initially given the anodyne name, the Office of Special Projects, which was shortly changed to the equally euphemistic name of the Office of Policy Coordination (OPC). Covert operations included propaganda. The directive talked of the "vicious covert activities of the USSR, its satellite countries and Communist groups to discredit and defeat the aims and activities of the United States and other Western powers." The use of the word *discredit* was important; this was a propaganda war.[141]

Operationally, the organization responsible for psychological warfare was the CIA. But the unit within the CIA that was in charge was the Office of Policy Coordination. And the OPC was an anomaly within the CIA because, although the CIA paid for it, housed it, staffed it, and supported it, the director of the OPC was selected by the secretary of state. State and Defense laid down policy, bypassing the director of Central Intelligence.[142] On September 1, 1948, Frank G. Wisner was appointed assistant director for policy coordination (ADPC). His background is important to the story of the founding of RFE. He was a brilliant lawyer, a Southern gentleman who during the war had worked in the OSS in Europe. He had later become deputy to the assistant secretary of state for occupied areas. While he was in the State Department he had spent much time on problems involving refugees in Germany, Austria, and Trieste. In the 1976 Senate report on intelligence a major role in the foundation of RFE was attributed to Wisner:

> The combination of State's continuing interest and Wisner's personal experience led to OPC's immediate emphasis on Central European refugee operations. OPC representatives made contact with thousands of Soviet refugees and emigres for the purpose of influencing their political leadership. The National Committee for Free Europe, a group of prominent American businessmen, lawyers, and philanthropists, and Radio Free Europe, were products of the OPC program.[143]

Kim Philby, the British spy, had dealings with Wisner and does not seem to have thought much of him:

> The Office of Policy Coordination (OPC) was concerned with subversion on a worldwide basis. Its head was Frank Wisner, a youngish man for so responsible a job, balding and running self-importantly to fat. He favoured an orotund style of conversation which was disconcerting. I accompanied a mission which he led to London to discuss with SIS

[Secret Intelligence Service] matters of common interest. When the discussions touched on issues of international concern, the Foreign Office sent representatives to watch the proceedings. At one such meeting, attended on behalf of the Foreign Office by Tony Rumbold, Wisner expatiated on one of his favourite themes: the need for camouflaging the source of secret funds supplied to apparently respectable bodies in which we were interested. "It is essential," said Wisner in his usual informal style, "to secure the overt cooperation of people with conspicuous access to wealth in their own right." Rumbold started scribbling. I looked over his shoulder and saw what he had written: "people with conspicuous access to wealth in their own right = rich people."[144]

In light of this story it seems very likely that it was Wisner's idea to camouflage Radio Free Europe's funding with rich people.

Wisner described his propaganda apparatus as his "mighty Wurlitzer." He boasted that he could sit himself down at his organ and play almost any tune he liked from eerie horror music to light fantasias.[145] There was no lack of funds to get the Free Europe Committee going, and the source was not primarily people with conspicuous access to wealth in their own right.

Why the secrecy? As Thomas Braden said, "In the early 1950's, when the cold war was really hot, the idea that Congress would have approved many of our projects was about as likely as the John Birch Society approving Medicare."[146] And NSC 10/2 instructed that the operations be "so planned and executed that any U.S. government responsibility for them is not evident to unauthorized persons and that if uncovered the U.S. Government can plausibly disclaim any responsibility for them."[147]

On the marble wall of the main lobby at CIA headquarters at Langley, Virginia, was inscribed:

AND YE SHALL KNOW THE TRUTH
AND THE TRUTH SHALL MAKE YOU FREE
John, viii: 32

The paradox of RFE was that an organization dedicated to truth was founded on a lie. That was the consequence of the secrecy.

The U.S. government did not hesitate to lie. When in 1954 the Czech government asked that the radio and balloon leaflet operations sponsored by the Free Europe Committee be halted, the reply read in part:

The Crusade for Freedom, an organization of private citizens, is supported by millions of Americans and expresses the aspirations of the American people for the freedom of all peoples. . . . The [radio and balloon leaflet] operation was undertaken by this private organization and neither the U.S. government nor the U.S. authorities in Germany were involved. The U.S. government rejects the protest of the Czechoslovak government which is without foundation.[148]

It became increasingly apparent that the restrictions on distribution of printed material and films meant that radio was almost the only way to reach East Europeans.[149] With the money flowing in from the CIA, the first need was someone to organize the radio operations and to recruit and train staff. The committee hired Robert E. Lang, formerly of the OSS, a young product advertising director of the Post Cereal Company, initially as a consultant and later as director. In December 1949 the Radio Committee became Radio Free Europe, a division of the Free Europe Committee. During the first year of its existence the Free Europe Committee changed its tack. It started out by thinking of leasing airtime from existing broadcasters. It approached the commercial stations, Radio Luxembourg, Radio Monte Carlo, and Europe Number One, but they all declined. RFE, therefore, had to set up a radio station from scratch. The committee had not initially envisaged a news service or music or drama. But "our friends in the south"—the OPC—wanted a more ambitious program. And that was what started broadcasting on July 4, 1950.[150]

The climate was getting rougher as evidenced by directive NSC 68, issued on April 14, 1950, which called for covert operations to subvert communist regimes.[151] The Korean War broke out only ten days before RFE started transmissions.

The broadcasters' objectives for RFE were very varied. Frank Altschul believed:

In the initial stage its purpose is to prevent, or at the very least to hinder the cultural, political and economic integration of the target area with the Soviet Union. In a later stage it may prove useful as a means of inviting or of stimulating positive and effective action. . . . For the time being the programs of Radio Free Europe are designed to keep hope alive among our friends, and to confuse, divide and undermine our enemies within the satellite states.[152]

Cord Meyer, who succeeded Thomas Braden as chief of the International Organizations Division of the CIA in September 1954, said:

I had no naive belief that the broadcasts of RFE and Radio Liberty (RL) could quickly bring the walls of the dictatorship tumbling down like those of Jericho. But I did strongly believe and remain convinced that persistent efforts to expose those within the bloc to both external and internal reality make aggressive foreign adventures more difficult for the regimes and incrementally over time improve the chances for gradual change toward more open societies.[153]

4

STARTING RFE AND RL
(1950–1953)

RFE: Harder than Popularizing Cornflakes

RADIO FREE EUROPE EXECUTIVES recruited nationals of the five countries to which they planned to broadcast—Bulgaria, Czechoslovakia, Hungary, Poland, and Romania—and trained them in New York. RFE acquired a 7.5 kilowatt transmitter and installed it at a former Luftwaffe air base at Lampertheim, south of Frankfurt. They nicknamed it Barbara. On July 4, 1950, RFE sent its first broadcast over that tiny shortwave transmitter. It consisted of thirty minutes of news, information, and political analysis for Czechoslovakia. It was a remarkable achievement only thirteen months after forming the Free Europe Committee and seven months after founding RFE. On July 14 broadcasts started to Romania, on August 4 to Hungary and Poland, and on August 11 to Bulgaria.

The programs were prepared in New York and either shipped across the Atlantic or broadcast by shortwave radio, always subject to noise, interference, and fading. It seems a Heath Robinson or Rube Goldberg approach today but would not have seemed so at the time. Nevertheless, it plainly was better to have the production facility near the transmitter, near the pool of European émigré labor, and near the target countries. So the Free Europe Committee built a facility on the borders of the magnificent English Garden, a park in Munich, still today one of the finest settings any radio station in the world could have had. And bigger transmitters were installed at other nearby sites. By November 1950 programs were being broadcast over three 10-kilowatt transmitters and one 50-kilowatt.

In May 1951 a 135-kilowatt medium wave transmitter started broadcasting to Czechoslovakia and Hungary.[1] These facilities were still inadequate. RFE needed more powerful transmitters with a better array of antennae. The shortwave transmitters needed to be farther away from the receivers because shortwave radio is reflected from the ionosphere; it needs to create a good wide angle with the ionosphere for the up and down paths of the signal. On July 4, 1951, transmission started from more powerful transmitters in Portugal.

Not surprisingly, there were formidable teething problems, the biggest of which was lack of news. RFE wanted to transmit to each country for at least eighteen hours a day to become the surrogate media of the target countries, unlike the BBC and the VOA, which transmitted only for short periods and then mainly international news. RFE's greatest need was for local news. The OPC had promised it but failed to deliver. (At one point the OPC suggested they might actually prepare the newscasts and commentaries. Not surprisingly this was greeted with horror in RFE, and the OPC did not pursue the idea).[2] RFE only got the news it wanted when it subscribed to wire services such as Reuters, started monitoring broadcasts and domestic news agencies' transmissions from behind the Iron Curtain, and built up its own reporting network to gather information from recent refugees.[3] Monitoring was important, but not until August 15, 1951, was the monitoring station at Schleissheim inaugurated.

At eleven o'clock in the morning on October 24, 1950, the Freedom Bell rang out from the Berlin Rathaus for the first time. It was the culmination of an extraordinary exercise in razzmatazz carried out with the panache, drive, and success at which the Americans are past masters. Similar in appearance to the Liberty Bell in Philadelphia, the Freedom Bell was the focus of a fund-raising campaign that earlier had rolled across the United States.

Some four hundred thousand people attended the inauguration ceremony in the Schoenberger Platz; one hundred thousand of the crowd were estimated to have come from East Berlin. Women wept, and General Lucius Clay was close to tears as he made his speech. Chancellor Adenauer was present, and Ernst Reuter, the mayor, spoke. The tones of the bell were subsequently used as a station break for RFE. "The rope of the death bell will become the gallows rope for those who ring it," was the comment of Hans Jendretsky, a member of the East German Politburo.[4]

Inspired by Madison Avenue and the leadership of General Clay, the Free Europe Committee launched the Crusade for Freedom to finance and support its activities. They appointed Abbott Washburn, a former OSS man with good public relations experience, as director. General Dwight D. Eisenhower inaugurated the campaign on September 4, 1950, Labor Day.

The opening of his speech, which was broadcast over all the major radio networks, encapsulated America's propaganda problem:

> Americans are dying in Korea tonight. They are dying for ideals they have been taught to cherish more than life itself. But it will be written and said tonight in Warsaw, in Prague, in Moscow that they died for American imperialism. Unfortunately, millions of people will believe this devilish libel against American soldiers, who have taken up arms in defense of liberty a second time in a tormented decade. Those millions will hear no other version but a hissing, hating tirade against America.

His solution was the Crusade for Freedom:

> We need powerful radio stations abroad, operated without Government restrictions, to tell in vivid and convincing form about the decency and essential fairness of democracy. . . . One such private station—Radio Free Europe—is now in operation in Western Germany. . . . The Crusade for Freedom will provide for the expansion of RFE into a network of stations. They will give the simplest, clearest charter in the world: "Tell the Truth."[5]

More than sixteen million signed "freedom scrolls" and contributed "truth dollars."[6] "You know we're actually helping to prevent World War Three," said Bing Crosby in a promotional film. "But that takes dollars. Truth dollars, all we can spare."[7] Ronald Reagan and Henry Fonda also made films. And Barbara Stanwyck, Frank Sinatra, and Rock Hudson made radio broadcasts. "Radio Free Europe is supported entirely by contributions by American citizens," listeners to the Rock Hudson broadcast were told.[8]

In fact the Crusade for Freedom was financially not that successful. From 1951 to 1976 receipts totaled about $50 million, costs about $20 million, and the net about $30 million. But it was good publicity for the efforts of the Free Europe Committee, which perhaps stood RFE in good stead when they came under attack in Congress later. One of the reasons for the campaign was to provide a front, to show that RFE had nothing to do with the U.S. government. But were that many fooled? A report for the director of the Psychological Strategy Board in 1952 said listeners in Czechoslovakia and Hungary believed RFE was sponsored by and had "the backing and financial support of the American government." He said that listeners to RFE and other Europeans could not conceive of such a big enterprise as RFE, with its powerful station and hundreds of staff, not being officially sponsored by the American government.[9]

Wanda Allender, a secretary in the early days of the crusade recalled the CIA subterfuge: "It was like a relative in the closet. Everyone knew he was there but no one commented on it." One of her jobs was to go down to Wall Street each week to the offices of the investment bankers, Henry Sears and Co., where General Charles Saltzman would give her the check to keep the crusade going.[10]

Benefiting from the experience of the Allies in World War II, the Crusade for Freedom dropped some three hundred million leaflets over Eastern Europe from balloons. The campaign started in Czechoslovakia on August 13, 1951. Some of the leaflets included the frequencies and broadcast schedules of RFE.[11] The slogan was "Winds of Freedom blow from west to east." Unfortunately, that was true of higher but not lower altitudes. Abbott Washburn, director of the crusade, recalled later the horror of the party inaugurating the launch of the balloons from a hill at Hof in West Germany when they started to drift back over their heads to the west. The group breathed again when the balloons rose higher and turned to the east. Only then could the party open the bottles of German lager they had brought with them for the celebration. Present were the columnist, Drew Pearson, the politician, Harold Stassen, and the president of RFE, C. D. Jackson.[12]

The CIA spared the Crusade for Freedom from involvement in the little exercise in which they put onto the trains going from Vienna to Hungary toilet paper printed with the picture of the communist leader, Matyas Rakosi.[13]

The only closure of an RFE service during the cold war was that to Albania in 1953. The service started with some difficulty in 1951, but the U.S. government had great hopes for resistance in Albania and even thought the regime might be overthrown. But there was no evidence the broadcasts were being heard. Albania had less than twenty thousand radio receivers in a population of more than one million.[14]

RFE did not broadcast to Yugoslavia. The BBC and the VOA did. Their broadcasts to Yugoslavia seem to have played no role in the cold war. They did not influence the break between the Soviet Union and Yugoslavia, which had nothing to do with Western pressure, but arose from the relationship between Stalin, Tito, and Djilas.[15]

The Americans' problem with propaganda was set out by Frank Altschul in a note to DeWitt C. Poole on August 15, 1950:

In the broad domain of propaganda, the United States has not until now been conspicuously successful. There is much evidence to indicate that we have been losing the war of words to the Soviet Union on many fronts. Although our government is one of the most liberal and forward-looking to be found anywhere, we have been convincingly portrayed to more than half the world as the prototype of reaction, of capitalist imperialism, even of Fascism. Meanwhile the Soviet Union, which is in the grip of an oriental despotism of the most vicious kind, has contrived to get itself accepted in vast areas, and even by some fuzzy-minded people in our own country, as the fountainhead of liberalism. Theirs is the Workers' Paradise, the peace-loving People's Democracy; ours is the land in which the worker is enslaved and the people the servants of a war-mongering ruling clique.[16]

Things had not changed much since the war. The U.S. Army General Board, in its final report on the war, concluded that propaganda had been "a neglected and ineptly used political and diplomatic weapon."[17]

Fifteen years later Lyndon B. Johnson did not think the situation had improved. In 1961, as vice-president, he returned from a foreign tour and said: "The United States has not sold itself to the world. A nation that knows how to popularize cornflakes and luxury automobiles ought to be able to tell the world the simple truth about what it is doing and why it is doing it."[18]

In Altschul's view one of the biggest problems was that in a total-itarian state government policy and propaganda were very closely linked. But in a democracy like that of the United States government policies were often initiated without regard to their propagandist implications. He be-moaned the propaganda problems that attended United States involve-ment with Chiang Kai-shek, Syngman Rhee, Franco, and even, curiously enough, the pope. But RFE could show Europeans that policies which the United States government might feel obliged to pursue did not always reflect the beliefs of the great mass of United States citizens. What RFE needed to stress was the situation in the United States of "a rising stan-dard of living, an ever-widening horizon of opportunity, personal free-dom and national independence in a world at peace." RFE also had to show that Western imperialism was a thing of the past.

One year later the *RFE Policy Handbook* of December 12, 1951, took a rather different line from Altschul's on the relationship with American government policy.

As a non-governmental station responsible to the millions of American citizens who support it, RFE cannot take a line contrary to United States Government policy or to the beliefs of the American people reflected in the Constitution of the United States and in American institutions. It holds itself free, however, to express independent views concerning the omission [*sic*—mission?] of the U.S. Government to and in respect of the countries to which its broadcasts are addressed, as well as views concerning the timing of acts and pronouncements.[19]

Altschul was very conscious of the dangers of association with the National Councils of émigrés that had been set up under the auspices of the Free Europe Committee. The desk staff of RFE had been recruited with the assistance of these National Councils. And those councils represented the past and, to some extent, the unpalatable past, of the peoples RFE wanted to influence. "It would be self-defeating to attempt to expound the gospel of twentieth century liberalism through the recognized voice of nineteenth century reaction," he worried. But a strong point was that RFE would be able to expose in countless ways the vast difference between Soviet promise and actual performance.

Altschul regarded RFE as no more than an experiment. Five weeks after broadcasting had started he was prepared to consider the possibility of closure. He concluded his report to DeWitt C. Poole:

> On the negative side is the circumstance that it is unlikely that we will be in a position to know the size of our audience, present or prospective. In this connection, the possibility of jamming must be given due weight. Furthermore, assuming reasonable success in reaching our listeners, it is unlikely that we will be able to determine how effective our programs really are. Whether in the light of all the foregoing the experiment will seem to continue to justify the very considerable capital and current expenditure involved is primarily a question for those to decide who have assumed the responsibility for defraying up to now our budgetary requirements.[20]

In the early days of RFE little policy guidance came from the OPC. But the Free Europe Committee evolved its own, and very bellicose it was, too. "It is the work of Gray-Black Propaganda to take up the individual Bolshevik rulers and the quislings and tear them apart, exposing their motivations, laying bare their private lives, pointing out their meannesses, pilloring their evil deeds, holding them up to ridicule and contumely." Thus said DeWitt C. Poole, the Freedom Committee president in November 1950.[21] The tone had become less shrill and strident in 1952 as the CIA got a better handle on policy. There was competition from the language groups to lay down policy too, and it was well into 1952 before the Americans in practice won this battle. They were not helped in this effort by the fact that C. D. Jackson, president of RFE, was reported to have told the émigrés at the dedication of the RFE building in Munich in 1951: "I'm turning over to you the keys of this building which is yours to operate as you see fit."[22]

The voluminous *RFE Policy Handbook* and a memorandum by William Griffith, political adviser, in February 1952 showed that the Americans had then no doubts about policy and who should lay it down. "This feeling of freedom is indispensible," Griffith said of the RFE exile staff. "That it is in fact an illusion, albeit a convincing one, is even more so."[23] This statement, however, has to be seen against the background of a need to reassure the nervous nellies in Washington that the émigrés were under firm American control. In fact the émigré broadcasting department directors had a great deal of responsibility and authority. There had been important organizational changes in the previous year or so. In September 1950 General "Beetle" Smith, had taken over as director of the CIA. A few days after taking charge he declared that Wisner and the OPC would in the future be under his sole administrative and policy control and would not take orders from the State Department. On January 2, 1951, Allen Dulles became deputy director of the CIA, responsible for the OPC and, hence, RFE and communication of its policy.[24] The policy handbook was marked "Secret. Not to be taken from the Offices of RFE." It was wide ranging and detailed, covering such topics as "After Liberation," "Anti-Semitism," "Broadcasting to Youth." The most important section said that RFE policy was based on "acceptance of the assumption that the West may display sufficient military power and skill in diplomatic negotiation for the Soviet tide to be forced to recede from our target countries without recourse to world war."[25]

The document shows great realism and responsibility vis-à-vis resistance. RFE was not addressing resistants or resistance groups as such, it said. It restricted comment on resistance news in broadcasts to warning against isolated acts of impulsive individuals and to assuring militant anti-Communists that "they will be given the means to fight for the liberation of their country when the time comes."[26]

Americans had difficulty finding something concrete with which to counter the Communists' peace movement. They hit on European unity as an aspiration for East Europeans, and it became a recurrent theme in papers on how to counter Soviet propaganda. Altschul talked about it, and the *RFE Policy Handbook* said: "The importance of this activity for propaganda purposes cannot be overestimated: It is the only Western movement comparable in moral attractiveness to the Soviet 'peace' movement." In recounting the advantages the authors of the handbook forecast that "thanks to the strength that resides in union, Russia would be at first discouraged from imperialistic adventures and later perhaps transformed into a friendly neighbor."[27] They were right although it took four decades. Rather less certain is the prediction: "If what has happened in America can be brought about in Europe, then we shall see, as in America, the abolition of the very idea of a proletariat by a progressive approach to a true classless society—a society of equal opportunity and equal advantages for all—without the sacrifice of spiritual and personal liberties."[28]

The section on anti-Semitism is interesting because it singled out the Romanian service as the one where the subject should not be discussed for fear that the regime might cancel the arrangement whereby Jews could leave for Israel.[29]

Surprisingly, Bulgaria was recommended as the first country on RFE's list to which Titoist arguments might usefully be broadcast. The authors of the policy document seemed to be unaware of the long historical ties that bound Bulgaria and Russia together, communist or not, and made it the last country where such arguments might have succeeded at that time.[30]

"Broadcasting to Youth" is a sophisticated and elegantly written chapter. "It is unquestionable that we do not need to *defend* democracy; we need only to be able to define it and illustrate it (in the etymological sense of 'illustrious') by examples drawn from the West."[31] The negatives of the communist regimes for youth were seen as Russification, ineptitude, favoritism, and the boredom of indoctrination. It must have been comforting for young listeners to know that except for "brutes and proven traitors" membership in communist youth organizations would not on liberation be held against them.

Literature on the Radios is surprisingly deficient in conveying what material they were actually transmitting. Apparently, the Radios retained few materials in archives. One RFE/RL executive said, "We were not prepared to retain back files just in case some academic researcher turned up." In administrative documentation, however, a note to the board of November 6, 1950, by Frank Altschul on a few of the programs he was preparing gives a sense of what was being transmitted.

1. What the Kremlin is Planning for You.
   A ten-minute program once a week.
   Format: A lecture by an economic expert in which, each week, a different aspect of the Soviet attempt to organize Eastern Europe as a single economic entity is discussed.
   Purposes: To demonstrate the dangers of the Soviet attempt to unify Eastern Europe economically, and to demonstrate how the Soviet plan is leading the satellite countries into inevitable economic collapse.
   Potential Audience: The intelligentsia of the satellite countries, both Communist and non-Communist.
2. Colonel Bell.
   A ten-minute program once a week.

Format: A lecture by a military expert under the pseudonym "Colonel Bell," who explains, each week, a different aspect of the military strength of the West and the weakness of the East.

Purpose: To demonstrate why the Russian aggression must fail in the long run.

Potential Audience: Primarily the military of the satellite countries. Secondarily, the educated elements of our audience.[32]

The style of each station varied according to national characteristics. The Voice of Free Hungary used more satire, more emotional patriotism, than the Voice of Free Czechoslovakia.[33] Altschul had no illusions about objectivity. He wanted "intelligent and vigorous slanting."[34]

A Psychological Strategy Board (PSB) was created in April 1951 to coordinate government policy. Its members included the under secretary of state, the deputy secretary of defense, and the CIA director.[35] By December of that year the board had decided to undertake an evaluation of RFE. The topics to be covered were

1. Is it necessary to continue RFE?
2. Is it desirable to continue at a lower level?
3. Is it advisable to step it up?
4. Is this the best method of accomplishing the particular aim and objectives and how do we develop a comparison of its effectiveness with that of other media?

An important supplementary question was what resistances or unfavorable reactions were being set up in its attempts to attain its objectives. And the overall question was If it is found advisable to continue RFE, how should it be continued, under what sponsorship, at what level and on what scale?[36]

Mallory Browne, the assistant director of Evaluation and Review of the PSB, went on a quick evaluation swing through Frankfurt, Munich, Berlin, and Vienna and reported in a memorandum to Gordon Gray, the director, on February 12, 1952. He was very positive. His preliminary conclusions were

1. It is, if not absolutely necessary, at least highly desirable and advisable to continue RFE.
2. The scale and scope of RFE should be increased.
3. It is essential to institute a greater measure of responsible policy control at the operational level. The two recommendations above are conditional on modifications in the present set-up which will provide a greater measure of responsibility.[37]

He reported that "by and large there was an overwhelming consensus that RFE is one of the most effective elements in the free world's cold war strategy today." Based on the evidence of escapees from Hungary and Czechoslovakia, which was reported to him, he was convinced that a substantial majority of both the Czech and Hungarian populations heard the RFE broadcasts either themselves or from friends and neighbors. It is doubtful whether his conclusion that the VOA appealed more to intellectuals and high-level people while RFE appealed more powerfully to peasants and industrial workers would have stood up under further scrutiny.

Curiously, he says in the report that RFE broadcast only to Czechoslovakia and Hungary and relayed some programs from New York to Romania. They were planning a full-scale program similar to that for Czechoslovakia and Hungary addressed to Poland, which was expected to get under way about the middle of March. In fact RFE had been broadcasting to Poland since August 4, 1950, and to Bulgaria since August 11, 1950.

RFE had a policy handbook, but the agonizing over American propaganda and foreign policy continued. DeWitt Poole resigned as president of the Freedom Committee in January 1951 and was succeeded by C. D. Jackson, publisher of *Fortune* magazine and the former civilian leader of the Psychological Warfare Branch under General Eisenhower.[38] On May 10 and 11 Jackson chaired a secret meeting at Princeton University to lobby for a statement on U.S. foreign policy so that RFE could know where it was going. The list of those who accepted invitations included Allen Dulles, General Clay, DeWitt Poole, Frank Altschul, Joseph Grew, Lewis Galantière, Robert E. Lang, and Charles Bohlen, shortly to become ambassador to the Soviet Union.[39] At least seven of them were former members of OSS.

One observer at the meeting believed it manifested a groundswell in private circles for more aggressive political warfare activity by the government.[40] The Princeton meeting addressed as its central problem the fact that the United States was not doing a good job on political warfare and those involved in it did not know what their aims were. Bohlen took a different line from most participants: "What people are complaining about is not that the Western way of life is not attractive to them, but 'Why don't you do something to get us out of jail?' "[41]

Allen Dulles pressed for a statement of policy and that was drafted. It was generally liked, and Lang said that after RFE had been floating around in the air for two and one half years the statement now gave RFE plan, strategy, and thought. "This piece of paper limits us, and allows us to be responsible, instead of the two and a half years we had to be irresponsible," Lang averred. Bohlen took the paper away with him, but although he had been complimentary about it, he said there was nothing in it that had not been said before by the president and secretary of State. What the paper said, the declassifiers of documents have not yet revealed.

The Psychological Strategy Board considered the Princeton meeting report at its meeting on June 12, but there was a singular lack of enthusiasm for it. "I don't know what is proposed to be done with this thing," said General "Beetle" Smith, director of the CIA. "They wanted a paper that could be used as a statement of U.S. foreign policy in case they decided it would be appropriate for the President to issue a statement they could hang their hat on afterwards," said Under Secretary David K. Bruce. After some buck passing it was agreed that State would look at it and it would be considered again at the next meeting.[42]

RL: Implacable Struggle

Radio Liberation, later to become Radio Liberty, was the child of the same parents as Radio Free Europe. It was conceived for similar reasons. But the period of gestation was much longer and the birth much more difficult.

Its informal origins lay in the establishment in 1949 in Munich, with OPC support, of the Institute for the Study of the USSR. Its formal origins were in the American Committee for Freedom of the Peoples of the USSR, Inc., which was founded in 1951. The most common short name by which it was known through most of its life and name changes was Amcomlib. Franklin A. Lindsay, an assistant to Frank Wisner in the OPC, set it up with a board consisting of academics and Russian-speaking journalists as its nucleus. Allen Grover, a vice-president of Time, Inc., an assistant to the editor-in-chief, Henry R. Luce, helped him recruit the board and was chairman of its first informal meeting. Eugene Lyons, a former correspondent in the Soviet Union, was elected president and Grover, secretary. Isaac Don Levine came on the board and was sent abroad as European director in August 1951. Lyons was replaced as president in February 1952 by Admiral Alan G. Kirk, and he was replaced in August 1952 by Admiral Leslie C. Stevens, who had had some experience with the Soviet Union.

In contrast to the Free Europe Committee there was no public fund raising and little publicity. Potential directors were told that money would come from friends of committee members. The friends were, of course, the CIA. In Amcomlib the code for the CIA was, as an appropriate parallel to the "friends in the South" of the Free Europe Committee, "the Confederates."

The objectives of Amcomlib were stated in a press release. Its first aim was "to aid the worldwide Russian and nationalistic emigration in its effort to sustain the spirit of liberty among the peoples of the USSR." Its second aim was "to preserve and sustain the historic cultures of Russians and the nationalities." Its third objective was "to aid the emigration in seeking to extend understanding of the West within the USSR." Radio was not specifically mentioned.[43]

The idea of setting up a radio station in Germany to broadcast to the Soviet Union dates at least to 1946. But General Lucius Clay, then deputy military governor in Germany, protested against the State Department initiative. "I cannot agree that the establishment of a broadcasting station in Germany to broadcast to the Soviet Union in the Russian language is in the spirit of the quadripartite government," he said.[44] But he changed his mind.

The obstacles to the establishment of an unofficial radio to broadcast to the Soviet Union were formidable. The sponsors wanted its authenticity enhanced by inspiration that appeared to come from émigrés and its operation to be by émigrés. The émigrés, however, could not agree among themselves what their objectives were. Was the target Russia or communism? The different origins of the émigrés precluded cohesion: some were prewar émigrés, some postwar, and, of the latter, some had collaborated with the Nazis, and some had not. There were Russians, and there were other nationalities. There were adherents to different political parties. There were almost no existing or potential radio journalists to operate such a radio.

Radio Liberation was *Osvobozhdenie* in Russian. What did that mean? It had been part of the name of the political organization under which the army of General Vlasov, the Soviet general, had fought on Hitler's side during the latter part of the war. (Colonel Kromiadi, General Vlasov's aide, was one of the original members of RL's founding group.) Did it mean physical liberation? Perhaps not, but there was plenty of confusion. Names changed frequently. They included American Committee for the Liberation of the Peoples of Russia, Inc., and American Committee for the Liberation from Bolshevism, Inc. Not until January 1964 did Radio Liberation become Radio Liberty.[45]

Amcomlib wanted to achieve its aims through a Center for Unified Action in Europe. The center would establish a program to communicate with the peoples of the Soviet Union, and one of the instruments would be radio broadcasts of news and analysis. After many months of agonizing negotiations, on November 7, 1951, the anniversary of the 1917 revolution, an enlarged Council for the Liberation of the Peoples of Russia was announced. This consisted of five disparate Russian groups and six non-Russian organizations, including Georgians, Azerbaijanis, North Caucasians, Byelorussians, Armenians, and Turkestanis. The Ukrainians were not represented. This was intended to be the body that would start broadcasting to the Soviet Union. But by August 1952 one of the Russian groups had defected and the rest had split into two camps, one Russian and the other non-Russian. So Amcomlib decided to go ahead without this council, if necessary. Radio Liberation started broadcasting on March 1, 1953.[46]

RL was housed in the operations building of the prewar Munich airport. Ironically, it was there in September 1938 that Hitler had greeted Neville Chamberlain and Edouard Daladier, the British and French prime ministers, for the talks that led to the dismemberment of Czechoslovakia. RL staff later claimed that the RFE staff, who looked down on the "slouching tatterdemalion staff" of RL, called their organization "Radio Hole-in-the-Head." The organization of transmission was primitive; copy was moved by motorcycle to the Munich railway station, given to a train guard on a train going to Mannheim, more than three hours away, and thence again sent by motorcycle to the transmitter at Lampertheim.[47]

The initial guidelines set the tone of the broadcasts. They spoke of "implacable struggle against communist dictatorship until its complete destruction."[48]

Jon Lodeesen, at one time the head of the Radio Liberty Russian service, analyzed the early broadcasts of Radio Liberty, which are available:

> The programing was dominated by the assumption that the audience and radio shared a hostility toward Stalin which called for the radio to engage in the heated rhetoric which the audience could not. A 2 March programme by a Georgian who had conspired alongside Stalin chided the dictator for a long list of crimes. At this point Stalin was already dying, but that would not be known until the next day.
>
> The tone did not change with the dictator's death on March 5. On 28 March, in honour of Zhuvkov's restitution to rank, a former officer under his command praised Zhuvkov in terms not unlike those which the Soviet media reserved for Stalin. A veteran who had lost his hand in the war followed this up by recalling how happy he was to hear of Stalin's death and how, just as Stalin had tricked and abused the soldiers so now would Malenkov and company seek to trick everyone by pretending to want peace in Korea.[49]

VOA: Not if It's by Rimsky-Korsakov

The Korean War had a dramatic impact on the fortunes of the VOA. Its appropriation for fiscal 1951 increased by 47 percent to $13 million, and it received a further $51 million to build facilities. By fiscal 1952 the appropriation was $20 million, an increase of 124 percent over two years.

Staff almost doubled in about one year to a budget ceiling in late 1951 of nineteen hundred. The improved facilities included a transmitter ship, the *Courier,* which started broadcasting to Eastern Europe and the Soviet Union from the Mediterranean in September 1952. By mid-1951 the number of hours broadcast daily to Eastern Europe and the Soviet Union had risen by nearly two-thirds from 1949 levels to thirteen. Ten languages were added: Albanian, Armenian, Azerbaijani, Georgian, Tatar, Turkestani, Ukrainian, Estonian, Latvian, and Lithuanian. The tone of the broadcasts became sharper. One program, for example, exposed with biting satire the "weaknesses and evils of imperialist communism." Others "exposed the sham and hypocrisy of communism's pretense of a better life."[50] Such a tone did not stop Senator Pat McCarran, democrat of Nevada, chairman of the Senate Internal Security Subcommittee, from suggesting that Communist sympathizers had slanted VOA broadcasts.[51]

Little was known about who was listening or what the impact was, but that did not deter the great act of faith. After all, Barrett said, Procter and Gamble had spent $19 million on radio programs, which was slightly more than the cost of all his radio operations, and yet Procter and Gamble could not trace definitely and provably the sale of a single bar of soap to their radio broadcasts.[52]

In early 1952 Barrett resigned and was succeeded as assistant secretary of state by Howland Sergeant, the deputy. Sergeant received rather more press attention than might have been expected because of his wife, Myrna Loy, the film star. (Sergeant became president of the RL Committee in 1954.) During a reorganization of responsibilities Wilson Compton, president of Washington State University, became the first administrator of the International Information Administration (IIA), which included international broadcasting and which succeeded the International Information and Educational Exchange Program (USIE). Compton received policy guidance from the assistant secretary but reported to the secretary of state and was supposed to have a relatively free hand in operations. He did not and complained to Dean Acheson about a "formidable inertia" in the State Department.[53] He did not get much support from Acheson, whose negative attitude toward the information program is exemplified by his later statement that "world opinion simply does not exist on matters that concern us." He believed that an American was apt to stare "like Narcissus at his image in the pool of what he believes to be world opinion until he pines away; or else he makes himself over into the image he would like to see, only to have his shrewder self tell him that he looks like a fool."[54]

Some members of Congress were also getting restless in the budget hearings for fiscal 1953. "We have created something like a Frankenstein," said one. "Give us the picture. You sit there with your foot in your mouth. We have to drag that out of you," said another. The requested appropriation of $30 million was cut to $22 million.[55]

In March 1953 a VOA producer asked the music library of the Voice for a recording of "Song of India," which he wanted to broadcast. The librarian explained that the record was no longer available. "You see," she added, "it's by Rimsky-Korsakov, and we're not supposed to use anything by Russians." The ban was soon rescinded, but the incident was not untypical of the McCarthy era.[56]

General Eisenhower had called in 1950 for a "Marshall Plan of ideas," and he made the information program a major issue in the 1952 presidential election campaign. In his first State of the Union message in 1953 he promised to make more effective all activities related to international information because they were essential to the security of the United States. But hopes that his speech augured well for the VOA were soon dashed. Senator Joseph R. McCarthy saw to that. The international information program had the bad luck to be the guinea pig for the first McCarthy investigations. On February 16 the Permanent Committee on Investigations of the Senate Committee on Government Operations, chaired by McCarthy, opened raucous televised hearings on the VOA, charging gross mismanagement, Communist inspired. In any event, no Communists were found in the IIA program although six employees were discharged on grounds of unsuitability. After a pathetic performance before the McCarthy committee and amid a furor about what use could be made of writings by Communists, the ineffectual Compton was told his days were numbered and he resigned on February 18. He was succeeded on March 2 by Robert L. Johnson, a cofounder of *Time* magazine, who found the heat that McCarthy created in the kitchen intolerable. He resigned after four months.[57] VOA morale was at an all-time low after the McCarthy hearings and, as Johnson told the Congressional Appropriations Subcommittee shortly before he left, it was at a very low level of prestige. There were widespread cuts in staff and services except for Eastern Europe, which continued largely sacrosanct. The exception was the abandonment of construction of two large relay stations that were part of the network that was to ring the Soviet bloc.[58]

BBC: The Voice of Britain Must Whisper

"The Voice of America booms, the Voice of Stalin roars, the Voice of Britain must whisper," commented the *Daily Mail* on proposed cuts in the BBC's overseas budget.[59]

The External Services were under great financial pressure for the five years that followed the end of the war, and capital investment particularly suffered, but not until 1951 did the knives come out and cut so deep that services had to be reduced. The BBC's requested appropriations for 1951–52 were cut from $1,492,000 (£5,330,000) to $1,330,000 (£4,750,000) or 11 percent.[60]

A major preoccupation of the BBC in the early fifties continued to be jamming, which spread to Eastern Europe. Jamming of the BBC Polish service started in December 1951, the Czech in February 1952, and the Hungarian in March. By May the BBC was reporting to the Foreign Office that jamming of the Romanian, Bulgarian, and Albanian services had recently started. The press announcement about the Hungarian and Czech jamming said that it would be countered by the BBC by a battery of transmitters of the type successfully used in combating Russian jamming.[61] Reception reports from Budapest referred only occasionally to jamming. Jamming of the Polish service caused a number of small groups of listeners to congregate outside Warsaw to listen. The satellite countries sometimes put their jammers at the disposal of the Russians despite the fact that Russia then had more than one thousand jamming stations in operation, according to American engineers' estimates. All the jamming was remarkably efficient, the BBC said, except for that of the Czechs and the evening Hungarian transmission where, thus far, both shortwave-lengths were mainly clear. Retimed bulletins were usually located within five to fifteen minutes by one or more jammers when "agitated attention signals from a jamming control centre can sometimes be heard."[62]

The confusion about how much could be heard in the Soviet Union continued. A BBC report of May 23, 1951, said that three or four frequencies of the combined U.K. and U.S. transmissions were getting through to their target.[63]

Despite the cost of antijamming the government decided in 1952 that existing services should not be curtailed. Broadcasting "constitutes one of the main facets of the rearmament programme and is directed towards preventing war," said a parliamentary committee.[64]

Relations with the Foreign Office were close. A Foreign Office memorandum recorded:

The actual day to day association between the Foreign Office and the Overseas Services is a good deal closer than is suggested by the statements in the Licence and Agreement and the White Paper [of July 1946]. There is in fact constant cooperation between them at all levels and both the scope and the content of the various foreign language broadcasts and the nature of the other activities of the Overseas Services are determined as a result of joint consultation.[65]

A section of a briefing note, February 13, 1952, headed "Foreign Office Influence on the Political Content of Broadcasts," which had been prepared for Foreign Office appearance before the House of Commons Public Accounts Committee, said:

> We are satisfied that the B.B.C. do in general understand what kind of programme the Foreign Office wish to have transmitted and we have full confidence in their discretion and that they will consult us when they are in doubt. If pressed we must admit that it is very occasionally necessary to draw the B.B.C.'s attention to undesirable items and to request them to suppress them in future.[66]

The Audience: Is Anybody Out There?

Little was known about the audience for Western broadcasters in the Soviet Union in the late forties and early fifties. But it was clear that there were few regular listeners. There were, after all, fewer than two million shortwave receivers. Moreover, according to a survey of Soviet citizens by the COMCOM project of the Massachusetts Institute of Technology (MIT), few of the privileged few dared to listen during the Stalin period.[67] It was even forbidden to keep transcripts of foreign broadcasts for official analysis and monitoring.[68] An anonymous report of 1951 on the BBC files took a rather diffferent view:

> Most Russians are willing to admit to having listened to Western broadcasts—and indeed seem to be rather proud of the fact. On the other hand we have not heard any praise for the broadcasts and most of the educated Russians—and certainly all the Communists—say that the broadcasts are silly or lies. Not much of a distinction seems to exist in their minds between the BBC and the Voice of America. It is quite likely that the people who said they listened to the BBC had only done so once.[69]

The East European audience was better understood because of an analysis by the Columbia University Bureau of Applied Research of a group of interviews carried out by Foreign News Service, Inc., during 1951 and 1952. The work, entitled "Listening to the Voice of America and Other Foreign Broadcasts" was done under contract with the U.S. Information Agency (USIA) and was based on a thirty-seven-item interview guide prepared by the Division of Evaluation, International Broadcasting Service, Department of State.[70]

The surveys included interviews with 114 people from Poland, 108 from Czechoslovakia, 87 from Hungary, 46 from Romania, and 37 from Bulgaria, totaling 392. They were foreign broadcast listeners, mostly refugees and mostly aged twenty to forty. All educational levels were represented, and occupations ranged from unskilled workers to professionals. There were few women. Data was also collected from 29 people from the Soviet Zone of Germany, Latvia, the Soviet Union, and Yugoslavia. Researchers did not claim to estimate the size of the foreign broadcast audiences because they did not have data from representative samples. But they concluded that the amount of foreign broadcast listening appeared to be considerable. The researchers at Columbia University considered that "while nationals of those countries who can be interviewed are likely to differ from the home populations in a number of important background characteristics, interviews of this type are of more value than might be supposed because escape from this area seems due more to personal circumstances than to any basic difference in opinions and attitudes from the home population."[71] This was not the view of researchers later, who saw clear differences in the stated attitudes of, say, refugees and émigrés.

The communist governments of Eastern Europe had followed that of the Soviet Union in not making listening to foreign broadcasts illegal. Nevertheless, many people believed it was illegal, and there were tales of listeners being arrested, charged on other grounds, such as black-marketeering, and sent to forced labor camps or imprisoned without formal charges. A Czech reported that the owner of an inn in Tinec had been sentenced to five years of forced labor for listening to Western stations. There were suggestions that in Hungary listening per se could be construed as antistate activity.[72] An intriguing question is why listening was not made illegal. The Columbia University staff decided that it would have been difficult and unwise to enforce and that stopping foreign radio listening might have also reduced the audience for domestic regime-controlled radio.[73] A Soviet Army lieutenant said, "Russian propaganda against the Western radio stations is planned with utmost care because the Communist propagandists are afraid that by being too harsh in their condemnation of these stations they might unwittingly increase their popularity among the people."[74]

Discouragement came from informers who reported on listening, which was perceived as evidence of a negative attitude to the regime. Children in schools were instructed by their teachers to observe and to report on the listening habits of their parents. Propaganda was directed against the broadcasters in newspapers, theaters, and public places. One refugee reported that in Hungary small ducks—the word in Hungarian, as in French, meaning false news—had started appearing in Hungarian shops labeled BBC or VOA.[75] Children came home crying from school when teachers ridiculed their parents for listening.

Clearly illegal were activities such as spreading "war-mongering rumours," "imperialist propaganda," and inciting others against the regime. Group listening was treated as prima facie evidence of subversion. The danger was pointed out by a Bulgarian landowner:

> I used to visit my friends in the evening in order to listen to the radio with greatest precautions. I used to finish my work at 7:00 P.M., then I would linger longer at the office so that I could leave it when it was already dark. Then, choosing side streets, watching that I was not being followed, I used to enter the street on which my friend lived, always from a different direction. Sometimes I would circle so much that I would cross the street five or six times before I finally entered the house. The key to the door was always left for me in a hidden place.[76]

Group listening was common, no doubt for encouragement to share the danger. Listeners used great ingenuity to avoid detection. A young skilled worker from Budapest reported: "Our radio was fixed so that when the doorbell rang, we could hear it on the radio. That way we could always be reading a book before anyone got inside."[77] Listeners often had two radios, one tuned loudly to the regime station and one quietly to the foreign broadcaster.

The code word in Hungary for listening to London was "in the bath." That was where telephone callers were told the master of the house was if they called between 8:30 and 9:00 P.M.[78]

A woman from Bucharest told an interviewer, "The whole propaganda against listening made us just more curious to listen to Western stations."[79] A young skilled worker from Poland commented: "The VOA and the BBC achieved something the Communists were trying to do, but didn't succeed in all these years—to break down social barriers. Today all social classes, people of all political creeds, of all professions and religions, and all age groups are listening to Western broadcasts."[80]

In addition to jamming, the regimes restricted access to foreign broadcasters through the radio sets themselves. They were sometimes in short supply and always were expensive. Spare parts were scarce. Listeners often reported that when they took their sets to be repaired the mechanics blocked off access to shortwave. The owners did not dare to return to complain. Parts were substituted for inferior ones. Radio sets had to be registered with the government and a license fee paid. People known for their anticommunist attitudes were denied a license. Therefore, often they did not register old sets. A Polish schoolteacher reported, "Each prospective buyer must now produce not only a certificate from the trade union branch at the place of his work but also an additional approval from the local National Council where political aspects are taken into account."[81]

To limit the cost of jamming the Bulgarians hindered listening by cutting off electricity just before a BBC or VOA broadcast was about to start. Another technique was to lower the power supply at the beginning of the broadcast. The listener turned up the knob, the authorities suddenly increased the voltage, and the radio's vacuum tubes were blown.[82]

What were the listeners looking for? The refugees had been seeking a source of information, a focus for their hostilities to the regime and a source of hope for liberation.[83] The comparative report summed up the desires:

> Far more requests were made for news broadcasts of all kinds than for any other type of program. But this statement of preference was more than just an expression of a desire for "the facts." Respondents tended to emphasize that what they wanted was encouraging news; this was further defined as news showing determined and increasingly effective opposition of the West to the Communists, domestic news showing how resistance to the current regimes by the local populations would be possible and news which would indicate that the time of liberation from the Soviets was not far off. Many respondents, too, went out of their way to state that they did *not* want to hear news broadcasts which did not convey information of this type, or which were disappointing or disheartening. They expressed a desire for "the truth," but "the truth" was in their minds only the hopeful news.[84]

Many listeners denounced broadcasts, particularly from the BBC, of what they thought was irrelevant discussion of affairs of interest only in the West.[85] They did not want to hear music or jokes. "We won't risk arrest or getting on the black list just to hear music."[86] "There's nothing funny about living under a communist regime."[87]

Their general feeling was that the VOA and more especially the BBC, were not aggressive enough: "Their language in comparison with that of the Communist stations is too soft and unconvincing. People who are used to the violent communist attacks on the West, to their tough and often rude language, have to make a great effort to believe . . . what is presented in a soft, quiet language."[88]

Only the Romanians showed a slight preference for the BBC over the VOA. All the other countries came down heavily in favor of the VOA. The reason seems to have been that listeners saw it as a station of authority and hope.

The BBC was the most popular other station among VOA listeners. They valued its relatively unbiased character and its accuracy. RFE was generally the second most popular of the other broadcasts although in Bulgaria and Romania Paris was preferred to RFE. Madrid, surprisingly, did better than both RFE and Paris in Poland.[89]

5

UPRISINGS
(1953–1956)

East Germany and Czechoslovakia: Better Pay—Less Talk

JUNE 1, 1953, MARKED A NEW ERA for Eastern Europe. On that day large-scale riots broke out at the Skoda works in Pilsen in Czechoslovakia and spread quickly to a number of other cities. In Pilsen the demonstrators trampled portraits of Stalin and Klement Gottwald, the Czech leader, underfoot. The police quickly suppressed the demonstrations and arrested about five hundred workers and others across the country.[1] There was a dispute in RFE management on whether to call for a general uprising, but opposition to such a call by William Griffith, RFE political adviser in Munich, and Lewis Galantière, policy adviser to Free Europe, prevailed over the views of Robert E. Lang, director of RFE, and Ruben Nathan, policy adviser in New York.[2]

On June 16 workers' demonstrations turned into a general strike in Berlin, and that eruption also spread quickly to many other places in the Eastern Zone of Germany. The Soviet army put it down bloodily on June 17. Nineteen men and women died in East Berlin, and the total for the whole of East Germany was 125. Demonstrations and riots in more than four hundred cities and towns rumbled on throughout the summer of 1953. RFE was vociferous in its support for the protests in the Eastern Zone, but John Foster Dulles did not follow up with American troops his brave words of 1952 about liberating Eastern Europe.

Recent research in East German archives shows how great was the influence of Radio in the American Sector, RIAS Berlin (RIAS) on the riots.[3] In October 1952 the U.S. Psychological Strategy Board had adopted a comprehensive psychological warfare plan against the East German Communists to encourage disaffection. RIAS was regarded as the most effective instrument for penetrating the Curtain.[4] Nevertheless,

67

RIAS had the same problem getting guidance from the State Department that RFE was to have later about the Hungarian uprising. Gordon Ewing, the political director of RIAS in Berlin, could get advice neither from the State Department nor from the American officials in Bonn about what to broadcast on the Berlin general strike. He went ahead and broadcast what had happened.[5] The coverage was ambivalent, at first cautious, but later repeated the workers' demand to continue the strike the next day.[6] RIAS had frequently reported on labor unrest before the uprising and had commented on successful strikes. When the government had backtracked on its forced construction of socialism on June 11 in a communiqué called "The New Course," local party officials had reported increasing numbers of pro-RIAS statements such as "All stations were lying, RIAS alone says the truth, our shackles are broken, we are free people again."[7] RIAS played an important role in spreading the strikes after June 16, and an internal East German study blamed RIAS broadcasts for creating the impression that the strikes of the construction workers in East Berlin were becoming a broad movement among the entire population.[8]

The riots in Czechoslovakia and East Germany were important for the broadcasters because they were the first of the uprisings; they had the delicate task of laying down policies for their staffs on how to deal with them. Like volcanoes, these uprisings thereafter erupted at intervals across much of Eastern Europe, culminating in the fall of communism in 1989.

RFE issued a staff briefing, "Czechoslovakia: Guidance no. 10," on June 30 that outlined a plan to undermine police and army loyalty to the regime.[9] RFE had reported that when the German Volkspolizei were called into the street to suppress rioters, they held their fire because they could not shoot down their brothers. Some even put their guns into the hands of the workers. Czech and Slovak soldiers were asked: "If that day should come for you, . . . would you do less than the East German Vopos did?" The message to the workers was that their strength was increasing while the rulers were becoming confused and disorganized. Officials were to be told by RFE that they could use their positions to sabotage the Russians, or they could defect to the West, one of the few instances in which RFE supported defection. RFE had always told young people to keep a low profile but to learn about firearms and how to handle a platoon of soldiers because some day Czechoslovakia might need their skills. They were told after the riots that one day they would reap their reward of freedom and would also be able to buy something—"an English motor-bike, a French literary review, a novel by Hemingway, a honeymoon on the Italian lakes."

RFE continued to develop its propaganda techniques in the run-up to the Czech elections of 1954 and combined the voicecasts with pamphlets dropped by balloons. It launched an "action program" called Operation VETO.[10] The plan was to encourage the Czechoslovak people to work for specific short-range reforms to erode communist authority gradually. It was now made clear that liberation as a consequence of an aggressive war waged by the West was unrealistic and as a result of voluntary Russian withdrawal, a fantasy. The Czechoslovaks must have been mystified by the philosophizing that "liberation of the Soviet satellites is likely to occur only as a result of a favorable confluence of events within and outside of the country. Inside this means that coordinated mass opposition must evolve and gather strength during the preliberation period." They would have better understood the ten-point demands, ranging from "better pay—less talk" to "goods for the people, not for the Soviets." The campaign sufficiently annoyed the regime that it attacked the exiles in RFE who "strive to sell the independence of Czechoslovakia to the American imperialists." When nearly four decades later Czechoslovakia said it wanted to join the European Community, those who could remember must have smiled wryly at the attack of 1954 on those who sought to force it to join a "German dominated European Federation." RFE launched a similar campaign in Hungary called Operation FOCUS.

Poland and Hungary: Crisis for RFE

RFE'S propaganda coup of the early fifties came from the defection to the CIA on December 5, 1953, of a colonel in the Polish secret police, Josef Swiatlo, while he was on a shopping trip to West Berlin. He had been deputy director of the department for security of the Party in the Polish Ministry of Public Security. He had had access to the private files on all the leading Communists in Poland. Indeed, in many cases he had actually compiled them. From September to December 1954 RFE broadcast more than one hundred taped interviews with Swiatlo in which he revealed detailed and accurate information on the corruption and personal rivalries of the leadership of the Polish Communist Party. The State Department believed the broadcasts were the single most effective political warfare operation since 1945.[11] On December 23 the chief of the Polish secret police was fired and three of his executives were arrested.[12]

The power of the police and security forces was curbed. Cord Meyer, the chief of the International Organizations Division of the CIA from September 1954 and, therefore, in charge of oversight of RFE and RL, believed it was "a startling demonstration of the effective influence of RFE within Poland and an important step in the sequence of events that finally led to the establishment of the more moderate Gomulka regime in the autumn of 1956."[13]

In the mid-fifties RFE emphasized throughout Eastern Europe three stories that set the scene for the uprisings of 1956. The first was the Swiatlo exposures. The second was the agreement between Khrushchev and Bulganin and Tito in May 1955 that there could be different roads to socialism. The third was Khrushchev's attack on Stalin at the Twentieth Party Congress in February 1956. The CIA secured a copy, which it passed to RFE, which broadcast it extensively.

On June 28, 1956, the RFE service to Poland again came into its own when the communist workers of the Cegielski works in Poznan rioted in the streets. Fifty-three men died in two days of fighting between the workers and the militia.[14] The two themes of the banners, "Bread and Freedom" and "Russians Go Home," under which they rioted were all the more potent because they were soon censored out of the official media for whom the events became nonevents and the dead, unpersons.[15] But they could not censor the Western Radios.

The importance of the Western Radios to the rioters was pointed up by the fact that they shattered to smithereens and trod underfoot a whole set of jamming equipment they had hurled out of the windows of the radio station. Soldiers looked on and did nothing. This station, one of Poland's most powerful, was used to jam broadcasts from the West. It was the last stronghold of the demonstrators.[16]

RFE showed great responsibility and restraint and avoided encouraging its listeners to engage in bloody but useless sacrifices. One of the first guidance notes said: "We understand and appreciate the motivations which have driven the workers of Poznan to desperate measures. However, riots and revolts are not likely to improve matters in Poland, for the police may be given an opportunity for reprisals which only make things worse. No government which bases itself exclusively upon the tanks and bayonets of the armed forces will endure. But the Polish people must husband their strength and hold on for the time of freedom."[17]

The suspension of jamming by the Poles in the aftermath of the riots was, no doubt, a sop to the rioters. But it perhaps also shows how important the authorities regarded the moderating influence of RFE and also the BBC to be.[18] A Polish Communist Party official and Gomulka supporter told an RFE reporter in Stockholm, "Had RFE not told our people to be calm, I am not sure whether we alone would have managed to cope with the situation."[19] The correspondent for *Le Monde* reported on December 26 that one of the most representative regime journalists praised the broadcasts of RFE, which appealed to Poles to preserve discipline and calm and recommended that the Poles avoid demonstrations and public disorders. *Zycie Literackie* of November 11 also complimented RFE and the BBC for recognizing that prudence and calm were fundamental prerequisites for gaining any kind of escape from Soviet domination.

The signals of the Western Radios got through despite continued jamming of the BBC Polish service by East Germany, Czechoslovakia, and the Soviet Union, and presumably also of RFE and VOA.[20]

The eventual aftermath of Poznan was that a "thaw" set in between the Polish government and the people with promises of an investigation into the wrongs against striking workers; there were concessions to peasants, and an emergency plan to raise the standard of living was proposed. In the power struggle that ensued Khrushchev suddenly arrived in Warsaw and threatened to use force against the Poles. But he caved in. The Poles had won. On October 21 it was announced that Gomulka had been elected first secretary of the Polish Communist Party, and the composition of the new Politburo showed clearly that the "thaw" faction was victorious.

General Bem was a Polish officer who commanded Hungarian troops against the Russians in Hungary's War of Liberty in 1849. It was to his statue in Budapest, two days after Gomulka's election, on October 23, that protesting Hungarian students and writers marched. It was the beginning of the Hungarian revolution. From Western Radios the Hungarians had learned of the Poznan riots and the thaw in conditions in Poland that had followed them. And they marched to General Bem's statue to express their admiration for the Poles and their determination to achieve the same freedoms.

The U.S. government set up a Special Committee on Soviet and Related Problems under the chairmanship of Jacob Beam, a member of the Policy Planning Staff, to exploit the Polish situation in the rest of Europe.[21] On October 26 Brigadier General C. A. Dolph, chief of the Joint Subsidiary Activities Division of the Joint Chiefs of Staff, proposed to the assistant secretary of defense that an emergency meeting of the Operations Coordinating Board consider immediate diversion of broadcast time and facilities beamed at other areas to Hungary, particularly over the critical coming weekend. Hard Polish news should be furnished to

Hungary, but Hungarian news should be withheld from Poland for the time being. The Beam committee should develop a plan for similar and other actions as the ferment spread to other satellites, he recommended.[22] Voice of America news broadcasts to Eastern Europe were immediately put on an around-the-clock schedule.[23]

But the outcome in Hungary was very different from that in Poland. Russian tanks crushed the uprising, with many dead. Imre Nagy, the Hungarian reformer, was removed from power and eventually was executed.

Radio Free Europe did not achieve glory, as it had in Poland, but justifiably or not, shame. It was the most traumatic experience in its history, and it did not recover from it until the glories of 1989, one generation later.

The first charge against RFE was that it attacked Imre Nagy. The main proponent of this accusation was Leslie B. Bain, an American journalist of Hungarian parentage. As he put it in his book, *The Reluctant Satellites,* some years later: "After Nagy assumed the premiership, he was violently and incessantly attacked by foreign radios, principally by Radio Free Europe and the Voice of America, as having brought in the Russians. Inasmuch as nearly all radios in Budapest were tuned to Munich senders during the days to follow, the effect of this culumny was tremendous and contributed most importantly to the inability of Nagy to control events and thus avert the major catastrophe of November 4th."[24]

Careless reading of a Radio Budapest broadcast caused RFE to broadcast that Nagy had called in the Russian troops. Nagy later made clear that he had not.[25] This was confirmed in documents that President Yeltsin gave the Hungarians when he visited Budapest in November 1992. Yuri Andropov, the Soviet ambassador to Hungary, forwarded the Hungarian government's request for intervention on October 28, retroactively dated October 24. It was signed by Andras Hegedus, the Hungarian prime minister.[26] RFE expressed no doubts; on the contrary, in an internal memorandum RFE called it a "fact." The policy line laid down for staff on October 24 said, "That Nagy called upon foreign troops to restore 'order' is a fact he will have to live down."[27] The BBC did not commit the error of saying Nagy called in the Russian troops.[28]

The second charge was that RFE had incited the rebellion. On November 3 the principal Romanian newspaper, *Scinteia,* said that hundreds of Hungarian soldiers from the West were flying to Budapest and the general headquarters of the Hungarian Fascists had been set up on the Austro-Hungarian border under the direct control of the Free Europe

American broadcasting station. At the United Nations Vasily Kuznetsov, the chief delegate of the Soviet Union, said that RFE had been on the air continuously for weeks giving instructions and orders to Hungarian rebels. The Hungarian White Book, an official report on the revolt issued later by the Kadar regime, said: "The subversive broadcasts of Radio Free Europe—backed by dollars, directed from America, and functioning on the territory of West Germany—played an essential role in the ideological preparation and practical direction of the counter-revolution, in provoking the armed struggle, in the non-observance of the cease-fire, and in arousing mass hysteria which led to the lynching of innocent men and women loyal to their people and their country."[29] Toward the end of November the Free Europe Committee issued a statement denying that RFE had incited the rebellion.[30]

In his autobiography, *Facing Reality*, Cord Meyer recounts that he and his staff reviewed the taped broadcasts that had been made in the weeks before the revolution. They could find no evidence that in this period RFE had violated the standing instructions against inciting to violence or promising external assistance. The German government and the Council of Europe both conducted investigations into RFE behavior and both absolved RFE of having incited the revolt by promising Western assistance.[31]

Chancellor Adenauer told a press conference on January 25, 1957: "This investigation has shown that the assertions which appeared in the press, that Radio Free Europe promised the Hungarians assistance by the West—armed assistance by the West—are not consistent with the facts. However, remarks were also made which were liable to cause misinterpretations."[32]

It is not clear from this quotation whether Adenauer was talking about the period before the revolt or during it. On the one hand, the report in the *Times* of London puts it in the context of the period during the revolt, not before it.[33] On the other hand, the *New York Times* said that Adenauer absolved RFE of charges that its broadcasts incited the insurrection.[34] The attitude of the German government was important because RFE could only operate in Germany if licensed by the German government.

The more widespread charge was that RFE had promised the Hungarians armed aid or intervention by the United States and the Western powers after the revolution had begun. The accusation was that this caused the fighting to be prolonged and many died who would have given up were it not for these promises.

Five days after the Russians launched their final attack on Budapest,

Freies Wort, the official organ of the Free Democratic Party (FDP) in West Germany carried this attack on RFE: "We are convinced that . . . RFE's aggressive propaganda is responsible to a large extent for the bloodbath that has occurred in Hungary for the last two weeks. A propaganda whose opportunistic agitation has to be paid for finally with the blood of people who have been led astray is a crime against humanity, no matter from whom it may come or to whom it may be addressed."[35] This theme was taken up by many newspapers in Germany and the United States.

A Special Committee on the Problem of Hungary, set up by the General Assembly of the United Nations, reported on the events of October and November 1956 in mid-1957. "It would appear that certain broadcasts by Radio Free Europe helped to create an impression that support might be forthcoming for the Hungarians," it said.[36]

In an interdepartmental meeting on November 13, 1956, Cord Meyer refuted the charges that RFE had stirred the Hungarians to revolt.[37] In his autobiography Cord Meyer's assessment of the RFE tapes broadcast during the revolution was that their tone was "more exuberant and optimistic" than the situation warranted. He makes no reference to incitement to violence.[38]

In a secret memorandum on November 20, 1956, the CIA drew these conclusions:

> a. Policy guidance provided to RFE and by RFE to its Hungarian desk was consistent with U.S. policies toward the satellites. RFE broadcasts were generally consistent with such policies.
>
> b. From all information available to date, RFE did not incite the Hungarian people to revolution.
>
> c. From all information available to date, RFE did not directly or by implication offer hope that American military help would be forthcoming to the patriots.
>
> d. RFE broadcasts went somewhat beyond specific guidances in identifying itself with Hungarian patriot aims, and in offering certain tactical advice to the patriots.
>
> e. The chronology and nature of events in Hungary and the statements of the Hungarian Government itself prior to its overthrow make it clear that the uprising resulted from ten years of Soviet repression and was finally sparked by the shooting on 23 October of peaceful demonstrators, and did not result from any external influence, such as RFE broadcasts or Free Europe leaflets.[39]

To find out what really happened one must turn to RFE itself. The frankest account is contained in a sober and balanced internal report by

William Griffith, political adviser, RFE Munich. It was addressed to Richard Condon, RFE European director, under the heading "Policy Review of Voice of Free Hungary Programing, 23 October—23 November 1956."[40] It shows that for much of the time neither the American management of RFE nor the head of the Hungarian service was in control of what was transmitted.

Each morning during the revolution, Andor Gellert, the head of the Voice of Free Hungary (VFH), or Laszlo Bery, his deputy, together with other senior members of the desk, met Griffith at a policy meeting. They told Griffith what they were planning to broadcast, and he gave them instructions. Frequently, their account of what they were planning to broadcast was misleading, policy directives were not conveyed to the commentators, and on at least one occasion Griffith's instructions were not carried out. The situation was aggravated by the fact that Gellert was ill much of the time. He returned to work after a long and serious illness but collapsed again at the end of the first week of November. Moreover, he had failed to implement Griffith's advice of two years earlier to replace inadequate members of his staff.

Griffith set the scene: "The tone of the broadcasts was over-excited. There was too much rhetoric, too much emotionalism, too much generalization. The great majority of programs were lacking in humility and subtlety. VFH output for the first two-week period in particular had a distinct 'émigré' tone; too little specific reference was made to the desires and demands of the people in the country."[41]

The internal inquiry analyzed 308 scripts broadcast by the Voice of Free Hungary from October 23 to November 23, covering some 70 percent of all programming, excluding news, from October 24 to November 3 and 50 percent from November 4 to 23, according to the memorandum. The possibility exists that some scripts were destroyed. Because the tapes carried a regular time signal, however, that is unlikely. Of the 308 programs analyzed RFE found that four programs were in violation of RFE's standing policies or daily guidances on the Hungarian revolt and a further sixteen programs involved some distortions of policies or failure to implement constructive techniques of policy application. Three of the stories that RFE considered to be in violation of policies offered military advice.

One program, on October 27, was by a supposed military commentator under the radio name of "Colonel Bell," who encouraged sabotage of rail and phone lines. He advised the local authorities in Hungary to secure stores of arms for freedom fighters and advised the population to provide them with food and supplies. The script also fairly clearly implied that foreign assistance would be forthcoming if the revolutionaries succeeded in setting up a central military command. Griffith had been given a misleading description of the plan to broadcast a program on resistance. Griffith reported:

> I considered the program as summarised inappropriate when it was presented at the morning meeting. I pointed out that such a program could be permitted only if it dealt with the topic in purely theoretical terms without any reference to current events in Hungary. Gellert gave assurance that this would be done. This broadcast was approved for broadcast by Bery. There is no evidence that Gellert read it in its completed form.[42]

It is difficult to understand how any listener at that time could think of a theoretical program on partisan war in any other context than that of Hungary. Griffith was big enough to acknowledge in his report that in retrospect it appeared to have been a mistake to have permitted the Hungarian service to broadcast any programs on military topics during the revolution. These programs were permitted because it was felt that to broadcast information on the theory of partisan warfare, tank defense techniques, and elementary principles of civilian defense during a civil war might help save lives during the revolution and at least would remind Hungarian listeners to be cautious and avoid sacrificing themselves in foolish gestures of resistance.

A second program by Colonel Bell on October 28 gave detailed instructions to Hungarian soldiers on the conduct of partisan warfare. He said that Hungarians had to continue to fight vigorously because this would have a great effect on the handling of the Hungarian question by the Security Council of the United Nations. He implied that the United Nations would give active support to the Hungarians if they kept on fighting. There was no mention of the inevitability of a Russian veto. In an indirect piece of propaganda Bell recounted how a small band of Yugoslav partisans fought and beat back much larger forces of German Nazis in South Serbia in 1943.

A third program on October 30 by another editor tried to instruct the Hungarians on the techniques of antitank warfare by illustrations drawn from successful Soviet tactics in World War II.

RFE had decided that the extent to which it should encourage the Hungarians to continue fighting should be dealt with by letting the Free Radios be heard increasingly so that they could be the guide. Griffith considered the most serious violation of all was the following report that

RFE carried twice in the Hungarian service on Sunday, November 4, in a program called "A Short World Press Review":

> This morning the British *Observer* published a report of its Washington correspondent. This situation report was written before the Soviet attack early this morning. In spite of this the *Observer* correspondent writes that the Russians have probably decided to beat down the Hungarian Revolution with arms. The article goes on: "If the Soviet troops really attack Hungary, if our expectations should hold true and Hungarians hold out for three or four days, then the pressure upon the government of the United States to send military help to the freedom fighters will become irresistible." This is what the *Observer* writes in today's number. The paper observes that the American Congress cannot vote for war as long as the Presidential elections have not been held [elections were scheduled for Tuesday, November 6]. The article then continues: "If the Hungarians can continue to fight until Wednesday [the day after the elections] we shall be closer to a world war than at any time since 1939." The reports from London, Paris, the United States and other Western reports show that the world's reaction to the Hungarian events surpasses every imagination. In the Western capitals a practical manifestation of Western sympathy is expected at any hour.[43]

Griffith believed this program was undoubtedly the one that several Hungarian refugees and correspondents had referred to as "the promise that help would come which RFE broadcast on the weekend of November 4."[44] It was especially reprehensible in Griffith's eyes because it had been agreed in RFE that any Western reactions that indicated promise of more than moral support would be misleading and should not be put on the air.

A broadcast of RFE on November 1 told its audience not to surrender their weapons. It said these weapons meant victory because he who had the arms also had the power. General Bela Kiraly, who had been commander in chief of the Hungarian National Guard and subsequently of the Freedom Fighters, later recalled a broadcast by RFE that he considered was addressed specially to him, which said his patriotic duty was to fight the Russians to the last. Although the broadcast did not promise that the American Marines would come, he believed that "if that voice encourages me to resist, there must be a government decision or plan behind it."[45] On another occasion, however, he said: "I would have gone out of my way to establish a settlement acceptable to the Soviet Union because I knew that Western Military power would *not* come at all, and I have dreaded a war on Hungarian soil." Kiraly recounted that the *New York Times* correspondent in Vienna, John MacCormac, asked him: "Should I print that you want the Marines?" He replied: "No sir, we do not want the Marines. We want peace with the Soviet Union." The freedom fighters who later charged that the West had let them down were "hotheads," he said.[46]

Bela Kovacs, former secretary of the Smallholders' Party, sheltered overnight in the American Legation on November 4 because of the heavy shelling. The legation reported: "Kovacs left little doubt that in his opinion the U.S. for the attainment of its selfish goals, had cynically and cold-bloodedly maneuvered the Hungarian people into action against the USSR."[47]

The importance of RFE and, therefore, of any failings during the revolution was enhanced by the fact that it relayed the transmissions of many of the local radios of the revolutionaries. This broadcast by Radio Free Rakoczi at 1352 on November 5 gives a sense of RFE's role: "Peoples of the world! Hear the call for help of a small nation! . . . This is Radio Rakoczi, Hungary. We have read an appeal. Radio Free Europe, Munich! Radio Free Europe, Munich! Answer! Have you received our transmission?"

As in Poland, one of the first actions of the rebels had been to shut down the detested jammers so that Western Radios could be heard without interference.

In December 1956 and January 1957 RFE continued its postmortem of its coverage by giving self-administered questionnaires to some eight hundred Hungarian refugees. Eighty-five percent denied that any outside influences had been responsible for the uprising, and less than 3 percent thought that radio and balloon-leaflet operations were an element of incitement. Only 6 percent felt that Western broadcasts specifically led to expectations of aid from the West.[48]

But these generally favorable replies for RFE and other broadcasters were not evident in interviews with 1,007 Hungarian refugees in a USIA sponsored survey in early December 1956. Ninety-six percent said they expected aid from the West, and 77 percent said they expected military aid. In reply to the question, "What led you to expect such aid?" 8 percent said RFE broadcasts, 20 percent said Western broadcasts aroused hope for aid, and 10 percent said Western propaganda.[49]

The survey asked respondents to rank the reasons why the Hungarians had been willing to attempt an uprising. The most popular reason was the example of Poland with 40 percent placing it first. A Western broadcaster would, no doubt, have wished to have been able to claim that only because of the Western Radios were the Hungarians aware of what was happening in Poland. That was not the case. The newspaper, *Szabad Nep,* started publishing reports of what was happening from October 19.[50] But, given that 93 percent of the respondents in the RFE survey said foreign radio was their most important source of news and only 1 percent said regime press and 1 percent regime radio, Western broadcasters could feel justly proud of their importance.

The U.S. Legation in Budapest had no doubts. "We are still faced with the fact that the Hungarians for the most part did interpret our broadcasts in a manner probably never intended or forseen," it reported on December 18. "When Hungarians charge us with not having come to their aid they in general refer to RFE 'promises'."[51]

Some RFE commentators, such as Allan A. Michie, deputy European director of RFE and coordinator of RFE's coverage of Hungary in Vienna during the revolution, surprisingly thought that it was significant that the percentage of culpable stories in the RFE file was so small. In fact, even if just one story was at fault, it was a matter of great gravity. It is well accepted in international journalism that quotation of a source does not absolve the transmitter of the information from responsibility for its content. The very fact of transmission gives it a certain authenticity.

The contrast is inevitably drawn between RFE's handling of the Polish story and the Hungarian story. There were, of course, great differences in the circumstances. Griffith kept himself well informed on Poland by asking Philippe Ben, the correspondent in Warsaw of *Le Monde* and *Ma'ariv,* to telex his reports to RFE. In July 1956 Seweryn Bialer, private secretary to Jakob Berman, who had earlier been in charge of culture and the police, defected and was an invaluable source of information. Hungary had been more tightly sealed and from outside it was more difficult to know what was going on. The Hungarian void was deepened, Griffith later recalled, by the fact that for reasons he could never discover, the American Embassy had dismantled its transmitter some time before the uprising. We now know that the United States had agreed to shut down its transmitter in exchange for the Hungarians agreeing not to install one in Washington when they opened a legation there. Griffith received almost no guidance from RFE's office in New York, the State Department in Washington, or the CIA. The only way he could find out what was happening was from the British, by talking to Norman Reddaway, head of the International Research Department (IRD) in the Foreign Office in London, who was a friend.[52] Moreover, Hungary experienced a popular revolt, and violence was on a completely different scale than in Poland. In Hungary the pressures came from outside the Party, but in Poland the pressures for liberalization were principally inside the Party apparatus.[53] But in the final analysis the difference lay in the people handling the story. The Polish story was handled impeccably because of the integrity and iron hand of the head of the service, Jan Nowak. Griffith later said that he made a mistake in sending off to the Hungarian border the only American on his staff who knew Hungarian, Bill Rademaekers, instead of keeping him in Munich to vet the Hungarian service.[54]

According to Griffith's memorandum, RFE believed itself much more culpable than did the outside investigators. Both Griffith and Cord Meyer share the view that the analyses of the RFE files by the West German government, the Council of Europe, and the United Nations Committee were something of a whitewash because they all had political reasons for not damning RFE.[55]

Frank Wisner went to the Austro-Hungarian border and saw the thousands of refugees streaming across. He met resistance leaders. Richard Bissell, who was to succeed Wisner as CIA's chief of covert operations in January 1959, said Wisner felt "we had done a lot to inspire and encourage the event."[56] Wisner had a nervous breakdown soon afterward. He shot himself on October 29, 1965.

What was the responsibility of the U.S. administration? RFE itself believed General Eisenhower and Foster Dulles had gone too far during the presidential campaign of 1952. The policy adviser issued a Special Guidance for Broadcasts on Liberation on September 2, 1953. It said:

> We of RFE . . . cannot comment upon these statements [on liberation by General Eisenhower and Dulles] with unqualified optimism, for to do so would be to deceive our listeners by inspiring in them exaggerated hope of Western intervention. . . . Not one word in these statements [on liberation] can be used to encourage militant anti-communists to go over from passive to active resistance in the expectation that such resistance will be supported by Western elements.[57]

On one occasion Eisenhower made a fiery speech and Lewis Galantière, policy adviser to Free Europe, issued a directive saying that RFE had to underplay it. John Dunning, a senior executive of RFE, later commented: "It was excessive and would have misled the people of Eastern Europe. What you say for U.S. consumption is one thing, what you say for overseas is another."[58]

When the Hungarian uprising was over, Dulles told the president that "we always said we are against violent rebellion."[59] But there was much ambiguity. C. D. Jackson advised the president's speech writer that the president should deliver a policy speech condemning the Russian armed intervention and declaring that the United States would "not tolerate European youth, European students, or the European worker, to be crushed." Jackson said such a statement was "sufficiently vague not to be a commitment, but has the kind of ring that is needed now."[60]

The president's staff secretary, Colonel Andrew J. Goodpaster, believed that the president had "never ridded himself of some feeling that our government, elements in our government—and specifically the CIA—had gone beyond their authority and in fact had carried out a line of propaganda which was not in accord with his policy."[61]

The problem was not that the CIA was pursuing its own policy but that the administration's was ambiguous. And there was also the problem of the control of the Hungarian desk in Munich. The two senior executives of the Free Europe Committee who went to Munich at the time of the revolution made a good point: "We must bear in mind that no parallel situation where an outside radio voice was the principal means of communicating internal as well as external facts during a major national uprising, has ever occurred before in history."[62]

It took RFE years to live down the Hungary story. Cord Meyer reported that when President Kennedy took office, Meyer found that some of his key advisers were initially hostile to RFE and RL because they believed that RFE had irresponsibly caused the Hungarian revolt and had innocent blood on its hands.[63]

The VOA was also charged with inciting and encouraging the riots, but there seems to be no evidence of this. Indeed P. Nadyani, chief of the VOA Hungarian desk at the time of the riots, claimed to have toned down what the U.S. delegate said in the United Nations about Hungary because his exact words might have sounded inflammatory.[64] The USIA assured the president that "certain programs even warned the freedom fighters to be cautious and not go too fast."[65] Subsequent internal reviews of the broadcasts claimed that there had never been a hint of any possibility of American aid in arms or men except for American assistance through the Red Cross or to the refugees who had fled across the border.[66]

The BBC was described by one student as being too objective at times. "Inspiring news items that might have been broadcast were, in fact, often not put out. All the same, the BBC was very good in informing the people and maintaining their morale, without, however, sending out propaganda."[67] Why "inspiring news items" had often to be sacrificed was explained by the head of the Foreign Services News Department:

We have always to be scrupulously careful in checking facts, but we had to be even more cautious and sceptical about details reaching us from Hungary. If we said something was happening in a certain town or factory, the people in that area knew whether we were correct or not. But people in the next town could not check the correctness of our reporting and they might have acted on our information—an inaccurate report, in those circumstances, could have had very serious consequences. We often had to sacrifice interesting news because we were not absolutely certain of its truth. And sometimes this meant throwing away news that afterwards proved to be true.[68]

The sobriety of the BBC did it no harm in Hungary. On the night of October 30 the Council of Free Hungarian Radio decided that it should follow in the footsteps of the BBC, which they considered had acquired an influence far in excess of that of other Western broadcasting stations. The council decided that "the new radio should emulate the factual, sincere and friendly tone of the BBC in its comments, and the BBC's outstanding reliability in its news service."[69]

Almost the last word on the Hungarian revolution should lie, perhaps, with the *Soviet Encyclopedia*, which in the 1951 edition said:

> Being unable to suppress the Hungarian revolution, Austria in April 1849 asked Tsarist Russia for help. Nicholas I readily lent his assistance to the Austrian oppressors. As Lenin wrote in 1900: "The Tsarist Government not only keeps the Russian people in slavery but also sends it to subdue other peoples which rebel against their slavery, as happened in 1849 when the Russian troops were engaged in suppressing the revolution in Hungary." (Lenin, *Collected Works*, 4th ed., 4: 351–52.)[70]

Λ　Λ　Λ

Forty years later the mystery of what RFE broadcast in 1956 has deepened. Maria Wittner, known as the Saint Joan of the revolution, stood up at a conference in Budapest in September 1996 and shocked the international audience with her denunciation of RFE.[71]

> Imre Nagy agreed to the invasion of Soviet troops. Already on this very day this step of his is put down as one of the greatest acts of treachery in Hungary's history. And this will be remembered for ever.
> Imre Nagy, who covered his hands in Hungarian blood. . . .
> Where are the traitors . . . Who are the murderers? Imre Nagy and his government . . . only Cardinal Mindszenty has spoken out fearlessly.

Such were typical quotations of what Maria Wittner, jailed for fourteen years for her part in the revolution, claimed were broadcast by RFE. She was quoting from what her friend from the revolution, Zoltan Benko, had written down as he listened to the radio during the fighting.[72]

Paul Henze, deputy political adviser for RFE in 1956, who listened to Maria Wittner, later commented, "We question the accuracy of these quotations."[73] An assistant in New York of Jan Nowak, the head of the Polish desk of RFE, compiled for him a dossier of broadcast summaries written by the RFE Hungarian staff. The dossier contains no direct quotations, but the tenor is more violent than that in the Griffith report. Nagy is described as a "traitor,"[74] a "Moscow puppet,"[75] and a "liar."[76] Jan Nowak's comment on Maria Wittner's quotations was, "They are absolutely true."[77]

Andras Mink, a research fellow of the Open Society Archives, Budapest, who has studied the transcripts the archives acquired from the RFE/RL Research Institute, confirmed that a considerable part of the quotations Maria Wittner cited from Zoltan Benko were contained in those transcripts.[78]

There have been suggestions that they were quotations from local radio stations relayed by RFE. The Free Europe Committee published a 112-page booklet, *The Revolt in Hungary: A Documentary Chronology of Events Based Exclusively on Internal Broadcasts by Central and Provincial Radios, October 23, 1956–November 4, 1956.*[79] It contains no attacks on Nagy.

Some believed at the time that either the secret police, with mobile transmitters, or an East German radio station were pretending to be RFE. Identification of radio stations is not always easy. Raisa Maksimovna, Mikhail Gorbachev's wife, gives a good illustration of that problem in her diary on the attempted 1991 Soviet coup. "Around seven in the morning Anatoly and Irina managed to get the following information over the transistor (it was not Mayak, probably the World Service of the BBC)."[80]

As to the charge that RFE incited the revolution, Mink commented: "The encouragement to fight, to stand firm, the proclaiming of the sympathetic feelings of the Western World, and their financial help is unambiguous, but I could not find even now a part of the text which would refer to concrete military intervention or something which would offer any prospect of this."[81]

Nevertheless, an old Hungarian rose to his feet at the Budapest conference and told the men on the platform who had been in charge of

RFE in Munich at the time of the revolution that RFE was to blame for the deaths of thousands of young Hungarians.

VOA: Why the VOA Should Be Abolished

On August 1, 1953, the United States Information Agency (USIA) was created, absorbing the IIA and other international information activities of the government. The creation of the USIA was the outcome of three committees that had been investigating information activities: the Senate Committee on Foreign Relations (the Hickenlooper committee); The President's Advisory Committee on Government Reorganization (the Rockefeller committee) and the President's Committee on International Information Activities (the Jackson committee). The most important for the VOA was the Jackson committee. Its chairman was William H. Jackson, a New York investment banker and former deputy director of Central Intelligence, and it was created on January 26, 1953, shortly after President Eisenhower took office.

The Jackson committee report, submitted on June 30, 1953, incorporated proposals from the other committees. It recommended that the program's primary purpose should be "to submit evidence to the peoples of other nations that their own aspirations for freedom, progress and peace are supported and advanced by the objectives and policies of the United States." It wanted broadcasts and printed materials to concentrate on objective, factual news reporting, avoiding a propagandist note but making forceful and factual refutations of false Soviet accusations when required. It was critical of the VOA, whose programs had been "widely criticized and discredited."[82] It bemoaned the fact that the national information program had suffered from a lack of effective central direction. "Too often, the program has been merely defensive. Lack of coordination has resulted in the haphazard projection of too many and too diffuse propaganda themes. No single set of ideas has been registered abroad through effective repetition. This is in sharp contrast to the technique of the Soviets, who have consistently hammered home a few carefully selected central themes: land reform, peace, anti-imperialism, youth."[83]

It questioned the rightness of spending one-third of the budget on broadcasting to the Soviet Union because little was known about the audience. It thought shortwave broadcasts appeared to be of little use because of inaudibility and the limited size of the audience. Transmissions in Tatar, Turkestani, and Azerbaijani were stopped.

The VOA disagreed with the Jackson committee recommendation to avoid a propagandist note. To the communist world, at least, the VOA insisted on a "hard-hitting anti-Communist message."

The USIA was structured so that the director reported to the president through the National Security Council, but the secretary of state directed the policy and controlled the content of the information program and provided guidance on the foreign policy of the United States. The first director was Theodore C. Streibert, former chairman of the Mutual Broadcasting System radio network.[84]

In the statement of mission for the USIA on October 22 the president said, "The purpose of the United States Information Agency shall be to submit evidence to peoples of other nations by means of communication techniques that the objectives and policies of the United States are in harmony with and will advance their legitimate aspirations for freedom, progress and peace."

The means by which this purpose would primarily be achieved were

> Explaining and interpreting to foreign peoples the objectives and policies of the United States Government.
>
> Depicting imaginatively the correlation between United States policies and the legitimate aspirations of other peoples of the world.
>
> Unmasking and countering hostile attempts to distort or to frustrate the objectives and policies of the United States.
>
> Delineating those important aspects of the life and culture of the people of the United States which facilitate understanding of the policies and objectives of the U.S. Government.[85]

Streibert told the president that the agency would avoid a propagandistic tone and concentrate on objective, factual news reporting and appropriate commentaries.[86] There were, nevertheless, still influential Americans who believed the country would be better off without the VOA. Walter Lippmann wrote an article that appeared in *Readers Digest* in August 1953 under the headline "Why the Voice of America Should Be Abolished."[87] Lippman wanted to broadcast internationally just a selection of domestic newscasts. He wrote:

> To set up an elaborate machinery of international communication and then have it say, "We are the Voice of America engaged in propaganda to make you like us better than you like our adversaries," is —as propaganda—an absurdity. As a way of stimulating an appetite for the American way of life, it is like serving castor oil as a cocktail before dinner. It will be said, I know, that if we abolish the Voice of America, if

we limited our overseas broadcasts to straight news, we shall "lose the battle for men's minds" to the Communists who conduct incessant propaganda. I do not think there is any evidence that the Voice of America has been winning that battle. On the contrary, there are all sorts of reasons for thinking it does much more harm than good to our influence abroad.

The VOA gradually moved out of the slough of despond of the McCarthy era. In September and October 1954 it transferred its headquarters from New York to Washington, D.C. Output increased, and it concentrated its efforts on the war against communism by directing 85 percent of all transmissions behind the Iron Curtain.[88]

BBC: Hobbled but by No Means Crippled

By 1955 the Soviet Union had wiped out the BBC's position as the world's leading international broadcaster in terms of broadcasting hours. Looked at from the point of view of super-power politics it is, perhaps, surprising that Britain had held this position for as much as ten years after World War II. The weight of international broadcasting was shifting from the West to the East. The Warsaw Pact countries had increased their broadcasting by 100 percent between 1950 and 1955.[89]

The recurring theme of the fifties, sixties, and seventies was challenge, review, and doubt as the British government tried to fit the BBC overseas services into the country's postwar economic situation and changing role in the postcolonial era. Time and again the government tried to cut back the overseas services. As Lord Strang, a former head of the Foreign Office, said in February 1957, "The art of hobbling an organisation without entirely crippling it is one which is well understood and practised in Whitehall."[90]

The BBC contended with three reviews in the fifties: from 1952 to 1954 the Drogheda committee and in 1957 and 1959 two by Charles Hill. The Drogheda Committee was set up in July 1952 after an outcry over freezing the 1952 External Services budget at the 1951 level. Lord Drogheda gave his report to the government in July 1953. The cabinet Committee on Information Services had difficulty at their meeting of July 5 in deciding on the line to be taken during the House of Commons debate on the report. The government had been advised to limit expenditure on information services, but the report suggested an increase. Harold Macmillan, minister of housing, soon to become prime minister, felt it would be best to follow Benjamin Disraeli's advice and be "prolix and obscure."[91] The report was not published in full until years later. Extracts were published in April 1954.[92] The full report contained an extraordinary piece of British arrogance: "The popularity of the British Broadcasting Corporation External Services depends above all on its high reputation for objective and honest news reporting. We believe this to be a priceless asset which sets the British Broadcasting Corporation apart from other national broadcasting systems."[93]

The report set the priority on large-scale capital investment, mainly in overseas relay transmitters. It also recommended restoration of some of the cutbacks of previous years. It had no doubt that broadcasting should continue to Russia, Czechoslovakia, Hungary, Poland, Albania, Bulgaria, and Rumania but thought the French, Italian, Dutch, Portuguese, and Scandinavian services should stop. In 1952–53 the BBC was spending only 9 percent of regional costs on Russia and the satellites compared to 34 percent on the rest of Europe.[94] The Foreign Office thought the broadcasts to Russia were generally rather dry and dull. The Information Research Department was responsible for offering guidance to the BBC on services to the Soviet Union and the satellites. They considered the services to the latter satisfactory.[95] The Drogheda committee recognized the necessity of concentrating all possible resources on broadcasting to Russia and the satellites. "A great war is now being fought in the air," they opined in the report. They considered it almost the only form of propaganda capable of penetrating the Iron Curtain.

In early 1956 the Foreign Office was asked to consider if money could be reallocated to meet the special threat of Soviet propaganda. They replied that one way of doing it would be to abolish most services to Western Europe. "Our Embassies in most European countries . . . do not believe that people of any prominence listen to them and regard their influence as negligible." The BBC was holding on to what was largely a fetish, the officials thought.[96] The Drogheda committee wanted broadcasting to cater to the needs of the "influential few" rather than the masses. This assertion brought down the wrath of the BBC. "Wireless has given to governments direct means of access to audiences overseas which enables them to influence foreign governments by and through direct contact with the masses," the board of governors lectured the noble lord and the government in a paper on the report.[97]

Before the government got around to implementing the Drogheda committee recommendations the Suez invasion intervened, bringing with it the biggest conflict ever between a British government and the BBC.

The scene was set on July 25, the day before Nasser nationalized the Suez Canal, when the British government's Policy Review Committee met and discussed a request by the foreign secretary that they consider "by what means the government could secure a larger measure of control over the content of broadcasts to the Middle and Far East, against the background that the BBC was thought to attach too much importance to impartiality." Possibilities were "either to arrange with the BBC that its broadcasts should be used as an instrument of government policy, or to make use of a different organisation and reduce government expenditure on BBC overseas broadcasts."[98] Ministers at the meeting concluded, "Overseas broadcasts . . . were paid for by the Government and it was reasonable that they should reflect Government policy."[99]

The sort of incident the government did not like occurred on August 8 and 14 when the BBC broadcast in its Arabic services what the prime minister and foreign minister had said on the air; then on August 15 gave broadcasting time to Egyptian Minister of National Guidance Salah Salem, the "dancing major." The prime minister complained about it to Sir Ian Jacob, the director-general of the BBC, on August 20.[100] Sir Ivone Kirkpatrick, the permanent under secretary at the Foreign Office, saw Jacob on August 28 and told him that ministers were preoccupied about the state of the overseas services. He said that "there were two powerful schools of thought, one of which was disposed to favour governmental control in the Overseas Services and the other, the curtailment of the £5 million [$14 million] grant in aid to the BBC, and its expenditure in other propaganda enterprises." Kirkpatrick reported, "Sir Ian Jacob looked stricken like a mother about to be deprived of her child."[101] But for all this desk thumping C. C. B. Stewart, the head of the Information Policy Department in the Foreign Office, said in a report on September 20 that "the BBC's Arabic Service has represented our case pretty well."[102]

That was not the view of the prime minister, and in the cabinet on September 26 Anthony Eden expressed his continued dissatisfaction with the Overseas Service of the BBC. The cabinet approved the establishment of a new committee of ministers under Lord Privy Seal R. A. Butler to review the existing arrangements for overseas broadcasting.[103] The first meeting took place on October 9, and Kirkpatrick put forward the view that there was no logical halfway position between no control of the BBC and total control, which would expose the government to the need to answer to Parliament in detail on the contents of the broadcasts.

When Butler reported to the cabinet on October 24, it decided to get the reactions of the director-general of the BBC to the provisional conclusions of the committee on overseas broadcasting. These conclusions included a cut in the grant-in-aid by at least $2,800,000 (£1 million), which was about one-fifth of the entire grant, which was to be achieved mainly by eliminating the European language services.[104] The cabinet minute is quite specific in its reference to "European language services"—not Western European language services—and in discussion the point was made that the complete elimination of the European services would be regrettable. But when Anthony Nutting, minister of state for foreign affairs, saw Sir Ian Jacob, he talked only of shutting down the Western European services with, not surprisingly, no reference to the services to Eastern Europe.[105] The money saved would be devoted in part to an intensification of the BBC's services to the Middle East and Southeast Asia. The government would not seek to impose any direct control over the BBC's External Services, but they would require the appointment of a Foreign Office liaison officer to advise the BBC on the content and direction of its overseas programs.

A Foreign Office minute said that the measures were taken "partly as a means of administering a shock to the BBC and inducing them to reconcile their independence with the need for greater care in conducting their services in the national interest."[106] According to two sources, William Clark, Eden's adviser on public relations, said that at this time the prime minister had instructed the Lord Chancellor to prepare an instrument that would take over the BBC altogether and subject it wholly to the will of the government.[107] Jacob doubted if matters could have gone so far.[108]

The government continued to bumble on. It first told the BBC the cut would be $2,800,000 (£1 million), then $1,400,000 (£500,000). It tried to get the BBC to agree to the cut. In fact, no cut was ever made. A Foreign Office liaison officer started work on November 2, but the arrangement lasted only a few months.

The BBC may have had a shock, but it did not affect its policy. It reported in its press review on October 31, the day when the Anglo-French bombing of the Egyptian airfields began, the *Daily Herald*'s headline, "This Is Folly," and the *Manchester Guardian* comment, "an act of folly without justification in any terms but brief expediency." It allowed Hugh Gaitskell, the leader of the Opposition, the right of reply after Eden's ministerial broadcast to the nation on November 3.

The complexity of the relations between the Foreign Office and the BBC is shown by the presence on an Egypt Committee—reminiscent of the Russia Committee founded in 1946—of Hugh Carleton Greene, controller, overseas services of the BBC. The secret Egypt Committee was concerned with propaganda. The BBC had agreed to a Foreign Office request to provide a representative on August 17.[109] The preparatory Foreign Office paper for the meeting of October 12 began with the statement: "In the long-term, we aim to get rid of Colonel Nasser. In the short-term, we must prepare the Arab world, and the rest of the world, for negotiations with him—the result of which must be represented as a success for us."[110] A review of the use made of the propaganda themes said they were all used by the normal organs of information of the Foreign Office. These organs are listed and included the press at home and the BBC overseas services.[111]

In a later meeting of the committee Donald Stephenson, who had succeeded Greene as controller, overseas services of the BBC, and as the BBC representative on the committee, explained the BBC's policy: "The BBC would always work on the assumption that the Government was right; but it needed to give a fair reflection of public opinion and to be believed by its listeners."[112]

Such is the Foreign Office control of some procedures of the BBC that the Foreign Office did not allow the BBC to release some of the internal BBC memoranda on Suez until 1994, and even then some were still withheld. If a government department writes to the BBC and classifies its letter as, say, "Confidential," "that classification applies not only to that letter but also to any other papers dealing with the same topic, including the BBC's internal discussions and the reply," according to the BBC. The BBC says this affects only a small proportion of its archives and for the most part is likely to arise in papers relating to the BBC World Service. "In practice this means that the BBC would not release material at the Written Archives Centre which has not similarly been released at the Public Record Office, normally after 30 years," the BBC states.[113]

The BBC came through the Suez crisis unscathed from its clashes with the British government and with its reputation enhanced.

1. The offices of the BBC Overseas Service at Bush House in London in the fifties. The BBC engaged in some self-censorship with this photograph. The inscription "To the Friendship of English Speaking Peoples" was removed when it was published on the Continent of Europe. Courtesy of the BBC.

2. Major-General Sir Ian Jacob, who was controller of the European service of the BBC early in the Cold War. He was a member of the secret Russia Committee in the Foreign Office, which devised propaganda strategies against the Soviet Union. Jacob became director-general of the BBC. Courtesy of the BBC.

3. An RFE transmitter station. Western broadcasters used relay stations at strategic points in Europe to ensure the best reception in Eastern Europe and the Soviet Union. Courtesy of the Associated Press.

4. British politicians were out to cut the BBC's overseas broadcasting budget despite the strength of Russian propaganda against Western democracy. Cartoon by Low, the *Daily Hearld*, February 22, 1952. Courtesy of the Centre for the Study of Cartoons and Caricature, University of Kent, Canterbury.

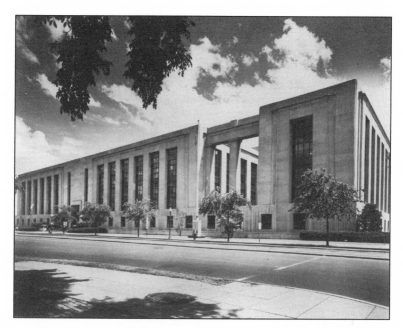

5. The headquarters of the VOA in sight of Congress in Washington, D.C. They moved from New York to Washington in 1954 after the establishment there of the United States Information Agency (USIA) of which the VOA was made a part. Courtesy of Voice of America.

6. Edward R. Murrow, appointed USIA director by President Kennedy in 1961. As a renowed broadcaster from the London blitz in the Second World War, Murrow gave the agency and the VOA a high profile, which against all the vicissitudes of its previous seven years, it greatly needed. Courtesy of Voice of America.

7. A poster attacking Russian listeners to Western Radios. "Bad enough you should believe that rubbish, ears flapping. Worse still, that you should swallow the lies and sing a foreign song." By kind permission of Sherwood Demitz, Washington, D.C.

8. Allen W. Dulles, *center,* the first president of the Free Europe Committee and the intelligence man most involved in the establishment of RFE and RL. He later became director of the CIA. Courtesy of the John F. Kennedy Library. Photo no. KN 18945.

9. The BBC started a radio soap for the Russian service similar to a well-known British soap, *Mrs Dale's Diary.* Cartoon by Emmwood, the *Daily Mail,* February 16, 1962. Courtesy of the Centre for the Study of Cartoons and Caricature, University of Kent, Canterbury.

10. RFE/RL offices in Munich, Germany, after being bombed in February 1981. Four members of the staff were injured but no one was killed. The Czech Secret Police; Carlos, "The Jackal," in the pay of President Ceaucescu of Romania; and the KGB working with the East Germans, have all been suggested as the perpetrators. Courtesy of Radio Free Europe/Radio Liberty.

11. Lech Walesa in Gdansk in 1983 listening to a live RFE broadcast from Oslo of his wife accepting the Nobel Prize on his behalf. Courtesy of the Associated Press.

12. The nuclear accident at Chernobyl. Russians heard of the disaster from Western Radios. The accident took place on April 26, 1986, but the Russian government said nothing for nearly three days. The embarrassment of the cover-up, exposed by Western broadcasters, helped drive Gorbachev into full-scale glasnost. Courtesy of TASS/Associated Press.

13. President Ronald Reagan delivering his 1986 holiday message to the people of the Soviet Union from the VOA control center. It was jammed. Courtesy of Voice of America.

14. Cartoon from a book of anti-Western cartoons called *A Shattering Blow* by Boris Efimov, Plakat, Moscow, 1985. The caption reads: "Radio Liberty and Radio Free Europe—These two old toads love croaking loudly. Their base in an old rubbish bin containing provocations, lies, slander, inventions."

15. The computerized master control center of RFE/RL in Munich, feeding all RFE/RL programs to five transmitter stations across Europe via land lines and satellite communications. Courtesy of Radio Free Europe/Radio Liberty.

16. Cartoon by Rogers, *Pittsburgh Press*, on the end of jamming, which stopped on November 29, 1988. It had started on February 3, 1948, and had at times stopped for some broadcasters, depending on the temperature of the cold war. © 1988 The Pittsburgh Press/United Feature Syndicate. Reproduced by permission.

17. The end of the cold war. A Berliner doing his bit to demolish the wall separating East and West Berlin after the opening of the checkpoints at midnight on November 9, 1989. Radio in the American Sector (RIAS) had kept East Berliners in touch with the world since the Wall was built in 1961. Courtesy of the Associated Press.

18. The president of Bulgaria, Zhelyu Zhelev, on a visit to England in 1991 at the grave of Georgi Markov, who was murdered by the Bulgarian secret police in 1978 because the Bulgarian rulers did not like his broadcasts. Courtesy of *The Independent*/Chistopher Jones, February 22, 1991.

19. A tired-looking President Gorbachev arriving back in Moscow on August 22, 1991 from house arrest during the attempted coup when he had kept in touch with the outside world by listening to Western Radios. Courtesy of Reuters.

20. "Thank you VOA for your truthful information"—graffiti scrawled on a wall near the Russian White House in Moscow just after the unsuccessful coup against Gorbachev in August 1991. Courtesy of the Voice of America.

6

THE BEGINNINGS OF
DÉTENTE
(1956–1963)

USSR: Shooting Themselves in Both Feet

FROM THE TIME of the Geneva Summit Conference of 1955 the history of Western broadcasting followed the ups and downs of détente. The Soviet Union suspended jamming of the BBC after Khrushchev's visit to Britain in the spring of 1956 then started it again during the suppression of the Hungarian revolution in November.[1] Because English language broadcasts were not jammed, Moscow University students transcribed the BBC's slow-speed English news bulletins and posted translations on university notice boards.[2]

In an interview for broadcast by CBS on June 2, 1957, Khrushchev said that if the VOA would change its programming, it would not be jammed. In the years of talks that followed the Russians made it clear that they were really after changes in RL and RFE, rather than the VOA, which had already modified its strident tone. There were many U.S.–Soviet talks about jamming and the programming relationship over the next six years. The talks took place, inter alia, at the periodic negotiations of the U.S.–Soviet cultural exchange agreements and almost continuously at the International Frequency Registration Board (IFRB) of the secretariat of the International Telecommunications Union (ITU).

By 1958 the Russians were devoting more resources to jamming than to their own domestic and international broadcasting. The total power of the jamming transmitters was three times that of the Western Radios. A report to the Central Committee said that for short periods of the day up to fifty to sixty radio stations of 5,500 to 7,500 kilowatts each were working against the Soviet Union. The Russians were jamming with 1,660 stations with a power of 15,440 kilowatts. At 0330 they were jamming nine transmitters with a power of 780 kilowatts, using 167 stations with a power of 6,592 kilowatts. That figure excluded hundreds of local jamming stations. These statistics have to be treated with reserve, however, because Russian propagandists seem to have used different counting methods in different years. The report plaintively continued:

> But despite all efforts and the expenditure of billions of roubles, jamming is not achieving its aim. Hostile radio stations are listened to all over the country, with the exception of the centers of Moscow, Leningrad, Kiev, and Riga. Jammed stations can be heard with the aid of a simple internal amateur radio-aerial. Testing carried out by the KGB and local Party organizations shows that even in certain districts of Moscow, Leningrad, and Kiev, as well as in the suburbs, BBC and VOA programs can be heard.[3]

The memorandum then described one of the most extraordinary snafus of the cold war—the production of short wave receivers by the Soviet Union, which enabled its citizens to listen to the very Western Radios it was jamming. According to the memorandum's estimates, before the war there were about two hundred thousand short wave receivers in the Soviet Union. In 1949 there were up to five hundred thousand; by 1958 there were more than twenty 20 million receivers capable of picking up Western stations. More short wave sets had been sold in the Soviet Union than in all other countries of the world.

> By order of the USSR Council of Ministers of February 17, 1953, it was proposed that the Ministry of Communications and Industry stop, as of 1954, production of receivers capable of picking up hostile broadcasts. But industry sharply increased its production of such receivers—in 1954 four million a year were being produced without any objection from the Ministry of Communications. Thus our technical measures directed against hostile radio broadcasts were brought to nothing by the mass production of short wave receivers. There was certainly no necessity for such production, which was governed merely by commercial considerations. It is enough to point out that at present, up to 85 percent of short wave receivers are located in the European part of the USSR, where our own short wave broadcasts cannot be heard and where it is possible to listen only to hostile radio.

Not only were the Russians shooting themselves in the left foot, they were hitting the right too; they were jamming a large number of their own stations.

The salt in the wound was that in the United States, England, West Germany, and other countries mass production of shortwave radios, on which Soviet programs could be heard, had stopped, according to the Russian propagandists. Less than 0.1 percent of sets could receive Soviet stations in the United States and in Germany 15 percent. Because of their high price, shortwave sets abroad could be found only among the richer section of the population.

The report recommended an end to the mass production of short-wave sets and spares; improvement of domestic radio programs and development of television; negotiation with the Americans and British so that jammming could be ended and the jamming transmitters diverted to domestic use. The report had some effect, and after 1958 the authorities forbade the sale of receivers with higher frequency short-wave bands of 19, 16, and 13 meters, the best for long-distance listening in certain circumstances. But ingenious citizens had the receivers adapted to receive the higher frequencies.

The Soviet Union did end jamming of the VOA when Khrushchev came to the United States in September 1959. The subject was raised at the Camp David talks. The Soviet foreign minister, Gromyko, proposed that the United States and the Soviet Union each limit its broadcasting to the other to three hours a day. The head of the USIA, George V. Allen, replied that such an agreement would be against America's policy of spreading information and the United States did not care if the Soviet Union broadcast twenty-four hours a day. The Russians then indicated they would stop jammming if the VOA would stop its "hostile and provocative" broadcasts.[4] Subsequently, the Russians told the President's Committee on Information Activities Abroad (PCIAA) that they were most concerned about references in the VOA programs to slave labor in the Soviet Union and a comment about the state of Khrushchev's health.[5] The president told Secretary of State Christian Herter and the director of the USIA, George Allen, to modify the VOA programming. Gordon Gray, special assistant to the president, reported on a meeting he had with the president on September 30, 1959:

> He said that in the recent Camp David talks Mr. Khrushchev had indicated that the Soviet Union would not jam what he referred to as legitimate broadcasts such as speeches of government officials. Mr Khrushchev indicated that the Soviet Union would jam broadcasts which were calculated to defy the Soviet government or to reach over the head of the Soviet government to the Soviet people. The President felt that he

wished the U.S. now to show some initiative in bringing the Voice of America in line with this kind of prescription.[6]

Allen told the president in response that the USIA had taken steps to be certain that the general tone of VOA broadcasts would not give cause for legitimate objection.[7]

Jamming resumed but was greatly reduced at least for a few months. Very light jamming of the VOA and the BBC lasted until the Russians shot down the American U-2 spy plane in May 1960. Jamming then intensified and was variable and selective until June 1963. The intensification of jamming on the morning of May 5, 1960, came before the announcement of the downing of the U-2. It coincided with a Politiburo and Central Committee meeting that marked the beginning of the fall of Khrushchev. So the decision on jamming was an integral part of an important political development.[8]

The jammers received instructions on which transmissions to jam, according to the international situation.[9] The broadcasters were learning a few tricks on ways to avoid selective jamming. The BBC did not trail items unless they were noncontroversial. They kept political commentaries short and varied the placing.[10]

On January 19, 1961, the Central Committee of the Communist Party of the Soviet Union (CPSU) decreed a large increase in jamming operations, the creation of a new special department in the Ministry of Communications to control it, and an improvement in local radio and television services in Russian and local languages to make listening to foreign broadcasts less attractive.[11]

The decree, "On Measures to Intensify the Struggle against Enemy Radio Propaganda," said that during the previous ten years the imperialist powers had made radio the main tool of hostile anti-Soviet propaganda, the distribution of disinformation, provocative fabrications, and rumors. They had set up a network that broadcast under the names of individual countries and more often under the names of allegedly independent anticommunist organizations. They broadcast malicious programs in the languages of the peoples of the Soviet Union in parallel around the clock. Ten to thirty stations with a total power of 800 to 3,000–4,000 kilowatts were continuously transmitting, and during some short periods up to sixty-eight stations with a total power of 8,000 kilowatts were at work. To isolate the population from hostile radio propaganda a broad network of jamming stations had been created that caused considerable interference with anti-Soviet broadcasts. There were local protection systems in eighty large cities using more than one thousand low-powered transmitters that made it difficult to listen to enemy broadcasts for tens of kilometers around. In addition there was a long-distance network. The total number of jammers, both local and long distance, was fourteen hundred with a total power of 14,000 kilowatts. (These figures cannot be reconciled with those of 1958, which were reported as higher, but the 1961 figures line up with those given in a 1959 report.) In recent years around $250 million (one billion roubles) had been spent on building new jamming stations and tens of millions of roubles were spent each year to support the networks, the decree reported.

Despite all that the decree bemoaned the fact that it was impossible to paralyze enemy broadcasting by jamming alone, given the vast size of the country and the existence of many millions of radio receivers. At some times the jammers were overwhelmingly more powerful than the enemy transmitters.

Examples were:

Time	No. of Jammers	KW Power	No. of Enemy Transmitters	KW Power
0030	120	1,120	13	1,090
0230	192	6,637	12	1,120
0430	150	5,500	10	770

Jamming also caused significant interference with domestic broadcasts and transmissions to other countries. Enemy radio propaganda penetration had also increased because of shortcomings in the management of television and radio in some of the republics and lack of program choice in Russian and in national languages.

To improve protection the CPSU Central Committee decided that

1. The CPSU Central Committees of the Union republics and regional and district committees would be obliged to take effective measures to reduce the influence of radio propaganda and to organize varied TV and radio programs, particularly at the enemies' peak broadcasting times.
2. The USSR State Planning Committee and the USSR Ministry of Communications would be obliged to increase the power of the jammers and to see that previous decisions on jamming were carried out.
3. The jamming of certain named stations, including Radio Liberty, which worked for so-called independent anti-Soviet and anticommunist organizations, would be increased.

4. A special department of forty-five people in the Ministry of Communications with control groups in Moscow and Khabarovsk would be created.
5. The special department's tasks were
   a. Constant checking of the VOA and BBC.
   b. Reporting monthly to the CPSU Central Committee on the character, content, and aims of the VOA and BBC broadcasts so that decisions could be taken on selective jamming and suggestions made for guidelines on Soviet counterpropaganda. The jamming of loyal broadcasting, that is, sport, art and literature, scientific, medical, and informational programs could be lifted.
6. The new department should, jointly with the KGB [Komitet Gosudarstvennoy Bezopasnosti (Committee for State Security)]
   a. Complete within three months proposals to stop jamming broadcasts in minor languages of the Soviet Union—Finnish, Hebrew, Farsi, Pushtu, Persian, Beludgi, and so forth.
   b. Check every three months on the content of broadcasts by Rome, Athens, Canada, Madrid, the Vatican, and the Voice of Zion and report on the need for further jamming. During the checking periods jamming should stop.
7. Named departments should, within two months, submit proposals on the organization of well-aimed return broadcasts to those countries hosting pirate anti-Soviet radio stations (Greece, the Federal Republic of Germany, Okinawa, and the Philippines) under the names of organizations not formally owned by the Soviet Union.
8. Decisions on jamming were to be submitted to the Ministry of Communications jointly with the KGB. The KGB was to
   a. find any new stations putting out anti-Soviet broadcasts;
   b. check the quality of jamming of anti-Soviet broadcasts.[12]

These measures were useful when the Cuban missile crisis of October 1962 caused the Russians further to increase jamming to cover 70–80 percent of all news items. But it still was not complete enough. For example, the following year P. Morozov, the secretary of the Amur Oblast Party Committee, reported that a check on the jamming of the VOA and Radio Liberty in five towns showed that jamming was unsatisfactory and part of these transmissions had been received.[13]

News was not much used as a term in Soviet journalism before the late 1950s. It was equated with the bourgeois concept of sensationalism.[14] "The traditional Party view was that news should be used only to provide illustrative material for predetermined didactic and propagandistic themes and otherwise ignored."[15] The attitude toward news changed because of the increase in listening to foreign broadcasting.

In 1959 two members of the Propaganda Department of the Central Committee, G. Kazakov and A. Romanov, analyzed VOA and BBC propaganda under seven headings:

1. Attempts to convince Soviet citizens of the advantages of life in the United States and in capitalist Western countries—living conditions, consumer goods, service network

2. Propaganda about American economic might

3. Attacks on Soviet democracy and praise of bourgeois democracy—attacks on communist dictatorship and alleged desire by Soviet citizens for more freedom to travel, write, and exchange ideas

4. Distortion of Leninist national policy—Baltic peoples as having been "enslaved" by Soviet imperialism

5. Stress on American technical progress, especially in the use of nuclear energy, and on the desire of the United States and Great Britain for international collaboration by scientists

6. Allegations about the Western capitalist powers' peaceful foreign policy, the Soviet Union being accused of not wanting firm peace, plus allegations that the Soviet Union wants to subjugate West Berlin

7. Tendentious portrayal of life in the people's democracies, showing Soviet supremacy as being based on force

The propaganda experts considered the programs "lively and radiophonic," which attracted listeners. They took particular exception to the assertion on the VOA that "nineteen million American negroes own more cars than the inhabitants of the whole of the Soviet Union."[16]

Khrushchev saw that to counter foreign broadcasting Russia had to compete with it. On January 29, 1960, the Central Committee issued a resolution, "On the Improvement of Soviet Radio Broadcasting." In a development reminscent of the failure of the attempts by the British newspapers in the thirties to stop the BBC from reporting news before they did, Soviet radio was to be allowed to provide news before it appeared in the newspapers. TASS was told to provide its news directly to local radio stations. And the main radio channel, the First Program, put a news broadcast into the peak listening hours for the first time. Local radio stations complained against TASS for its slowness because it diminished their ability to compete with foreign radio broadcasts.[17]

Gennadi Shishkin, a TASS correspondent who had returned from London to become the appointed editor of TASS, determined to speed the news by introducing the open floor plan newsroom that he had seen in Reuters. But when the author visited TASS in Moscow in 1966, most of the journalists were still in small rooms, two by two. "That's so that they can play chess," said Shishkin.

A further Central Committee directive was issued on June 6, 1962. Soviet radio was told to put itself in a position to compete with "hostile radio propaganda." Some progress was made, and the local radio administration of Estonia reported in 1963 that if the "Latest News" program were put on the air at the same time as the VOA's Estonian program, it would be listened to instead of the VOA.[18]

The impact of Western broadcasting was very visible at the funeral of Boris Pasternak, the author of *Doctor Zhivago*, in 1961 when thousands poured into his village to attend because they had heard about it on the BBC.[19]

RFE and RL: Doubts and Disputes

The State Department continued to have reservations about RFE and RL. The PCIAA was told that those opposing the continuation of the Radios believed their low credibility affected belief in VOA broadcasts. They had not adjusted to conditions in the Soviet bloc nor to changes in U.S. policy.

A report for the PCIAA of April 22, 1960, stated that RFE should dilute the polemical theme. RL need not change its content. Consultation with the USIA by RFE and RL should be more continuous and deal with tactical items. Diplomatic missions should be associated earlier, more directly and systematically with policy guidance. Retirement programs should be offered to aliens on the staff because they had difficulty in adjusting to the milder more factual tone that was now desirable. They should be replaced with Americans where possible.[20]

There were doubts and disputes at many levels during the late fifties and sixties. C. D. Jackson, who had been president of the Free Europe Committee in 1951 and 1952, did not think much of the attitude of John Foster Dulles toward RFE and told him after he resigned from the board in December 1958 that if Dulles did not support RFE, he might as well let it go out of business.[21]

Internal squabbles were endemic. In November 1960 the European director, Eric Hazelhoff, fired eighteen editors on the Czech desk because of a campaign of insubordination. In December Hazelhoff and his two deputies were fired and the eighteen editors reinstated.[22]

Staff were subject to pressure and to physical attack. Through double agents infiltrated into RFE/RL the KGB and their satellite services were able to identify exiled personnel and then take reprisal actions against members of their families behind the Iron Curtain.[23] In September 1954 the first apparent assassination took place when an RL employee, Leonid Karas, a journalist on the Byelorussian desk, was found drowned in the Munich area in mysterious circumstances.[24] Two months later the chief of the RL Azerbaijani desk, Abo Fatalibey, was murdered. He was found dead in his apartment bound with wire and mutilated with a sign attached to his body warning "traitors of the motherland."[25] A defector who was a double agent tried to kill Jan Nowak with a gift of poisoned vodka.[26]

The CIA had doubts about RFE and RL, according to the former CIA operative, Victor Marchetti, and John D. Marks, formerly of the State Department:

> [In the mid-sixties] the spirit of East-West détente was growing, and many officers in the CIA thought that RFE and RL had outlived their usefulness. Supporters of the stations were finding it increasingly difficult at budget time to justify their yearly costs. Even the East European governments were showing a declining interest in the stations, and the jamming efforts fell off considerably. The agency carried out several internal studies on the utility of RFE and RL, and the results in each case favored phasing out CIA funding. But after each study a few old timers in the CIA, whose connections with the stations went back to their beginnings, would come up with new and dubious reasons why the radios should be continued.[27]

The Radios' boards of directors consisted of influential persons who also defended continuance.

There was also a conflict between the analysts in the CIA and the covert action staff, who were concerned with RFE and RL. Cord Meyer had been proud of the record of RFE in predicting the Hungarian uprising. The State Department had been sceptical. Allen Dulles had criticized Meyer for not having brought RFE's advice more forcefully to his attention.[28]

But Marchetti and Marks claimed that much of the RFE and RL analysis was thought to be of doubtful value at CIA headquarters and was held in low esteem throughout the U.S. intelligence community. RFE and RL émigré personnel used letters from listeners in Eastern Europe and other information. By the mid-1960s "the general view at CIA headquarters was that the two facilities were widely penetrated by communist agents and that much of the analysis coming out of Munich was based on false information planted by opposition agents."[29] Plants in

RFE and RL were not only from the communist bloc but also from North Atlantic Treaty Organization (NATO) countries.

Cord Meyer recalled that there was occasional pressure from within the CIA to use the Radios for disinformation campaigns. Meyer declined. He did not want to compromise their reputation for accuracy.

What other uses did RFE and RL have? The Russians had no doubt that they were centers of espionage, and Marchetti and Marks agreed with them. "The two radio stations, with their large staffs of Eastern European refugees, are a ready-made source of agents, contacts, information and cover for operations," they said.[30] Cord Meyer said he did not allow American and exile staffs to be used for secret agent operations.[31] Nevertheless, Gene Mater, who was news director of RFE from 1961 to 1965, was approached by the CIA to be an agent, a proposal he rejected.[32]

Who dictated policy was neither consistent nor clear. Cord Meyer said the CIA could not delegate to American management the CIA's responsibility for providing policy guidance and control. "We finally worked out an arrangement with the Department of State under which we cooperated in drafting an annual guidance directive for each country to which the radios broadcast and then we hammered out agreement with the radios on its provisions. In times of violence this general collection of do's and don'ts was supplemented by daily advice."[33] But Jan Nowak, the head of the Polish service of RFE, said Meyer was wrong and that guidance directives were written by the State Department. There was a change when Allen Dulles stepped down as head of the CIA in November 1961, claimed Nowak. When he was in charge, minions could not give instructions, Nowak asserted. Nowak believed that RFE was much less a creature of the CIA than was RL, which needed much greater control.

But journalists know what their superiors want. Ralph Walter, who held many senior positions in RFE, said that CIA control was very light. Contact was an exchange of information, not instructions on what to broadcast. At the time of the Warsaw Pact invasion of Czechoslovakia in 1968 he received only one instruction.[34] "Our decisions were much more likely to be based upon what we considered to be right and proper rather than on some spectre of Washington 'peering over our shoulders'."[35] Representative Ogden R. Reid was to tell the Senate Hearings in May 1971 that guidances emanated from Munich and then went to Washington, where they were reviewed by the State Department and the CIA and, in some cases, were changed, but rarely. William Griffith said the reason RFE and RL executives effectively ran the Radios was because the State Department was not interested in them and, therefore, rarely laid down policy; the CIA in theory was not allowed to and in practice did not. He considered the six-hour time differential between Munich and Washington an important factor. Half the European day was gone by the time Washingtonians got to the office. RFE and RL staff had to have taken decisions.[36]

David Taylor, an Englishman, one-time leader of the trade unions in RFE/RL, likened the CIA's lack of control over RFE to that of the British government over the East India Company in the eighteenth century.[37]

VOA: Hard Sell or Soft Sell?

VOA, unlike its cousins in RFE, acquitted itself well at the time of the Hungarian revolution. Already from 1954 on the VOA programming had become less strident.[38] After Hungary it became even more moderate. The USIA instructed the VOA to avoid value judgments, argument, rhetoric, polemics, loaded or purple adjectives, and a tone that was excitable, emotional, sarcastic or self-righteous. The aim was believability and avoidance of the appearance of propaganda.[39]

Four years after the assaults of McCarthy on the VOA the USIA was again under attack from Congress. The Senate Appropriations Subcommittee, led by Chairman Lyndon B. Johnson, savaged Arthur Larson, who had succeeded Streibert as director in November 1956. Larson had been politically foolish and had performed badly in the hearings on the fiscal 1958 budget.[40] The fiscal 1958 USIA appropriations were cut, and the consquence for the VOA was a reduction in the operating budget of 16 percent from the previous year to $17,134,000. Not until fiscal 1963 did the VOA get back to the level of expenditure and staffing of fiscal 1957.[41]

Scarcely had the USIA finished licking its wounds from the Senate hearings than it had to bear external assaults from two propaganda disasters: the mob demonstrations against school integration in Little Rock, Arkansas, and the Russian Sputnik rocketed into orbit before the Americans had launched their satellite. Despite the attempts of the USIA to play down the significance of these events USIA polls showed that large numbers outside the United States believed that negroes were badly treated throughout the country and that Russia was ahead of the United States in technical development.[42] The U.S. Advisory Commission on Information believed the United States was thirty years behind the Soviet Union in propaganda effectiveness.[43]

Larson lasted only one year and was succeeded by George V. Allen, whose "soft sell" approach contrasted sharply with the "hard sell" of Streibert. After he had been in the position for three years, Allen said:

> I'm not quite certain I'm yet ready to go along with the notion that it's good per se for the government to have an official radio for news broadcasts. . . . Secondly, is our purpose to present the government's foreign policy persuasively, or just present it and let people make up their minds about it? The President and the Secretary of State should of course be persuasive, and when we report them we'll presumably be persuasive too, but should VOA itself try to persuade? If so, it becomes an advocate, not a reporter.[44]

The BBC would have had no problem in agreeing with his thesis. But there were many important people in the USIA who disagreed. Thomas C. Sorenson, at this time deputy director, believed that Voice officials in the late 1950s pushed too hard and too far in the name of objectivity and credibility so that much VOA broadcasting became merely pointless.[45]

President Eisenhower thought, at least in one instance, that balance had gone too far.

> I had been told that a representative of the Voice of America had tried to obtain from a senator a statement opposing our landing of troops in the Lebanon. In a state of some pique I informed Secretary Dulles that this was carrying the policy of "free broadcasting" too far. The Voice of America should, I said, employ truth as a weapon in pursuit of free world objectives, but it had no mandate or license to seek evidence of lack of domestic support of America's foreign policies and actions.[46]

Henry Loomis, director of the VOA from July 1958 to March 1965, contributed much to the objectivity debate and believed that in many ways the VOA charter was the most significant contribution he made to the Voice. He instigated the charter because he believed the Voice needed a formal statement of principles from which it could fight its battles. George Allen approved it in late 1960 just before he left, but it did not receive presidential sanction. It said:

> The long-range interests of the United States are served by communi-cating directly with the peoples of the world by radio. To be effective, the Voice of America must win the attention and respect of listeners. These principles will govern VOA broadcasts:
> 1. VOA will establish itself as a consistently reliable and authori-

tative source of news. VOA news will be accurate, objective, and comprehensive.

2. VOA will represent America, not any single segment of American society. It will therefore present a balanced and comprehensive projection of significant American thought and institutions.

3. As an official radio, VOA will present the policies of the United States clearly and effectively. VOA will also present responsible discussion and opinion on these policies.[47]

Sorenson represented a counter view; he thought it was generally unobjectionable as far as it went but that it did not go far enough and was "ambiguous and vague."[48]

President Kennedy appointed Edward R. Murrow USIA director in March 1961. As a renowned broadcaster from the London blitz in World War II Murrow gave the agency a high profile, which after all the vicissitudes of its previous seven years, it greatly needed. The VOA resented the supervision that the USIA imposed on it during the Cuban missile crisis in October 1962, and Murrow, while affirming the charter, put in a caveat:

It is vital that our broadcasts not mislead either our enemies or our friends about the nature, intent, and implications of our actions and purposes. Therefore, VOA commentaries and analyses on foreign affairs should at all times, and especially on subjects involving vital U.S. interests, reflect the nuances and special emphases, as well as the main thrust, of the policies and intentions of the U.S. Government. Commentaries should give as accurate a picture of U.S. public policy as can most persuasively be presented up to air time.[49]

So the pendulum was swinging away from the "no propaganda" of the Allen era. This trend was underlined when in January 1963 the president issued a new Statement of Mission for the VOA "to help achieve United States foreign policy objectives." One way this was to be done was by "influencing public attitudes in other nations."[50]

BBC: Be Beastly to the Communists—or Not?

In the aftermath of the Suez crisis the BBC was concerned to see how liaison with the Foreign Office could be improved. "The Corporation intends to ask its senior staff to keep more closely in touch with the heads of the geographical departments of the F.O.ign [sic] Office, for it is at this level where there is probably more room for improvement. This should ensure that broadcasting, as an instrument of foreign policy, is as effectively exploited as it can be by the Department," a Foreign Office official recorded. The same paper said there was no set channel for communicating major or long-term policy, but information was usually passed by the assistant under secretary, or his nominee, to the director or assistant director of the BBC's External Services. Tangye Lean, assistant director of external broadcasting, has plaintively written in the margin: "As far as I am concerned I don't think I have had 'information on major policy'—certainly not as a normal thing."[51]

The British government continued its pastime of producing reports on its propaganda activities. A review of all overseas information services, including the BBC External Services, by Charles Hill, chancellor of the Duchy of Lancaster, and the minister in charge of the coordination of government information services was published on July 15, 1957. Overall the recommendations produced a reduction of the BBC's total hours of broadcasting. Arab and African services were increased and those to Western Europe reduced. Transmissions to Eastern Europe were regarded as broadly adequate. The Russian service had been increased by fifteen minutes to 2 hours 15 minutes a day from November 1956, and the Polish service was increased likewise from September 1957. The net increase in recurrent expenditure was $162,000 (£58,000) compared with the $1,400,000 (£500,000) the BBC claimed it needed to restore cuts made in the early fifties.[52]

Poland was broadcasting more to Western Europe than was the BBC. The Copenhagen newspaper, *Dagens Nyheder,* reported: "With some regret and a touch of dismay it must be affirmed that it is the voices of the West that are disappearing and becoming muted. And it is the propaganda blast of the East—where no dictator needs to request Congress or Parliament for grants—which is increasing in stridency."[53]

The Drogheda report had gone into limbo. But on one issue its view had been reversed. "While the sympathy of the influential few must always be sought, it is no less important, in many areas, to seek to enlist the good will of the general population," the Hill document said. The following week the debate on elitism continued combined with the allegation that the Russian service was trimming its sails in order not to displease even the touchiest of its listeners and in order to get jamming lifted.[54] The attack was launched in the *Spectator* on July 21, 1957, by Peter Wiles, a Fellow of New College, Oxford, who accused the service of "moral compromise and appeasement" and charged Anatol Goldberg, its programme organizer, who became one of the most respected and best-known commentators in Russian broadcasts from the West, with "esoteric right-wing Marxism." Goldberg's reply was, "The line we have adopted since Stalin's death has been to welcome any change for the better and to suggest openly or by implication that the politically minded Soviet citizen should ask for more." The distinguished historian, Leonard Shapiro, felt the service was "more concerned with the Soviet establishment than with the growing number of Russians who are aware that there is much wrong with communist rule."[55] Goldberg believed that the target audience should be the intellectuals as distinct from the actively dissident minority, who were few and had little influence. He believed that any change that would occur in Soviet society would come from the intelligentsia.[56] Goldberg did not regard the dissidents as the intelligentsia. He wanted to address the intelligentsia within the nomen-klatura.[57] Certainly, Soviet analysts believed that the BBC's policy was to concentrate on the Soviet technical intelligentsia—"those who play an important part . . . in scientific and technical progress in our country."[58]

The Suez conflict between the British government and the BBC was well publicized. An important conflict, which received no publicity, surfaced in 1960. Ralph Murray of the Foreign Office called a meeting with senior executives of the BBC External Services on March 30, 1960. A summit meeting of Khrushchev, Eisenhower, de Gaulle, and Macmillan was scheduled for May. There were high hopes for an East-West rapprochement, and against that background Murray was concerned at the content of BBC services to countries of Eastern Europe, which, he said, contained comment on their internal affairs, attacks on members of governments with which Britain was in friendly relations, and satire. The BBC files do not show who attended the meeting for the BBC, but the BBC position was that it had a duty to comment on all affairs.[59]

The collapse of the summit because of the U-2 incident did not cause the BBC-FO conflict to go away. The BBC sent Murray a memorandum, which said: "It is vital that the Satellite audiences should be able to believe that the West continues to be interested in their plight. Besides, the West must also show that it judges events and ideas within the Communist bloc (or within a specific satellite state) not by Communist but by Western standards." The BBC conceded that it had to avoid personal abuse of particular representatives of the governments concerned, but maintained that satire could be useful.[60]

Murray circulated the BBC paper to the British ambassadors in the target countries. The ambassadors disagreed with the BBC. Far from attracting listeners by showing an interest in their internal affairs, they believed such commentaries risked repelling listeners by criticism that was outdated and by offending national pride.[61] At an inconclusive meeting with Murray the BBC told him they believed the British embassies were inclined to tell the BBC "not to be beastly" because they were trying to make friends and contacts. The BBC modified the note a little and sent it to the Foreign Office.[62] In it the BBC reiterated its position and pointed out that, in any case, programs on internal affairs took up less than 8 percent, at most, of the total broadcasting time of any service. The debate had lasted eighteen months.

The BBC believed that it was clearly Soviet policy to describe any Western attempt to influence opinion behind the Iron Curtain as "cold war" and any communist attempt to influence opinion in the free world as "peaceful competition." Despite its closeness to the Foreign Office the BBC had again shown that it would fight its corner and not give in, whatever the Foreign Office thought.

In 1948 the survey of British embassies showed they thought the BBC was not anticommunist enough. In 1961 the embassies thought the BBC was too anticommunist. But in 1961 the BBC was less accommodating of the Foreign Office view. Senior BBC staff found it increasingly easy to dismiss pressures and attempts at interfering as the years went by.[63]

The BBC usually resisted attempts by the British government to influence individual broadcasts. But an incident in the Russian service in 1967 was to show that was not always the case. On the eve of the Six Day War, George Brown, the foreign secretary, was in Moscow for talks to try to avert the war. The Russians threatened to break off the talks if the BBC went ahead with a planned transmission of a reading from *Letter to a Friend*, by Stalin's daughter, Svetlana Alliluyeva. Under pressure from 10 Downing Street the BBC agreed to defer the transmission so as not to jeopardize the efforts for peace. It restored it forty-eight hours later after the talks had failed.[64]

7

OTHER MAJOR
BROADCASTERS

Vatican Radio

THE "POPE'S RADIO" had broadcast intermittently in Ukrainian, Lithuanian, and Polish before and during World War II. It started broadcasting weekly in Russian on April 19, 1943. After the war it expanded its transmissions, broadcasting in Hungarian in 1946, Czech and Romanian in 1947, and Slovene and Latvian in 1948. But in 1948 the only daily transmissions to Eastern Europe were in German and Polish. Slovak, Bulgarian, and Croatian were added in 1949, and Russian was stepped up. Byelorussian came on the air in 1950, Albanian in 1951, and Armenian in 1966.[1]

On July 13, 1949, Pope Pius XII excommunicated Communists. In his 1949 Christmas address the pope laid out his information policy on totalitarian regimes and declared it was only too well known what the totalitarian, antireligious state demanded of the church as the price of its tolerance: a church that was silent when it should preach.[2]

In 1950 Vatican Radio officials announced plans to expand facilities to counter the "Moscow-inspired atheistic propaganda being poured into the ears of bewildered Catholics in Iron Curtain countries," as the *New York Times* reported.[3] It said the Vatican spokesmen recognized that the battle in the ether and in the press between Catholicism and atheism was very uneven.

But, as Father Pasquale Borgomeo, director-general of Vatican Radio, commented, "Despite the legendary wealth of the Vatican and the urgent need to broadcast, it was not until 1957 that a fully equipped transmitter was set up." After the Pontiff lobbied for funds, the faithful contributed some $2 million.[4]

Vatican Radio and the Catholics of Eastern Europe were fortunate that Pope Paul VI was the son of a journalist and interested in news. In 1967 he changed the orientation of Vatican Radio from emphasis on the technical to concern with content, and he staffed and structured it accordingly.[5]

Pope John Paul I well understood the power of news. He told journalists that if St. Paul returned to the world, he would head Reuters, the international news agency.[6]

The Vatican devoted more resources to Eastern Europe and the Soviet Union than to any other part of the world. In 1984, a typical year, one-third of all transmissions went to the Soviet bloc, a larger number than to anywhere else.[7] Expenditure on Vatican Radio increased nearly thirtyfold in real terms in the thirty years from 1950 to 1989, rising to $21 million (33,331 million lire). The most marked rise was in the first seven years of the pontificate of John Paul II when it more than doubled.[8]

The perennial question asked of all Radios: "Does he who pays the piper call the tune?" arises also with Vatican Radio. Its statutes of 1995 say that it is "expected to follow closely the directives it receives regarding its programming, doctrinal and informational content." "However," the statutes continue, "Vatican Radio is not the official voice of the Holy See and, therefore, the content of its broadcasts, which are prepared and transmitted with the speed and timeliness that radio demands, remains its own responsibility."[9] One example of Vatican Radio stepping out of line became apparent in January 1989 when a Czech government minister responsible for religious affairs complained to the Vatican about Vatican Radio's programming. In effect, the Vatican promised that Vatican Radio would in the future be good. "Vatican diplomacy made payment of a tribute to the Czech government," was Father Borgomeo's comment. "Vatican Radio stepped out of line several times," he went on. "It was difficult to stop some members of the staff, for example Lithuanians, from getting out of control."[10]

Not that Vatican Radio was always in the opposite camp. A cross-border oddity came in 1981 when Vatican Radio agreed to a request from Romania to shield one of the Vatican's omnidirectional transmitters because the Romanians wanted to use the same frequency to broadcast in Romanian to Moldova in the Soviet Union.[11] The Russians must have been very displeased.

Would Vatican Radio have been any different if it had not been run by the Jesuits but by a different order? Father Borgomeo was emphatic that it would have been different. "Jesuits believe in the spirituality of discernment and the exercise of the critical faculty. Jesuits have always emphasized dialogue with non-believers. So these beliefs corresponded to the medium—radio with no borders."[12] It was easier for Vatican Radio to be unaware of borders than many Radios because the Radio believed it was most unlikely that it would be subject to systematic jamming for any long period.

The Vatican received few letters from listeners in Eastern Europe and the Soviet Union while the cold war was on. In 1977 they received only 3,546 compared with 10,084 from Western Europe. But in 1990 letters from the East soared to 63,033, many coming from the Ukraine.[13] "They said thank you and testified to us the fidelity of their listening, which for some had lasted for more than 20 years," Father Borgomeo reported.[14] "Our purpose was not to destroy a political system, but to help create a new society," he explained.[15]

Radio France Internationale

At first glance it is curious that France should have played such a relatively small role in international broadcasting after 1945, given the fact that it was the leading broadcaster among the anti-Axis powers before World War II and given the high profile it always tried to maintain on the world stage. After the war the Alliance Française was everywhere active in education and Agence France Presse ranked with Reuters of Britain and the Associated Press of the United States as one of the big three international news agencies. But for much of the postwar period French international broadcasting ranked around twentieth in the world.

At the end of 1944 the de Gaulle government set up a department in the Ministry of Information, Emissions vers l'Etranger (EVE), to handle overseas broadcasting other than to the French colonies.[16] Broadcasts started on January 1, 1945, and during the early part of the year EVE started broadcasting in Arabic, Bulgarian, Czech, Danish, Dutch, English, French, German, Greek, Hungarian, Italian, Norwegian, Polish, Portuguese, Romanian, Serbo-Croat, Slovak, Slovene, Spanish, and Swedish. A Yiddish service for the Jews of Eastern Europe started in 1958.[17] Most East European services suffered stops and starts from 1947 onward. The only service free of a hiatus was the service to Poland, where French cultural ties were particularly strong. For three years from the end of 1950 the Polish service was subsidized by the Marshall Plan in return for broadcasting support for Western values and the American way of life.[18] But the Russian service, which had been a feature of French international broadcasting before the Second World War, did not start until 1963.[19] And neither the Russian service nor the Polish service were spared in the greatest bloodletting in the history of French international broadcasting when, in August 1974, all services were closed except for those in English, French, German, and Spanish.[20] Not until the early eighties did broadcasting to Eastern Europe take on a new life. Polish started again in 1981, Russian in 1983, and Romanian in 1985.[21]

The political tone of the broadcasts varied. In 1949 an American journalist commented that French radio was full of sarcasms about communism that even the VOA would not dare to broadcast.[22] But over the years the tone mellowed and the message became more of an explanation of the values on which French democracy was based.[23]

The vicissitudes of French international broadcasting were the result of organization, finance, and politics. Organizationally, it shuffled between ministries and was buffeted about by changes in the structure of domestic broadcasting. It did not achieve stability until 1983 when Radio France Internationale (RFI) was established as a national subsidiary company of Radio France, and it benefited from a five-year development plan for the years 1983 to 1987.[24] Financially, the extraordinary feature of French international broadcasting was that for much of its history it was financed, at least in part and sometimes wholly, by the French domestic listener through the radio license fee. Not surprisingly its budget received particular attention from the members of the Chamber of Deputies. Politically, as far as services for Eastern Europe and the Soviet Union were concerned, there was strong left-wing resistance to broadcasting propaganda to the Communists of the Soviet bloc. And often, whatever the political color of the French government, the French Ministry of External Affairs saw its priorities as asserting French influence outside Europe to Africa or Asia or Latin America.

For all that, the role of French international radio in Eastern Europe and the Soviet Union during the years in which it was broadcasting should not be underestimated. As a samizdat (underground publication) said in 1972, some of the smaller radios were growing in importance in the Soviet Union because they were listened to when the jammers were at work on the big radios. It cited the French and Canadian radios as in the first rank of these smaller radios.[25]

Radio Canada International

"One, two, three, four. Is it snowing where you are, Mr Thiessen? If so telegraph back and let me know." Thus, on October 23, 1900, the Canadian, Reginald Aubrey Fessenden, broadcast the first voice message by radio. One year later Guglielmo Marconi received, in Canada, the first transatlantic message by radio.[26]

But in international radio Canada did not continue pioneering. Not until early 1945 did Canada start regular international broadcasting. The first languages used were English, French, German, Dutch, and Czech. Russian was added in 1951, Ukrainian in 1952, Polish in 1953, and Hungarian in 1956.

The International Service of the Canadian Broadcasting Corporation (CBC), which was eventually called Radio Canada International (RCI), was responsible to the Canadian Parliament through the Department of External Affairs. It was run and managed by the CBC. The 1942 Order-in-Council establishing the service laid down that the CBC's work in this field should be carried on "in consultation" with the Department of External Affairs.[27] In 1950 this consultation went as far as the attachment of an external affairs officer to the International Service for six months to give policy guidance on psychological warfare.[28] Thirty years later the government was more relaxed, and it then agreed that "programming and editorial policies are wholly the responsibility of the CBC."[29] Soon there was no day-to-day relationship with the Department of External Affairs, according to Terry Hargreaves, executive director.[30]

Canada did not start broadcasting in Russian until five years after the British did. The motivation for starting it was curious. Jack McCordick, who was in charge of psychological warfare in the Department of External Affairs at the time put it this way: "The Canadians have a special relationship . . . with both the United States and the United Kingdom. We were privy to their most secret councils in matters of intelligence and planning. They value our input but we are junior members of the club and we mustn't fall behind in our dues."[31]

The services to Czechoslovakia and Germany were hangovers from World War II. To take the initiative to start a new service broadcasting behind the Iron Curtain was another matter, which caused much heart searching in government. Moreover, Canada had 350,000 citizens of Ukrainian origin. It was Canada's largest ethnic group and the largest émigré group of Ukrainian origin in the world. The government, therefore, came under pressure from this group to start broadcasting in Ukrainian, which, reluctantly, it did on Canada Day, July 1, 1952. It was concerned that the Russians might feel Canada was encouraging Ukrainian separatism. The British had no Ukrainian service for that reason.

The total weekly number of hours broadcast in the fifties to Eastern Europe rose from 16 hours 45 minutes in 1951 to 34 hours 15 minutes in 1959. Western European hours went down.[32]

The government continued to attach great importance to the broadcasts to Eastern Europe in the early sixties. To maintain the emphasis on

Eastern Europe, transmission times to Western Europe and Latin America were further reduced, and broadcasts in Danish, Dutch, Italian, Norwegian, Swedish, and Finnish were discontinued. In the early seventies it still considered the Soviet Union its top shortwave priority, followed by Japan, West Germany and China.[33]

For much of the cold war Radio Canada International was not jammed. This worried some observers who thought it meant that the programs were too bland to be worth the cost of jamming. Others thought that it was a quid pro quo for Canada relaying some programs of East European broadcasters on its own network. In that it was unique among Western broadcasters. Nevertheless, the Russians attacked RCI. A notable foray was on March 20, 1976, when the magazine *TRUD* described named announcers in the Russian and Ukrainian services as fascists, drunks, and criminals. The Russian ambassador complained to External Affairs officials that the RCI programs were worse than the BBC and Radio Liberty.[34] The absence of jamming may have been the reason why at one time the volume of Russian language mail sent to the Canadian international service was larger than that sent to the BBC.

Canadian broadcasters were not spared the attacks from within which other broadcasters experienced. On November 30, 1976, the government announced that for reasons of economy it intended to abolish the entire International Service. The International Service mounted its lobby troops, and after a press campaign the government reversed its decision.[35]

The Canadian reaction to the end of the cold war was more violent than that of any other country as far as broadcasting was concerned. On March 22, 1991, the Polish, Czech, Hungarian, and German services were closed.

Radio in the American Sector, RIAS Berlin

DIAS Berlin (Drahtfunk in the American Sector) started on February 7, 1946, transmitting through the Berlin telephone network to wired receivers. Its main purpose was to carry information on work opportunities, availability of food, fuel, and clothing, pickup points for ration coupons, and time schedules for electric current. But it also carried news and current affairs, music, and light entertainment. Radio Berlin was in the British sector, but the Russians had occupied it first and stayed there, refusing to let the other powers use it. So the Americans installed their own transmitters and toward the end of 1946 started broadcasting to East Berlin and East Germany on medium and shortwave frequencies. The new service was called RIAS, Radio in the American Sector. The

East Germans said it stood for Revanchism, Intervention, Anti-Bolshevism, and Sabotage. RIAS developed a large listenership in East Germany.

At the time of the Berlin blockade in 1948 it started a cabaret program called *The Islanders*, which became one of the most popular German cabaret programs after World War II.[36] Unemployed musicians, some formerly with the famous Berlin Symphony Orchestra, were recruited to a new orchestra—eventually called the Radio Symphony Orchestra of Berlin—which became equally famous. A youth orchestra, a chamber chorus, and dance orchestra also became illustrious. The news programs included feeds from the VOA.[37]

RIAS was headed by Americans working with German management led by a German Intendant. The controls on the station from Washington were loose. One commentator wrote in the fifties: "The staff makes a reasonably conscientious effort to hew to the official line, but since directives from headquarters reach Berlin from two days to two months after the events that inspired them, RIAS has to develop most of its strategy as it goes along."[38]

The East German government regarded RIAS sufficiently dangerous for the government to try to poison and abduct an interviewer, Lisa Stein. In March 1955 someone she regarded as a friend fed her candy containing the highly dangerous poison scopolamine while they were chatting in a West German cafe. The lady was expected to become ill while walking from the cafe to her nearby residence, where agents in a car would then abduct her. But the plot went wrong because she did not become ill until she was nearly home, and some neighbors helped her and sent her off to hospital where she was severely ill for forty-eight hours but recovered when an antidote was found.[39]

RIAS expanded in the fifties, adding FM, and starting broadcasts from Hof in Northern Bavaria so that it could be heard throughout East Germany and even in parts of Czechslovakia and Poland.

When the Berlin Wall went up in August 1961, RIAS became even more important. After the wall sealed off the East, RIAS was still receiving more than fifteen hundred letters each month from East Germany. Typical comments were "You are our only contact with the West"; "Your programs are a ray of hope"; "Do not forget us."[40]

Listening to RIAS was illegal, and some violators were given prison terms. But that did not stop secret listening, particularly when RIAS started to broadcast rock music in the sixties to attract the younger generation. They could mail requests to a series of frequently changing addresses, forcing the secret police to change constantly their mail intercept operations.

RIAS cooperated with U.S. intelligence agencies operating in Berlin to collect intelligence and facilitated the recruitment of covert sources and agents in the Soviet Zone.[41] From 1972 it was funded jointly by the German and American governments. Television started on November 10, 1986.

RIAS was dissolved after forty-six years on May 19, 1992. The station had had three broadcast channels. RIAS was incorporated in a new national public radio network. RIAS 2, directed at young people, became a commercial station. RIAS-TV joined Deutsche Welle.[42] The appreciation of the German government for what RIAS had done was shown by the establishment of a commission to promote exchanges of broadcast journalists and broadcasting information between the two countries. It was financed at $13 million (DM 20 million) each year by Germany.[43]

Deutsche Welle

The Russians jammed Deutsche Welle (DW); they did not jam Radio France Internationale. That is the best indication of the importance they attached to Germany's international radio in the cold war although it did not play as important a role as the Radios of the Americans and the British.

The vituperation against DW was even more intense than against the VOA and the BBC. The DW commentators looked at the Soviet Union "through the spectacles of a lunatic and the prism of the most obdurate prejudice," Radio Moscow said. They were a "Goebbels breed."[44] The Russians were so upset by what they considered to be the violently anti-Soviet character of the DW Russian service when it started on July 1, 1962, that they considered introducing even more intense jamming than they employed against the VOA and the BBC. Commentaries in August 1962 that particularly troubled them were those entitled "The True Face of Communism," "Sunset of the Leipzig Fair," "Are they really getting rid of the Stalinists?"[45] But they eventually rejected substituting blanket jamming for the selective jamming they were using against the VOA and the BBC because it would demand considerable additional technical resources.[46]

The curiosity of West German international broadcasting is that there was not one organization, but two, whose services, uncharacteristically for the German sense of order, overlapped. Deutsche Welle was founded in 1953 as a joint venture of the domestic radio network, ARD, the association of West German radio stations, to broadcast internationally by short wave. Deutsche Langwelle was founded in 1952 to broadcast by long wave to all Germany, as a counter to the broadcasting from East Germany, which had started in 1948. It was not much of a counter for the first four years, broadcasting only music. Not until November 3, 1956, at the time of the Hungarian uprising, did it start broadcasting news. It was succeeded by Deutschlandfunk (DFL) on January 1, 1962, which had an expanded mandate to transmit a European language service.

The change was embodied in the federal government's "Legislation on the Establishment of Broadcasting Organizations under Federal Law," which the federal Parliament passed on October 26, 1960.

The socialist SPD party voted against. The legislation established Deutschlandfunk and reestablished Deutsche Welle under federal law. The anomaly was that two organizations were to broadcast to Eastern Europe.[47]

They both broadcast in Polish, Czech, Slovak, Hungarian, Romanian, Bulgarian, Serbo-Croat, and Slovene. DW also broadcast in Macedonian and Russian. DW broadcast mainly by shortwave and DFL by long and medium waves. Not until January 1977, when the Socialists were in power, was there rationalization. DW dropped Polish, Czech, Slovak, and Hungarian, and DFL dropped Romanian, Bulgarian, Serbo-Croat, and Slovene. This change was not just rationalization. The law established the precept that broadcasters should be independent of the government. Nevertheless, DW lost the most important services because the socialist government believed that DFL was more inclined toward the socialist line and DW was too right wing.[48] Specifically, Botho Kirsch, head of the East European desk, was considered unsympathetic to the Ostpolitik of rapprochement.[49]

Despite the 1977 events, Dieter Weirich, director-general of DW from December 1, 1989, considered German government not very interested in DW because "there are no votes abroad."[50] Pressures came more from the German Foreign Office. Michail Antonow, head of the Bulgarian desk of DW, recounted how during the cold war the Foreign Office would complain to the director-general about particular stories carried in the Bulgarian service. Not all directors-general took any notice. But if one did, he explained, "I would get a good drubbing from the director-general. The pressure was toothless. They had no way of making us do something."[51]

Deutsche Welle took over the foreign language programs for Europe of Deutschlandfunk in 1993.

8

CLEARER AIRWAVES
(1963–1968)

USSR: No Longer Saturday's News on Monday

JAMMING AGAIN became involved in détente. In the aftermath of the Cuban crisis and the negotiations on a limited nuclear test ban treaty jamming was reduced in stages. On June 10, 1963, all jamming of the BBC ceased, and on June 19 the VOA was clear again.

The end of jamming came in curious circumstances. To the surprise of both the Russian military and the American delegation the Soviet deputy minister of communications, Ivan Vassilevich Klokov, in Geneva for talks on the protocol for establishing the "hot line" between Washington and Moscow, took aside some of the Americans and started talks on ending jamming of the VOA. He dropped the demand that curtailment of RL had to be included in any arrangements. Jamming could be ended if there were restraints on VOA programming and the VOA's long wave transmitter near Munich was shut down. It is not clear if the Americans gave any quid pro quo to end jamming of the VOA, but they reduced the power of the Munich transmitter from 1,000 to 50 kilowatts. The Russians subsequently claimed that jamming was ended as a result of the agreement of the United States to restrain the content of the VOA programs. The following January the Americans reached agreement with the Hungarians to shut down the Munich transmitter in exchange for the end of Hungarian jamming of the VOA. Hungary stopped jamming the VOA and also the BBC and RFE on February 1, 1964. Czechoslovakia stopped jamming both the VOA and BBC on April 1 but continued to jam RFE. Romania had stopped jamming the VOA, the BBC, and RFE on July 29, 1963. Bulgaria stopped jamming the BBC in 1964 but did not suspend jamming of the VOA until September 1974. Since 1964 the United States opened and closed down the

116

Munich transmitter in step with Soviet resumption and suspension of jamming.[1]

The British were certainly prepared to give quid pro quos for cessation of jamming. Ralph Murray told the Communists in Warsaw in 1956 that if they stopped jamming, the tone of the BBC broadcasts would naturally change. "They stopped, and it has," he reported. At its extreme, the communist attitude was contained in the quip, "If you stop broadcasting, we'll stop jamming."[2]

The Senate Foreign Relations Committee had a good laugh about what the State Department thought it was doing with the Munich transmitter in the hearings on the future of RFE and RL in May 1971. It broadcast on the same frequency as Radio Moscow, but Martin Hillenbrand, assistant secretary for the European bureau of the State Department, denied that the VOA was jamming in the technical sense. "They were merely broadcasting a perfectly intelligible program on the same wavelength," he said. The frequency—173—had been allocated to Radio Moscow by the 1948 Copenhagen Convention, but the State Department argued that because Germany was not a party to the Copenhagen Convention, it was in order for the VOA to use it.[3]

In *Broadcasting to the Soviet Union: International Politics and Radio,* one of the most important books written on cold war broadcasting, Maury Lisann says:

> The decision to end most jamming in mid-1963, in addition to its role in furthering foreign policy, appears to have been based on a belief that the Soviet sociopolitical system had stabilized to the point that it could safely absorb additional uncontrolled information and that improvements in Soviet media would enable the Soviet information services to compete openly with foreign radio broadcasts and handle questions raised by them.[4]

But surely the sequence of events was "We want détente. Détente makes the end of jamming desirable. We should, therefore, compete with the foreign radio stations. Even with jamming we must compete because many people listen anyway."

In 1963 a radio station of one of the Soviet Union republics boasted that it had stopped writing the Sunday and Monday newscasts on the preceding Saturday.[5] But it took the Russians until 1964 to mount a major counterattack on international Radios. On August 1, 1964, the twenty-four-hour a day radio program *Mayak* (Beacon) went on the air. It consisted of frequent newscasts interspersed with short irregularly placed items of music, interviews, and commentary. Its purpose was to meet the demand for news caused by foreign radio. It was designed to counter the Western speciality of "agitation by naked facts."[6]

Mayak was the most important weapon in the fight against foreign broadcasting. The second was regular newscasts on other programs. The third was specially designed anti-American programs and the fourth, prompt commentaries and analyses.[7]

In mid-1965 *Mayak* was broadcasting more than seven hours of news and commentary each day and the other principal program, the *First Program*, was transmitting a total of almost three hours a day.[8] The extent of this revolution is shown by the fact that four years earlier no news at all had been broadcast in prime time.

Just less than one year after *Mayak* started, *Kommunist*, the main theoretical journal of the Central Committee, explained the policy on foreign Radios. It said:

> Bourgeois propagandists are trying to use foreign radio, press, tourism, as channels of penetration of alien views in our midst. It would be rash on our part to be satisfied that these channels have not justified all the long-range hopes of the anti-Soviet propagandists. It is necessary to study the tactics of enemy propaganda and actively counteract them. And this demands the elimination of those shortcomings of ideological work that in contemporary conditions are becoming especially intolerable. Usually such shortcomings appear where the most important demands of the Leninist tradition of propaganda work are forgotten.
>
> In our time, when there is a radio receiver in almost every house, to be silent about this or that event, not to illuminate it from the position of socialist ideology, means to give "freedom of action" to the falsifications of bourgeois propagandists.
>
> More than that it is important not only to explain correctly this or that fact, but it must be done promptly. It must be recognized that bourgeois information agencies have achieved a high operational efficiency, immediately responding to everything happening in the world, while we are sometimes late. This means that the false version flies around the world faster than the truthful and exact one. And the first report produces sometimes the greater impression! In contemporary conditions the spread of information and its operational effect is becoming the most important sphere of ideological struggle, and in this, complacency is inadmissible.[9]

They clearly agreed with Adlai Stevenson, former Democratic presidential candidate, who once said: "A lie can run round the world before the truth has got its boots on."[10]

Journalists on Soviet radios had a lot to contend with in trying to become efficient, particularly from Glavlit, the censorship organization. Boris Belitsky, a science and technology presenter on Moscow Radio, recalled later:

I remember one occasion when I interpreted for one of our cosmonauts—I think it was Leonov, the first man to perform a walk in space in 1965. I returned to the radio in a rush and wrote something up—only to have it rejected by Glavlit. The reason was that it hadn't been published yet. So I argued with the chap, saying, "How could it possibly have been published when the man only said this half an hour ago and I rushed here to put it on the air as soon as I could?" And the answer was, "Until I see it in black and white, such sensitive information cannot go on the air."[11]

The article in *Kommunist* paid particular attention to the VOA and BBC, which it said glorified the material wealth of the West and which used techniques such as the deceptive appearance of objectivity created by casual references to Western shortcomings. It also mentioned by name RL, RIAS, RFE, and DW. It complained that the foreign broadcasting services of Italy, France, Spain, and Japan also echoed the anti-Soviet line.

The Communists could never win on speed in news; they needed political referral. Russian journalists in TASS so often had to sit on a story while they went up the political heirarchy to get a decision on how to handle a sensitive topic. In Reuters, for example, journalists editing stories had no relationship with the British Foreign Office. They decided how to handle a story solely on their own professional judgment. But even this puzzled communist visitors to Reuters. "What is your news policy?" they would ask. "Our policy is to have no news policy," this author and other executives would reply.

The chairman of the Radio and TV State Committee, N. Mesyatsev, was worried about the commentaries broadcast on Western Radios and the lack of response to them in the Soviet press. In a memorandum to the Central Committee of July 2, 1965, he explained:

At present enemy radio propaganda is being intensively waged against the Soviet Union. In the Western radio stations' programs about 30–40 percent of the time is occupied by talks and commentaries on current international topics and by news bulletins composed of tendentiously selected material. Because these broadcasts go on all day long and are particularly intensive in the evening, the Soviet press does not have the chance to react immediately to enemy attacks. Unlike the press, however, radio and television can give timely comments on the Western stations' propaganda.[12]

He clearly did not think it practicable for the newspapers to go to bed earlier, as in the West. He asked for permission to recruit three commentators. The Central Committee Propaganda Department took eight months to reply. On March 9, 1966, they said no, there were enough journalists already who could do the work.[13]

A party that Erik de Mauny, the BBC correspondent in Moscow, gave there for winners of a radio competition on December 18, 1965, so concerned the KGB that its chairman, V. Semichastny, wrote a report on it to the Central Committee Propaganda Department.[14] The importance attached to the foreign broadcasts is indicated by the many notes on the subject in the Central Committee archives signed, not by minions, but by successive heads of the KGB. "One of the main aims of the competition was to attract radio listeners' attention to BBC broadcasts and to seek new unofficial contacts with Soviet citizens," the report said. Semichastny was concerned that de Mauny had organized the party without the knowledge of the USSR Foreign Ministry or any other Soviet organizations. Two Soviet citizens from Moscow were present among the fifty or so diplomatic and press corps guests. The KGB had clearly thoroughly grilled the two prize winners:

> During the reception the Englishmen showed great activity in detailed questioning of the two Soviet citizens about life in the Soviet Union, about how often they listen to the BBC in Russian, what the reception of broadcasts is like, what class of the population listens to them, how they like them, and so on.
>
> An analysis of the questions put to the Soviet citizens shows that the Englishmen are actively trying to establish unofficial contacts with Soviet citizens with the aim of discovering through them the degree and character of the influence of British propaganda on Soviet people and also with the aim of studying matters that interest them.
>
> It should be noted that the Moscow diplomats and foreign correspondents were pleased with this reception, regarding it as a new form of unofficial contact with Soviet citizens, avoiding the Foreign Ministry's Press Department, the Committee for Cultural Links, and other Soviet organizations; they hope to hold further such parties in the future.[15]

One BBC prize winner, Boris Glukov, who won a fortnight's holiday in Britain, had to wait until 1994 to claim his prize. He had been refused permission to travel to the West because he worked for a top-secret Russian company installing radar. Although he correctly answered a series of questions in a quiz, letters to the BBC in London to claim the prize were mysteriously lost.

"I am not impressed at all by the number of young people who have to sleep on the streets. This will simply not do and would not be allowed in Russia," was his comment when he finally got to London.[16]

One of the most interesting accounts of attitudes toward Western Radios came from a young American student, William Taubman, who studied at Moscow University in 1965 and 1966. In his book, *The View from Lenin Hills,* he recounts how surprised he was at how freely and fearlessly students listened to and quoted the Voice of America. They told him that before buying a shortwave radio, people would test it to see if it could pick up the VOA through the jamming. If it could, it was a good radio. The students listened mostly to music on foreign broadcasts but could not always ignore the news. The cultural impact of the West was exemplified by one student: "It's a nightmare," he cried out in delight at the sight of mini-skirts, mesh stockings, and brightly colored stretch pants in a *New York Times* color magazine. One Party member told Taubman how clever the VOA was not to suppress criticism of the United States. Taubman had no doubts that the conversations he had with the students would not have been possible twenty years earlier, and even five years earlier they would not have talked to him so freely.[17]

In April 1966 a press campaign attacking foreign Radios started. The opening shot was an article in *Izvestia* on April 14, 1966, describing RL, an organization rarely mentioned before. Thereafter, attacks on RL were largely concentrated in the provincial press. In September *Izvestia* started a feature called "Muddy Waves of the Ether," replying to individual programs. It compared the VOA to the liar, Baron Munchausen. In the period to the end of 1967 it attacked the VOA nine times and DW twice.[18] The BBC was treated differently because it was thought to have a narrower, although not less influential, appeal. It used a subtle insinuating flattery and a 60:40 formula for and against capitalism and the Soviets.[19] The main publication that dealt with the BBC was the intellectuals' *Literaturnya Gazeta.*

Simultaneously with the press campaign, a glossy radio magazine called *RT* was launched in April 1966. Its first issue said that *RT* would teach its readers how to listen to foreign radio and to distinguish the half-lies and half-truths of the broadcasts of VOA, BBC, DW, and RFE in a column called "Caution, Falsehoods in the Air." But it published few articles about the Western broadcasts and their faults; circulation declined, and it folded in December 1967.[20]

So great was the concern of Party propagandists with foreign radios that the questions posed by workers because of what they had heard on Western broadcasts became known as "sharp questions." "It seems to me that the main attention of our mass-political work today must be to ensure that people are not left with any uncertainty on the so-called sharp questions," said a commentator in *Pravda*.[21]

Opinion polls were started in 1965. Lisann analyzed them as follows:

> The salient facts of those investigations, insofar as the limited raw data that were disclosed can be interpreted, are as follows. About 40 to 60 million people, with varying degrees of regularity, listen to foreign broadcasts. Major questions of public interest that are known mainly through foreign radio coverage reach and are of interest to 50 to 75% of various population groups. From 30 to 50% of the population consider the response of Soviet broadcasting to be inadequate. In addition, from 20 to 30% of the population, perhaps more, seem generally to doubt the credibility of all Soviet information sources, and by inference, much of the basic ideological legitimacy of the system.[22]

In 1968 the first survey of the readership of *Pravda* was carried out. It is significant that the results were not published and only became available in the West after Vladimir Shlapentokh, who had headed the project, emigrated to the United States. The survey showed that 6–8 percent of the respondents got information from foreign radio. Among the college-educated that percentage rose to 10 percent. The listenership was, in fact, probably higher because Shlapentokh believed respondents would have been cautious about revealing the amount they listened to foreign radios.[23]

A watershed in foreign broadcasting came in February 1966 when Andrei Sinyavski and Yuli Daniel were put on trial for sending works abroad to be published. It gradually dawned on their supporters that by giving reports of the trial to Western news agency correspondents they could be assured of a hearing across the Soviet Union. The medium was Western Radios. Nothing like that had ever before happened in Russia. The carefully prepared propaganda scenario toppled. Crowds appeared outside the courtroom—they had learned of the time and place of the trial from Western Radios. Listeners heard the unthinkable—that defendants did not admit their guilt. The Soviet media were thrown onto the defensive and had to try to uphold their version of the trial.[24]

Ludmilla Alexeyeva, a leading dissident, has described how the dissidents slowly realized the value of using the correspondents and the Radios. She recalled the first day of the Daniel and Sinyavski trial:

> When I sensed a reporter or an operative near me, I quieted down and turned away. I didn't want to be overheard, and I didn't want to be quoted in a Western newspaper. I remember thinking: We are here because our friends are on trial. It's our problem; it's our grief. For reporters, this is just a political thriller. I don't want my life to be the subject of someone's curiosity.[25]

But at the first break in the hearings the wives of the accused came out of the courthouse and told the waiting dissidents what had happened. The correspondents listened in, filed their stories, and back they came on the Radios to be heard, unjammed, across the whole vast country. "Thus," Ludmilla Alexeyeva explained, "future human rights activists discovered the only means available to them to spread ideas and information under Soviet conditions."[26] Soon the dissidents were approaching the correspondents directly and on the last day of the trial took them off to a cafe to buy hot dumplings.

By 1968 the dissident Andrei Amalrik was quite clear on the role of the Western Radios. "Our aim was to give the world a better idea of the state of affairs in the USSR and to reach the Russian people via Western radio. And in that we succeeded. The number of listeners to foreign radio broadcasts increased several times over."[27]

When Larisa, Daniel's wife, visited him in prison as he started his five-year sentence, she wanted to tell him of the international stir the judgments had created, which she had heard of on the Radios, but did not want the guard to understand. "Grandmother Lillian Hellman asked me to say hello. Uncle Bert Russell also sends regards. Your nephew, Guenter Grass, talks about you a lot, and so does his younger brother, little Norman Mailer." "It's nice that you Jewish people have such large families," said the guard.[28]

The aftermath of the trial was even more worrisome to the authorities. The protests led to more trials, and so the circuit repeated itself. Samizdat became more political and more popular because of rebroadcasting. The broadcasting of the names of the dissidents strengthened them because they overcame their sense of fear and isolation.

The dissidents believed that the government's inconsistencies in the ways in which it handled cases showed that the dissidents' actions could still make a difference to the trials. It was, therefore, that much more important that through the Radios they knew what was happening in the trials. Ethnic and religious groups learned through the Radios that they could use the Moscow samizdat and Western press connections of the dissidents to publicize their struggles.[29]

When the Galanskov-Ginsberg trial took place in January 1968, *Komsomol'skaya Pravda* admitted that its commmentary on the trial was in response to "fussing" of foreign radio broadcasts.[30] More than one decade later, in April 1979, when Ginsberg was taken from his labor camp in Mordovia to Moscow's Lefortovo Prison to be told he was to be deported, his wife, Irina, heard the news as she lay in bed listening to the VOA. "A few minutes later friends and relatives started knocking on my door. Western journalists came round and we gave a press conference at 3:00 A.M. I'll never forget the excitement," she said.[31]

A dissident gave a copy of the "Appeal to World Public Opinion" of Larisa Bogoraz and Pavel Litvinov to Reuters; it was broadcast on the BBC, and Litvinov received letters supporting him for weeks.[32] It was unusual because it was addressed to Soviet citizens and not to officials. It was also addressed to the West.

On April 30, 1968, the first issue of the *Chronicle of Current Events* appeared, a factual account of human rights violations with great concern for accuracy. It was the first samizdat link between geographically isolated segments of the human rights and other movements. Activists learned of the publication from the Radios, sought it out, and provided it with information.[33] The *Chronicle* carried a lot of information about prisons. The guards often told prisoners about the prisoners' own situation from what they had heard on the Radios. That they were not forgotten was a comfort to the prisoners.[34]

From 1963 dissident Vladimir Bukovsky spent twelve years in prisons, labor camps, and psychiatric hospitals. A recurrent theme in his autobiography, *To Build a Castle: My Life as a Dissenter,* is the important role that Western Radios played in prison and other places of incarceration. Prison guards and officers twiddled the knobs of their radios at night to get Western radio stations. Their worry was that prison abuses would be reported by the BBC, RFE/RL, and the VOA, who would be "kicking up a stink again." Then a commission would come from Moscow, which would be bound to find blemishes and blunders, reprimand the staff, and sometimes even sack them. So in the morning the staff asked each other if they had heard anything on the Radios. There could scarcely be a more specific example of the benefit of the Radios to the dissidents in the treatment they received. The guards were intrigued by the radio war and would whisper to the prisoners the content of a broadcast about a hunger strike that they had just finished.[35]

Bukovsky describes life in a psychiatric hospital:

> Every morning when we sat down to breakfast, I tuned in to the BBC and while the loonies gulped down their gruel, the epileptics writhed in convulsions and the schizophrenics sat motionless over their bowls, staring unseeing into space, we listened to the news from London: letters and protests over the Sinyavsky-Daniel case, a transcript of the trial itself, Tarsis' interviews and statements in London. My underworld friends simply shook their heads—the things that go on! But they began listening with particular interest after my name also came up a few times. From then on I no longer needed to worry about switching it on in time—the orderlies did it for me and we all stopped talking.[36]

In the Bor labor camp, 300 miles south of Moscow, Bukovsky got a renowned pickpocket, Pyotr Yakovlevich, who was also a radio mechanic, to build him a shortwave receiver. They ordered the parts through one of the free workers, a "courier" who used to bring tea into the camp. It was an excellent radio, which picked up the BBC, VOA, RL, DW, and even Radio Monte Carlo. The only station it had been built to exclude was Radio Moscow. Bukovsky kept the radio hidden in a camp schoolroom, disguised as a piece of physics apparatus. "The school steward, a prisoner, used to let me into that room secretly every evening and there I would plunge into a completely different life. I was back with my friends, deploring their arrests, accompanying them to Red Square to protest against the occupation of Czechoslovakia, writing protest letters."[37]

The recurrent theme in Andrei Amalrik's account of his periods in camp in his *Notes of a Revolutionary* was the role of the Western Radios. The use of radio receivers was forbidden in Talaya camp, but transistor sets found their way in from outside, just as vodka did. All the free workers in Talaya listened to the Voice of America, Amalrik wrote, and when VOA reported that he was there, the commotion was incredible. Everyone stopped felling timber and crowded round the radio. "Now the whole world knows about Talaya," they said with pride. A woman came up to Amalrik's wife when she was there later and said, "Please tell the Voice of America right away that I've been fired."[38] A young hold-up man expressed great pride in sharing Amalrik's cell because he had heard about him on the Voice of America.[39] A woman prison doctor, Captain Raisa Tsarko, saw it differently, had no time for Amalrik, and was jealous of his fame: "Why does the Voice of America talk about you and not about me?" she shouted at him.[40]

At first reading it would appear that the dissidents had the Constitution on their side. Article 125 stated:

> In conformity with the interests of the workers and in order to strengthen the socialist system, the citizens of the USSR are guaranteed by law:
> a) freedom of speech;
> b) freedom of the press;
> c) freedom of assembly and meetings;
> d) freedom of street processions and demonstrations.[41]

But, as Bukovsky and Litvinov and Amalrik and others found, the courts decided the preamble meant that the rights were only exercisable in accordance with the interests of the working class and with a view to strengthening the socialist system. The aim of the information was also relevant, and one propaganda pamphlet stated, "Bourgeois propagandists may in certain cases libelously utilize actual facts and statistical data."[42]

The cards were all stacked against the dissidents. During the 1978 examination of the UNESCO MacBride Report on the global flow of information, the International Commission for the Study of Communication Problems, one of the delegates explained that balanced information demanded that alongside official statements those of the opposition should also be reported. Leonid Zamyatin, the head of TASS, retorted: "There is no opposition in the USSR. There are criminals who oppose the Constitution."[43]

But Amalrik had no doubt about the justification for the dissidents' actions and their appalling suffering: "Lots of flour, and only a little yeast; but it's the yeast that makes the dough rise."[44]

RFE and RL: O What a Tangled Web the CIA Wove

The temperature of the cold war can be judged quite well by studying the name changes of RL, its services, and its parent. On March 16, 1953, the American Committee for Freedom of the Peoples of the USSR became the American Committee for Liberation from Bolshevism. In 1958 RL's revised policy manual talked of "liberalization" instead of "liberation." In 1959 RL began to refer to itself as "the freedom stations." Finally, in 1964, Radio Liberation became Radio Liberty. The tenor of the broadcasts of RFE and RL also changed. An interesting comparison has been made between the treatment by RFE of the fall of Malenkov in 1955 and of Khrushchev in 1964. In 1955 the position had been not that the facts were distorted but that RFE broadcasters had found it too much to disguise their delight over the downfall of the leader. By 1964 the file was merely to give broad information on the Khrushchev removal and its probable effects in the West, at home, and in the communist orbit. "The new voice of RFE was an end to the negativism and slogans of the past, the use of the Communists' mistakes and sins only to point to the way to stop their repetition."[45]

When the author negotiated a contract to supply the Reuter news service to RFE in the early sixties, Gene Mater, news director of RFE, used the charitable nature of RFE funding as an argument to try to keep the price low. The Reuter view, shared by many in the media and in government, was that it was obviously largely funded by the CIA although it would be tactless in negotiations to mention it. It came as no surprise when all was revealed in 1967.

On February 14 the *New York Times* carried a full-page advertisement placed by *Ramparts,* a counterculture magazine published in San Francisco, proclaiming that its March issue would carry a story about the CIA's relationship with the National Students Association (NSA). On the same day the *New York Times* carried a front-page story referring to the *Ramparts* advertisement, which said that an executive of the NSA had admitted that the association had been receiving funds from the CIA. The item also said *Ramparts* would carry the full report in its March issue. The next day the *New York Times* said President Johnson had instructed the CIA to stop secret aid to student groups. The president had also called for a review of all other anticommunist programs funded by the CIA. "It is believed that the Agency provided clandestine aid to anti-Communist labor unions, publications and radio and television stations." But not until February 21 was RFE identified. Even then there was no mention of RL. the *New York Times* described how money was disbursed through dummy channels to legitimate foundations that passed funds on to agencies dependent on the CIA. Among the five organizations that received money from the Hobby Foundation of Houston, Texas, was RFE. RFE received $40,000 in 1964 and $250 in 1965. William P. Hobby, Jr., executive editor of *The Houston Post* and a member of the Board of Trustees of the Hobby Foundation, told the *New York Times* the foundation had very carefully not filed in duplicate that part of its 990-A tax return related to its sources of funds. If the law had said it had to, it would have shown the sources to be known CIA front foundations and would have exposed the RFE-CIA connection. Under the banner headline "O What a Tangled Web the CIA Wove" the *Washington Post* ran a detailed story on the methods of funding in its Sunday edition on February 26.

The British MI6 believed the *Ramparts* story originated with the Czechoslovak secret service, the StB, although there is no evidence that the *Ramparts* staff knew this.[46]

CBS News waded into the story with a major documentary on March 13. Mike Wallace described CIA support of RFE as "the strangest of CIA's penetration into private groups, a project which, in effect used you, the individual American, as a cover. . . . If you responded to the many appeals for Radio Free Europe on television, in magazines, even on buses and subways, then you became a part of a CIA cover."[47] It is curious that Wallace still did not seem to be aware that the CIA had not penetrated RFE but had set it up in the first place.

The furor that followed the program, which centered on CBS carrying public service announcements appealing for funds for Radio Free Europe, had extra force because the president of CBS, Frank Stanton, was also chairman of the Executive Committee of the Radio Free Europe Fund.

A strange aspect of the brouhaha of early 1967 was that the CIA connections with the Radios had been disclosed in the *New York Times* in April 1966 and neither in 1967 nor since did the story receive attention. It said:

> In Munich, the C.I.A. supports a variety of research groups and such major propaganda outlets as Radio Free Europe, which broadcasts to Eastern Europe, and Radio Liberty, aimed at the Soviet Union. Besides entertaining and informing millions of listeners in the Communist nations, these nominally "private" outlets provide employment for many gifted and knowledgeable refugees from Russia, Poland, Hungary and other countries.[48]

Admiral Raborn, director of Central Intelligence, declined to tell an Executive Session of the Senate Foreign Relations Committee in 1966 whether or not RFE was or was not connected with the CIA.[49]

Surveys of East European refugees indicated that RFE credibility was raised by allegations of its CIA connections, particularly among Hungarians.[50] Comments in the Soviet Union indicated that on balance the effect of awareness of the intelligence connection was more favorable than unfavorable.[51] But, according to David Taylor of RFE, the past deceit created staff problems. "We were lied to," he said.[52]

President Johnson was concerned about its legality and set up a committee under the chairmanship of Nicholas Katzenbach, under secretary of state, John Gardiner, secretary of health, education, and welfare, and Richard Helms, director of the CIA. It took them only two weeks to complete their work, and they presented their report to the president on March 29. In it they said: "No federal agency, shall provide covert financial assistance or support, direct or indirect, to any of the nation's educational or voluntary organizations." And it categorically stated, "No programs currently would justify any exception to this rule."[53]

That seemed to be the end of RFE and RL. But a rather contrived contention was advanced that the Radios "were not private and voluntary organizations as defined by the Katzenbach report but rather government proprietaries established by government initiative and functioning under official policy direction." Influenced by Richard Helms and Senator James O. Eastland of Mississippi, the president decided they should be saved. But it was a close call.[54]

VOA: The New Sound

The conflicts between the USIA and the VOA at the time of the Cuban missile crisis continued after it was all over. The VOA paid little attention to President Kennedy's important American University peace speech of June 10, 1963, in which he changed the direction of America's cold war policies. Henry Loomis failed to tell his staff to interpret the speech along the lines laid down in a memorandum to the USIA from White House Assistant McGeorge Bundy. Only after four days did VOA hit the story hard.[55]

Loomis resigned in March 1965, chafing against USIA interference with the VOA to make it solely a mouthpiece of government. Some of the media said the interference continued after the departure of Loomis. The *New York Times* said, "The White House and the State Department have always tried to exert pressure on the VOA to some extent, but in this administration the situation has materially worsened." Carl Rowan, who had succeeded Murrow as director of the USIA in 1964, denied it. John Chancellor, an NBC news correspondent, took on the job of director of the VOA on September 1, 1965, and stayed there until the spring of 1967, and with him the acrimony ended. He made it clear the task of the VOA was to make the policies of the U.S. government clearly and explicitly understood around the world.[56]

Chancellor also changed the programming of the VOA with a "new sound," making it livelier and brighter. "Yankee Doodle" replaced "Columbia, Gem of the Ocean" in station breaks. The tough language of the cold war, already toned down, almost entirely disappeared.[57]

The debate over objectivity resumed with the appointment of Chancellor's successor in September 1967, another broadcaster, John Daly. Daly was quoted in Congress as saying he intended that the VOA report should reflect "fully and fairly the division in the country [over Vietnam]." Representative Charles Joelson (Democrat, New Jersey) asserted: "The Voice of America is to promulgate our Government policy."[58] Daly resigned in June 1968, in part "because he felt he could no longer serve as an effective shield for the career news employees against pressures from self-interested policymakers."[59]

Chancellor summed up the perennial problem of USIA-VOA conflict well:

> The USIA suffers, and it probably always will, from too many career employees suspended in a sort of civil service aspic, who go on for years defining truth on their own terms. This takes various forms: too much interference by policy officers, for example, with writers and newsmen at the Voice of America; or, conversely, an effort to achieve too much independence from policy guidelines by those writers. There have been times in the Agency's history when the policy people were allowed far too much control over what we might call "creative output," and there has been savage infighting as a result of that overcontrol.[60]

It was the conflict between the journalist and the diplomat and the journalist and the propagandist.

BBC: To Fill the Bucket of Misinformation

In October 1963 the BBC reported that farmhands on a collective farm in Poland had asked that the BBC Polish service be relayed on the farm's loudspeakers. The farm management acceded to their request.[61] Such an incident, unthinkable not long before, plus the end of Russian jamming, caused Maurice Latey, head of the BBC's East European Service, to ask rhetorically in a lecture he gave in November 1964: "Now that we are, so to say, officially on speaking terms with our audience what should we be telling them?" His answer was not much different from what had been said earlier. Give the audience what they want—straight news and honest and objective comment and background information on it. Give them news about everyday life in Britain, at work and play, the arts, science and technology, sport and music.

What changed with the end of jamming was scheduling so that longer continuous time on the air allowed for more ambitious programming. The Russian service launched a "University of the Air," which included a series on the latest developments in British philosophy, and its "do it yourself" jazz lesssons were popular. The Polish, Czechoslovak, Hungarian, and Yugoslav services ran competitions for the 1964 Shakespeare Quatercentenary, with the prize, a visit to Britain, also unthinkable not much earlier.[62] Style was changing at this time with "livelier journalistic presentation in which impromptu everyday speech took over from the polished scripted performances of the past."[63]

Latey believed the most valuable part of the BBC's audience was the technical intelligentsia, estimated in the Soviet Union to be about twenty million people and a similar proportion of the population in Eastern Europe. They ranged from high officials, factory managers, writers, artists, scientists to school teachers, skilled workers, and the equivalent of evening-class attenders and readers of serious paperbacks in Britain. The class was growing because of the generally high standard of education in communist countries. The young people had a contempt for the cant and hypocrisy of their elders and a passion for truth and sincerity.

Latey's review stressed that the BBC was not trying to convert the new generation of Russians to capitalism because if it were to try it would certainly fail. It was not trying to drag away from Russia Eastern Europeans, who he believed had an interest in retaining some kind of special relationship with the Soviet Union. So he asked himself what good the broadcasts could do and answered with considerable prescience:

> They can help in remaking Europe, in healing the great schism of the past half-century, in creating a new Europe stretching from the Atlantic to the Pacific. This is the optimum aim, a very long-term one, which may well seem Utopian at the present time. It depends on the prediction—always perilous—of great and continuing changes in the nature of European communism. The difficulties in the way are obvious, difficulties of communication across the ideological gulf, difficulties of filling up the bucket of ignorance and misinformation with the small drops of truth which we can pour into it. Yet no one could have predicted ten years ago the remarkable changes that have already taken place. At present we are pushing at an open door. The door may close again. In that case we have our minimum objective. Broadcasting can still keep our foot in the door. It can guarantee that the Stalinist model of a completely isolated communist world can never again be attempted with any hope of success; and that is a great service to the cause of peace.[64]

A sad parenthesis to this measured message of hope came in 1967 with the closure of the BBC Albanian service. Despite the small number of radios there were some listeners to Western broadcasts; a Swedish journalist who visited Albania in 1958 said a senior radio official in Tirana told him there was extensive listening to the BBC Albanian service, which was the chief competition for Albania's domestic broadcasts.[65]

The Audience: An Occasional Worthwhile Thing on the BBC

RFE created an Audience Analysis Section in 1954 to start systematic research. It evolved into the East European Audience and Opinion Research Division (EEAOR). Radio Liberty began gathering empirical evidence of listening habits soon after it started broadcasting and in due course established the Soviet Area Audience and Opinion Research Division (SAAOR) in Paris. The work of these two organizations became recognized as the best available and became the bible of the international broadcasting industry, heavily used by the other major broadcasters, such as the VOA and the BBC.[66] The two research organizations were merged into Media and Opinion Research (MOR) in the RFE/RL Research Institute in Munich in November 1990.

The most important question for RFE when it set up its Audience Analysis Section was quite simply, "Is RFE listened to by the people behind the Iron Curtain?" But, according to Robert Holt in his book *Radio Free Europe*, it also wanted to know:

1. What role does radio (including regime radio) play in the lives of the target audiences?

2. What do the target audiences get from Western radio?

3. In what manner is the behavior and attitude of the target audiences affected by Western broadcasts?

4. What would be the effect if RFE stopped broadcasting?

5. What actions and attitudes of the peoples do the regimes attribute to Western broadcasting and particularly to RFE?

6. How do regime attacks affect RFE effectiveness?

7. Are some aspects of RFE's activities more disturbing than others?[67]

RFE interviewed nationals outside their home countries and then analyzed the interviews with mail received by RFE. Holt studied three of the early reports based on material gathered in 1954 and 1955.[68] The Polish report was based on 127 interviews and 107 letters, the Czechoslovak on 190 interviews and 93 letters, and the Hungarian on 238 interviews and 203 letters. Those interviewed were generally refugees, emigrants, repatriates, or legal travelers in the West. There were usually a good range of different classes, including the intelligentsia, white-collar workers, workers, farmers, and peasants, and a number of nationalities. Most were less than sixty-five. Letters were mostly not of much interest because they were mainly concerned with matters unrelated to RFE, and RFE did not consider the data they provided reliable for listener research. RFE was guarded about drawing too many general conclusions from the small interview samples, particularly bearing in mind possibilities of bias among those who wanted to please the interviewer.

RFE considered that it had an unqualified "Yes" to the question on whether people listened. It was not foolish enough to try to project listener statistics from the interviews although it did deduce that RFE was the most popular of the Western Radios. It considered the BBC and the VOA about tied in second and third place. RFE was popular first because it was on the air all day, whereas the BBC and the VOA only broadcast for a few hours. Second, a Hungarian lawyer explained, "RFE is like a secret broadcasting station operating in Hungary, while VOA and BBC represent the official broadcasts of the American and British governments respectively."[69] RFE, however, conceded that the BBC outranked RFE in prestige and popularity among the better-educated elements of the population in Czechoslovakia, Hungary, and Poland because of its objectivity, reliability, and high intellectual level and popularity dating from World War II. RFE was criticized for lacking objectivity, speaking in an exaggerated and immoderate tone, raising false hopes, and reporting inaccurately on internal affairs.

Holt made only modest claims for the importance of RFE: "In the main, however, the role of RFE (and other Western stations) seems to be that of supporting and reinforcing certain existing attitudes and beliefs, contributing, one might say, to the maintenance of an attitudinal status quo."[70]

Surprisingly enough, one of the most important backhanded compliments to RFE came from Imre Nagy, the prime minister and first secretary of the Communist Party in Hungary, at the end of 1953. He blamed RFE for the fact that almost 50 percent of the peasants in agricultural collectives had abandoned them during the previous six months and returned to individual farming.[71]

By March 1959 the VOA's parent, the USIA, was bold enough in a survey of surveys to estimate that Western broadcasts had an audience numbered by millions in each of three or four countries: East Germany, Poland, Hungary, and probably Czechoslovakia. In proportion to their smaller numbers of radio sets, the audiences in Bulgaria, Romania, and Albania were probably similar. The boldness of the estimate was a result of the greater information obtained as a result of the opening of the windows in Poland and Hungary in 1956 although Hungary's soon slammed shut.[72]

Hungarians questioned after the revolution showed that at the time of the uprising 84 percent of the Hungarians had a radio in working order in the home. Of these radios, 74 percent could receive shortwave broadcasts and 39 percent longwave. During the year before the uprising 90 percent of the people had listened to foreign broadcasts. Of those who had not, 30 percent gave as the reason nonpossession of a radio and fewer than 5 percent gave reasons relating to fear. Ninety-six percent had listened to RFE in the previous year, 82 percent to the VOA, and 67 percent to the BBC. Ninety-one percent thought the BBC was generally reliable, 85 percent VOA, and 69 percent RFE. But 21 percent thought RFE not reliable against 4 percent for the VOA and 2 percent for the BBC.[73]

Six years later the USIA reported on a survey of Poles that pointed up the different attitudes toward the broadcasters of refugees and visitors; the latter naturally were likely to be more sympathetic to the regime. Blue collar workers made up the largest occupational group among the refugees. The visitors were older, better educated, included a higher proportion of women, and were mostly professional and white collar workers. Ninety-one percent of refugees said they had heard a Western radio program during the year before they left Poland compared to only 71 percent of the visitors. Asked if they thought a particular broadcaster was always truthful, 76 percent of the refugees said yes to the VOA compared to 44 percent of the visitors; 82 percent of refugees said yes to the BBC compared to 52 percent of visitors; 61 percent of refugees said yes to RFE compared to 42 percent of visitors.[74]

The 1959 USIA sponsored survey of surveys showed that the high point of listening to Western Radios in Eastern Europe in the fifties had been in 1951 and 1952, presumably because the Korean War raised hopes of liberation, which the populations wanted to hear about from the West. Ruefully, the American organization noted that "BBC achieves its fairly large audiences (usually at least equalling those of the VOA) in spite of having a total transmitting effort considerably less than that of VOA." It also commented that in East Germany in the fifties there was a remarkable and almost unbroken upward trend in listenership to the BBC. The BBC proverbially had a greater appeal to intellectuals than did the American stations, but the report considered this assumption exaggerated. Certainly, the Western broadcasters reached the elite more than they reached the masses.[75]

The Soviet Union was more worrisome to American audience analysts than was Eastern Europe. Keen to justify their budgets to Congress, they had to contend with an American Embassy in Moscow, which reported that they met few Russians who said they listened to Western Radios and whose diplomats said they could not hear the Western broadcasts because of jamming. Since October 1954 the Office of Scientific Intelligence (OSI) had been issuing secret reports that only about 10–20 percent of the frequencies of the VOA could be heard in rural areas and that reception was considerably worse in the towns.

Salvation for the broadcasters, concerned about the paucity of listeners, came with the Brussels World Fair in 1958, where Radio Liberation conducted its first major interviewing effort. More than 300 Soviet citizens were contacted. Of the 138 who discussed radio at all, 92 percent said they had listened to foreign radios. The most listened to was the BBC with 66 percent; close behind came VOA with 64 percent. Only 47 percent listened to Radio Liberation. Less than 50 listeners were prepared to say how often they listened. More than one-half of them said they listened less than once a month, about one-quarter or less listened several times a week, and a similar proportion tuned in more than once a month. They were not against the regime, and they attacked anti-Soviet propaganda.

Typical comments on Western Russian language broadcasts were:

Middle-aged Soviet pavilion executive: "I prefer BBC because they broadcast dry facts and leave us to make the conclusions—but the facts are presented in such a manner that we can only draw certain conclusions (said with a smile). On the other hand, take VOA and Radlib. They draw the conclusions themselves and don't leave it to us to do so. Also they tend to be too biased— one can feel too much bitterness in their programs."

Forty-five-year-old Moscow engineer: "You must remember that there are more important things than material ones—ideology for instance. What has the West to offer us in this field? Capitalism would never achieve success in our country."

Twenty-three- to twenty-five-year-old Ukrainian mechanic from the Donbass: "They paint too rosy a picture of conditions in the West, and there is too much hatred in some of their broadcasts."[76]

They apparently regarded listening to Western broadcasts at least occasionally and openly admitting such listening as not inconsistent with being a good Communist.[77]

The USIA thought that occasional listening to Western broadcasts had become a sign of sophistication and that a switched-on remark in interparty conversation would be: "Of course I've heard Western broadcasts, from time to time, out of sheer curiosity. But—except for an occasional worthwhile thing on BBC—they're just a pack of lies; I get bored with them and don't listen often."

The USIA concluded on the basis of interviews with repatriates that probably between 2.5 percent and 5 percent of the Soviet population listened to Western broadcasts once a week. That meant between 5 and 10 million listeners in a population of 200 million and with 25 to 35 million with easy access to shortwave radios. USIA doubted if hardened Communists listened enough to Western Radios for it to affect their outlook appreciably. But the indirect impact by way of the climate of opinion in which the Soviet leaders moved might be considerable.[78]

The boom in radio listening came in the late fifties. From about six million in 1955, the number of radios rose to twenty million by 1960 and by 1964 had overtaken the number of wired speakers at about thirty-five million. Statistics became uncertain after 1962 when the annual registration and subscription tax on receivers was abolished and replaced by a once-only 15–20 percent surcharge on the purchase price. Annual production was more than four million sets for a number of years.

Curiously, the authorities' attitude toward individual stations was that they frequently attacked RFE, which did not broadcast to the Soviet Union, but for a number of years did not mention its sister station, RL, which did, presumably because they did not want to draw attention to RL.[79]

The Radios played a role in defections although they were not allowed to encourage them. Four of a group of ten defectors from the Soviet Union in January 1955 said foreign broadcasts were an important factor in their decisions to escape.[80]

In August 1969 a Russian fisherman, fed up with the regime, put a letter in a bottle and threw it overboard. It washed up on the Swedish seashore, and a pensioner found it. He took it to a Russian friend, an engineer named V. Kunnos, who photocopied it and sent one copy to the BBC and one to Radio Liberty. The fisherman said he listened to the BBC and RL as often as possible when at home and wanted them to mention his letter in a broadcast. "Your broadcasts are very necessary for us," he wrote. "Only from them can people learn the truth about what is going on in the world, including our own country." His letter was a tirade against "this huge concentration camp known as the USSR."[81]

9

CZECHOSLOVAK INVASION
AND AFTER
(1968–1979)

Helsinki: Hoist with Their Own Petard

Ⱥт 0222 on august 21, 1968, the BBC World Service reported that the Soviet Union and other Warsaw Pact countries had invaded Czechoslovakia. The BBC was the first external service to broadcast the news. A commentary in the Russian service of the BBC at 0445 was heard loud and clear. But then old transmitters were brought out of mothballs and jamming started again.[1] It was directed against the VOA, the BBC, and DW as it had been in 1963. RL had, of course, been jammed all along. It was at first at a lower level than it had been in the early sixties, but in March 1969 it began to intensify and in May it had reached the peak levels of early 1963 of 70 or 80 percent.

The need to intensify jamming was underlined by an extraordinary incident when Minister of Trade Struyev went on television to counter Western reports of a possible price increase in the Soviet Union.[2]

In *Broadcasting to the Soviet Union*, Maury Lisann puts forward the interesting theory that the failure of the Soviet media in competing with the Western Radios meant that the Russians were planning to introduce jamming anyway and that the invasion of Czechoslovakia merely dictated the timing. He believes it would have been reimposed in 1969. He does not give any proof for this theory.[3]

RFE had learned its lessons from the Hungarian revolution. When the Warsaw Pact armies moved into Czechoslovakia, preplanned procedures to ensure the measured content, tone, and quality of the broadcasts were put into effect. RFE got nothing but praise for its broadcasting during that period.[4]

Although the invasion of Czechoslovakia seriously set back détente, negotiations in the years that followed led to the Helsinki Final Act of August 1, 1975, which had an important role in the lead-up to the fall of communism fourteen years later. The Helsinki Final Act had a long history.

In February 1954 at the Berlin Four Powers Conference the Soviet Union had called for a treaty establishing a "general system of European security." By a curious twist of the ironies of history, this proposal led twenty-one years later to the Helsinki Final Act, which provided for the "freer and wider dissemination of information." As Richard Davy put it in *European Détente: A Reappraisal*:

> In short, the Final Act as it emerged was almost the opposite of what the Soviet Union had wanted. Instead of endorsing the status quo it was a charter for change. Instead of legitimising the Soviet sphere of influence it legitimised Western intrusion into it. Instead of making frontiers immutable it specifically affirmed the principle of peaceful change. Instead of putting contacts under official control it emphasised the role of individuals.[5]

The Russians saw it differently at the time. Vladimir Kryuchkov, then head of the First Chief Directorate of the KGB, in charge of operations beyond the Soviet Union, told members of the KGB staff that the Helsinki agreements were "one of the Soviet Union's greatest triumphs since World War II." He boasted: "Poor fools! It will take years for them to understand. We will sell their books, magazines and newspapers to foreigners in hotels reserved for foreigners, and we will burn the rest."[6] In fact, it took him sixteen years to understand. In August 1991 he was head of the KGB and was arrested for his part in the coup.

The first act toward freer and wider dissemination of information was the obligation on the signatories to publish and disseminate the text of the Final Act and to make it known as widely as possible. Soviet newspapers published the complete text in August 1975 to the amazement of their readers.[7]

The NATO ministers' Brussels meeting in December 1969 had called for the freer movement of people, ideas, and information. "Ideas" had to be dropped in the negotiations leading up to the Final Act, but "information" alone was of importance to the cause of international broadcasting because it gave it a further legitimating anchor.

The specific reference to broadcast information said: "The participating states note the expansion in the dissemination of information broadcast by radio, and express the hope for the continuation of this process, so as to meet the interest of mutual understanding among peoples and the aims set forth by this Conference."[8]

The Americans had tried to have a specific reference to jamming included. This was as far as they got, but, to the West at least, it referred to the ending of jamming of the BBC, VOA, and DW in 1973 and meant that the jamming of RFE and RL should cease.

The Russians saw it otherwise. If some people regarded the provisions of the Helsinki final document as "an invitation to fling open the door to subversive anti-Soviet pro-violence propaganda, or to fan national, and racial strife, then they are labouring in vain," said Georgiy Arbatov, head of the Institute for the Study of the United States of America and Canada.[9] In the same vein, *Pravda* carried a major article in January 1976, charging RL and RFE with trying to change the communist system in the Soviet Union and Eastern Europe.[10]

A Helsinki Watchdog Group was founded in Moscow on May 12, 1976, led by Yury Orlov, a leading non-Jewish campaigner for human rights. Another member was Anatoly Shcharansky, who in July 1978 was found guilty of espionage against the Soviet Union and sentenced to three years in prison and ten years in a labor camp. His crime had been to apply for an exit visa to emigrate to Israel. At his trial he was accused of assembling and disseminating Helsinki Watchdog Group documents, which had served as the basis for programs that had been broadcast by radio stations hostile to the Soviet Union, such as the VOA, RFE, RL and the BBC.[11]

The broadcasting of Helsinki Watchdog Group documents by the Western Radios had great impact in the Soviet Union. Typical was a document about Soviet children being taken away from their parents. The law said parents had to bring their children up in a spirit of "communist morality." The document gave details of six heartrending cases of parents, mainly Baptists, whose children had been taken away into the State's care because they had brought up their children according to religious rather than communist principles.[12]

Yuri Zhukov, *Pravda*'s senior commentator, who regularly answered viewers' questions on a television show, warned against listening to foreign Radios when much of the jamming ceased.

Those who touch this mud that is pouring through the airwaves on alien radio beams pollute themselves and besmirch the dignity of a Soviet citizen. And others do more than just listen. Either wishing to boast before their friends of how well they are informed or simply because they misunderstand the alien voices conveyed to us on the radio, these people, by all kinds of gossip, pollute others as well. But we, comrades, come out for cleanliness![13]

But the Central Committee was still concerned about the uncompetitiveness of its own media and in 1979 issued a directive calling for a more persuasive approach and less "gray" attempts at window dressing.[14]

The review meeting on the Final Act in Belgrade in 1977 and 1978 showed up the many sharp differences on jamming. Sergei Kondrashev launched a vicious attack against RL, calling it operated by "traitors whose hands were dripping with blood." Western delegates pointed out that jamming violated the terms of the Final Act.[15]

The antibroadcaster pressure did not let up and communist representatives pressed the International Olympic Committee into revoking RFE's accreditation to the 1976 Innsbruck Olympic Games and prevented reporting by the West German Radios, Deutsche Welle and Deutschlandfunk, from the March 1976 Leipzig Fair.[16]

RFE and RL: To the Graveyard of Cold War Relics

The first major domestic attack on RFE was over Hungary in 1956, the second, which also included RL, was at the time of the *Ramparts* revelations in 1967. The third came from a surprising source, President Johnson, which was unknown to those two organizations at the time because it was delivered in secrecy within the confines of the White House. In an interview with this author years later Richard Helms, director of the CIA from June 1966 to February 1973, recalled the occasion.[17] He could not remember the date but thought it was in 1968.

President Johnson held so-called Tuesday lunches. They were so called despite the fact that they were sometimes breakfasts and sometimes took place on days other than Tuesdays. They were usually held in the president's family dining room off the living room at the west end of the second floor of the White House. Certain members of the administration became members of the Tuesday lunches although they had to be invited on each occasion. They were people whom the president particularly wanted to talk to: the secretary of state, the secretary of defense, the chairman of the Joint Chiefs, the president's press officer, the national security advisor, and the director of Central Intelligence. Tom Johnson, the president's assistant, later to become president of CNN, took notes. The members were not allowed to take notes.

After one of these lunches the president asked Helms to stay behind.

"I'm going to close down those Radios," he told Helms. Helms was amazed. "But you can't do that," Helms replied. He later recalled that he afterward regretted how he had reacted—without even a "Mr. President"—but he had been very surprised. Helms explained to the president that the Radios were doing a lot of good, and they had a protracted discussion. "All right," President Johnson said, "If you think they're so important, you go up to Capitol Hill and get them financed. But you must tell those Senators and congressmen that you do not have my support." Helms said in the interview that he was startled by this decision. "Everything that the Executive branch puts in Government budgets theoretically has the president's approval. So if it does not, it changes the convention." Helms added, "But since I had no choice, that is what I had to do."

Helms prepared his brief well and was finally able to persuade the appropriate senators and congressmen to support the continuation of the Radios. "Mind you," said Helms, "I don't want to give the impression that I was the most persuasive fellow since Abraham Lincoln or Winston Churchill. But I had to make all the arguments; I did not want to be turned down."

Cord Meyer believed the reason for President Johnson's stance was budgetary. "He had not really thought through how the Radios could be funded," Meyer commented.[18] Helms supported the Radios because they were one of the few things that the United States could do to try to alter events and attitudes. His reasoning was as follows:

> Diplomacy had no effect, and the iron fist of the Red Army was very evident. We didn't know exactly where our efforts would lead. But we hoped to encourage opposition. Contrary to what was largely felt in the West, the Agency was trying to support the noncommunist Left. If we had shut down the Radios, it would have given the people of Eastern Europe the impression that we had given up on them. They would have believed that there was a permanent division of Europe and that we had decided to wash our hands of the whole affair.

The fourth major attack on RFE and RL came four years after the assault that started with *Ramparts*. That there was a lull from 1967 to 1971 was the result, no doubt, of the preoccupation with the Vietnam War. When the attack did come, it once again almost cost the two organizations their lives. On January 25, 1971, Senator Clifford Case of New Jersey delivered in the Senate a blistering attack on the two Radios. He charged them with deceiving both American taxpayers and listeners in

Eastern Europe and the Soviet Union. He expressed his concern for those hundreds of thousands of Americans who had contributed to the Crusade for Freedom drives during the fifties. "Several hundreds of millions of dollars in United States government funds had been expended from secret CIA budgets to pay almost totally for the costs of these two radio stations broadcasting to Eastern Europe. . . . [At] no time was Congress asked or permitted to carry out its constitutional role of approving the expenditures."[19] Case referred to the Katzenbach committee report of 1967 and its damning clauses that would rule the Radios out of court.

Case then introduced Senate Bill 18, which would amend the United States Information and Educational Exchange Act of 1948 to Provide Assistance to Radio Free Europe and Radio Liberty. It included an appropriation of $30 million for fiscal year 1972 to provide grants to the Radios for administration by the secretary of state.

There were three important background elements to the Case démarche. First, he hired as a member of his staff John Marks, a disgruntled former State Department employee, who later helped write a book unsympathetic to the Radios. Second, Senator Frank Church of Idaho was particularly upset because before he had been elected to the Senate he had been recruited as a principal in a Crusade for Freedom drive in Idaho without being told that the CIA financed RFE. Senator Stuart Symington of Missouri also supported the anti-Radios lobby. Third, and by far the most important element, was the increasing disillusionment with U.S. foreign policy of Senator Fulbright, chairman of the Senate Foreign Relations Committee.

His attitude toward the Radios, which at first sight is remarkable from this great liberal, is better understood in the light of his overall view of the developments in American foreign policy. He had expounded his views on American foreign policy in his lectures in 1966 for the Christian A. Herter Series at the Johns Hopkins School of International Studies, which he later published under the title *The Arrogance of Power.* His thesis was that the United States was moving toward a more strident and aggressive foreign policy. America was suffering from the tendency of great nations to try to remake other countries in their own shining images and was succumbing to the human failing of telling other people what to do.[20]

President Johnson agreed with the theory put to him by Richard Helms that Fulbright had been soured by his disappointment at not being made secretary of state by President Kennedy.[21]

The State Department and the CIA wanted the Radios to continue. But the State Department did not want responsibility for RFE and RL, whose aims did not always coincide with the department's short-term policies and caused diplomatic embarrassment. It was the same thinking that made the British Foreign Office happy to have no responsibility for the content of the External Services of the BBC. So the State Department and the CIA put together an alternative, which was an American Council on Private International Communications (ACPIC), which Senator Chase tabled on May 24, 1971, as S.1936, an alternative to S.18.

The council would be appointed by the president with the advice and consent of the Senate. The Senate threw out the ACPIC bill and looked at S.18 again. But Fulbright delayed matters by proposing that the General Accounting Office (GAO) and Congressional Research Service (CRS) of the Library of Congress be asked to prepare research reports to be used in determining whether "it is in the public interest to support them with tax dollars." Only by the passing of a continuing resolution were the Radios able to carry on operations into the next fiscal year. The GAO and CRS reports turned out to be favorable to continuation of the Radios.

The full Senate passed S.18 on July 30. The House considered the ACPIC bill on September 14 and 21 and rejected it. They passed an amended S.18 on November 19. It provided for a study commission, which would also temporarily receive appropriations and supervise grants to the Radios. The House and Senate met in conference committee on January 16 and January 26, 1972. Fulbright and Thomas E. ("Doc") Morgan of Pennsylvania, chairman of the House Foreign Affairs Committee, clashed, and the House and Senate failed to reconcile their differences.

On February 17 Senator Fulbright delivered in the Senate his most powerful attack on the Radios and made his famous comment: "Mr. President, I submit these Radios should be given an opportunity to take their rightful place in the graveyard of cold war relics."[22] His speech was a wide-ranging attack on the administration:

> Mr. President, the history of these radios, particularly the covert funding and policy direction of them, provides, I think, an example—a good example—of how and why people lose faith in their Government and their elected officials. Fundamentally, this is a matter of credibility and the public's expectations that its Government is so structured that the "big lie" cannot be perpetuated indefinitely; that the separation of

powers is a real safeguard, if not an immediate one; and that our system of checks and balances does, over a period of time at least, work much as the Founding Fathers said it would.

The case of Radio Free Europe and Radio Liberty indicates, I suppose, that given a long enough period of time, the checks and balances are there; the separation of powers does exist; and the "big lie" can be exposed.

While this case "proves" all of these things, I cannot help but think that it has, nevertheless, taken an exceptional toll in the people's faith and credibility in their Government—a faith and credibility already overtaxed by U-2 flights that we did not know anything about; by an invasion at the Bay of Pigs that we were not involved in; by Tonkin Gulf incidents that we were innocent of; and the list goes on and on . . .

But through all of this—through all of the deception and falsehoods heaped on the American public—there was Radio Free Europe, keeping the "truth alive behind the Iron Curtain."

Moving away from the great deception, he turned to the specific foreign policy issue: "Regardless of the label attached to the Radios, the fact is this activity, even if it entails nothing more than 'straight news reporting,' raises a number of foreign policy issues not the least of which is the extent of our meddling in the internal political affairs of other countries by means of directing and supporting broadcasting activities in behalf of political refugees."[23]

Tension was mounting; the latest continuing resolution was due to expire on February 22 and there could be no extension. There was enough money in the operating accounts to run for a short period. On February 23 the conference committee met again but broke up in total disarray. On the same day, however, a resolution signed by fifty senators urged Fulbright to drop his opposition. The resolution had been initiated by the bipartisan team of Senator Hubert Humphrey of Minnesota and Senator Charles Percy of Illinois.

Finally, David M. Abshire, assistant secretary of state for congressional relations, got agreement to a compromise providing for State Department oversight, no commission to study the future and no commission supervision. The Senate and the House approved $36 million for the fiscal year 1972. On March 30 the president signed the bill.[24] It had been a close call.

Six weeks later, on May 10, President Nixon announced that he had asked the secretary of state to submit a bill that day that would continue government support to the Radios through fiscal year 1973. He strongly recommended that the bill be given favorable consideration before the beginning of the new fiscal year. He also announced that he planned to appoint a Presidential Study Commission on RFE and RL with instructions to render its report and recommendations by February 28, 1973, so that the administration and Congress could take them into consideration when formulating authorizing legislation for fiscal year 1974.

He gave the following as the background to these decisions: "The decision to continue Government support for these radios was approved by large majorities in Congress and reflects the judgment that has been expressed overwhelmingly by newspapers throughout this country and by leading citizens in all walks of life that Radio Free Europe and Radio Liberty continue to perform a unique and valuable service."[25]

Hearings by the Senate Foreign Relations Committee on the fiscal year 1973 appropriations bill included testimony by Dirk Stikker, a former secretary-general of NATO and former foreign minister of the Netherlands. He was a member of RFE's West European Advisory Committee (WEAC), and Fulbright had invited him to testify so that Fulbright could attack the lack of financial support for the Radios by the European allies of the United States. European financial support never materialized despite vague promises. The fiscal 1973 bill was passed without significant opposition in either the House or Senate.

To the BBC, a competitor of RFE and RL, Fulbright's view of the Radios was a fundamental and dangerous misreading of the situation that would lead to depriving millions of people in Eastern Europe of their main source of information about the outside world.[26]

The president appointed Milton S. Eisenhower as chairman of the commission on August 9, 1972. He was a brother of the former U.S. president and president emeritus of Johns Hopkins University. The other members were chosen from the lists of the great and the good in the fields of diplomacy and academe. The brief was rather discursive:

I believe the Commission should undertake a critical examination of the operation and funding question and recommend methods for future maintenance and support of the radios which will not impair their professional independence and, consequently, their effectiveness. Determination of proper support mechanisms will, of course, involve considerations of the relationship of the radios to the national interest and to this Nation's foreign policy objectives, the relationship of the radios to executive branch agencies, financial and other supporting requirements of the radios, as well as any other matters having a bearing on radio operations or objectives. Throughout the study, the Commission should discuss these matters thoroughly with concerned members of Congress.[27]

The commission was not specifically asked to recommend whether the Radios should be continued. Nevertheless, the report, *The Right to Know,* commendably delivered ahead of the deadline on February 5, 1972, did so. It contained a strongly implied reproof to Senator Fulbright.

> The Commission is convinced that Radio Free Europe and Radio Liberty, by providing a flow of free and uncensored information to peoples deprived of it, actually contribute to a climate of détente rather than detract from it. Experience in the last few months has shown that "relaxation of tensions" on the government level does not necessarily lead to a relaxation of internal controls. In fact, since the summer of 1972, quite the contrary has occurred. We therefore recommend that the stations be continued until the governments of the countries to which the stations are broadcasting permit a free flow of information and ideas, both internally and between the East and the West.[28]

The report elaborated many arguments on the benefits of the Radios, some incontrovertible, some that some people would regard as debatable. In the incontrovertible category was the statement that because the Radios reported particular stories, the communist media were frequently compelled to report them also, albeit belatedly. It paid tribute to the research by the Radios, "the best of its kind available." In the debatable category was the view that if the international community was to make true and lasting progress toward East-West détente it would come about through pressure exerted on their own governments by an informed citizenry. Likewise debatable was the statement that over a long period of time the cost of the Radios could obviate military expenditures many times greater.[29]

Good quotations supporting the case for the Radios were liberally scattered throughout the report. It led with one from Aleksandr Solzhenitsyn, "If we ever hear anything about events in this country, it's through them [Radio Liberty broadcasts]."[30] Another was from Andrei D. Sakharov, the Soviet nuclear physicist and human rights campaigner, who wrote, "Freedom to obtain and distribute information, freedom for open-minded and unfearing debate and freedom from pressure from officialdom and prejudices . . . is the only guarantee against an infection of people by mass myths, which in the hands of treacherous hypocrites and demagogues, can be transformed into bloody dictatorship."[31]

The commission plainly took great delight in including a quotation from Senator Fulbright of some years earlier, which went directly counter to all his attacks on the Radios in the Senate:

We must try to convey accurate information to the Russians about Western life, about the aims of Western policy, and about the heavy price that the Cold War exacts from both their people and ours. I do not know whether we can influence Russian public opinion and strengthen it as a brake against dangerous and adventurous policies, but I believe we must try to do this as a matter of responsibility not to the Russians but to ourselves.[32]

The commission answered the organizational problem by proposing a Board for International Broadcasting, which would "in effect serve as a nexus between the public, Congress, the Executive Branch and the stations." It was not greatly different from that proposed by the State Department and the CIA in May 1971 and rejected by the Senate. It would include the following features, the report said:

• The Board would receive Congressional appropriations and make grants to RFE and RL.
• The Board would be responsible for assuring that the stations do not operate in a manner inconsistent with broad United States foreign policy objectives.
• The Board would be vigilant on behalf of the professional independence of the stations, whose primary function is to promote a free flow of relevant information and interpretation to the Soviet Union and the nations of Eastern Europe.
• The Board would be responsible for assuring that adequate fiscal controls are maintained and that funds are used in an effective and efficient manner for the purposes intended.
• There would be seven directors of the new Board; five, including the Chairman, would be appointed by the President with the advice and consent of the Senate from Americans distinguished in such fields as foreign policy and mass communication. The other directors would be the chief operating executive of Radio Free Europe, Inc. and the chief operating executive of the Radio Liberty Committee. They would be ex officio, non-voting members.
• The Board would have a minimum staff, drawing on the stations for much of its administrative support.
• Headquarters of the new Board and the executive staffs of both stations should be located in contiguous space, preferably in the Washington, D.C., area.[33]

The commission provided a rider on journalistic ethics:

The Commission realizes that there may seem to be an inconsistency in speaking of "professional independence" and then of operations "not inconsistent with United States foreign policy objectives." Fully professional independence could not have limits placed upon it. What the Commission advocates is professional independence with the sole limitation that the stations not operate in a manner inconsistent with broad United States foreign policy objectives.[34]

On possible improvements and economies, the commission, in the context of the need for renovation and modernization of facilities, suggested a study of joint technical broadcasting facilities, including the VOA. It thought the functions and space of RFE and RL might be consolidated. It rejected financial support from Western governments because it could lead to confusion in operational policies. It welcomed private contributions, both American and non-American.[35]

The report recommendations were implemented through Public Law 93–129, the Board for International Broadcasting Act, enacted on October 19, 1973. The BIB had been created by the end of April 1974. The chairman was David Abshire, executive director of Georgetown University's Center for Strategic and International Studies and former assistant secretary of state. On October 1, 1976, the two Radios merged as RFE/RL, Inc. The president was Sig Mickelson, a broadcaster with a great reputation, who had been the first president of the CBS News Division. In February 1978 most of the administrative functions moved to Munich.

The political tone of the new regime is given by an extraordinary proposal made by the BIB board at the beginning of 1978 that, in an attempt to get jamming stopped, it was prepared seriously to consider making RFE/RL airtime available to officials of the Soviet Union and Eastern Europe for responses to specific complaints about the content of the RFE/RL broadcasts that had merit. Congress quickly decided that if that happened it would deny RFE/RL all funds.[36]

The Voice Is Not Muted

The aftermath of the Czech invasion brought no easing in the struggles between the VOA and its masters in the USIA, the State Department, and the White House that had chequered its history. Debates on détente versus confrontation were added to those on objectivity versus propaganda. On the one hand was the U.S. ambassador to the Soviet Union urging a "crisper anticommunist line" and, on the other, the State Department advising the VOA to play down the twentieth anniversary of the Hungarian revolution.[37] The State Department did not like the VOA referring to Soviet "duplicity" in connection with the introduction of Soviet antiaircraft missiles into Egypt in September 1970. On September 21 the secretary of state, William Rogers, sent a memo to the USIA director, Frank Shakespeare, telling him that under the law the USIA had to receive formal policy guidance from the State Department. Shakespeare replied that he considered general policy guidance sufficient. He said he had dropped the practice of clearing any specific news items with the State Department shortly after he had taken office. He told Rogers that he reported directly to the president. The struggles were no longer consistent; positions and their advocates changed like sunspots changing radio reception.

Two areas that the VOA exploited in which there was little dispute on coverage were ethnic minorities and dissidents in the Soviet Union. Shakespeare regarded the discontent of the national groups as a great blessing to the USIA.[38] The view of the VOA diverged from that of others, including congressmen, on how to handle Solzhenitsyn's *Gulag Archipelago* when it was published in 1973. The VOA decided to broadcast only excerpts, unlike RFE/RL, which broadcast readings daily. Shakespeare, by then the former director, said the book should be given the most extensive coverage.[39] But the new director, James Keogh, laid down this policy, which prevailed:

> VOA has covered this developing story just as it traditionally covered other aspects of the dissident movement in the USSR. USIA's approach is exactly the same now as it was before the Soviet Union ceased jamming in September without our foreknowledge and without explanation. Soviet officials are criticizing this policy. We are holding to it. What we do not do—as the official radio voice of the United States—is to indulge in polemics aimed at changing the internal structure of the Soviet Union. To read from the book would be far outside the normal style of Voice of America programing and would tend to reinforce Soviet charges that the United States is utilizing these events as a political weapon and is intervening in the domestic affairs of the USSR. USIA has not muted its Voice. At the same time, we have not acceded to suggestions that we turn backward to the old cold war style of broadcasting.[40]

Nothing points up more sharply the differences between the relations beween the VOA and the U.S. government and between the BBC and the British government than the VOA handling of the Vietnam story and the BBC's treatment of Suez nearly two decades earlier. The VOA was part of a government agency; there were lines of command and channels for instructions. The BBC was an institution independent operationally from government to which there were no lines of command and no channels for instructions. The BBC received no instructions about how to handle Suez although there were plenty of threats. Given the structures it would have been surprising if the VOA had received no instructions on Vietnam. It received them and agonized over the conflicts with its charter, but it carried them out.

In July 1976 the charter was entered into law as Public Law 94–350. The terminology was different only in minor respects except, perhaps, for the deletion of the phrase "as an official radio," from the internal document of 1960.

In 1978 the VOA distanced its foreign correspondents a little from the government by making them administratively separate from U.S. embassies and missions. They started to travel on regular and not official passports and leased office space overseas as did commercial news organizations.[41]

BBC: Russia Is Not for Dancing

The period that followed the broadcasters' traumas of the Prague Spring found the BBC again battling against reviews. (It had had to contend with three minor ones since the Hill report in 1959: Vosper 1961–62; Rapp 1964–65; Beeley 1967.) This time it was first of all the Duncan report, published in July 1969, which recommended a switch to commercial and cultural promotion of Britain from explanation of Britain's political policies, which was what they believed was then the emphasis. The Duncan committee went back to the elitist line of the abortive Drogheda report and also wanted concentration on broadcasting in English, except in Eastern Europe and the Middle East. The managing director of the External Services, Oliver Whitley, wrote to the Foreign Office in April 1970:

> The main value of the External Services is not that they may help to sell tractors or nuclear reactors, nor even that they so influence people in other countries, nobs or mobs, as to be more amenable to British diplomacy or foreign policy. Their main value is that because they effectively represent and communicate this British propensity for truthfulness or the adherence to the individual right to the perception of reality, they help to increase the instability of political systems based on the total inversion of morality and reality for ideological purposes. Countries which have such political systems are for that reason less amenable to British diplomacy, more difficult to trade with, and particularly if pow-

erful or proliferating, liable to be a military threat to Britain, whose contrasted liberties constantly give the lie to their fictitious universe.[42]

Peter Fraenkel, one-time controller of the European services of the BBC, recalled interviewing a Bulgarian industrial worker who had defected to the West, who had been amazed by hearing a BBC report that had shown this propensity for truthfulness. In January 1972 a German woman threw an inkpot at the British prime minister, Edward Heath, which, naturally, the BBC reported. The Bulgarian worker knew the Bulgarian media would have suppressed such an item. That was when he started listening to the BBC.[43]

Periodic collisions between the Foreign Office and the BBC continued despite the generally close working relationship. After a row about a BBC report on the status of Bahrain, Minister of State Goronwy Roberts told Charles Curran, director of external broadcasting, that he wanted a system of "vetting" BBC news. Curran gave him short shrift.[44]

Little changed as a result of the Duncan report. Nor did much change as a result of the report of the British Government's Central Policy Review Staff—the think tank—seven years later in August 1977. They wanted cutbacks and the end of all broadcasting in European languages except to Eastern Europe. Once again the BBC fought back and was strongly supported by the British press. In the leftwing *New Statesman* magazine a commentator, Anthony Howard, wrote that "the net result of any such cut-back would be to relegate the BBC to the same status as 'Radio Liberty' and 'Radio Free Europe', in other words to make it an overt, anti-communist propaganda agency." "Nothing," he said, "could be better calculated to destroy 'at a stroke' the reputation for editorial integrity that the BBC has patiently (and sometimes as at the time of Suez in 1956, painfully) managed to build up over the years."[45] "More think, less tank," demanded the *Economist*.[46] The government effectively rejected the report except for the proposed program of increased capital investment.

There was no public outcry about the closure on April 30, 1977, of the Information Research Department; the public did not know about it. The IRD, which at one time had grown to a staff of four hundred, had been the subject of cutbacks in 1971 and in 1973. David Owen, the Labour foreign minister, closed down the propaganda machine that his Labour predecessor had started thirty years before as Owen's contribution to open government. Brian Crozier, a consultant to MI6 and to the CIA, later wrote: "Thus the Labour Government had destroyed the only active instrument of counter-subversion in the United Kingdom (as distinct from the passive observation of MI-5) as a sop to the Left. The KGB had won, possibly when it least expected victory."[47] Not until January 1978 was the story of IRD told when the *Guardian* broke the story under the headline, "Death of the Department that Never Was."[48]

Senior BBC External Services staff were still able to keep in touch with Foreign Office thinking. They were allowed to read ambassadors' dispatches in a private room to get the essence of the Foreign Office line. They normally agreed with it, anyway, according to Mary Seton-Watson, formerly head of the Russian service.[49]

By 1979 the BBC External Services budget was again under attack. The government wanted a cut of 10 percent for the next financial year, ending March 31, 1981. Again there was a public and parliamentary outcry, and eventually only the Spanish, Italian, and Maltese services were killed off. But the ending of the Spanish service was shown to have been remarkably shortsighted when the Falklands war broke out less than one year later.[50]

One piece of common sense that ran through all the frequently stupid governmental reviews of the BBC was that services to Eastern Europe should not be cut back.

When Aleksandr Solzhenitsyn visited the BBC in 1976, he was critical of the soft tone of the broadcasts. He said that the approach of the Anatol Goldbergs of this world was no better than "water trickling through your fingers." When the BBC tried to improve their presentation, he had earlier declared: "Russia is not for dancing." The Russian dissident, Andrei Amalrik, complained when he visited the BBC that its output showed "a certain wishywashiness: on the one hand . . . on the other . . . I suppose that is how the British are."[51]

Despite his reservations about the British character Amalrik valued what the BBC was doing. "Foreign broadcasts into Russia play an enormous role," he said in an interview in 1977.[52] "It is the only alternative information available to millions of Soviet citizens."

The Russians believed the BBC had close links with the Secret Intelligence Service (SIS). In December 1968 a series of articles in *Izvestia* claimed coded messages were transmitted for agents in Eastern Europe. Listeners' letters were forwarded to the SIS and SIS agents worked in the BBC, A. Panfilov wrote in *Radiovoyna* (Radio wars).[53]

In 1979 what seems to have been the first monograph to have been published in the Soviet Union about the BBC appeared. In *Bi-Bi-Si: Istoriya, apparat, metody radiopropagandy* (The BBC: History, apparatus, methods of radio propaganda) Vladimir Artyomov and Vladimir Semyonov aimed to show the BBC as a "biased, unreliable source of information."[54] The gentlemanly tones of the BBC were different from the crude anticommunism of the VOA. The essence of the BBC technique was "factological propaganda," which was based on "information without comment," "the dramatization of a fact," and "balanced information," even though the balance was not genuine. The two Vladimirs gave an example of the technique:

> Thus, alongside a politically orientated program about the relationship between religion and the state in the Soviet Union, there is a program "about a new cookery book." And alongside an item that falsifies our country's history there is a long and rather dull item about meteorology. However, both sets of scripts are read by the same announcer in the same way and without any change of tone. The listener is, as it were, made to feel that the important political commentary is as "impartial and truthful" as the less important item. For how, indeed can there be anything ideologically subversive about a cookery book![55]

They quoted the BBC commentator, Lindley Fraser, who in his book *Propaganda*, revealing the manufacturing secret, said that what mattered for the propagandist was not truth for its own sake but a reputation for truthfulness.

Markov: Murdered Because He Told the Truth

The most tragic and bizarre event in the history of the international broadcasting of the BBC and RFE, or indeed of any international broadcaster, was the murder of the Bulgarian defector, Georgi Markov, who was hit by a tiny poisoned pellet as he was crossing Waterloo Bridge in London.

Markov, who defected in 1971, was one of Bulgaria's most distinguished writers. He worked for the Bulgarian service of the BBC, where he met the English girl he married, Annabel. They lived in Clapham and had a daughter, Sasha. Life was normal for this small family until in 1977 Markov started to write his memoirs, which were broadcast on the Bulgarian service of RFE. It was after the chapters called "Meetings with Todor Zhivkov," in which he spoke scornfully of the Bulgarian leader, that Markov started to get death threats. Typical of the contempt which Markov displayed is this account of a conversation Markov had with Zhivkov while they were walking together in the mountains near Sofia: "Zhivkov said that, for him, the model of a real Communist Party leader was Khrushchev. Here I must mention that only two days after our walk Khrushchev was toppled, but it was all too clear that Zhivkov had no idea what was happening in the Soviet leadership."[56]

Annabel Markov has recounted how in January 1978 a Bulgarian living in the West telephoned to warn Markov that if he continued to write for Radio Free Europe, he would be killed. There were a number of warnings over a period of five months until toward the end of May 1978 the Bulgarian who had given the warnings himself visited the Markovs. He said Markov was to be poisoned with a substance that had been tested in Moscow and had been transferred to the West.[57]

On September 7, 1978, President Zhivkov's birthday, Markov was walking over Waterloo Bridge to the headquarters of the BBC External Services in Bush House when he felt a sharp pain in his right thigh. He looked around and saw a man bend down and pick up an umbrella. Markov said later that he believed the attacker did so to hide his face. It has been generally believed that the umbrella fired the pellet, but Markov did not believe that. Markov died four days later on September 11. The inquest found that the pellet shot into his leg contained 0.2mg of ricin, a substance twice as poisonous as cobra venom, for which there is no antidote.[58] "Georgi was murdered because he told the truth," Annabel Markov wrote.[59]

After the downfall of Zhivkov, Annabel Markov visited Sofia, and at the beginning of 1990 Alexander Lilov, later head of the ruling Bulgarian Socialist Party, promised her a full investigation of her husband's death.[60] In the following eighteen months she made eight more visits.[61] Bulgarian police came to London and British police visited Sofia. In February 1991 the President of Bulgaria, Zhelyu Zhelev, on a visit to Britain, drove down to the ninth-century parish church of Whitechurch Canonicorum in West Dorset to pay his respects at the grave of Markov. He told Annabel and Sasha, by now 14, that the assassination would be thoroughly investigated.[62] Bit by bit parts of the story came out.

In November 1991, General Leonid Katsamunski, who was in charge of the investigation, could reveal on television that Bulgaria's secret services were directly involved in Markov's murder.[63] The following month he disclosed that he had unearthed a Politiburo decree from July 1977 that said that all measures could be used to neutralize enemy émigrés. That political stamp of approval freed the hands of the secret police, he said. But he could not find the file on the Markov case. General Stoyan Savov, the former deputy interior minister, and General Vladimir Todorov, the former chief of the secret police, were charged in January 1992 with removing the Markov file. On January 6, two days before he was due to go on trial, Savov was found dead, shot in the right temple with a Colt pistol. It has not been determined if it was murder or suicide. The following June Todorov was sentenced to fourteen months—later reduced to nine months in prison—for destroying the files. He said they were uninteresting.

A KGB General, Oleg Kalugin, wrote in his autobiography published in 1994 that the KGB became involved in the preparations for the murder at the request of the Bulgarians.[64] A KGB officer discussed with the Bulgarians three ways of liquidating Markov silently and without a trace: poisoned jelly, poisoned food, and a poisoned pellet. The poisoned jelly had been tried on Aleksandr Solzhenitsyn in a shop in Russia in the early 1970s. An agent had rubbed some on him. It made him violently ill, but did not kill him. The poisoned jelly appealed to the Bulgarians. They thought of rubbing it on the handle of Markov's car door, but decided not to go ahead when they realized it might kill Annabel instead, which would scare off Markov.

They then planned to follow Markov on a planned vacation to a seaside resort in Italy, have an agent bump into him on the beach and smear him with the poisoned jelly. But in the first of a series of failures, which read like something from a spoof spy film, the agent had to report back to his superiors that the weather was cold, the beach was half-empty, Markov was clothed, and he could not work out how to get at him to rub on the cream. The next attempt at assassinating Markov was to poison his food during a visit to Germany. But for undisclosed reasons that also failed. So they tried shooting the poisoned pellet at a horse. The horse died so they then tried it on a prisoner who had been sentenced to death. He went hysterical, but survived. They then used the same technique on another Bulgarian defector, Vladimir Kostov, in Paris. That also failed. But when Kostov heard of the death of Markov, he alerted officials in London, they exhumed the body, and an autopsy revealed a tiny pellet lodged in a small wound in Markov's right thigh.[65] The KGB, evidently unable to buy a suitable umbrella in Moscow, or perhaps because they wanted to cast suspicion on the CIA, had got the KGB in Washington to send them several American umbrellas, which they then adapted with firing mechanisms. One of them was used to kill Markov.[66]

Markov was employed by the BBC but worked for other broadcasters. Peter Fraenkel, the controller of the BBC's European services when Markov was murdered, believed that Markov was killed because of what he broadcast for RFE, not the BBC. Fraenkel had been told to close his eyes to Markov working for RFE. "The Bulgarian secret police did not manage to shut me up and neither did Peter Fraenkel," said Markov.[67]

Media speculation continued through the early nineties on the identity of the killer, but no one was arrested. In 1994 Vladimir Bereanu and

Kalin Todorov published in Sofia their book, *The Umbrella Murder*. They said a Bulgarian diplomat living in Sofia was the killer. They believed Markov was not a dissident but an agent for the Bulgarian Secret Service. They claimed he had been killed because he had been recruited by the British Secret Service and was working as a double agent.[68]

10

SOLIDARITY
(1979–1989)

Poland: "If You Would Close Your Radio Free Europe . . . "

THE HARBINGER of the momentous events of the eighties was the Polish pope, Karol Wojtyla, who visited Poland in June 1979 just after his election. He was the first non-Italian pope since Hadrian VI, a Dutchman, who was elected 450 years earlier. Gorbachev had no doubts about the role the Polish pope played. In March 1992 he wrote, "What has happened in Eastern Europe in the last few years would not have been possible without this Pope, without the great role—including a political one—which John Paul II played in the events of the world."[1]

More than one million people gathered to greet the pope on a disused airfield outside Gniezno, Poland's religious cradle. That showed them that "we," the people, were more numerous than "they," the Communists. The participants heard accurate reports of the event from the Western Radios. Vatican Radio mounted massive editorial operations for the pope's visits, sending as many as eighteen staffers.[2] Polish television showed only old ladies and nuns at the pope's open-air masses. "That combination—awareness of our numbers and tangible proof of communist duplicity—helped to produce the Solidarity revolution the following year," commented Radek Sikorski, a dissident, later a member of a postrevolution government.[3]

Nevertheless, the CIA believed the Russians regarded the pope as a moderating force in Poland.[4] And the West also wanted no disruptions. Adam Michnik, the Polish historian and dissident, complained that RFE became overly cautious and stopped giving information about arrests of members of the opposition, who were disgusted by this censorship.[5]

The position of the Catholic Church in Poland was unique. Catholicism was part of Polish national identity because through its history the

157

country had felt itself assailed on one side by Prussia and Protestantism and on the other by Russia and the Orthodox Church. Even when others became resigned to living with the repressive regime, the Polish pope kept alive the spirit of Solidarity, praying every Wednesday and Sunday to the Black Madonna of Czestochowa. And he had his own radio station to carry his message. "The Church is on the side of the workers," he declared.[6] Between 1979 and 1985 listeners to Vatican Radio increased sevenfold.[7] Laypeople and clerics would post on church doors the Vatican Radio schedules and frequencies.[8]

"If you would close your Radio Free Europe, the underground would completely cease to exist," said Jerzy Urban, the Polish government spokesman.[9] He was quoted on August 14, 1984, four years to the day after a strike started at the Lenin Shipyard in Gdansk, which marked the beginning of the troubles in the eighties. One month later, on September 17, 1980, Solidarity was founded. Representatives of independent trades union founding committees agreed to apply jointly for legal registration as a nationwide Independent Self-Governing Trades Union. The 1981 year of troubles culminated in a "state of war," which Prime Minister General Wojciech Jaruzelski declared on December 13. Solidarity leaders and activists were interned.

The eighties was the decade of achievement of the Western Radios, above all in Poland, where the ground swell of East European revolution started. The Radios had not always been held in high esteem. Adam Michnik wrote from prison in 1982:

> In our youth, in the 1950s and 1960s, the community of émigrés did not have a good reputation. They were considered something alien. There existed a stereotype of the émigré as someone who turned his back on his country, who placed himself outside his nation, who did not share its good and bad times, who hopelessly yearned for a return to old times and privileges for himself—the émigré who chose easy earnings, security and prosperity and who, for American money, told lies about Poland on Radio Free Europe.[10]

But that attitude changed as official propaganda became increasingly annoying and censorship increased. Michnik's letter from prison continued: "Masses of people listened to Radio Free Europe, searching not only for information about parts of the world not covered by the Polish media but also for honest news about their own country—about the follies of censorship and the protests of the intellectuals. The rebellious intelligentsia sought to communicate with Polish society via London and Paris—and they succeeded."

The key was communications. Jacek Kuron, the activist of the Committee for Social Defense (KOR) recounted how earlier, whenever anyone was arrested, his friends could call Kuron. He, in turn, would notify RFE or other news organizations, and the information would be broadcast back into Poland.[11] From August 1980 Solidarity used RFE to announce times and places of meetings. It was easier to telephone internationally than domestically. One day Kuron was on the telephone giving a live interview to RFE when there was a knock at the door. He opened up and it was the police. "Excuse me," he told the interviewer, "I have to go to prison."[12]

Reuters staff in Warsaw frequently had visits from men who would give them news. "When will it be transmitted by RFE?" they would ask.

It was ironical that RFE programs were cited in evidence in trials of dissidents, including Kuron. Anna Skowronska, the lawyer defending Anna Walentynowicz, said it was a paradoxical situation that "in the course of a criminal trial where the rules concerning presentation of credible evidence are particularly tight, a representative of the prosecutor's office quotes [as evidence] transcripts monitored from a radio station which is assessed by the official propaganda as mendacious and subversive."[13]

In 1982 President Reagan signed a secret National Security Decision Directive (NSDD 32) that authorized a range of measures to neutralize efforts of the Soviet Union to maintain its hold on Eastern Europe. The measures included increased propaganda. Shortwave radios were smuggled into Poland via channels established by priests, agents, and representatives of American trade unions.[14] The dissident, Alexander Malachowski, listened in prison to the Polish service of the BBC on a small radio hidden under his long bushy beard.[15] Lech Walesa drove his guards in prison so crazy with the radio turned up full blast listening to the BBC, Radio Free Europe, and the Voice of America that at one point they told him it was broken.[16] On another occasion Walesa was incarcerated in an old hunting lodge. His guards discovered he was listening to the BBC and Radio Free Europe, and they changed his radio for a less-powerful set. Walesa, who was, after all, an electrician, took it apart and managed to make it pick up London. The guard would change it when Walesa was out of the room, and when he came back, Walesa would change it back again.[17]

When Walesa visited the United States in November 1989, he was asked how important RFE had been in the cause of Polish freedom. He replied that the degree could not even be described. "Would there be earth without the sun?" he asked.[18]

Radio had an important impact on *Zamizdat*. The circulation of *Zamizdat* rose from a maximum of eighty thousand when distributed on paper to many millions when transmitted by radio.[19]

Even members of the government got their information from the Radios. At the height of the crisis when a Central Committee member was asked whether Kuron and the other jailed dissident intellectuals had been released, he answered with a bitter smile: "I have just heard on the BBC that five more KOR members have been arrested."[20]

The impact was clearly seen. Stanislaw Kania, leader of the Polish Communist Party, told the Central Committee that it was no accident that leaflets circulating in Poland increasingly resembled broadcasts from RFE.[21] Deputies in parliament in August 1980 began to talk in the language of RFE.[22] Lech Walesa summarized the RFE achievement:

> When a democratic opposition emerged in Poland, the Polish Section of Radio Free Europe accompanied us every step of the way—during the explosion of August 1980, the unhappy days of December 1981, and all the subsequent months of our struggle. It was our radio station. But not only a radio station. Presenting works that were "on the red censorship list," it was our ministry of culture. Exposing absurd economic policies, it was our ministry of economics. Reacting to events promptly and pertinently, but above all, truthfully, it was our ministry of information.[23]

The Western Radios played an important role in Solidarity, but the repercussions were also felt beyond the Polish borders. Indeed, some believed that without the Western Radios and their impact in Poland there would have been no revolution in Russia. Bronislaw Geremek, the leader of the Solidarity caucus, said of Jan Nowak, the former director of RFE's Polish service, "We are here thanks to him."[24] In turn, Lev Timofeyev, the Soviet dissident and leader of the human rights group, Press Club Glasnost, said, "Without Poland's Solidarity, there would be no Gorbachev, nor Sakharov in Paris."[25]

USSR: The End of the Lie

"Solidarity was a manual for all citizens of the USSR," said Georgui Vatchnadze, a Georgian specialist in Moscow on Western Radios.[26] The manual was put to good use in 1980 and 1981 when there were wildcat strikes at car and tractor factories and other industrial plants and in coal mines in the Soviet Union. The CIA considered the resumption of jamming of the BBC, VOA, and DW in August 1980 after a gap of seven years (despite the risk of giving the West an additional grievance that could be used against them at the Conference on Security and Cooperation in Europe [CSCE] Review Conference due in Madrid the following November) and showed that the Russians were more concerned about their own domestic labor and economic situation than the CIA had previously imagined.[27] But the jamming did not stop the Polish story from being heard throughout the Soviet Union. Curiously enough, the chief censor of the Soviet Union approved the publication of a book by Vatchnadze in 1981 on the role of the Western press and international Radios in the events in Poland. The print run was three hundred thousand. Vatchnadze's view is that perestroika would not have taken place without Western Radios.

Senior members of the nomenklatura received transcripts of the highlights of the foreign radios and, therefore, knew well what was being broadcast. To receive the transcripts was an honor. In Georgia, with a population of five million, only three copies were distributed, according to Vatchnadze. Vitaly Korotich, one-time editor of the influential magazine, *Ogonyok*, recounted how every day a gun-carrying man from the office of the Central Committee of the Communist Party would deliver to him the transcripts.[28] For Korotich the paradox was that jamming tried to prevent unimportant people from hearing the news from the West. But the very people who were powerful enough to influence change were those who got the contents of the Radios in the transcripts. The fish rotted from the head.

The transcripts took on a new role in 1987 and afterward, according to Leonid Kravchenko, head of Soviet television until the 1991 coup.[29] He believed that Deutsche Welle wanted to cause problems between the conservative Yegor Ligachev and Gorbachev. They created an image of Ligachev as a dangerous opponent of Gorbachev. Yegor Yakovlev, the liberal strategist, they portrayed as the only person on whom Gorbachev could really rely. Kravchenko continued:

> This work of Deutsche Welle was very effective because the people who were passing on this information to them were quite influential people in the Soviet Union. The time came when I began to feel some of our leaders became very nervous when they read some of this information. I think that when the well-known conflict came between Ligachev and Yakovlev, maybe not a decisive role, but a very important role, was played by the Deutsche Welle broadcasts and the broadcasts of some other Radios that focused on this theme. Sometimes you will see in

Gorbachev's speeches phrases such as "people are trying to make me believe." That is purely a reference by him to what he has been reading in these monitoring reports.

Botho Kirsch, head of the East European editorial desk of DW, later denied that anyone passed information to DW. The broadcasts were based on published material, he said.[30]

The Russians had dusted off in 1982 a League of Nations convention they had signed in 1936, but never ratified, which urged states to prohibit any transmission detrimental to international understanding. They ratified it on September 17, 1982. The United States had never been a party to the convention. Other Western countries repudiated it. By 1985 the Russians were admitting they jammed.[31]

In the early eighties the Soviet press became increasingly preoccupied with countering the Radios' propaganda. Questions the newspapers felt they had to deal with included:

1. Why does the Soviet Union not set an example in the matter of radical disarmament?[32]

2. Why is there only one candidate in elections to the Soviets in the Soviet Union, whereas in other countries there are several?[33]

3. In view of the present shortage of labor, why are workers from capitalist countries not invited to take jobs in the Soviet Union?[34]

4. How do you regard the assertions of anti-Soviet propaganda that we are incapable of feeding ourselves?[35]

The Russian military considered the Radios dangerous exploiters of Soviet areas of vulnerability. In an article in *Izvestia* in 1984 General Aleksei Epishev, chief of the main political directorate of the Soviet Army and Navy, listed areas of vulnerability that included campaigns in defense of human rights, publicity about Poland, and support for national self-determination. Fanning nationalist sentiments, Western Radio stations persistently stressed the uniqueness of the nationalities' culture and customs, the purity of their language. Attempts to sow the poisonous seeds of religious fanaticism and playing on the feelings of believers for subversive purposes were being stepped up, he wrote. RFE/RL was especially dangerous to the Soviet Union because of their "inflammatory and hostile activity," said Epishev. He quoted President Chernenko's warning of June 1983 of "attempts to organize a real information and propaganda intervention against us and to turn radio and television channels into an instrument of interference in states' internal affairs and the execution of subversive acts."[36]

The Soviet government admitted the role of the Radios in specific incidents. The Soviet press mounted an unusually bitter attack on Western Radios for their role in publicizing nationalist demonstrations in the Soviet Baltic republics on August 23, 1987.[37] The demonstrations were to mark the forty-eighth anniversary of the Hitler-Stalin pact, which handed the republics over to the Soviet Union. Officials said Western Radios had incited the demonstrations, which RFE/RL denied.[38] Janis Rozkalns, an organizer of the demonstration in Riga, the Latvian capital, estimated that more than five thousand people attended the event. "Without the Western radio, we might have had 100 or 200," the *New York Times* quoted him as saying.[39] Juarak Juriado, working for an Estonian émigré group based in Stockholm, said: "Those who want to arrange a demonstration don't have any possibility to get out their information, so, of course, the role of the radios is very big."[40]

It was only on the foreign radios that people could learn the truth about the war in Afghanistan and about Sakharov's protests. "We heard about him by foreign radio," said Sergei Stankevich, later to become a senior adviser to President Yeltsin. "At that time, everybody listened to foreign radio. Our reaction was blaming: We blamed the whole system and Brezhnev personally."[41]

It is, of course, impossible to be precise about the timing of the growth of disillusionment with Soviet propaganda and increasing reliance on the Western Radios. Two retired journalists from Radio Moscow, who did not want to be identified, had been ardent Party members when they started work in the fifties.[42] But they said in an interview in June 1991 that under the influence of Western Radios they began to experience doubts at the beginning of the seventies and to tell each other about them. By the beginning of the eighties not only did people in general believe news from Western Radios but they had also ceased to believe Soviet propaganda. Not everyone listened to the foreign Radios, but they would hear of it from others, for example, when they traveled to work on the metro in the morning.

Soviet Area Audience and Opinion Research (SAAOR) at RFE/RL estimated in 1984 that VOA reached 14–18 percent of the adult population during an average week. RL had 8–12 percent, the BBC 7–10 percent, and DW 3–6 percent.[43] A CIA report of late 1985, which looks as if it might have come from an émigré, gave an unusual slant on such figures:

> In addition to being harder to listen to due to jamming, Radio Liberty was less popular because of its pervasive pessimism about events in the Soviet Union and Soviet life. Stories about arrests, for example, tended

to subdue rather than rally those who opposed the government. [DELE-
TION] listening to Radio Liberty was seen as masochistic, because it focused the listener on the negative aspects of his surroundings rather
than providing an optimistic view of alternatives. VOA and the BBC, on
the other hand, were more optimistic and broadcast more of a variety of
stories about the positive aspects of Western life and achievements.
They had a much more positive impact on their Soviet listeners.[44]

The disaster at the Chernobyl nuclear plant on April 26, 1986, was
"the end of the lie," as the French historian, Hélène Carrère d'Encausse,
termed it.[45] Western Radios saw to it that nothing could ever be the same
again. It was not that the Radios had never exposed a lie before. What
made this lie a turning point was the effect of the explosion on so many
citizens and the length of time before their government told them the
truth. The repercussions of Chernobyl pointed up Solzhenitsyn's adage
that "one word of truth is of more weight than all the world."[46]

Solzhenitsyn considered the lie had become a pillar of the state, and
there had been many lies.[47] Even while the Kremlin was still denying on
September 1, 1983, that they had shot down the Korean Airlines pas-
senger plane, KAL flight 7, Radio Liberty was broadcasting tapes of the
airliner's last minutes. Later, after the Kremlin admitted it had shot it
down, but claimed it was flying without lights, Radio Liberty aired the
tape of the interceptor pilot's report that he could see its strobe lights.[48]
Eight years later the pilot, Lieutenant Colonel Gennadi Osipovich, admitted to *Izvestia* that he had been ordered by high Soviet officials to lie.[49]
In fact, if the Russians had come clean from the start, they would largely
have denied the Americans the propaganda triumph. The inquiry of the
International Civil Aviation Organization in 1993 concluded that the
USSR air defense command assumed that the aircraft was a U.S. military
reconnaissance plane before they ordered its destruction.[50]

There were plenty of jokes about the lies:

Q: Is Comrade Nyetyev the greatest and most important inventor of all time?

A: In principle, yes. Comrade Nyetyev invented toilet paper, the
electric razor, the registry office, the automatic fleatrap, the ul-
tra–short wave, and the beer glass. But Comrade Potalov was an
even greater inventor.

Q: Why? Did he invent more things?

A: No. He invented Comrade Nyetyev.[51]

The humor was not always intentional. Andrei Sakharov, the dissident Soviet academician, and his wife, Elena Bonner, once got into a taxi in Moscow manned by a loquacious driver. He gave them a rambling account of his family problems and their history. He tried to recall the date of one particular incident. "You know," he said. "It was the year the Czechs invaded the Soviet Union."[52]

Sometimes the lie was a sin of omission, which people learned about from Western Radios. Such was the caviar scandal in 1979. Caviar was hidden in cans labeled as herring and sold to luxury stores or exported at the price of caviar. The price difference between herring and caviar was pocketed by the organizers of the network, the Western Radios explained.[53]

Yevtushenko said the truth had been replaced by silence and silence was a lie.[54] The silence was censorship although censorship did not legally exist in the Soviet Union.[55] Indeed, Karl Marx had pointed out its dangers in 1842: "A censored press only serves to demoralize. That greatest of vices, hypocrisy, is inseparable from it. The government hears only its own voice while all the time deceiving itself, affecting to hear the voice of the people while demanding that they also support the pretense."[56]

Censorship was precisely regulated. The list of what was to be omitted was laid down to every censor.[57] It included:

- The itineraries of trips and locations of stopovers or speeches of members and candidate members of the Politburo.
- Information about the organs of Soviet censorship that discloses the character, organization, and method of their work.
- Activities of the organs of state security and Soviet intelligence organs.
- The amount of crime, the number of people engaged in criminal behavior, the number arrested, the number convicted.
- Information about the existence of correctional labor camps.
- Facts about the physical condition, illnesses, and death rates of all prisoners in all localities.
- The number of illiterate people.
- Reports about the human victims of accidents, wrecks, and fires.
- Information about the consequences of catastrophic earthquakes, tidal waves, floods, and other natural calamities.
- Calculations of the relative purchasing power of the ruble and the hard currency of foreign states.
- The size of the total wage fund [i.e., wages paid to the population], or the amount of money that comprises the population's purchasing power, or the balance of income and expenditure of the population.

- Information about hostile actions by the population or responsible officials of foreign states against representatives or citizens of the Soviet Union.
- The correlation between the cost of services for foreign tourists in the Soviet Union and the selling price of tourist trips in the Soviet Union.
- Information about export to foreign countries of arms, ammunition, military technology, military equipment.
- Information suggesting a low moral political condition of the armed forces, unsatisfactory military discipline, abnormal relations among soldiers or between them and the population.
- The number of drug addicts.
- Information about occupational injuries.
- Information about the audibility of the radio stations of foreign states in the Soviet Union.
- Information about the duration of all union training sessions for athletes; information about the rates of pay for athletes; information about the money prizes for good results in sports competitions; information about the financing, maintenance, and staff of athletic teams.

At the time of the Afghanistan war the Politiburo permitted only one report of a death or of a wound per month among Soviet service personnel.[58]

There were also abundant instructions on what should be published. A twenty-five page guidance manual published by TASS in a limited edition of only 350 laid down that acquired immunodeficiency syndrome (AIDS) had to be angled to show it was a disease of the West.[59] The purpose of newspapers was to propagandize the Soviet way of life. It was a newspaper's duty to tell of the joy of freely given labor. Entertainment for entertainment's sake was forbidden. In fact, censorship was the ally of the Radios. Its existence was one of the main reasons why people listened to radio.

A. O. Udachin was a soldier stationed in East Germany. In 1984 he was convicted of high treason, refusal to return from abroad, and participation in an anti-Soviet organization. The verdict said he had listened to foreign radio broadcasts on the BBC and the VOA. Under their impact he formed a negative attitude toward the Soviet state. He decided to go to the West and reached the Berlin Wall. "I looked at the guards, spotlights and barbed wire and realized it was impossible to cross. I sat for a while on a bench in Alexanderplatz and then stood up and started walking back. Six hours later I was arrested by the East German police."[60] The reference to listening to foreign radios was not untypical in such cases.

Article 32 of the Principles of Criminal Legislation of the USSR and the Union Republics obliged judges to take such matters into account in a character appraisal that weighed in the sentencing. Writing to foreign radios and even having a friend who had gone to work for Radio Liberty were cited in such cases, not that measures were taken against all who wrote to Western radio stations.

There seem to have been very few cases where Western radio stations were the basis of the main charge in an indictment. But Dmitrii Mazur, the Ukrainian dissident, was accused of switching on a radio at a bus stop in January 1980. He listened for two minutes to a broadcast by an unidentified station that said that Soviet troops were responsible for atrocities in Afghanistan. He got six years in strict-regime camps and five years in exile for "anti-Soviet agitation and propaganda."[61]

Victor Davydov, a law student, was picked up by the KGB on February 9, 1984, at his family's apartment in the city of Kuybyshev and was informed several hours before the official announcement that President Yuri Andropov was dead. "They detained me because they did not want me to listen to what Western radio commentators would say about Andropov and pass it on to my friends at university," Davydov said. He was well known as a devoted listener. In 1976 he was arrested for tape-recording readings of Aleksandr Solzhenitsyn's novel, *The Gulag Archipelago*, and passing on copies. He was committed to a psychiatric hospital for one month.[62] As late as 1986 the sentence against A. N. Mironov started by declaring that he "systematically listened to broadcasts of foreign radio stations, including subversive ones."[63]

No one knows how many Soviet citizens learned of Chernobyl from Western Radios. But it is unlikely to have been very different from percentages in Eastern Europe, where some figures are available. According to an RFE/RL survey, 28 percent heard of it by word of mouth and 24 percent from local media. But by far the largest group heard of it from external broadcasts, 45 percent.[64] The explosion took place at 0123 on Saturday, April 26, but not until nearly three days after the disaster struck, at 2100 on Monday, April 28, did the Russian government make a terse announcement. It was the seventh item in the main evening television news program. On May Day a fuller announcement appeared, but that gave little idea of the seriousness of the disaster. The Soviet media were more preoccupied with a cycle race in Kiev than with Chernobyl.

A reporter from Soviet television interviewed some British tourists outside the Rossiya Hotel in Moscow on May Day. Ian Smith, a Devon businessman, told him they had cut short their tour around the country.

A representative of Thomson Holidays had told the the tourists that an atomic explosion had allegedly taken place in the Soviet Union. The city of Kiev had been evacuated. "The situation in Kiev is normal," retorted the interviewer. Meanwhile in Kiev officials were helping to coordinate the relocation of tens of thousands of refugees. Extra cashiers had to be put on duty at the ticket booths at the railway station to cope with the long queues. Aeroflot offices also had to cope with long lines.[65]

Clips of cows grazing near the reactor, which had been broadcast on television in the days following the accident, were now revealed as false.[66] In the previous February Gorbachev had appointed the liberal-minded Alexandr Yakolev as the Central Committee secretary in charge of the media, and he had put his own allies in charge of important national publications.[67] The embarrassment of the cover-up helped drive Gorbachev in late 1986 into full-scale glasnost.[68] With good reason academician Valery Legasov, the chemist who went to sort out the mess, likened the historical significance of Chernobyl to the eruption of Mount Vesuvius that buried Pompeii in hot ashes in A.D. 79.

A Soviet embassy official in Washington excused the cover-up as an attempt not to demoralize people. "In this regard we treat the population as children," he said.[69]

The minister of energy and electrification, A. I. Mayorets, had only one year earlier, on May 19, 1985, issued an order stipulating: "Information about the unfavorable ecological impact of energy-related facilities (the effect of electromagnetic fields, irradiation, contamination of air, water, and soil) on operational personnel, the population and the environment shall not be reported openly in the press or broadcast on radio or television."[70]

As Grigori Medvedev, a nuclear engineer, commented on Chernobyl, "Failure to publicise mishaps always has unexpected consequences: it makes people careless and complacent."[71]

The news of the Chernobyl disaster brought to Russians by the Western Radios was the most shattering blow to communist belief they had ever experienced. The superiority of Soviet science, epitomized in the first man in space, was a basic tenet of communism. The destruction of Chernobyl destroyed that tenet.

Leszek Kolakowski, the Polish philosopher, explained the communist lie thus:

> Communism lives on inevitably impossible promises. Because its legitimacy is based upon expectations which necessarily will not be fulfilled. Because its inherited ideology cannot be dismissed, and at the same

time it is in glaring contradiction to reality. So, in order to keep this legitimacy principle alive, they have to keep the mendacious facade without which they would fall apart. It is perhaps the most oppressive part of life under communism. Not terror, not exploitation, but the all-pervading lie, felt by everybody, known to everybody. It is something which makes life intolerable for people under communism.[72]

The Marquis de Custine, who traveled in Russia under the czars in the nineteenth century, would have said the lie was endemic in Russian society. Custine met a young Englishman whose two younger brothers had drowned in a ferry accident while sailing for Peterhoff. Some of the rumours about the drownings on that day said two thousand had drowned. An Italian painter who later recounted the story—his tally was four hundred drowned—would talk only in a whisper "because the Emperor has forbidden that it should be spoken of." "A silence more frightful than the evil itself everywhere reigned," wrote Custine, "and only two lines about it in the *Gazette* and no details."

The French nobleman condemned Russian society: "Hitherto I had been accustomed to believe that a man could no more dispense with truth for his mind than with sun and air for his body; but my Russian journey has undeceived me. Truth is only needful to elevated minds or to advanced nations; the vulgar accommodate themselves to the falsehoods favorable to their passions and habits; here, to lie, is to protect society, to speak the truth is to overthrow the state."[73]

Suffering under a similar burden nearly one and one-half centuries later, the Russian poet, Yevgeny Yevtushenko, said, "One day it will be normal, not courageous, to write the truth."[74]

Glasnost brought that day nearer, but, paradoxically, the Western Radios were needed to help bring about glasnost. In late 1987 several dozen independent publications started of which the largest was the magazine *Glasnost*. But when the editor, Sergei Grigoryants, tried to register it with the appropriate authority, he was told he could not because his magazine did not represent anything, that is, no official Soviet entity. Therefore, when the typed copies were sent by post, they were confiscated. Grigoryants commented, "What really counts is that foreign radio stations broadcast our material in Russian-language programs beamed to the Soviet Union."[75]

Glasnost opened up the international airwaves. In October 1987 there was a live television linkup between Moscow and Washington in which Senator Daniel Moynihan was able to tell the Soviet audience that they lived in a "human rights hell" where restrictions on emigration and press freedom were worse than those under the czar. The program was seen by an estimated 150 million Soviet viewers. During the previous March Margaret Thatcher, the British prime minister, on a visit to Moscow gave a long uncensored interview on Soviet television.[76]

The government continued to debate whether or not jamming should be ended. Sergei Lapin, one-time head of TASS, although a conservative, wanted it to end, as did the liberal Yakovlev. Kryuchkov, the KGB chief, and Ligachev, wanted it to continue. There was even a hassle about who should pay for it. The KGB wanted it transferred to Gostelradio, the Soviet broadcasting authority, who refused. "The cemeteries have never belonged to the Ministry of Health," Henrikas Yushkiavitshus, vice-chairman of the TV and Radio Committee told them.[77]

Jamming started to decrease from January 1987, when the BBC Russian service was clear. Most VOA transmissions to the Soviet Union and the communist bloc were not jammed after May 1987. Polish transmissions of the VOA, RFE, and BBC were clear after January 1988.[78] But the jammers that had been released were used to increase the jamming of RL, and it was not until 2100 Central European time on Tuesday, November 29, 1988, that RL and the Estonian, Latvian and Lithuanian transmissions of RFE were clear.[79]

The Central Committee had become accustomed to seeing CNN during the Moscow Summit in May 1988. So Gostelradio transmitted it on channel 24 in Moscow. They did not announce the frequency, but it soon became widely known. And so the needs of the rulers for the most important TV news station in the world gave a news bonus to the person in the street with important repercussions three years later.[80]

RFE/RL: Kitchen of the Stinking Fish of False Reports

At 2147 on Saturday, February 21, 1981, the headquarters of RFE/RL in Munich was rocked by a bomb. It did extensive damage, particularly to the Czech studios, and four employees were injured. The tape machines kept rolling, and all services continued on the air. The technicians on duty in the central control room, Nestor Bahrjanyi and Heinrich Lutz, picked themselves up off the floor and calmly loaded extra tapes. At about 2300 the West German police evacuated the building. As the tapes in the unmanned control room ran out, the transmitting stations took over the compilation of the programs with tapes. The total number of minutes lost on all services was limited to less than one hour.[81] By 1445 on the Sunday, Glenn Ferguson, president of RFE/RL, could issue a notice to his staff telling them that all normal programming was progressing and all studios were operational.[82] Police estimates of the size of the bomb ranged as high as twenty-five kilos. The explosive was of a type unavailable anywhere in Western Europe except, perhaps, to the military.[83] The damage exceeded $2 million.[84]

Who did it? German police and American investigators believed at the time that the Czechs were most probably responsible.[85]

On January 3, 1991, however, the American ABC TV network ran a program in the *Primetime Live* series on the Venezuelan terrorist, Carlos "the Jackal" (Ilich Ramirez Sanchez), and claimed he was responsible for the RFE/RL bombing.[86] He had done it at the instigation of President Nicolai Ceausescu of Romania. Carlos met Ceausescu and soon went off on a spree, killing the president's critics. When Carlos got back to Romania, he was a welcome guest at the Diplomats Club. The ABC correspondent Pierre Salinger described his life style:

> He drank heavily at this club almost every night. Ceausescu made sure it was well stocked with eager to please dancers and prostitutes. Sometimes Carlos was summoned to Ceausescu's bedroom. There the brooding president listened for hours to Radio Free Europe's attacks on his rule and then pleaded with Carlos to do something about it. Finally Carlos did: he slipped past security at Radio Free Europe headquarters in Munich and placed more than 40 pounds of plastic explosives near the foundation of this building. Those on duty on February 21st 1981, remember a sudden flash of white light.[87]

Salinger gave no sources for the story. Similar reports, also unsourced, appeared in the German newspaper, *Bild Zeitung,* on January 13, 1991, and in a book on the Jackal published in 1993. In *To the Ends of the Earth: The Hunt for the Jackal* David Yallop said Carlos planned the attack from East Berlin. Yallop erroneously states that the Carlos group demolished the radio station.[88] Richard Cummings, RFE/RL director of security, said in September 1993 that documents from the former East German Intelligence Service and other sources showed that Carlos was paid $1 million by Ceausescu with the support of other East European intelligence services to carry out the bombing, which Carlos planned while in Budapest.[89] A 1981 Hungarian secret police report said a Hungarian telephone tap had intercepted a call from Munich to Budapest on the day of the bombing in which an associate of Carlos in Munich reported the successful detonation to Carlos.[90]

On August 16, 1991, however, Oleg Kalugin, the former KGB general, had visited the RFE/RL headquarters in Munich, with, as he told the staff, "a certain amount of trepidation," and he claimed the KGB had been behind the bombing. Kalugin said there had been no intent to injure anybody, but he said the KGB hoped the explosion would scare the German neighbors. He said the KGB had hoped the neighbors' complaints would cause the German government to tell RFE/RL to leave Germany.[91] Kalugin later wrote that the bomb had been planted by an East German agent.[92]

A Czech spy who had infiltrated RFE had drawn up plans to bomb RFE earlier. On September 14, 1993, Pavel Minarik was sentenced in Prague to four years in prison for planning to blow up the Munich headquarters while working there in the seventies. Minarik submitted to Jaroslav Lis (code-named "Necasek"), his boss in the State Security Agency, at least three detailed plans. One of the plans explained: "The janitors in the RFE building are foreign workers. They use carts for their work. I will place the explosive in one of the carts and push it near the broadcasting panel. I assure you I would prepare the operation carefully and wisely."

He had the decency to propose telephoning fifteen minutes before the explosion to allow the staff to leave the building. But when he put forward his final scheme in 1973, his boss, Necasek, told him that the international situation was not favorable for the execution of the plan; nothing ever came of it.[93] Unless, of course, it was the Czechs who blew up the building in 1981.

Oleg Tumanov, the head of the Russian service of RL, was also a plant, this time by the KGB. Kalugin thought Tumanov's main contribution to the work of the KGB was in helping the KGB to spread rumors and disinformation and create conflict among the RL staff. He also told the KGB which of his colleagues might be suitable for recruitment or susceptible to blackmail because of their sexual proclivities. Through Tumanov the KGB recruited two other Radio Liberty employees. Polish intelligence also had two Polish émigré agents on the staff. Tumanov eventually had to flee from Germany when a KGB officer, who knew about his KGB ties, defected. Tumanov subsequently asked RFE/RL for his pension. They did not give it to him.[94] Many spooks were planted in many news organizations during the Cold War, but it is difficult ever to determine that they corrupted the news. Most news organizations' checking systems prevented it.

An attack of a milder kind on Radio Liberty came in 1985 in a Russian film *Can-Can in the English Park*. It was a thriller about a KGB man who infiltrated RL in its building alongside the English Park in Munich that attracted big audiences. The CIA financed RL, the film declared, and it showed how the station was manned by liars and traitors. The agent broke into the archives and obtained the names of the station's informants. One critic commented: "It shows in a new light the kitchen in which the stinking fish of false reports is prepared."[95]

By a curious irony the reconstruction of the RFE/RL headquarters, equipment replacement, and improved security measures after the bombing soaked up most of the $4 million supplemental appropriation that the new Reagan administration had intended would give a new lease of life to RFE/RL through improved programming.[96] There had been a number of calls for a reinvigoration of RFE/RL, including one from former President Nixon.[97] On July 19, 1982, President Reagan announced:

> We intend to move forward consistent with budgetary requirements with a program to modernize our primary means of international communication, our international radio system. This plan of modernization for a relatively modest expenditure over a number of years will make it easier for millions of people living under Communist rule to hear the truth about the struggle for the world going on today between the forces of totalitarianism and freedom. The sad fact is that the Voice of America, Radio Free Europe and Radio Liberty have been neglected for many years. Their equipment is old and deteriorating, their programming resources strained. Little has been done to counter the jamming that has intensified in recent years.[98]

The Board for International Broadcasting, while admitting that the costs of the long-term modernization effort would be substantial, wanted them seen in perspective. The cost of the proposed MX missile would be some $26 billion, but the total federal expenditure since 1949 on RFE and RL had barely exceeded $1.2 billion, it said in its 1983 report.[99] RFE/RL got $21.3 million for facility modernization and program enhancement, and the annual appropriation was also increased. For the first time in fifteen years RFE/RL could increase rather than reduce its activities.[100]

The new administration brought in right-wingers to run the stations. Frank Shakespeare, a former USIA director, became chairman of the Board for International Broadcasting. Shortly after his appointment the boards of the BIB and the Radios were merged after the Pell Amendment, which was introduced into the Senate in the autumn of 1982. Shakespeare brought in James L. Buckley, the former New York senator, as president of RFE/RL. George Bailey, an American who had worked for the right-wing Springer press group in Germany, became head of Radio Liberty, and George Urban, a former BBC broadcaster of Hungarian origin, became head of RFE. "Shakespeare, Bailey and I cleared out the détenteniks from RFE," Urban later recalled.[101]

The RFE executive, Ralph Walter, believed that domestic political pressures on RFE/RL only came after the formation of BIB.[102] In other words, the Radios were more independent politically when they were financed by the CIA.

Congressman Larry Smith visited RFE/RL in Munich in February 1985 at the request of Congressman Daniel A. Mica, chairman of the Subcommittee on International Operations, in preparation for the upcoming budget authorization request for fiscal years 1986 and 1987. He was accompanied by subcommittee staff. The report was scathing:

> It is apparently common knowledge in Munich that the Directors of the radios were hired by the Chairman of the Board for International Broadcasting. In fact, some even volunteered the fact that George Urban, Director for RFE, was hired in total disregard of the views of the President of RFE/RL Inc. Other [sic] intimated that, as a result, both Directors of the radios "beat up" on Buckley.
>
> In the end, it appears that greater latitude may have devolved to the Directors of the radios, the direct opposite of what Congress had intended, as a result of both the change in the Boards and the reshuffling of senior management. BIB, in an attempt to involve itself in the daily operations of RFE/RL, has weakened the position of the President, eliminated the Vice President for Program Policy, resulting in a de facto increase in the independence of the individual radios.
>
> Finally and most importantly, in our estimation BIB can no longer objectively oversee, as directed by law, the radios as a result of its active involvement in its daily operations.[103]

The reviewing party felt there were instances of questionable programming, partly because of a lack of overview. There was evidence that the two directors had moved the Radios to a much less subtle, uniform anticommunist line. The directors considered the situation in Eastern Europe and the Soviet Union so tenuous that the Soviet Union could be on the verge of collapse, and they implied that the West should push harder to precipitate the fall of the Soviet Union. The review team did not appreciate the prescience of Urban and Bailey and thought their views almost too dramatic.

VOA: Provocative Insinuations

President Reagan not only gave a new lease on life to RFE/RL when he took office in January 1981 but also showered the VOA with his munificence. The allocation was $1.3 billion, mainly to modernize transmitters, beginning in fiscal 1984 and running through fiscal 1989. But spending money can sometimes be more difficult than allocating it. By the beginning of fiscal 1989 not one shortwave relay station had been built, and the total then obligated was only $360 million. Three mediumwave stations were on the air.

The USIA inspector general blamed the VOA because its approach to modernization was too time consuming. "VOA has frittered away its opportunity to modernize," Donald Levine, a former official in VOA's engineering division, charged.[104]

The increase in broadcasting hours to the Soviet Union and Eastern Europe was more successful than the capital expenditure program. It rose sharply, with an increase of 30 percent, from 255 hours 30 minutes a week in December 1980 to 332 hours 30 minutes in December 1984. A new service in Azerbaijani started on July 4, 1982, and hours of transmission were increased in the services in Estonian, Georgian, Latvian, Lithuanian, Polish, Russian, Ukrainian, and Uzbek.[105]

Despite the brouhaha about more propaganda the VOA operating budget obligations increased by less in percentage terms in the period from fiscal 1982 to fiscal 1988 than in the same prior period. They went up by 56 percent from 1976 to 1982 to $116,000,000 and by 52 percent from 1982 to 1988 to $168,000,000. Staff numbers increased by a slightly higher rate in the Reagan period at 14 percent to 2,836 compared with 10 percent to 2,269 in the prior period.[106]

Quality improved. The VOA admitted that in the past there had been listener perceptions of triviality or cultural insensitivity in projecting America, which it was seeking to correct.[107] Even Solzhenitsyn, from a particularly partial point of view, believed by 1984 that the VOA had improved.[108] He had attacked the VOA in May 1980 because they were "constantly trying not to arouse the anger of the Soviet leadership. In their zeal to serve détente they remove everything from their programs which might irritate the Communists in power."[109] Religious broadcasting, particularly evangelical, increased as did business programming. A new style of editorial was introduced in 1982, which was intended to forcefully advocate the values of the West.[110]

In October 1985 the VOA restarted its broadcasting to Western Europe after a hiatus of twenty-five years.[111] This gap points up an important difference between the policies of the BBC and the VOA. One of the reasons the BBC served the world, at least with its English-language services, and did not only broadcast to, say, Eastern Europe, was that it did not want to appear to be anticommunist. The VOA had no such qualms.

The resurgence of the VOA was part of President Reagan's determination to combat the Soviet propaganda offensive. National Security Decision Directive 45 (NSDD 45) of July 15, 1982, stressed that international broadcasting constituted an important instrument of U.S. national security policy. It instructed that VOA's commentary and analysis should incorporate "vigorous advocacy of current policy positions of the U.S. Government."[112] National Security Decision Directive 77 (NSDD 77) of January 14, 1983, outlined the structure of the NSC's Special Planning Group on Public Diplomacy (SPGPD). Its high-powered membership included the secretary of state, the secretary of defense, and the director of the USIA. The SPGPD had four interagency committees, one of which was the International Broadcasting Committee (IBC). According to NSDD 77, the committee was responsible for the planning and coordination of international broadcasting activities sponsored by the U.S. government.[113] "The truth is mankind's best hope for a better world," said President Reagan in 1983. "That's why in times like this few assets are more important than the Voice of America and Radio Liberty as our primary means of getting truth to the Russian people."[114]

Having a close friend and confidante of the president as director of the USIA during most of the eighties was very good for the VOA. Charles Z. Wick, former business representative of Tommy Dorsey, had his fair share of mistakes, including secretly taping telephone calls. But he expanded the activities of the Voice and ensured there was plenty of money available to do it.[115]

Strange use of VOA broadcasts to transmit messages via music during the USIA directorship of Wick, the former music arranger, came to light in the nineties. Nodar Djin claimed in a court hearing against the VOA that in 1985 he had been fired because he complained about an order to broadcast a suspicious message. The message, according to Djin, was to someone in the Soviet Union. As ABC News put it:

> The secret message said that a listener in a remote village in the Soviet republic of Georgia requested to hear a popular Georgian folk song—a song that the broadcast said had been played the night before at a concert in Washington, D.C. But there had been no concert and Djin said the folk tune was so popular it was heard every day in Georgia, so why request it? The message was a fabrication, which Djin said he had been ordered to keep secret.[116]

According to court documents, the order to broadcast the clandestine message came from Charles Wick. ABC claimed VOA broadcast at least five covert messages during Wick's tenure. Alan Silverman, another broadcaster, was ordered to play a song at a specific time from the Rod Stewart album, "Foolish Behavior." Wick did not remember the Silverman incident, but said it would be appropriate under those conditions of national security and the U.S. national interest. Mary Bittermann, however, who ran the VOA under President Carter, said clandestine messages had no place there.

The CIA used the VOA to transmit information to Solidarity, using complex codes or music. Wick recalled: "They would come in with a request for a message to be sent. Because it was in the national interest, so long as it didn't hurt the integrity of the Voice, we would broadcast it."[117] Every week at a different time a message on U.S. policies was transmitted over the VOA.[118]

RFE/RL were also involved in transmitting a coded message in 1982, although the senior executives only acceded under protest to what they considered to be an outrageous request and after an assurance that it was a one time exception and not the start of a slide down a slippery slope.[119] BBC executives have disclaimed any knowledge that they were used by MI6 to transmit coded messages.

Nikita Khrushchev attacked jazz as "the kind of music that gives you a feeling of nausea and a pain in the stomach." He thought it sounded like "a streetcar screeching to a halt."[120] Most of the young people of the bloc did not share his views. Popular music was important for the Radios because it attracted people to a part of Western culture. Moreover, they tuned in to listen to the music, but the news and other programs were woven in with the music and they heard them too. The unstructured character of jazz in itself represented freedom for many.

Willis Conover who hosted "Music USA" for the VOA from 1955 until he died in 1996, was the best known of the music presenters. "For much of the world over the past 40 years, Willis Conover was jazz and he was the Voice of America," Geoffrey Cowan, the VOA's director, said when Conover died.[121] During the height of the cold war, Conover may have had as many as 30 million listeners, he added. When he started broadcasting, some foolish Congressmen attacked his program, which they said was wasting taxpayers' money and giving the United States a bad image.

When the western Radios started broadcasting rock and pop music, young people recorded it on x-ray film and later on tapes.

Eventually the radios of the communist bloc had to give in and start broadcasting big beat music. On May 7, 1966, *Izvestia* complained that Soviet radio was "permeated with blatantly vulgar song counterfeits of every kind, oriented toward 'foreign fashions.' "[122] Twenty years after Andrei A. Zhdanov had launched for Stalin an offensive against "American influences" (including music), the battle had been lost on the music front.

Minsk, Pinsk. From his Hollywood days President Reagan would have appreciated the wonder that in 1988 in one day VOA had telephone calls to its call-in show from these two cities, so often the butt of the comics. Broadcasting had been revolutionized after the ending of jamming. The VOA was able to present panels and round tables, radio bridges to discuss such topics as legal changes in the Soviet Union and a weekly call-in show with young people phoning in to talk about Michael Jackson and pop music. "It's really quite remarkable," said Gerd von Doemming, head of the Soviet service, "Even Soviet operators help out in the conversations when we can't quite catch the name of the caller."[123]

The new atmosphere did not stop the Soviet Union from lodging a formal diplomatic protest on February 29, 1988, accusing the VOA of inciting public unrest in broadcasts to the Baltic republics of Lithuania, Estonia, and Latvia. "Among other things, these broadcasts have been crudely distorting historical facts, making provocative insinuations about the growth of nationalist sentiment in the Baltic republics of the Soviet Union and expressing U.S. support for forces that do not accept the social system in the country," TASS said.[124]

The USIA started a satellite television network, WORLDNET, in 1983. Hungarian state television was the first to take the programs in 1985.[125] Satellite television began to be received in homes in Eastern Europe, often with homemade dishes.

BBC: Mongooses Trying to Destroy Everything Snakelike

A listener in Kiev wrote to the BBC: "The BBC reception has been bad here, whereas the Voice of America and Deutsche Welle are much better heard—but we prefer your broadcasts."[126]

The Thatcher government in Britain followed the same policy as the Reagan administration in the United States by taking measures in 1981 to step up the audibility of its international broadcasting transmissions. The government approved a ten-year program of $207 million (£102 million).[127]

Despite cutbacks in the overall External Services current account budget, transmissions in Russian were increased in January 1980 after the invasion of Afghanistan, raising the total daily Russian output to 5.5 hours.[128] And ten days after the imposition of martial law in Poland in

December 1981 Polish language broadcasts were increased by about 25 percent. A week later jamming of Polish programs from jamming stations located on Soviet territory began. All shortwave transmissions were affected, but medium wavelengths remained free. The jamming of mediumwave transmissions would have had to have been done from within Poland.

Evidence of listening in Czechoslovakia came from a trade fair in Prague where one British exhibit included projection of slides with a voice track. A large proportion of the visitors recognized the voice as belonging to a member of the BBC Czechoslovak Section.[129] After, the Afghan invasion attacks on the BBC in the Soviet press increased and were more hostile than for some time. One article in *Izvestia* mentioned the Russian service's increase in transmission time and alleged that Britain was switching to an even more anti-Soviet style in its international radio programs.[130]

The debate on the nature of the BBC had continued throughout the cold war. Vladimir Artyomov dealt again with the BBC in magazine articles in November 1983: "The BBC is Fanning Psychological Warfare."[131] The theme was that the BBC surrounded itself with a "halo of objectivity and justice yet [is] striving at the same time to achieve its reactionary aims." When the BBC broadcast facts unfavorable to British policy, this was an example of "the jesuitically refined methods of the English bourgeoisie, the oldest in the world."[132] The purpose of broadcasting such news was to befuddle the listener into believing in the BBC's objectivity so that it might better infiltrate other items favorable to capitalism and subversive of the Soviet system.[133]

Some attacks, like this one by Vitaly Korotich, editor of the magazine, *Ogonyok*, were more direct and, indeed, positively vituperative:

> Sometimes BBC people behave like mongooses striving to destroy everything snakelike, like ferocious and exclusive exterminators of everything it is their job to combat. But whereas the mongoose's hatred is ultimately of use to people, the hatred of unobjective propagandists engenders chauvinism. The arrogation of the exclusive right to judge, pardon, execute, and sentence are throwbacks to bygone days and the black sails of British pirate admirals or the thick soles of colonists' shoes churning the dust on foreign roads.[134]

But the reactions of the Russian in the street were not necessarily the same as these extracts from letters of listeners and former listeners show:

I know that all radio stations lie, but you seem to me to be lying less than others.[135]

When I come home I open the window to receive oxygen for my lungs and turn on the BBC for oxygen for my mind.[136]

Reception is very bad, but people manage to hear: some in their dachas and some in the country, some under bridges and some on improved radio sets. Your work is not in vain.[137]

The policy laid down some years earlier by Alexander Lieven, then head of the East European services, on broadcasting to communist audiences evidently still worked: "We should not adopt an automatically hostile attitude, avoid the 'black and white' approach and, at all costs abstain from pettiness, pinpricks, rubbing salt into the wounds, sarcasm, polemics or superior 'holier than thou' or 'you are always wrong' attitudes. A cool detached, almost clinical approach is called for."[138]

The BBC also benefited by continuing to follow the policy laid down in World War II in dealing with Goebbels—never answer attacks. To do so gives the attacker the initiative.[139]

But glasnost eventually made an impact, and soon at least some officials were willing to be interviewed in Polish on the telephone from London.[140] By February 1986 a major reporting breakthrough came when a Russian-speaking specialist from the BBC External Services was allowed to attend the Twenty-seventh Party Congress of the CPSU.[141]

The opening up of Eastern Europe coincided within the BBC with the appointment in 1986 as managing director, BBC External Broadcasting, of John Tusa, an experienced broadcaster of Czech origin. He tackled the BBC's "pyschosis of poverty" and reinvigorated the organization with a new budgeting system, a renewal of the World Service, and systematic program evaluation.

11

REVOLUTIONS
(1989)

Poland: Influence of the Bagel-shaped Round Table

POLAND LIT THE TORCH that flamed throughout Eastern Europe in the 1989 Year of the Revolutions. The peculiarity of those East European revolutions was that it was communist countries in Europe that fell like dominoes and not capitalist countries in Asia, as the Americans had feared.

The photograph of the enormous bagel-shaped round table with a large floral centerpiece that was used for the "Round-Table" talks in Poland in February 1989 went round the world, including Eastern Europe. And soon dissidents in other countries in Eastern Europe were wanting and having their Round-Table talks.[1]

Students in Bucharest used the same slogans as had been used in Prague. RFE did programs on the role of the students in Prague and how the military had stayed in their barracks.[2]

The domino metaphor is, of course, misleading to the extent that neither the fall of the pieces nor the factors that caused them to fall were even and sequential. The Soviet Union played a sometimes anomalous role—at first ahead in reform and then slipping behind. The words *perestroika* and *glasnost*, born in the Soviet Union, were banned in the media of East Germany. During the Polish Round-Table talks, at one point a senior party official jokingly asked Lech Walesa to stop Adam Michnik from reading Soviet newspapers. But the flow of reform again changed direction when the Berlin Wall opened. The *New York Times* quoted the reaction of a Russian student, twenty-year-old Yuliana Pogosov: "Even with this it could take ten or twenty years for us to get so far."[3]

The extent to which governments permitted domestic media to cover revolutionary events in other East European countries and their treatment of them greatly varied. Some thought it was difficult to tell the difference between the programs of Budapest's Radio Kossuth and those of the VOA.[4] The official press and television of Hungary gave the Polish elections in June rapt attention. But in East Germany and Czechoslovakia coverage was sparse and hostile.

Cross-border Television: The Smuggled Camera

The relationship between Hungary and Romania in the run-up to the revolutions showed that the influence of radio and television was not only important when broadcast from outside Eastern Europe but also from within. Alajos Chrudinak, a Hungarian TV producer, said he had received many letters from Romanians saying, "You have made the revolution."[5]

Chrudinak was thrown out of the university after 1956 at the age of nineteen because of his association with the views of Imre Nagy, the Hungarian prime minister who was executed for his part in the revolution of 1956. He became a TV producer and in 1975 started a program called *International Studio* in which both journalists and politicians from both East and West participated and expressed wide-ranging views. The Party tried to stop it, and when that failed, they tried to censor it. Chrudinak justified the program by referring to the third basket of the Helsinki Accords. The agitprop head, who was in charge of agitation and propaganda, said that he was "spitting in the face of Hungarian foreign policy."[6]

He then made films for a weekly program called *Panorama*. In particular he addressed the question of minorities. The subject of the minorities in the Eastern bloc was at that time taboo and included, of course, the three million Hungarians in Romania. He got around the ban by shooting films on, for example, minority rights in the Sahara. Those programs were seen by the Hungarians across the border in Romania because they were able to watch Hungarian television. Hungarian television tended to be watched by groups of twenty to thirty people crowded around a TV set. The Hungarian viewers in Romania translated for the Romanian speakers.

Chrudinak interviewed Thatcher, Chancellor Kohl of West Germany, and President Mitterrand of France on what they thought of Ceausescu. He interviewed Eugène Ionesco, the playwright, and King Michael of Romania, even persuading the latter to make some remarks in Romanian. Then in May 1989 he went to Timisoara and shot a program on Laszlo Tokes, the Lutheran priest, then little known, who said: "It is enough that I shall speak. I shall destroy this wall of fear." The Hungarian program was seen in parts of Romania and the Romanian government decreed Chrudinak persona non grata. Four days before the uprising in Timisoara he found three Romanians who described on Hungarian television what had happened in the uprising in Brasov in 1987. That interview also was seen in parts of Romania.

When the Timisoara uprising started on December 15, the Romanian secret police, the Securitate, were amazed to see news reports on Hungarian TV received in Romania of what had happened in Tokes' church. How had a video camera got into the church? The answer was that Chrudinak had left it with the priest against precisely such an eventuality when he had interviewed him the previous May. Chrudinak was not only concerned with Romania. He also conducted a three-hour interview with Alexander Dubcek, the Czech leader who had been ousted by the Russians in 1968. And Czechs drove down to the Hungarian border to watch it.

East Germans watched Hungarian television to identify the best border crossings for their escapes. In Prague people who had never bothered to buy a television set to watch generally boring Czech television bought one to watch Soviet programs, which had become so interesting.

The flow of material between the communist countries had its slightly bizarre aspects. For example, on November 6, Soviet television broadcast an interview with Dubcek that had been supplied to it by the Czech samizdat videojournal. The sycophancy of Zhivkov, the Bulgarian leader, who arranged for Bulgarian television to relay the programs of the first Soviet television channel, blew up in his face when the Soviet media became engaged in glasnost and what were to him seditious sentiments were disseminated throughout Bulgaria.[7]

The country that had been most influenced by television, not from within the bloc but from the West, was, of course, East Germany. "The enemy of the people stands on the roof," said Walter Ulbricht, the East German leader. So dangerous did the Communists consider the impact on their people of the television from Western Germany—"electronic imperialism"—that at one period fighting brigades of the Communist Free German Youth (FDJ) clambered up onto roofs and cut down the antennas. But there were too many and they gave up.[8] Indeed, eventually the demand for West German television was so great that East Berlin fed the two main television stations, ARD and ZDF, into its cable television system.

The speed of playback from abroad of a story was well exemplified when the East Berlin police attacked the crowd during Gorbachev's visit on October 7. Television pictures were immediately beamed back into East Berlin by the West Germans.[9]

A survey of émigrés in 1985 showed that 82 percent of East Germans watched West German television regularly, 17 percent often or occasionally, and only 1 percent seldom. The contrast with East German television was startling. Only 10 percent tuned in often or daily, 18 percent occasionally, and 72 percent very seldom or never.[10]

An analysis of the attitudes of those peoples of Eastern Europe who listened to Western Radios and also watched Western television and those who could only listen to Western Radios would make a fascinating thesis.

Manipulation of the Radios: Mysterious Deaths

On November 18, 1989, the Voice of America and Radio Free Europe carried from Prague a report that a student had died in a police attack on Czech students at a rally the previous day.[11] The report was wrong. But it started a sequence of events that eventually brought down the communist government.

Czechs have traditionally had their feelings focused by youthful martyrs. Jan Palach burnt himself to death in 1969, and the rally on November 17 was the fiftieth anniversary of the funeral of Jan Opletal, the Czech student killed by the Nazis in 1939. What seemed highly likely was that it was a classic case of someone manipulating international radio to his own ends.

Where did the story come from? Was it from the government who wanted to scare the students off further protests? Or was it from the students or other opposition who wanted to provoke further protests? Or was it a plot by a group of Czech secret police, perhaps supported by the KGB? The Czech government of Vaclav Havel was so concerned to find out that it set up a ten-man parliamentary commission to investigate the violence of November 17, still called "the massacre."

The interim report of the commission, published in mid-1990, said that toward the end of 1988 a group of leading party figures met in secret, among whom was General Alois Lorenc, the head of the StB (the Czech secret police). They decided that the leadership of Milos Jakes and Miroslav Stepan could not survive and that eventually it would have to negotiate with the opposition. So they planned to remove the old leadership and infiltrate the dissident movement. Then a moderate leadership would negotiate with a divided and weakened opposition. The infiltration plan, code named Operation Wedge, was very successful. But removing Jakes and Stepan proved more difficult. So they decided to stage the killing of a student by the riot police on the revered Opletal anniversary date of November 17. They calculated that the public anger would be so great that it would topple the government.

Lieutenant Ludvik Zifcac, a secret police officer, infiltrated the student leadership. The students assembled at Opletal's grave in Vysehrad cemetery on the afternoon of November 17. One of the voices that advocated a march on the center of Prague was Zifcac's. When the students marched along the river bank of the Vltava, Zifcac led them up Narodni Street toward Wenceslas Square. The street was a police trap from which there was no escape. They attacked the students; 561 were injured and one faked death. In all the turmoil Zifcac fell to the ground, and his body was covered with a blanket. He was taken away in an unmarked ambulance.

A woman, Drahomira Drazska, who subsequently disappeared, went to Vaclav Benda, a well-known Charter 77 movement signatory, and told him the dead man was Martin Smid from the Faculty of Mathematics and Physics at the university. She said he was a friend of hers since childhood. Benda told Petr Uhl, a Civic Forum activitist who ran a news agency for foreign journalists. Uhl telephoned Michael Zantovsky, a Reuter correspondent, and told him. Zantovsky said, "I asked him if he was sure and he said he had an eyewitness and that the eyewitness is completely reliable and that he was 100 percent certain that a student was dead." Zantovsky filed his story, and it was quickly broadcast back to Czechoslovakia by the VOA and RFE.

There were two Martin Smids studying at the faculty. One of them was away. The other had been at the demonstration and went on television to show that he was uninjured.

The commission determined that on the night of November 17 General Lorenc had dinner at a safe house of the secret police with General Teslenko, the KGB's head of station in Prague, and General Viktor Grushko, who had flown in from Moscow three days earlier. During the meal they were interrupted by twenty-five phone calls. Later Lorenc and Grushko drove to the StB operational headquarters, where they spent much of the night. The next morning Grushko flew back to Moscow.

The commission believed that the Soviet leadership was involved in the plot. Grushko's reporting line was to General Kryuchkov, a member of Gorbachev's Politburo and head of the KGB.

"This incident probably as much as anything else caused huge demonstrations on November 20—about 200,000 people," Zantovsky said. "That started the whole thing and got the ball rolling." Zantovsky subsequently became Vaclav Havel's press secretary and later ambassador to the United States.[12]

So the communications vehicle that started the Czech revolution rolling was U.S. radio stations. But the mystery of the plot continued to thicken as the years went by. On January 30, 1992, the final report was presented to Parliament. It was published in full in *Rude Pravo* from February 5 to 7. It received little or no publication outside Czechoslovakia, and journalists and authors were writing articles and books about the plot based only on the interim report at least three years later. That was the more remarkable, given that the final report completely contradicted what had been said in the interim report.

In the summary of the interim report Milan Hulik, one of the most senior figures, said: "There is no doubt that the leading personality of the whole operation . . . was General Lorenc. . . . The contacts between Lorenc and KGB officials which have been discovered couldn't in my opinion point to any other conclusion than KGB connivance in the whole action."[13]

The main points of the final report were[14]

• The KGB were informed about what was going on, but it was not proved that they influenced events.

• The police action against the protesters was not planned in advance.

• The action was not undertaken to overthrow the conservative communist leadership.

• Ludvik Zifcak, who said he was ordered to pretend to be a dead student, was lying.

• Drahomira Drazska invented her whole story. She habitually invented stories and had a history of drug abuse.[14]

On May 2, 1995, Ludvik Zifcak began an eighteen-month jail term for abuse of power.[15]

The second great lie of the revolutions also, curiously enough, involved death. It was a question of the number who died in the revolution in Romania, although some would say it was not manipulation, only misinformation.

The story started with a Hungarian radio report on Tuesday, December 19 of brutal repression during demonstrations in Timisoara. The source was a Hungarian whose relatives were doctors in Timisoara. The radio broadcaster spoke of a real manhunt with soldiers going into houses and carrying out summary executions. On Wednesday, December 20, the day of Ceausescu's return from Iran, the East German news agency, ADN, announced that 3,000 to 4,000 people had been killed in

Timisoara. The source was Romanians living in East Germany who had telephoned relatives in Romania. The dead had been transported in trucks outside the town and been buried in a communal grave. Soldiers had fired on women with children, including pregnant women. The center of Timisoara was completely destroyed. The Yugoslav press followed up with more detail—demonstrators cut down with bayonets, children crushed under armored cars. By Friday, December 22 ADN had 4,600 dead in Timisoara, 1,860 wounded, 13,000 arrested, and 7,000 condemned to death. Hungarian television had 4,630 bodies discovered in a communal grave. Yugoslav television showed pictures of mutilated and tortured bodies.[16]

On Saturday, December 23 the *New York Times* carried an Associated Press story datelined Timisoara, December 22,[17] which said:

> Hundreds of people today were digging up mass graves discovered in the forest district of Timisoara, trying to find the remains of friends and relatives killed in last weekend's crackdown.
>
> Three such mass graves are believed by townspeople to be holding as many as 4,500 corpses massacred by the security forces on Saturday, Sunday and Monday. There was no independent confirmation of the number of dead.
>
> West German television, apparently showing footage provided by Romanian television, showed muddy naked corpses being dug out and placed on white sheets, one after the other.
>
> All had their feet tied together. The body of a boy, 3 or 4 years old, was shown lying on the ground.

The death figure had reached 5,000 to 12,000, according to the Yugoslav news agency, Tanjug, on Saturday, December 23. The detail showed assiduous reporting. According to TASS, 800 children under the age of fourteen had died, 45 of them coming out of a puppet show.

But on December 28 Mary Battiata, reporting from Timisoara, told readers of the *Washington Post* that doctors at the city hospital said that several hundred was a more realistic figure than the 4,500. Strong doubts had also begun to surface there and in Bucharest about the figures of up to 80,000 dead throughout the country, which had been broadcast on Romanian television. The French minister of humanitarian aid, Bernard Kouchner, said in Bucharest he had been told by Romanian health officials that the total number of known dead in fighting around the country in the previous two weeks was 746.[18]

On January 19 a letter from Dr. Milan Dresler of Timisoara was published in which he claimed there had clearly been manipulation. The most recent corpse was more than ten months old.[19] On January 24 three doctors from Timisoara appeared on the RTL-Plus TV channel and said that corpses of people who had died from natural causes had been taken from the hospital by "revolutionaries" and presented to the TV cameras as Securitate victims. The body of a woman who had been photographed with a child lying across her stomach, had in fact died of alcohol poisoning and the child was not hers.[20]

Reporting from Bucharest on December 26, John Lloyd of the *Financial Times* explained the impact of the stories: "Even in this most closed of the closed societies (Albania apart) enough filtered in to subvert. Broadcasting from abroad, Radio Free Europe, Voice of America and the BBC World Service were able to circulate news of dissidence and, last week, to beam in the news of Timisoara which went round Bucharest like a flash."[21]

An official report, leaked in December 1994, said that most of the 1,036 people killed during the troubles were innocents caught in the cross fire between panic-stricken soldiers and civilians firing at imaginary terrorists. "The army shot about five million rounds and the population as many as they could lay their hands on—at first out of joy, then against the 'terrorists,' then because they were drunk," according to Valentin Gabrielescu, leader of the enquiry team. The popular uprising was hijacked by a clique of reformist communist conspirators who had been plotting Ceausescu's overthrow for years.[22] One year after the leak, the report had still not been published.

It is clear that the misleading stories were designed to manipulate the media that broadcast into Romania in order to advance the revolution. Who, specifically, the manipulators were is not known.

Impact of the Radios: Froth on the Milk Rises

"If my fellow citizens knew me before I became president, they did so because of these stations," said Vaclav Havel.[23]

The Western Radios were a forum for dissidents: dissidents in Romania like Doina Cornea, a former university professor in Cluj, under house arrest for her critical letters to Ceausescu, and Dan Petruescu, a writer in Iasi, could not meet in Romania, but met through the medium of RFE.[24] The *Times*, reported from Bucharest that the handful of dissident intellectuals were isolated figures who knew of each other's existence mainly from listening to the BBC and Radio Free Europe; they seldom met to discuss ideas face to face. Without the knowledge dissidents gleaned from foreign radio broadcasts, it probably would not have been possible for the new Romanian provisional government to have come up with such a diverse membership for its ruling thirty-nine-member council, according to Coen Stork, the Dutch ambassador.[25]

The *New York Times* quoted Sergei Secuescu, a Bucharest student, as saying: "We can see TV from Bulgaria, from Yugoslavia. We listen to the foreign radios, to Voice of America, Radio Free Europe, BBC. The phone was working. People have brothers, friends."[26] As Blaine Harden put it in the *Washington Post* in a report from Bucharest: "shortwave foreign broadcasts, including those of the Voice of America and Radio Free Europe, as well as British, German, and French stations, helped to undermine the Orwellian repression. Romania's conspicuous silence for most of the past year was not the dismal quiet of hopelessness. Rather, it was the stillness of people paying attention."[27]

Even the Romanian military got their intelligence from RFE during the revolution. In December 1989 RFE broadcast the name of the town that had an airport through which Ceausescu might escape. The Romanian Army General Staff telephoned RFE in Munich to ask for the name of the town, as they had not been able to hear it properly. They left a telephone number for RFE to call back.[28]

The Radios were also a substitute for a domestic opposition. As Tamas Palos, the director-general of MTI, the Hungarian News Agency, said: "It was RFE that was the opposition in Hungary for many years."[29]

Shortly before a demonstration in Prague on October 28, someone leaked a tape recording of a speech that Milos Jakes gave at a provincial Party meeting. The recording was broadcast into Czechoslovakia by RFE. The *New York Times* described it as rambling and clumsy and quoted a dissident as saying it was "a laugh a minute" and undercut Jakes' public standing.[30]

Broadcasters were sometimes restrained in the coverage. The BBC, for example, did not advertise the time and place of demonstrations.[31]

But it was not only news broadcasts that had an impact. It was also entertainment and fictional programs that showed, for all its corruptions, the delights of the consumer society. East Europeans listened to overseas broadcasts to confirm that they were not forgotten and that they could maintain European cultural links.

Once the tide began to rise it was difficult to stop it. As Gavril Popov, the Soviet economist who was one of the five cofounders of the Interregional Group of Reform Deputies, put it: "Everyone who has boiled milk knows that if you miss the right moment, you suddenly find out that froth has begun to rise of its own accord, no matter what you do with the fire or the pot."[32]

The impact of the Radios varied from country to country because the character of the revolutions varied. Miklos Vasarhelyi, a Hungarian writer, reckoned that in Hungary the revolution was the will of the people and had not been figured out by the intellectuals or politicians or diplomats.[33] Czechoslovakia followed its nineteenth-century tradition that social movements were always ignited by the intelligentsia, according to Vaclav Havel.[34] Without the students there would have been no revolution in Czechoslovakia. It was they who cajoled the workers to participate.[35] It was different in East Germany. When the citizens of Greifswald mounted a vigil outside the courthouse on December 4, 1989, to stop the Stasi from burning documents, only a handful of the town's three thousand students took part. Thomas Meyer, a physics professor at the university, believed it was because most of the students were too indoctrinated to believe that the Stasi could be, or should be, overthrown.[36]

But perhaps the most important role of the Western Radios was continuously to broadcast the thoughts on democracy of the three intellectuals of outstanding calibre of Poland, Hungary, and Czechoslovakia: Adam Michnik, Gyrogy Karoly, and Vaclav Havel.

The Audience: Education in Another Spirit

RFE was the dominant broadcaster in Eastern Europe in 1989, followed by the VOA and the BBC. In Czechoslovakia and Romania RFE was the most important and most listened to Western radio station just before and during the revolutions of 1989, according to audience research. It was followed by the VOA and the BBC in that order. In Poland the pecking order was the same. In Hungary RFE was the leader with VOA and the BBC equal at second. Bulgarian research has always been considered unreliable.[37]

Two factors that favored RFE, as always, were that its hours of transmission were much greater than those of the other broadcasters and that it was a surrogate domestic radio station that was strong in domestic news of the target country.

In Romania 48 percent of those interviewed thought RFE was the most important of all the stations, foreign and domestic, in the three months before the revolution, with 17 percent favoring the VOA and 4 percent the BBC.[38] Comparable figures during the revolution were 10 percent, 2 percent, and 0.4 percent. The reason for the decrease during the revolution was that Radio Bucharest moved up from 20 percent to 77 percent.

The Romanian survey asked for an evaluation of the factors influencing public opinion in the lead-up to the overthrow of the Ceausescu regime. Sixty-one percent thought political change in other East European countries was very important, 53 percent the Soviet policy change toward the East European countries, 33 percent the RFE broadcasts, 28 percent Romanian dissidents' activities, and 18 percent Western Radio broadcasts.

In July 1990 RFE published the results of a postal questionnaire conducted in Romania on the Romanian revolution and the role of radio in Bucharest. Typical comments were:

> I consider RFE had a decisive role in the success of our revolution. RFE's broadcasts focused on details about the massacre in Timisoara. During that time I listened to RFE daily in the morning and the evening. After hearing about the genocide in Timisoara in RFE's broadcasts, the population of Bucharest, particularly our young people, rose against the Ceausescu regime. (Male economist, 54)
>
> The most important station for me after the revolution is VOA because of its complete, objective, and verified newscasts. (Male doctor, 66)
>
> BBC is the most important radio station because of its professionalism, programming variety, and objectivity. (Male teacher, 35)[39]

Twenty years earlier audience researchers determined that 59 percent of the adult population listened to RFE once a week or more often and 23 percent to the VOA and BBC.[40] In Czechoslovakia before the revolution RFE scored 13 percent, the VOA 6 percent, and the BBC 2 percent. During the revolution the figures were 10 percent, 4 percent, and 1 percent.[41]

A focus study group in Czechoslovakia in February 1990 produced this comment: "[Western stations] supported our hopes for change. . . . The reversal wouldn't have been possible so quickly if we hadn't been educated by these stations in another spirit, and if we had not gotten the information."[42]

The 1970 figures for Czechoslovakia were RFE 37 percent, BBC 28 percent, and VOA 24 percent.

The BBC commissioned the first systematic study of the radio audience in a Warsaw Pact country, which was carried out in Poland in February and March 1989 and consisted of 1,946 face-to-face interviews of nationals over sixteen in respondents' homes.[43] The survey showed that 7.2 percent of the population listened to RFE at least once a week, 6.8 percent to the BBC, and 6.6 percent to the VOA. Those who listened, depending on events, amounted to 17.9 percent for RFE, 13.9 percent for the VOA, and 10.7 percent for the BBC. Total audiences were 33.9 percent for RFE, 26.4 percent for the VOA, and 23.1 percent for the BBC.

The BBC survey was important because it showed up substantial discrepancies with earlier surveys. According to the usual way Western broadcasters judged their audiences, by researching visitors to the West, from 1983 to 1988 80–90 percent of adult Poles were foreign radio listeners and the BBC had a regular audience of 30 percent. Polish internal research found that in this period 20–30 percent of adult Poles sometimes listened to foreign radio and the BBC had an occasional audience of about 10 percent. The Western broadcasters' research had overestimated the audience because travelers were usually educated and, therefore, were more likely to listen to foreign Radios than were the mass of the population. The Polish internal research underestimated because of the blunt and even intimidating way the question was asked.

In 1969–70 the estimates were 38 percent for RFE, 18 percent for the BBC, and 12 percent for the VOA. A survey similar to that of Poland carried out in Hungary in June 1989 gave RFE 9.7 percent of adult Hungarians listening regularly and the VOA and the BBC 2 percent each. The figures were lower than from previous surveys of visitors to the West.[44] The Hungarians had done surveys internally as early as 1967, but had not published them then. Listeners were inclined to say that they tuned in to the BBC and DW rather than to RFE because those Radios were less hostile, according to Tamas Szecsko, a researcher. He believed RFE surveys were favorable to RFE because RFE was fighting for survival.[45] In 1969–70 RFE scored 41 percent in Hungary, the BBC 16 percent, and the VOA 14 percent.

RFE did not broadcast to East Germany, and the top of the league there in the summer of 1989, according to a study of travelers, was RIAS Berlin with a regular audience of 63.4 percent. Deutschlandfunk had 37.1 percent, Deutsche Welle 9.3 percent, and the BBC 6.5 percent. Nearly one in five listeners claimed to have listened to "Flutlicht," a program that did not exist.[46]

12

EPILOGUE: GORBACHEV LISTENS TO THE VOICES

RADIO LIBERTY and the BBC defeated the plotters of the coup of August 1991. That was the view of Leonid Ionin, the political commentator, writing in *Nezavisimaya Gazeta*.[1] He believed the importance of the media, especially shortwave, could not be overstated. "If the high-level plotters had followed the tested recipe of General Jaruzelski [in declaring martial law in Poland]—seized the newspapers, radio stations, television, cut off the telephones and isolated the White House from Moscow and Moscow from the Soviet Union and the world—they would likely have succeeded. Any other way they were doomed."

Yeltsin knew how much he needed the Radios. In the previous April he had commented that Russians received more correct information about the work of the Russian Supreme Soviet, its leadership, and the Russian government from Radio Liberty than from the Soviet media. "This radio station reports objectively and fully, and we are generally quite thankful to them," he said. One of his aides sent this fax to the Center of Democracy in Washington on August 9:

> 11:14 A.M. (EDT): Did Mr Bush make any comments upon the situation in this country(?). If he did, make it known by all means of communication, make it known to the people of this country.
>
> The Russian Government has no NO way to address the people. All radio stations are under control.
>
> The following is BY's address to the Army. Submit it to the USIA. Broadcast it over the country. Maybe "Voice of America." Do it! Urgent![2]

Interviews carried out by RL after the attempted coup showed that in Moscow 30 percent of the respondents listened to RL during the attempted coup, 18 percent to the BBC, and 15 percent to the VOA. In most centers polled outside Moscow the VOA was ahead of the BBC.[3] A poll carried out for the USIA in the Russian Federation between December 11, 1991, and January 2, 1992, showed that around 15 percent of those polled listened regularly (at least once a week) to foreign Radios, 7 percent to the VOA, 7 percent to RL, and 6 percent to the BBC. These figures have to be understood in the context of transmission hours. The VOA transmitted for ten hours each day, RL for twenty-four, and the BBC for eight. Questioned on the coup, those who said foreign radio was the first or second most reliable source, when asked to specify which, ranked the BBC first (28 percent), RL second (27 percent) and the VOA third (25 percent).[4]

The first act of the Committee for the State of Emergency when they staged the coup in the early hours of Monday, August 19 was to shut down all newspapers except eight hard-liners. Only one newspaper, the official trade union publication, *TRUD*, reported Yeltsin's condemnation of the coup. Radio stations were either closed down or played light music. Television was restricted to the first state channel.

At 1300 hours Yeltsin emerged from the White House, the House of Soviets, which housed the Russian government, and climbed up onto tank no. 110 of the Taman Division and appealed to the citizens of Russia to oppose the coup. Russians heard his address on the Western Radios. As the citizens of Moscow later that afternoon ransacked building sites by the Kalinin Bridge for scaffolding poles and steel rods to build the barricades to defend the White House, their news was coming from the Western Radios. "At five o'clock a familiar sound caught my attention," reported Iain Elliott, a senior Radio Liberty man, "the news from Radio Liberty emerged loud and clear from the center of a large cluster of umbrellas at the end of the bridge."[5]

On the Monday night the most important piece of television coverage of the entire coup came from CNN—the famous shot of Yeltsin on the tank. Sergei Medvedev, the anchor for the 2100 hours news program, *Vremya*, on the Monday night had put together a five-minute segment, which, to the fury of his bosses, showed democratic resistance to the coup. It included material from CNN, Medvedev's main source of information on TV, and material Medvedev and his crew had themselves shot: tanks rolling down the streets of Moscow, Yeltsin's "appeal to the citizens of Russia," the building of barricades, and the massing of people out to defend the White House from attack.[6]

Radio Liberty opened an office on the eleventh floor of the White House; their three Russian correspondents telephoned their reports to

Munich, whence they were relayed to transmitters ringing the Soviet Union and instantaneously beamed to listeners across the country. On the Tuesday night the RL correspondent, Misha Sokolev, telephoned Munich with an urgent and emotional eye-witness report of tanks moving in on the building. *"Proshayte* [farewell], I'm afraid this is my last report," he said, abruptly terminating the live broadcast. But the phone line to Munich was kept open, and he later came back on the air to report that the tanks were turning back. Millions of Soviet citizens, including soldiers, their ears glued to their radio sets, were listening.[7] There was no jamming, and no telephone lines were cut.

On the morning of Wednesday, according to *Rossiiskaia Gazeta*, "To relieve the pickets who had lived through those heavy hours, Muscovites began to arrive on the first metro trains, having spent the night at their receivers, listening on Radio Liberty to information about the attack that had begun."[8]

The other Western Radios had extended the hours of transmission of their Russian services: the BBC, for example, from 6.5 hours to 17 hours. But they could not compete with RL, broadcasting not only in Russian but also eleven other Soviet languages. "It was the main channel of information for the Soviet people," the deputy, Oleg Adamovich, said.[9] CNN put the pictures they were shooting outside the White House up to satellites, which relayed them to Atlanta and back via satellites to Moscow. There the television center, Ostankino, despite censoring of its own domestic news programs and being surrounded by troops, transmitted them via microwave to Moscow hotels and the Kremlin. Muscovites lucky enough to have the right antennae could see hazy pictures of what was going on.

At about 0200 hours on Thursday, August 22, the TU-134 presidential plane touched down in Moscow from the Crimea. The coup attempt defeated, a tired-looking but smiling Gorbachev waved from the top of the aircraft steps. Within hours he was giving a press conference on his house arrest ordeal in the dacha in Foros. "Seventy-two hours of total isolation," he said. "Everything was done, I think, in order to weaken me psychologically." The isolation and the attempt to weaken him psychologically may have been the intention, but it is not what happened. Western Radios broke the isolation.

This was his story:

Everything was turned off, but we found some old receivers in the service quarters and were able to set up antennas—the lads were able to figure out how to do that.

We were able to catch some broadcasts and find out what was happening. We got BBC, best of all—BBC best of all. They were the clearest signal. Radio Liberty, then Voice of America—at least that is what I was told, based on the information they had.[10]

Later, he wrote: "My son-in-law Anatoli managed to listen to a Western station on his pocket Sony. We started to collect and analyze information and assess the way the situation was developing."[11]

As an excited David Morton, head of the Russian service of the BBC, said: "It is phenomenal. It vindicates everything we have stood for in the last thirty years."[12]

Not surprisingly, the BBC took half-page advertising space in London newspapers to trumpet what Gorbachev had said about them. They omitted the reference to the clearest signal. It was a relay from Cyprus. Later in the same press conference Gorbachev said he had not seen the BBC correspondent there. He gave the BBC yet another tribute: "The BBC knows everything already."

In the dacha Gorbachev would have heard Yeltsin broadcasting his appeal to the people and other interviews with opponents of the coup that would have given him an idea of the strength of the resistance. He would have learned that the coup was not well organized. He would have concluded that he was getting support from President George Bush and Prime Minister John Major, who had telephoned Yeltsin. It would not have escaped Gorbachev's notice that if he had not ended the jamming of Western Radios in 1988 and sold off jamming equipment to independent radio stations for use as transmitters he might not have learned what was happening. If it had not been for the Radios, his resolve might not have strengthened. He might have signed away all his powers and changed the course of history.

CHRONOLOGY

1922   November 7: Russians inaugurate the Comintern Radio Station.

1924   Russians start foreign-language international broadcasting.

1932   December 19: BBC starts international broadcasting.

1942   February 24: VOA starts broadcasting.

1945   Start of the cold war.

1946   March 24: BBC starts Russian service.

1947   February 17: VOA starts Russian service.

1948   February 3: Russians start jamming.

1950   June 25: Start of Korean War.

           July 4: RFE starts broadcasting.

1953   March 1: RL starts broadcasting.

           March 5: Stalin dies.

1956   October 23: Hungarian uprising.

1967   February 21: CIA financing of RFE revealed.

1973   October 19: U.S. Board for International Broadcasting Act.

1975   August 1: Helsinki Final Act signed.

1976   October 1: RFE and RL merged.

1988   November 29: Russians stop jamming.

1989   End of the cold war.

1991   August 19: Gorbachev, under house arrest, listens to the Voices.

NOTES

Introduction

1. Problems of Soviet Literature, Reports and Speeches at the First Soviet Writers' Congress, Cooperative Publishing Society of Foreign Workers in the USSR, 1935, p. 73, quoted in George Bailey "The Perception Mongers: Reflections on Soviet Propaganda." Occasional Paper 44. (London: Institute for European Defence and Strategic Studies, 1990), 12.

2. Speech to English Speaking Union, Guildhall, London, AP Report in *Chicago Tribune,* June 14, 1989.

3. David Remnick, *Lenin's Tomb, the Last Days of the Soviet Empire* (London: Viking, 1993), 2.

1. Prologue

1. Burton Paulu, *Radio and Television Broadcasting in Eastern Europe* (Minneapolis: Univ. of Minnesota Press, 1974), 34.

2. A. Y. Yurovskiy and R. A. Boretskiy, *The Fundamentals of Television Journalism,* quoted in Paulu, *Eastern Europe,* 34.

3. Vsevolod N. Ruzhnikov, lecturer in the history of Soviet radio, Moscow Univ., interviewed by the author and Robert Evans, Reuters chief representative in the Soviet Union, Moscow, June 13, 1991.

4. V. I. Lenin, Polnoe sobranie sochinenii (PSS) (Moscow: Izdatel'stvo Politicheskoi literatury, 1958—), 51:130; V. I. Lenin, *Collected Works (CW)* (London: Lawrence and Wishart, 1960–), 35:437, quoted in Thomas H. Guback and Steven P. Hill,"The Beginnings of Soviet Broadcasting and the Role of V. I. Lenin," *Journalism Monographs of the AEJ,* no. 26, Dec. 1972, 12.

5. Lenin, PSS 52:54; idem, *CW* 35:473, quoted in Guback and Hill, *Beginnings,* 16.

6. Ruzhnikov, interview.

7. Guback and Hill, *Beginnings,* 31; David M. Abshire, *International Broadcasting: A New Dimension in Western Diplomacy* (Beverly Hills, Calif.: Sage Publications, 1976), 18.

8. J. A. Hale, *Radio Power: Propaganda and International Broadcasting* (London: Paul Elek, 1975), 16.

9. Lenin, PSS, 35:85–88 and Lenin, *CW* 26:315–18, quoted in Guback and Hill, *Beginnings,* 5.

10. Paulu, *Eastern Europe,* 199.

11. Ruzhnikov, interview.

12. Robert Conquest, *Stalin: Breaker of Nations* (London: Weidenfeld and Nicolson, 1991), xvii.

13. Will Irwin, *Propaganda and the News, or What Makes You Think So* (1936; reprint, Westport, Conn.: Greenwood Press, 1970), 130–31.

14. William Haley, "Broadcasting as an International Force" (speech, Univ. of Nottingham, Dec. 1, 1950).

15. Hale, *Radio Power*, 17.

16. Haley, "Broadcasting."

17. Vladimir Yaroshenko, "Broadcasting in Russia," in *Broadcasting Around the World*, ed. W. E. McCavitt (Blue Ridge Summit, Pa.: Tab Books, 1981), 52; John Tusa, *Conversations with the World* (London: BBC, 1990), 5; and Ruzhinkov, interview.

18. Fernando Bea, *Qui la Radio Vaticana . . . Mezzo secolo della Radio del Papa* (This is Vatican Radio: Half a century of the Pope's radio) (Vatican City: Ufficio Propaganda e Sviluppo, 1981), 46.

19. Bea, *La Radio Vaticana*, 19.

20. Félix Juan Cabasés, "El servicio publico eclesial de Radio Vaticano (1967–1992)" (The ecclesiastical public service of Vatican Radio [1967–1992]), (Ph.D. diss., Basque Univ., 1994), 957–63.

21. Frédéric Brunnquell, *Fréquence monde: Du poste colonial à RFI* (World frequency: From colonial radio to RFI) (Paris: Hachette, 1992), 12.

22. Tusa, *Conversations*, 29.

23. D. R. Browne, *International Radio Broadcasting: The Limits of the Limitless Medium* (New York: Praeger, 1982), 48–49.

24. Quoted in Rutger Lindahl, *Broadcasting Across Borders* (Lund: CWK Gleerup, 1978), 7.

25. Quoted in Hale, *Radio Power*, 1.

26. Abshire, *New Dimension*, 19.

27. Tusa, *Conversations*, 6.

28. Gerard Mansell, "Broadcasting to the World: Forty Years of the BBC External Services" (pamphlet, Jan. 1973), 41.

29. Introductory Memorandum to Correspondence and Relative Papers Respecting Cultural Propaganda, Foreign Office, 1935, FO 431/1, p. 1, quoted in J. B. Black, *Organising the Propaganda Instrument: The British Experience* (The Hague: Martinus Nijhoff, 1975), 2.

30. Harold Nicolson, "The British Council 1934–1955," in the Twenty-first Anniversary Report of the British Council (London: British Council, 1955), 4, quoted in Black, *Propaganda Instrument*.

31. Internal report by J. B. Clark, Oct. 24, 1938, quoted in Gerard Mansell, *Let Truth Be Told: 50 Years of BBC External Broadcasting* (London: Weidenfeld and Nicolson, 1982), 57–58.

32. Quoted by Robert Kee, *Munich: The Eleventh Hour* (London: Hamish Hamilton, 1988), 193.

33. H. Grisewood in *One Thing at a Time: An Autobiography* (London: Hutchinson, 1968), quoted in Asa Briggs, *The History of Broadcasting in the United Kingdom*, 5 vols. (Oxford: Oxford Univ. Press, 1961–95) 3:81–82.

34. C. A. Siepmann, *Radio, Television and Society* (Oxford: Oxford Univ. Press, 1950), 295–96.

35. John P. Foley, *The Jeffersonian Cyclopedia* (New York: Funk and Wagnall, 1900), 733.

36. Edward P. Lilly, "The Development of American Psychological Operations 1945–

1951," Dec. 19, 1951, Psychological Strategy Board, Harry S. Truman Library, Declassified Documents RP no. 1,742 of 1988.

37. Briggs, *History of Broadcasting* 3:18.

38. Siepmann, *Radio*, 296.

39. Merni Ingrassia Fitzgerald, *The Voice of America* (New York: Dodd, Mead, 1987), 4.

40. E. Tangye Lean, *Voices in the Darkness: The Story of the European Radio War* (London: Secker and Warburg, 1943), 46–60.

41. *Financial Times*, May 8, 1995.

42. Ruzhnikov, interview.

43. M. P. Mikhailov and V. V. Nazarov, *Ideologicheskya diversiya-vooruzheniye imperializma* (Ideological diversion is the armament of imperialism) (Moscow, 1969) 16, 24, 44–46, quoted in M. Lisann, *Broadcasting to the Soviet Union: International Politics and Radio* (New York: Praeger, 1975), 5.

44. Tusa, *Conversations*, 22–24.

45. Asa Briggs, *The BBC: The First Fifty Years* (Oxford: Oxford Univ. Press, 1985), 196–97.

46. Quoted in Briggs, *History of Broadcasting* 3:5.

47. Briggs, *History of Broadcasting* 3:433–34.

48. Briggs, *History of Broadcasting* 3:12.

2. The Start of the Cold War (1945–1947)

1. Briggs, *History of Broadcasting* 3:396.

2. Mansell, *Truth*, 218.

3. R. Pirsein, *Voice of America: A History of the International Broadcasting Activities of the United States Government 1940–1962* (New York: Arno Press, 1979), 127.

4. *Tribune*, Oct. 19, 1945, quoted in Hugh Thomas, *Armed Truce: The Beginnings of the Cold War, 1945–46* (London: Hamish Hamilton, 1986), 761.

5. Geoffrey Warner, "The Study of Cold War Origins," in *The End of the Cold War*, ed. David Armstrong and Erik Goldstein (London: Frank Cass, 1990), 14.

6. Hugh Thomas, *Armed Truce*, 369–70.

7. Warner, "Origins," 13.

8. John Ranelagh, *The Agency: The Rise and Decline of the CIA* (London: Weidenfeld and Nicolson, 1986), 91.

9. John Lewis Gaddis, *Russia, The Soviet Union and the United States: An Interpretive History*, 2d ed. (New York: McGraw Hill, 1990), 168.

10. Mansell, *Truth*, 218.

11. Memorandum to Ernest Bevin, secretary of state, Broadcasts in Russian to the USSR, PRO FO 371/56817.

12. Quoted in Mansell, *Truth*, 218.

13. Briggs, *History of Broadcasting* 4:149.

14. Report on Impressions of BBC Russian Service by Mr Tutaeff, Oct. 16, 1946, WAC E1/1265.

15. Ian Jacob's statement of policy for the European services, July 29, 1946, quoted in Mansell, *Truth*, 217.

16. *Komsomolskaya Pravda*, Jan. 3, 1957.

17. PRO CAB 128/5, C.M.16(46), Feb. 21, 1946.

18. White Paper on Broadcasting, Cmd. 6852 (1946).

19. BBC Licence and Agreement Clause 4(5), Cmd. 6975 (1946), 15(5), Cmd. 8579 (1952), 14(5), Cmd. 2236 (1963), 13(5), Cmd. 4095 (1969), 13(5), Cmd. 8233 (1981).

20. Hansard Parliamentary Debates, vol. 425, cols. 1076–98, July 16, 1946.

21. White Paper on Broadcasting, Cmd. 6852 (1946).

22. David Rodnick, member of the United States Social Services Research Council, "Through the Iron Curtain," supplement to London Calling, Aug. 28, 1952, 7, quoted in Briggs, History of Broadcasting 4:508.

23. Haley note for BBC board of governors Oct. 30, 1946, WAC R1/3/60.

24. PRO CAB 128/5, C.M.5(46), Jan. 15, 1946.

25. Russia Committee, meeting, Apr. 2, 1946, PRO FO 371/56885/N5169/5169/38G.

26. Warner memorandum, Apr. 2, 1946, PRO FO 371/56832/N6344/605/38G.

27. Kirkpatrick memorandum, May 15, 1946, PRO FO 371/56885/N6092/5169/38G.

28. Scott Lucas, "Government Information Services and Psychological Warfare after 1945," seminar, Institute of Historical Research, London, May 28, 1991.

29. Russia Committee, meeting, Sept. 17, 1946, PRO FO 371/56886/N12335/5169/38G.

30. Sir Orme Sargent to Sir M. Peterson, British ambassador in Moscow, July 28, 1947, PRO FO 371/66370/N8114/271/38.

31. Leonard Miall, former chief Washington correspondent, BBC, and member of the British Political Warfare Mission to U.S., interviewed by the author, London, Feb. 16, 1993.

32. Charles Richardson, From Churchill's Secret Circle to the BBC: The Biography of Lieutenant General Sir Ian Jacob (London: Brasseys, 1991), 228–30, 234.

33. President Roosevelt to the chairman of the Federal Communications Commission, James L. Fly, Nov. 16, 1943, quoted in Pirsein, Voice, 100.

34. Pirsein, Voice, 101–2.

35. Executive Order 9608, quoted in Pirsein, Voice, 108–11.

36. Department of State bulletin no. 323, publication 2381 (Washington, D.C.: USGPO), Sept. 2, 1945, 306, quoted in Pirsein, Voice, 111.

37. Arthur W. MacMahon, Memorandum on the Postwar International Program of the United States (Washington, D.C.: USGPO, 1945), 69.

38. Ibid., xvii–xviii.

39. Pirsein, Voice, 112.

40. December 31, 1945, quoted in Pirsein, Voice, 115.

41. Department of State, Departmental Order, effective Dec. 31, 1945, Organization and Functions of the Office of International Information and Cultural Affairs, Dec. 20, 1945. Pirsein, Voice, 115.

42. Subcommittee of the Committee on Appropriations of the House of Representatives, Hearings on Departments of State, Justice, and Commerce Appropriations for 1955, 83d Cong., 2d sess., Washington, D.C., USGPO, 1954, p. 546, quoted in Pirsein, Voice, i.

43. Louis Kruh, "Stimson, The Black Chamber and the 'Gentleman's Mail' Quote," in Cryptologia, 12, no. 2 (Apr. 1988): 65–80.

44. Hugh Thomas, Armed Truce, 223, quoting Admiral William Leahy, I Was There (London, 1950), 363.

45. C. Thayer, Diplomat (New York: Harper and Bros., 1979), 187.

46. E. W. Barrett, Truth Is Our Weapon (New York: Funk and Wagnalls, 1953), 54.

47. Pirsein, Voice, 114.

48. Ibid., 116–18.

49. Kent Cooper, The Right to Know: An Exposition of the Evils of News Suppression and Propaganda (New York: Farrar, Straus, and Cudahy, 1956), 257.

50. Frank Shakespeare, "International Broadcasting and U.S. Political Realities," in *Western Broadcasting over the Iron Curtain*, ed. K. R. M. Short (London: Croom Helm, 1986), 60.

51. Pirsein, *Voice*, 127.

52. Walter Bedell Smith, *Moscow Mission 1946–49* (London: William Heinemann, 1950), 168–69.

53. Ibid., 171.

54. Alex Inkeles, *Public Opinion in Soviet Russia: A Study in Mass Persuasion* (Cambridge, Mass.: Harvard Univ. Press, 1967), 251.

55. William E. Daugherty and Morris Janowitz, eds., *A Psychological Warfare Casebook* (Baltimore, Md.: Johns Hopkins Press, 1958), 736–39.

56. E. Sergeev, *Ogonyok*, no. 19, 31, May 8, 1949, quoted in Daugherty, *Warfare Casebook*, 739–40.

3. The Beginning of the Age of Jamming (1947–1950)

1. Paul Lendvai, *The Bureaucracy of Truth: How Communist Governments Manage the News* (London: Burnett Books, 1981), 164.

2. Ruzhnikov, interview.

3. M. Lisann, *Broadcasting*, 4.

4. Hale, *Radio Power*, 136–37.

5. George Urban, *The Nineteen Days: A Broadcaster's Account of the Hungarian Revolution* (London: William Heinemann, 1957), 270n.

6. CIA, note for the president, "Historical Developments in the Jamming of the VOA by the USSR," Jan. 20, 1950, 3, Harry S. Truman Library (HSTL), Independence, Mo., President's Secretary's Files, Declassified Documents, RP no. 185, of 1991.

7. Barrett, *Weapon*, 116–17.

8. J. A. [pseud.] "Radio in the Cold War," *The World Today* 10, no. 6 (June 1954): 253.

9. CIA, "Historical Developments," 4.

10. American Embassy report, Secret 507/3/49, WAC E2/119/1.

11. Barrett, *Weapon*, 117.

12. Department of State Appropriations Bill for 1950, Hearings, Senate, 182–83, quoted in Pirsein, *Voice*, 155.

13. *Hansard Parliamentary Debates*, vol. 468, cols. 159–60, Oct. 26, 1949, quoted in Briggs, *History of Broadcasting* 4:514.

14. *New York Times*, Nov. 17, 1949.

15. CIA, "Historical Developments," 1.

16. Letter to the Department, Feb. 24, 1950, PRO FO 953/654.

17. Briggs, *History of Broadcasting* 4:514.

18. Note by H. G. Venables, head of European programme operations, BBC, Sept. 30, 1955, WAC E2/978/1.

19. James Wood, *History of International Broadcasting* (London: Peter Peregrinus in association with the Science Museum, 1992), 165–66.

20. CIA, "Historical Developments," 8.

21. Letter from A. C. E. Malcolm of the Foreign Office Information Policy Department, Secret, Nov. 4, 1950, to Sir Ian Jacob, BBC, WAC E2/325/2.

22. CIA, "Historical Developments," 8.

23. USIA sponsored report, "The Impact of Western Broadcasts in the Soviet Bloc," Mar. 1959, 41, NARA.

24. American Embassy report 507/3/49, WAC E2/119/1, 1–2.

25. Letter of June 7, 1949, from R. L. Speight of the Foreign Office Information Policy Department, Secret, to Geoffrey Harrison at the British Embassy, Moscow, WAC E2/119/1.

26. CIA, "Historical Developments," 1.

27. Ibid., 10–11.

28. Barrett, *Weapon*, 119.

29. James Monahan, "Broadcasting to Europe," BBC Lunch-time lecture, Oct. 9, 1963, 11.

30. Briggs, *History of Broadcasting* 4: 513.

31. BBC, "The European Service of the BBC, 1938–1959" (pamphlet, Sept. 1959), 18.

32. Board for International Broadcasting (BIB) Report for 1987, 27.

33. Altschul to DeWitt Poole, Aug. 15, 1950, Altschul Papers, Lehman Collection, Columbia Univ. Library, New York, copied in the Mickelson Papers, Hoover Institution on War, Revolution, and Peace, Stanford Univ., Palo Alto, Calif.

34. Monahan "Broadcasting to Europe," 7.

35. BBC, "European Service," 18.

36. Sir Ian Trethowan, "The BBC and International Broadcasting," (lecture, London, Feb. 2, 1981).

37. Pirsein, *Voice*, 476 n. 31.

38. CIA, "Historical Developments," 3–10.

39. Pirsein, *Voice*, 155.

40. Ranjan Borra, "The Problem of Jamming in International Broadcasting," *Journal of Broadcasting* 11, no. 4 (Fall 1967): 359, quoting United Nations, General Assembly, Official Records: Fifth Session, agenda item 30 (b): Freedom of Information, Interference with Radio Signals. Resolution adopted by the General Assembly at its 325th Plenary Meeting on Dec. 14, 1950.

41. Abshire, *New Dimension*, 50.

42. *New York Times*, Nov. 17, 1949.

43. Hale, *Radio Power*, 137.

44. Christopher Mayhew, *Time to Explain: An Autobiography* (London: Hutchinson, 1987), 106–7.

45. Ibid., 55–58.

46. David Leigh, *The Frontiers of Secrecy: Closed Government in Britain* (London: Junction Books, 1980), 218–19.

47. Christopher Mayhew, interviewed by the author, London, Feb. 4, 1994.

48. Ibid.

49. "Future Foreign Publicity Policy," Jan. 4, 1948, PRO CAB 129/23, C.P.(48)8.

50. Ibid.

51. PRO CAB 128/11, C.M.3(48), Jan. 3, 1948.

52. Leigh, *Frontiers*, 219–20.

53. Russia Committee meeting, Jan. 15, 1948, PRO FO 371/71687/N765/38G.

54. No. 6 circular, PRO FO 1110/1 P/138/138/G, released Aug. 17, 1995.

55. "Anti-Communist Publicity—Memorandum by the Secretary of State for Foreign Affairs," Apr. 30, 1948, Top Secret, PRO GEN. 231/1, FO 1110/9, J. no. 18297, released Aug. 17, 1995.

56. Ibid.

57. "Memorandum—The B.B.C.'s broadcasts to Eastern European countries," July 15, 1948, PRO FO 110/49, released Aug. 17, 1995.

58. Letter from the Foreign Office to various embassies, Oct. 19, 1948, PRO FO 953/229A, and Christopher Warner memorandum to Christopher Mayhew, "BBC Broadcasts to Iron Curtain Countries," Aug. 13, 1948, PRO FO 953/229A.

59. Foreign Office circular no. 7, "Foreign Office Guidance to the B.B.C." PRO FO P899/8/950.

60. Letter from Murray to Group Captain Stapleton, who represented the Service Departments at a meeting to discuss liaison on propaganda, May 14, 1948, Top Secret PRO FO 1110/38, released Aug. 17, 1995.

61. Letter from the Foreign Office to various embassies, Oct. 19, 1948, PRO FO 953/229A.

62. Letter from Murray to Stapleton, May 14, 1948, PRO FO 1110/38.

63. Ian Jacob "Statement of Policy for the European Service," directive no. 1, July 29, 1946, WAC E2/132.

64. Ian Jacob, "The Place of Broadcasting in International Relations," *International Journal*, 1949–50, quoted in Frank Ward and Helen Koshits, "Radio Canada International and Broadcasting over the Iron Curtain," in *Western Broadcasting over the Iron Curtain*, ed. K. R. M. Short, 27–56 (London: Croom Helm, 1986), 30.

65. Letter from Jacob to Warner, Apr. 26, 1948, PRO FO 1110/16 18225, released Aug. 17, 1995.

66. Letter from Jacob to Warner, May 28, 1948, PRO FO 1110/16 18225, released Aug. 17, 1995.

67. Letter from Jacob to Warner, Apr. 26, 1948, PRO FO 1110/16, 18225; and letter from Murray to Lean, June 4, 1948, FO 1110/16 18225, released Aug. 17, 1995.

68. Russia Committee, minutes, Oct. 28, 1948, PRO FO 371/71687 8000.

69. "Anti-Soviet and pro-British Colonial Propaganda," June 16, 1948, PRO CAB 130/37, GEN 231/4.

70. Morgan to Keith and others, Oct. 12, 1949, PRO CO 537/5130.

71. Briggs, *History of Broadcasting* 4: 512–13.

72. Mansell, *Truth,* 220.

73. U.S. Moscow Embassy report, quoted in a report on monitoring the VOA and the BBC, Aug. 1, 1951, WAC E1/1265.

74. BBC report on evidence of a Russian schoolteacher, WAC E1/1265.

75. Haley, "Broadcasting," Dec. 1, 1950.

76. Ministerial Committee on Anticommunist Propaganda meeting, Dec. 19, 1949, PRO CAB 130/37, GEN 231/3d meeting.

77. Rae to Hankey, Dec. 17, 1948, and subsequent minutes, PRO FO 371/71632A/N13368/1/38G.

78. "Channels of Communication Between the Foreign Office and the BBC's External Services," memorandum drafted by J. L. B. Titchener, Foreign Officer Liaison Officer with the BBC External Services, and agreed with J. B. Clark, director of External Broadcasting BBC, Mar. 28, 1957, WAC R34/1580/3. (Titchener was appointed during the Suez crisis and was known in the BBC as "Titchener of Tartoum.")

79. Interview with Lyn Smith, "Covert British Propaganda: The Information Research Department: 1947–77," *Millennium: Journal of International Studies* 9, no. 1 (1980): 67–83.

80. W. Scott Lucas and C. J. Morris, "A Very British Crusade: The Information Research Department and the Beginning of the Cold War," in *British Intelligence Strategy and the Cold War, 1945–51*, ed. Richard Aldrich (London: Routledge, 1992), 106.

81. Letter from Ralph Murray of the Foreign Office to Ian Jacob of the BBC, June 20, 1950, Secret, WAC E2/325/1.

82. Letter from Tangye Lean to Murray, Oct. 2, 1950, WAC E2/253/2.

83. Note from Jacob to Tangye Lean, Mar. 16, 1948, WAC E2/206/8.

84. R. L. Speight, oral evidence to Beveridge Committee, June 1, 1950, PRO FO 953/621.

85. Letter from Paul Grey of the Foreign Office to J. B. Clark, director of External Broadcasting, July 26, 1956, and reply of Tangye Lean, assistant director of External Broadcasting, Aug. 16, 1956, WAC E1/2455/1.

86. Memorandum, "Eastern Zone Material" by BBC Berlin representative to assistant head of the German Service, June 21, 1949, WAC E1/756.

87. Memorandum, "Information Supplied by SPD," by assistant head of German Service to Berlin Representative, June 11, 1949, and replies of June 20, 29, 1949, WAC E1/756.

88. Letter from J. G. Ward, Private Office of the deputy U.K. high commissioner, Wahnerheide, to E. M. Rose, Office of the Deputy, British Military Government (Berlin), Apr. 30, 1952, PRO FO 953/1285.

89. Peter Johnson, former BBC correspondent in Berlin, interviewed by the author, London, England, May 6, 1996.

90. Charles Wheeler, interviewed by the author, London, England, May 2, 1996.

91. Letter from R. O'Rorke, head of the German Service of the BBC, to R. A. Harrison, BBC Berlin representative, Dec. 18, 1954, WAC E1/753/4.

92. Letter from D. B. J. Ambler to J. Monahan, Jan. 27, 1955, WAC E2/782/1.

93. Wheeler, interview.

94. Note by R. A. L. O'Rorke, assistant head of German Service, Dec. 4, 1957, WAC E1/753/5.

95. Summary of the Report of the Independent Committee of Enquiry into Overseas Information Services, Cmd. 9138 (1954), quoted in Mansell, *Truth*, 211.

96. B. Bumpus and B. Skelt, "Seventy Years of International Broadcasting," *Communication and Society*, no. 14 (Paris: UNESCO, 1985), 117, and Mansell, *Truth*, 221, 224.

97. Senate report no. 811 to accompany H. R. 3342, "Promoting the Better Understanding of the United States among the Peoples of the World and to Strengthen Cooperative International Relations," 80th Cong., 2d sess. (Washington, D.C.: USGPO, Jan. 7, 1948), 3, quoted in Pirsein, *Voice*, 131.

98. Pirsein, *Voice*, 132.

99. Senate Report no. 811 to accompany H. R. 3342, 4, "Promoting Better Understanding," quoted in Pirsein, *Voice*, 138.

100. 22 USC 1431 et seq., United States Information and Educational Exchange Act of 1948, As Amended (P.L. 402), 80th Congress, approved Jan. 27, 1948, quoted in Pirsein, *Voice*, 139–41.

101. Pirsein, *Voice*, 112, 133.

102. Ibid., 142–44.

103. Thayer, *Diplomat*, 191–92.

104. Pirsein, *Voice*, 145.

105. House of Representatives Fourteenth Intermediate Report, "Investigation of the State Department Voice of America Broadcasts," House report no. 2350, 80th Cong., 2d sess. (Washington, D.C.: USGPO, 1948), quoted in Pirsein, *Voice*, 145.

106. Pirsein, *Voice*, 145–46.

107. "U.S. Information Service in Europe, Implementation by the Department of State (as of 1/49) of the Recommendations Contained in the Reports of the Committee on For-

eign Relations (Smith-Mundt Congressional Group), January 1948," Feb., 1949, 10, quoted in Pirsein, *Voice*, 148–50.

108. John Albert, chief of German section of VOA, interviewed by R. W. Pirsein, n.d., quoted in Pirsein, *Voice*, 156.

109. Kenneth Paul Adler, Morris Janowitz, Douglas Waples, "Competitive Broadcasting to Germany," (a content analysis research report by the Committee on Communication, Univ. of Chicago, July 1950), quoted in Pirsein, *Voice*, 475.

110. Lilly, "American Psychological Operations," 80. Declassified Documents, RP no. 1742 of 1988.

111. Department of State Appropriations Bill for 1950, Hearings, House, 851, quoted in Pirsein, *Voice*, 154.

112. Inkeles, *Public Opinion*, 737.

113. Institute of Communications Research, "Comparison of the English Language Services of the Voice of America, the British Broadcasting Corporation, Radio Moscow, from Broadcasts during Dec. 1953," (Univ. of Illinois, Urbana, July 1954), quoted in Pirsein, *Voice*, 233.

114. Barrett, *Weapon*, 79.

115. Address on foreign policy at a luncheon of the American Society of Newspaper Editors, Apr. 20, 1950, Public Papers of President Harry S. Truman, 1950, 260–64, quoted in Hans N. Tuch, *Communicating with the World: U.S. Public Diplomacy Overseas* (New York: St Martin's Press, 1990), 15.

116. Barrett, *Weapon*, 78–79.

117. Lilly, "American Psychological Operations," 82–83. Declassified Documents RP no. 1742 of 1988.

118. Barrett, *Weapon*, 85.

119. Ibid., 77, 80.

120. D. R. Browne, *International*, 98, quoting Wilson Dizard, *The Strategy of Truth, the Story of the USIS* (Washington, D.C.: Public Affairs Press, 1965).

121. Robert T. Holt, *Radio Free Europe* (Minneapolis: Univ. of Minnesota Press, 1958), 15.

122. Memorandum by Altschul to DeWitt Poole, Aug. 15, 1950, Altschul Papers. See also n. 33.

123. CIA, "Suggested Replies to GAO Questions on RFE/RL," Feb. 1972, released after FOIA request Feb. 1993.

124. Thomas Braden, director of the International Organizations Division of the CIA with responsibility for Free Europe, 1951–54, in a telephone interview with Sig Mickelson, May 6, 1982, Mickelson Papers.

125. T. B. Macaulay, *History of England from the Accession of James II* (1848; reprint, London: Everyman, 1906), 1:393.

126. Holt, *Radio Free Europe*, 3.

127. Ibid., 52.

128. Ibid., 7.

129. Daniel Yergin, *Shattered Peace: The Origins of the Cold War and the National Security State* (London: Andre Deutsch, 1978), 87.

130. Ibid., 19.

131. Policy Planning Staff Records, box 33, "Chronological 1949," quoted in John Lewis Gaddis, *The Long Peace: Inquiries into the History of the Cold War* (New York: Oxford Univ. Press, 1987), 160.

132. Christopher Simpson, *Science of Coercion: Communication Research and Psychological Warfare, 1945–1960* (Oxford: Oxford Univ. Press, 1994), 25.

133. Ibid., 42.

134. Holt, *Radio Free Europe*, 10–11.

135. Ibid., 11–12.

136. James McCargar, interviewed by the author, Washington, D.C., Oct. 18, 1990.

137. McCargar, interview.

138. Sig Mickelson, *America's Other Voice: The Story of Radio Free Europe and Radio Liberty* (New York: Praeger, 1983), 19.

139. U.S. National Security Council, NSC 4: "Coordination of Foreign Information Measures", Confidential, Dec. 9, 1947, Record Group 273, NARA.

140. Christopher Simpson, *Coercion*, 38.

141. U.S. National Security Council, NSC 10/2: "Office of Special Projects," June 18, 1948, Top Secret, declassified Oct. 29, 1992, Record Group 273, NARA.

142. United States Senate, 94th Cong. 2d sess., final report of the Select Committee to Study Governmental Operations with Respect to Intelligence Activities, Supplementary Detailed Staff Reports on Foreign and Military Intelligence, book 4, Apr. 23, 1976 (Washington, D.C.: USGPO) 30; and Ranelagh, *Agency*, 134.

143. Senate Intelligence Report 1976 (see n. 139), 34–37.

144. Kim Philby, *My Silent War* (London: MacGibbon and Kee, 1968), 141.

145. Thomas Powers, *The Man Who Kept the Secrets: Richard Helms and the CIA* (London: Weidenfeld and Nicolson, 1979), 81.

146. Thomas W. Braden, "I'm Glad the CIA Is 'Immoral'," *Saturday Evening Post*, May 20, 1967, quoted in Ranelagh, *Agency*, 250.

147. U.S. National Security Council, NSC 10/2. See n. 141.

148. Department of State bulletin, vol. 30, no. 780 (June 7, 1954), 881, quoted in Holt, *Radio Free Europe*, 7.

149. U.S. Presidential Study Commission on International Broadcasting (Eisenhower Commission), "The Right to Know" (Washington, D.C.: USGPO, 1973), 2.

150. Mickelson, *America's Other Voice*, 23–28.

151. U.S. Department of State, *Foreign Relations of the United States* [hereafter *FRUS*]: *1950* (Washington, D.C.: USGPO, 1977) 1:237–92.

152. Altschul, "The Present Orientation of Radio Free Europe," Nov. 6, 1950, Altschul Papers. See n. 33.

153. Cord Meyer, *Facing Reality: From World Federalism to the CIA* (New York: Harper and Row, 1980), 114.

4. Starting RFE and RL (1950–1953)

1. Mickelson, *America's Other Voice*, 30–33.

2. Memorandum from DeWitt C. Poole to Frank Altschul, "Script Writing in Washington," May 28, 1950, Altschul Papers. Lehman Collection Columbia Univ. Library, copied in the Mickelson Papers, Hoover Institution on War, Revolution, and Peace, Stanford Univ., Palo Alto, Calif.

3. Mickelson, *America's Other Voice*, 35–41.

4. Free Europe Committee, *The Story of the World Freedom Bell* (Minneapolis, Minn.: Nate L. Crabtree, 1951), 33–37.

5. Ibid., 10–13.

6. Ibid., 44.

7. Philip M. Taylor, *Munitions of the Mind, War Propaganda from the Ancient World to the Nuclear Age* (London: Patrick Stephens, 1990), 223.

8. The Museum of Television and Radio Archive RB 7222, New York.

9. Supplementary memorandum, Feb. 15, 1952, to accompany a memorandum of Feb. 12, 1952, "Preliminary Evaluation of Radio Free Europe," by Mallory Browne to Gordon Gray, director of the Psychological Strategy Board, HSTL, declassified documents RP no. 2918 of 1988.

10. Wanda Washburn (neé Allender), interviewed by the author, Washington, D.C., Nov. 2, 1992. (Wanda Allender became Abbott Washburn's wife.)

11. Louis Galambos, ed., *The Papers of Dwight D. Eisenhower* (Baltimore, Md.: Johns Hopkins Univ. Press, 1989) 12: 492 n. 3.

12. Abbott Washburn, interviewed by the author, Washington, D.C., Nov. 2, 1992.

13. Bennett Kovrig, *Of Walls and Bridges: The United States and Europe* (New York: New York Univ. Press, 1991), 41.

14. John Foster Leich, "Great Expectations: The National Councils in Exile, 1950–60," paper, Dec. 1, 1988, author's collection.

15. David Wedgwood Benn, former head of the Yugoslav section of the BBC World Service, interviewed by the author, London, Jan. 15, 1996.

16. Note by Frank Altschul to DeWitt C. Poole, Aug. 15, 1950, Altschul Papers. See n. 2.

17. Thomas C. Sorenson, *The Word War: The Story of American Propaganda* (New York: Harper and Row, 1968), 12.

18. Arthur E. Meyerhoff, *The Strategy of Persuasion: The Use of Advertising Skills in Fighting the Cold War* (New York: Coward-McCann, 1965), 15.

19. "Radio Free Europe Policy Handbook," cover dated Nov. 30, 1951, but text dated Dec. 12, 1951, Department of State (incomplete), C. D. Jackson Papers, DDEL, declassified documents RP no. 1974, of 1986, section 1, 1.

20. Note, by Frank Altschul to DeWitt C. Poole, Aug. 15, 1950, Altschul Papers. See n. 2.

21. Memorandum by DeWitt C. Poole, "Radio Free Europe," for the Freedom Committee Board and approved by the Board, Nov. 15, 1950, Altschul Papers. See n. 2.

22. Mickelson, *America's Other Voice*, 42 n. 3.

23. Griffith memorandum, "RFE—Four Essential Ingredients of Its Success," Feb. 15, 1952, author's collection.

24. Ranelagh, *Agency*, 199.

25. RFE Policy Handbook, section 1, 3. See n. 19.

26. Ibid., section 14,1

27. Ibid., section 7,1

28. Ibid., section 7,9

29. Ibid., section 12a,1

30. Ibid., section 12,3

31. Ibid., section 15,7

32. Frank Altschul, supplement to note, "The Present Orientation of Radio Free Europe," Nov. 6, 1950, Altschul Papers. See n. 2.

33. Griffith memorandum, Feb. 15, 1952.

34. Altschul, note, Aug. 15, 1950, to DeWitt C. Poole, Altschul Papers. See n. 2.

35. Kovrig, *Walls and Bridges*, 41.

36. Memorandum by Gordon Gray, director of the Psychological Strategy Board to

Mallory Browne, "Evaluation of Radio Free Europe," Top Secret, Dec. 7, 1951, Declassified Documents RP no. 3545 of 1988.

37. Memorandum by Mallory Browne to the director of the PSB, "Preliminary Evaluation of Radio Free Europe," Feb. 12, 1952, Top Secret. HSTL, Declassified Documents RP no. 2918, of 1988.

38. Lawrence C. Soley, *Radio Warfare: OSS and CIA Subversive Propaganda* (New York: Praeger, 1989), 222.

39. Letter from C. D. Jackson to Allen W. Dulles, May 1, 1952, C. D. Jackson Papers, Dwight D. Eisenhower Presidential Library (DDEL), Abilene, Kansas, Declassified Documents RP no. 1094 and 1097, of 1988.

40. Minutes of staff meeting of PSB, May 12, 1952, C. D. Jackson Papers (DDEL), Declassified Documents RP no. 2908, of 1988.

41. Letter of Lewis Galantière to C. D. Jackson, June 6, 1952, enclosing his summary of the record of the Princeton Meeting on Political Warfare, C. D. Jackson Papers (DDEL), Declassified Documents RP no. 1165, of 1988.

42. PSB Minutes, meeting, June 12, 1952, PSB, Minutes, Top Secret, HSTL, Declassified Documents RP no. 1770, of 1988.

43. Mickelson, *America's Other Voice*, 50–62.

44. Jean E. Smith, *Lucius D. Clay: An American Life* (New York: Henry Holt, 1990), 285.

45. Jon Lodeesen, "Radio Liberty (Munich): Foundations for a History," *Historical Journal of Film, Radio and Television* 6, no. 2 (1986): 197–200.

46. Mickelson, *America's Other Voice*, 62–68.

47. James Critchlow, *Radio Hole-in-the-Head/Radio Liberty: An Insider's Story of Cold War Broadcasting* (Washington, D.C.: American Univ. Press, 1995), ix, 11, 91.

48. Library of Congress, 1972a:9, quoted in Abshire, *New Dimension*, 31.

49. Lodeesen, "Radio Liberty," 202.

50. Pirsein, *Voice*, 198–233.

51. *New York Times*, July 10, 1951.

52. Subcommittee of the Committee on Appropriations of the House of Representatives, hearings on Department of State appropriations for 1952, 82d Cong., 1st sess., (Washington, D.C.: USPGO, 1951), 1,972, quoted in Pirsein, *Voice*, i.

53. Sorenson, *Word War*, 29.

54. "The American Image Will Take Care of Itself," *New York Times Magazine*, Feb. 28, 1965.

55. Pirsein, *Voice*, 224–27.

56. Barrett, *Weapon*, 101.

57. Sorensen, *Word War*, 31–41; and Pirsein, *Voice*, 236–312.

58. Alan Heil, "The Voice Past: The VOA, the USSR and Communist Europe," in *Western Broadcasting over the Iron Curtain*, ed. K. R. M. Short, 98–112, (London: Croom Helm, 1986), 100.

59. *Daily Mail*, Mar. 31, 1951, quoted in Mansell, *Truth*, 223.

60. Mansell, *Truth*, 211–24.

61. BBC notes, WAC E2/119/2.

62. BBC Report on Jamming, Feb. 1952, WAC E2/119/2.

63. Quoted in BBC report, "Broadcasts to Eastern Europe," Sept. 26, 1951, WAC E2/119/2.

64. Ninth report from the Select Committee on Estimates Session 1951–52, Overseas Broadcasting, July 30, 1952.

65. Memorandum submitted to the Select Committee on Estimates Session 1951–52 by the Foreign Office and printed in the ninth report, no. 287, BBC Overseas Services, WAC E2/651/1.

66. Foreign Office briefing note, "Foreign Office Influence on the Political Content of Broadcasts," Feb. 13, 1952, PRO FO 953/1487.

67. Rosemarie S. Rogers, "The Soviet Audience: How It Uses the Mass Media" (Ph.D. diss., Massachusetts Institute of Technology, 1967), 167–68.

68. Artyom Panfilov, *Radio SShA v psikhologicheskoy voyne* (U.S. radio in the psychological war). (Moscow: Mezhdunarodnye otnosheniya [Novosti Press Agency Publishing House], 1967), 89–90, quoted in Lisann, *Broadcasting*, 4.

69. BBC Overseas Services, "Conditions in the Soviet Union," Apr. 16, 1951, WAC E2/147.

70. Columbia Univ., Bureau of Applied Social Research, "Listening to the Voice of America and Other Foreign Broadcasts" in Poland, Czechoslovakia, Hungary, Romania, and Bulgaria, plus a comparative report (6 reports total), (New York: Columbia Univ., Oct. 1953, Jan. 1954). USIA Special Reports, Record Group 306, NARA.

71. Columbia Poland Report, ii.

72. Columbia Hungary Report, 2, 4.

73. Columbia Romania Report 2 n. 1.

74. Columbia Comparative Report 3 n. 2.

75. Columbia Hungary Report, 3–5.

76. Columbia Bulgaria Report, 17.

77. Columbia Hungary Report, 13.

78. BBC, "Through the Iron Curtain: The BBC and the Cold War on the Air," *London Calling*, supplement, Oct. 9, 1952, WAC.

79. Columbia Romania Report, 15.

80. Columbia Poland Report, 3.

81. Ibid., 9.

82. Columbia Bulgaria Report, 10.

83. Columbia Romania Report, 34.

84. Columbia Comparative Report, 14.

85. Ibid., 15.

86. Columbia Romania Report, 33.

87. Columbia Czechoslovakia Report, 35.

88. Columbia Romania Report, 49.

89. Columbia Comparative Report, 18.

5. Uprisings (1953–1956)

1. Hans Renner, *A History of Czechoslovakia Since 1945* (London: Routledge, 1989), 28.

2. William Griffith, interviewed by author, Munich, Germany, June 8, 1993.

3. Christian F. Ostermann, "The United States, the East German Uprising of 1953, and the Limits of Rollback" (working paper no. 11, Cold War International History Project, Woodrow Wilson International Center for Scholars, Washington, D.C., Dec. 1994).

4. Ostermann, "East German Uprising," 13–14.

5. Griffith, interview.

6. Ostermann, "East German Uprising," 16–17.

7. "Analysis of the Preparation, Outbreak and Suppression of the Fascist Adven-

tures of June 16–22, 1953," July 20, 1973, SAPMO-BArch, 2/5/546; and report of District Headquarters, June 18, 1953, SAPMO-BArch, NL 90/437, quoted in Ostermann, "East German Uprising," 14–15.

8. The Role of Hostile Broadcasts During the Events in Berlin," June 21, 1953, SAPMO-BArch, NL 90/437, quoted in Ostermann, "East German Uprising," 18.

9. Quoted in Holt, *Radio Free Europe*, 147–49.

10. May 1954, quoted in Holt, *Radio Free Europe*, 149–62.

11. State Department telegram to Warsaw Embassy, Dec. 13, 1954, FOIA no. Poland 8302236, June 27, 1985.

12. A. A. Michie, *Voices Through the Iron Curtain* (New York: Dodd Mead, 1963), 165.

13. Meyer, *Facing Reality*, 120.

14. Norman Davies, *God's Playground: A History of Poland*, 2 vols. (1981; reprint with corrections, Oxford: Oxford Univ. Press, 1991), 2:584.

15. Timothy Garton Ash, *The Polish Revolution: Solidarity* (New York: Charles Scribner's, 1984), 10.

16. *New York Times*, June 30, 1956.

17. Holt, *Radio Free Europe*, 175.

18. Meyer, *Facing Reality*, 122.

19. Michie, *Voices*, 191.

20. Report by the BBC director of external broadcasting, Mar. 5, 1957, WAC R34/1580/3.

21. James D. Marchio, "Rhetoric and Reality: The Eisenhower Administration and Unrest in Eastern Europe, 1953–1959" (Ph.D. diss., American Univ. 1990), 351.

22. C. A. Dolph III to assistant secretary of defense, "Emergency Exploitation of the Hungarian Situation," Oct. 26, 1956, Papers of Admiral Radford, 1953–57, Record Group 218, box 9, NARA.

23. *New York Times*, Oct. 27, 1956, quoted in Marchio, "Rhetoric and Reality," 375.

24. L. B. Bain, *The Reluctant Satellites: An Eyewitness Report on East Europe and the Hungarian Revolution* (New York: Macmillan, 1960), 110.

25. Urban, *Nineteen Days*, 182.

26. *New York Times*, Mar. 25, 1993.

27. Memorandum, Dec. 5, 1956, William Griffith, political adviser, RFE, Munich, to Richard Condon, RFE European director, "Policy Review of Voice of Free Hungary Programming, 23 October–23 November 1956." Author's collection.

28. BBC, Hungarian Section News Bulletins 1956, WAC E35/2/1–4.

29. Report of a U.N. Special Committee on the Problem of Hungary set up by the U.N. General Assembly, 41, WAC E35/45/1.

30. *Editor and Publisher*, Nov. 24, 1956.

31. Meyer, *Facing Reality*, 126–27.

32. Report of a U.N. Special Committee, 51, WAC E35/45/1.

33. *Times*, London, Jan. 26, 1957.

34. *New York Times*, Jan. 26, 1957.

35. *Freies Wort*, Nov. 9, 1956, quoted in Holt, *Radio Free Europe*, 194.

36. Report of a U.N. Special Committee, 51, WAC E35/45/1.

37. *FRUS: 1955–1957*, 25: 436–37.

38. Meyer, *Facing Reality*, 129.

39. "Radio Free Europe," Eisenhower Library NLE MR case no. 80-502, doc. no. 4, declassified, Jan. 22, 1982, and released after FOIA request, Aug. 1994.

40. Griffith Memorandum. See n. 27.

41. Ibid.

42. Ibid.

43. Michie, *Voices*, 257–60.

44. Griffith Memorandum. See n. 27.

45. BBC program, *CIA: Berlin Cowboys*, June 24, 1992.

46. Michael Charlton, *The Eagle and the Small Birds: Crisis in the Soviet Empire: From Yalta to Solidarity* (London: BBC, 1984), 124–25.

47. Telegram from the legation in Hungary to the Department of State, Nov. 19, 1956, 11:00 P.M. *FRUS: 1955–1957*, 25:472.

48. Hungarian Refugee Opinion, Confidential Special Report no. 6, Jan. 1957, Audience Analysis Section, Radio Free Europe, Munich.

49. USIA sponsored survey "The Attitudes, Opinions, and Sources of Information Bearing upon the Hungarian Uprising of 1956," NARA, 1957.

50. USIA, "A Study of Communications and Propaganda Effectiveness in the Light of the Hungarian Revolution of October–November 1956, September 1957."

51. *FRUS: 1955–1957*, 25: 520–21.

52. Griffith, interview.

53. Paul A. Smith, Jr., *On Political War* (Washington, D.C.: National Defense Univ. Press, USGPO, 1990), 209.

54. Griffith, interview.

55. Griffith, interview; and Cord Meyer, interviewed by the author Oct. 7, 1992.

56. Evan Thomas, *The Very Best Men: The Early Years of the CIA* (New York: Simon and Schuster, 1995), 146.

57. Free Europe Committee staff paper, "Radio Free Europe and the Hungarian Uprisings," included with letter of Jan. 9, 1957, from Willis D. Crittenberger, president, Free Europe Committee, to Senator Hubert Humphrey, sec. 1, 2. "RFE's Responsibilities to the United States and to its Listeners, Hungarian Revolt and VOA and RFE, Foreign Relations Disarmament Subcommittee to Hunt, Lewis W.," file SEN 84A-F7, tray 12, Records of the Senate Foreign Relations Committee, 1952–58, Record Group 46, NARA.

58. John Dunning, director of Operations and Planning, Free Europe, 1955–75, telephone interview with Sig Mickelson, May 6, 1982, Mickelson Papers.

59. Marchio, "Rhetoric and Reality," 417.

60. C. D. Jackson to Emmet J. Hughes, Oct. 26, 1956, Time, Inc. file, Emmet J. Hughes, C. D. Jackson papers, DDEL, 1934–67, box 49, quoted in Marchio, "Rhetoric and Reality," 420.

61. Andrew J. Goodpaster, interview with Thomas Soapes, Oct. 11, 1977, Jan. 16, 1978, OH-378, transcript DDEL, quoted in Marchio, "Rhetoric and Reality," 427.

62. S. Walker, M. Delgado, memorandum to Willis D. Crittenberger, Dec. 7, 1956, "Review of the RFE and FEP Operations to Hungary and Poland October 1–December 1, 1956," included with letter from Crittenberger to Senator Humphrey, Jan. 9, 1957, Hungarian Revolt and RFE, Foreign Relations Disarmament Subcommittee to Lewis W. Hunt, file SEN 84A-F7, tray 12, Records of the Senate Foreign Relations Committee, 1952–58, Record Group 46, NARA.

63. Meyer, *Facing Reality*, 126.

64. Pirsein, *Voice*, 367.

65. Memorandum for the president, Nov. 19, 1956, "Voice of America Broadcasts to Hungary," by Abbott Washburn, acting director, Declassified Documents, RP no. 2014, of 1984.

66. Heil, *Voice Past*, 101.

67. Quoted in Urban, *Nineteen Days*, 64.

68. Ibid.

69. Ibid., 250.

70. *Soviet Encyclopedia*, 2d ed., 1951, 7:380, quoted in Urban, *Nineteen Days*, 1.

71. "Hungary and the World 1956: The New Archival Evidence," Sept. 26–29, 1996 (conference, attended by the author, organized by the Institute for the History of the 1956 Revolution, Budapest; Hungarian Academy of Sciences, Budapest; National Security Archive, George Washington Univ., Washington, D.C.; Cold War International History Project, Woodrow Wilson International Center for Scholars, Washington, D.C.).

72. Maria Wittner, interviewed by the author and Duncan Shiels, Reuter correspondent, Budapest, Sept. 28, 1996. She was quoting from Zoltan Benko's book *Tortenelmi Keresztut* (Crossroads of history) (Miskolc: Felso Magyarorszag Kiado, 1994).

73. Paul Henze, interviewed by the author, Budapest, Sept. 29, 1996.

74. Andor Gellert broadcast, Oct. 25, 1956.

75. Sandor Korosi Krizsan broadcast, Oct. 26, 1956.

76. Laszlo Bery broadcast, Oct. 29, 1956.

77. Jan Nowak interviewed by the author, Budapest, Sept. 29, 1996.

78. Andras Mink interviewed by Duncan Shiels, Budapest, Nov. 22, 1996.

79. Free Europe Committee, "The Revolt in Hungary: A Documentary Chronology of Events Based Exclusively on Internal Broadcasts by Central and Provincial Radios, Oct. 23, 1956–Nov. 4, 1956" (New York, n.d.).

80. Mikhail Gorbachev, *Memoirs*, trans. Georges Peronansky and Tatjana Varsavsky (New York: Doubleday, 1996), 633.

81. Andras Mink, report to Ilona Gazdag of Reuters, Budapest, at request of the author, Nov. 15, 1995.

82. Pirsein, *Voice*, 318–21.

83. Jackson committee report (abridged), "Propaganda and Information Activities in the Free World," Declassified Documents RP no. 1163, of 1988.

84. Sorensen, *Word War*, 28–47.

85. Statement by President Eisenhower, released to the press Oct. 28, 1953, quoted in Sorensen, *Word War*, 49.

86. Letter from Theodore C. Streibert, director of the USIA, to President Eisenhower, Oct. 27, 1953, quoted in Sorensen, *Word War*, 50.

87. Walter Lippmann, "Why the Voice of America Should Be Abolished," *Readers Digest*, Aug. 1953, 41.

88. Pirsein, *Voice*, 351.

89. Mansell, *Truth*, 236–37, 239.

90. House of Lords debate, Feb. 6, 1957, quoted in Mansell, *Truth*, 211.

91. Minutes of the Cabinet Committee on Information Services, July 5, 1954, PRO CAB 130 Ref. 102.

92. Summary report of the Independent Committee of Enquiry into the Overseas Information Services, Apr. 1954, White paper, Cmd. 9138.

93. Overseas Information Services: Report of the Drogheda Committee, PRO CAB 129/64 Secret C. (53) 305, Nov. 13, 1953.

94. Note by P. F. Grey, assistant under-secretary, Apr. 10, 1956, PRO FO 953/1641 B1011/17.

95. Memorandum, by C. C. B. Stewart, "Criticism of the External Services of the British Broadcasting Corporation," Sept. 20, 1956, PRO FO 953/1634.

96. Note by P. F. Grey, Apr. 10, 1956, PRO FO 953/1641 B1011/17.

97. Comments on the report of the Drogheda Committee, Board of Governors Paper G94/53, Sept. 25, 1953, BBC Archives, quoted in Mansell, *Truth,* 225.

98. Minutes of Policy Review Committee, July 25, 1956, PRO FO 953/1641.

99. Minutes of Policy Review Committee, July 25, 1956, PRO CAB 134/1215, quoted in W. Scott Lucas, *Divided We Stand: Britain, the US and the Suez Crisis* (London: Hodder and Stoughton, 1991), 167.

100. PRO FO 953/1642, quoted in Peter Partner, *Arab Voices: The BBC Arabic Service, 1938–1988* (London: BBC, 1988), 101.

101. Note by Ivone Kirkpatrick to J. O. Rennie, head of the Foreign Office Information Department, Aug. 28, 1956, PRO FO 953/1643, PB1011/43/G.

102. C. C. B. Stewart memorandum, PRO FO 953/1643.

103. Minutes of Cabinet Meeting, Sept. 26, 1956, PRO CAB 128/30 67(8).

104. Minutes of Cabinet Meeting, Oct. 24, 1956, PRO CAB 128/30 73(4).

105. Sir Alexander Cadogan diary, Oct. 25, 1956, Churchill College Archives, ACAD/1/27.

106. Foreign Office Minutes on government measures against the BBC, PRO FO 953/1645.

107. Mansell, *Truth,* 232, quoting Harman Grisewood, *One Thing at a Time* (London: Hutchinson, 1968), 199, and another unnamed BBC official. Grisewood was chief assistant to the director-general.

108. Mansell, *Truth,* 232–33.

109. Letter from Ivone Kirkpatrick to Ian Jacob, Aug. 16, 1956, and Jacob's reply, Aug. 17, Top Secret and Personal, WAC R34/1580/1.

110. Note by A. D. Dodds Parker, a Foreign Office minister, Oct. 11, 1956, WAC R34/1580/1.

111. Note undated, but annotated as "Late September or Early October," Top Secret, WAC R34/1580/1.

112. Record of meeting of Harvey's Advisory Committee, Top Secret, Feb. 8, 1957, WAC R34/1580/3.

113. Letter from Jacqueline Kavanagh, written archivist, to the author, May 5, 1995.

6. The Beginnings of Détente (1956–1963)

1. Lisann, *Broadcasting,* 9.

2. BBC report, Mar. 5, 1957, WAC R34/1580/3.

3. Report, Aug. 6, 1958, to the Central Committee, signed by L. Ilyichev, A. Romanov, and G. Kazakov, CPA, fond 5, Op. 33, case 75, 163–67.

4. Sorenson, *Word War,* 110–11.

5. Notes of staff meeting of the President's Committee on Information Activities Abroad (PCIAA), Apr. 25, 1960, DDEL, Declassified Documents, RP no. 1,065, of 1991.

6. Memorandum by Gordon Gray, special assistant to President Eisenhower, of his meeting with the president, Sept. 30, 1959, Top Secret, Oct. 1, 1959, DDEL, Declassified Documents, RP no. 1,107, of 1986.

7. Memorandum by George V. Allen for President Eisenhower, "Discussions with Soviets re Jamming and Other Radio Matters," Top Secret, Nov. 5, 1959, DDEL, Declassified Documents, RP no. 2,744, of 1992.

8. Lisann, *Broadcasting,* 9–10.

9. "Air Waves Without 'Black Holes'," report in *Pravda,* Mar. 15, 1989.

10. Note by Maurice Latey, head of the BBC East European service, "Russian Programmes and Selective Jamming," June 1, 1960, WAC E2/669/1.

11. Decree Jan. 19, 1961, CPA, fond 5, Op. 33, case 106.

12. Ibid.

13. Memorandum by P. Morozov to the Central Committee, May 16, 1963, fond 5 (7717), Op. 55, case 20, 180–81.

14. David Wedgwood Benn, *Persuasion and Soviet Politics* (Oxford: Basil Blackwell, 1989), 160.

15. Lisann, *Broadcasting*, 8.

16. Memorandum, Apr. 22, 1959, by G. Kazakov and A. Romanov, "On the Broadcasts of VOA and BBC in Russian and Other Soviet languages," fond 5 Op. 33, case 106, 23–26, 31–42.

17. Lisann, *Broadcasting*, 12.

18. "For the People's-Worker, the People's-Creator," *Sovetskaya Pechat*, Apr. 1963, 33–36, quoted in Lisann, *Broadcasting*, 13–14.

19. Note by Maurice Latey, Jan. 22, 1961, WAC E1/2455/2.

20. PCIAA note, 3, VOA/RFE/RL and RIAS, Secret, Apr. 22, 1960, DDEL, Declassified Documents, RP no. 2907, of 1986.

21. Rhodri Jeffreys-Jones, *The CIA and American Democracy* (New Haven, Conn.: Yale Univ. Press, 1989), 95.

22. Mickelson, *America's Other Voice*, 114–15.

23. Meyer, *Facing Reality*, 120.

24. Mickelson, *America's Other Voice*, 9.

25. Critchlow, *Hole-in-the-Head*, 55–56.

26. Jan Nowak, interviewed by the author, Washington, D.C., Oct. 19, 1990.

27. Victor Marchetti and John D. Marks, *The CIA and the Cult of Intelligence* (New York: Dell, 1974), 176.

28. Meyer, *Facing Reality*, 119.

29. Marchetti and Marks, *CIA*, 176.

30. Ibid., 175.

31. Meyer, *Facing Reality*, 118.

32. Gene Mater, former news director, RFE, interviewed by the author, Washington, D.C., Oct. 17, 1990.

33. Meyer, *Facing Reality*, 117.

34. Ralph Walter, former director, RFE, interviewed by the author, Munich, June 21, 1990.

35. Ralph Walter, "The New Voice of Radio Free Europe," annotation on manuscript by Donald Shanor (research paper, preliminary, Graduate School of Journalism, Columbia School of Journalism, Feb. 1968).

36. William Griffith, interviewed by the author, Munich, June 8, 1993.

37. David Taylor, interviewed by the author, Munich, June 19, 1990.

38. D. R. Browne, *International*, 101.

39. Memorandum from Arthur Larson, USIA director, to Robert Button, "Guidelines on VOA Objective, Content and Tone," July 22, 1957, quoted in Pirsein, *Voice*, 373.

40. Sorenson, *Word War*, 93–104.

41. USIA memorandum to the author, Oct. 28, 1992.

42. "Public Reactions to Little Rock in Major World Capitals" (SR-8), Research and Reference Service, USIA, Oct. 29, 1957, and "The Impact of Sputnik on the Standing of the

U.S. versus the U.S.S.R." (WE-52), Research and Reference Service, USIA, Dec. 1957, quoted in Sorenson, *Word War,* 100–104.

43. Thirteenth Report of the United States Advisory Commission on Information, Jan. 1958, 9, quoted in Sorenson, *Word War,* 103.

44. Sorenson, *Word War,* 236.

45. Ibid., 233.

46. Dwight D. Eisenhower, *The White House Years: Waging Peace 1956–1961* (New York: Doubleday, 1965), 278–79, quoted in Sorenson, *Word War,* 233.

47. "Directive to the Voice of America," USIA, Nov. 1, 1960, quoted in Sorenson, *Word War,* 235.

48. Sorenson, *Word War,* 236.

49. "Voice of America Policy," a directive from Edward R. Murrow, director of USIA, Dec. 4, 1962, quoted in Sorenson, *Word War,* 239.

50. Sorenson, *Word War,* 143.

51. Letter by J. L. B. Titchener of the Foreign Office to J. B. Clark, director of External Broadcasting, with an attached note, "Channels of Communication Between the Foreign Office and the BBC's External Services," Mar. 28, 1957, WAC R34/1580/3.

52. White Paper on Overseas Information Services Cmd. 225 (1957), quoted in Mansell, *Truth,* 233–37.

53. Quoted in the House of Commons debate, July 31, 1957, and quoted in Mansell, *Truth,* 238.

54. *Spectator,* June 21, 1957, quoted in Mansell, *Truth,* 261.

55. *Spectator,* Aug. 16, 1957, quoted in Mansell, *Truth,* 261.

56. Peter Fraenkel, "The BBC External Services: Broadcasting to the USSR and Eastern Europe," in *Western Broadcasting over the Iron Curtain,* ed. K. R. M. Short (London: Croom Helm, 1986), 139–157, 153.

57. Peter Fraenkel, former controller European Services, BBC, interviewed by the author, London, Mar. 9, 1994.

58. M. S. Solvyez, Leningrad Home Service, May 5, 1974, quoted by Peter Fraenkel, *BBC,* 152.

59. Gregory MacDonald, head of the BBC Central European service, notes on a meeting, Mar. 30, 1960, with Ralph Murray of the Foreign Office, WAC E2/669/1.

60. BBC memorandum, "Broadcasting to the Satellites", Oct. 10, 1960, sent to the Foreign Office Oct. 20, 1960, WAC E2/669/1.

61. Letter from Ralph Murray of the Foreign Office to Tangye Lean of the BBC, Mar. 2, 1961, WAC E2/669/1.

62. BBC memorandum, "Broadcasting to the Satellites," Aug. 14, 1961, sent by James Monahan of the BBC to Donald Stewart at the Foreign Office, Aug. 16, 1961, WAC E2/669/1.

63. Gerard Mansell, former managing director, External Services, BBC, interviewed by the author, London, May 17, 1995.

64. Mansell, *Truth,* 263.

7. Other Major Broadcasters

1. Father Pasquale Borgomeo, director-general of Vatican Radio speech, Moscow, Dec. 19, 1990, author's collection; and Cabasés, "Radio Vaticano," 1,003–19.

2. Quoted in Marilyn J. Matelski, *Vatican Radio: Propagation by the Airwaves* (Westport, Conn.: Praeger, 1995), 82.

3. *New York Times,* Sept. 24, 1950, quoted in Matelski, *Vatican Radio,* 81–82.

4. *New York Times,* Oct. 28, 1957, quoted in Matelski, *Vatican Radio,* 82.

5. Father Félix Juan Cabasés, Gregorian Univ., Rome, interviewed by the author, Rome, July 3, 1996.

6. Reuter report, Sept. 1, 1978, quoted in Donald Read, *The Power of News: The History of Reuters* (Oxford: Oxford Univ. Press, 1992), frontispiece.

7. Cabasés, "Radio Vaticano," 1,210.

8. Figures provided to the author by Vatican Radio, July 2, 1996. The actual expenditure was converted by Vatican Radio in 1993 terms. The actual expenses in 1989 were U.S. $19,590,000 (26,878 million lire).

9. Statuto della Radio Vaticana, approved by the pope Sept. 1, 1995, effective Oct. 1, 1995.

10. Father Borgomeo, interviewed by the author, Rome, July 5, 1996.

11. Father Borgomeo, interview, July 5, 1996.

12. Ibid.

13. Figures provided to the author by Vatican Radio, July 2, 1996.

14. Father Borgomeo, speech, Moscow, Dec. 19, 1990.

15. Father Borgomeo, interviewed by the author, Washington, D.C., Nov. 6, 1990.

16. Brunnquell, *Fréquence Monde,* 66–67.

17. Radio France Internationale. "Radio France Internationale 1931–92: Aux vents de l'histoire" (Radio France International, 1931–92—On the winds of history) (Paris: Apr., 1993), 15, 19.

18. Brunnquell, *Fréquence Monde,* 82.

19. Ibid., 96.

20. Ibid., 134.

21. *Radio France,* 26, 27, 28.

22. Brunnquell, *Fréquence Monde,* 83.

23. Ibid., 167.

24. *Radio France,* 27.

25. Deutsche Welle "Monitor," Aug. 24, 1972, quoted in Brunnquell, *Fréquence Monde,* 129.

26. Arthur Siegel, *Radio Canada International: History and Development* (Oakville, Ontario: Mosaic Press, 1996), 12.

27. Order in Council P. C. 8186, Sept. 18, 1942, quoted in Siegel, *Radio Canada International,* 81.

28. Siegel, *Radio Canada International,* 104.

29. Ibid., 169.

30. Terry Hargreaves, interviewed by the author, Montreal, Sept. 9, 1992.

31. Siegel, *Radio Canada International,* 107.

32. James Hall, "The Cold War Intensifies," in *Radio Canada* (East Lansing: Michigan State Univ. Press, forthcoming).

33. Report of the Radio Canada International Task Force, May 9, 1973, author's collection.

34. Siegel, *Radio Canada International,* 161–62.

35. Ward and Koshits, *Broadcasting,* 27–56.

36. *New York Times,* May 20, 1992.

37. USIA, *Four Decades of Broadcasting 1946–1986, RIAS Berlin* (Bonn: USIA, 1986).

38. Daugherty, *Warfare Casebook*, 146.

39. CIA memorandum, "Soviet Use of Assassination and Kidnapping," Feb. 1964, prepared for the President's Commission on the Assassination of President Kennedy (The Warren Commission), republished in entirety in *Studies in Intelligence*, 19, no. 3 (fall 1975), 9.

40. *Manchester Guardian*, Aug. 25, 1961.

41. M. C. Partridge, major general G-2, to Allen Dulles, Aug. 3, 1953, C. D. Jackson Papers, box 74, DDEL, quoted in Ostermann, *East German Uprising*, 14.

42. *New York Times*, May 20, 1992.

43. Agreement in Nr. 31 Tag der Ausgabe, Official Gazette, Bonn, Sept. 12, 1992.

44. Botho Kirsch, "Der Kampf um die Freie Meinung" (The struggle for freedom of thought), in *Auftrag Deutschland, Nach der Einheit: Unser Land der Welt vermitteln*, ed. Dieter Weirich (Mainz: v Hase und Koehler Verlag, 1993), 169.

45. Memorandum from E. Mamedov, deputy head of the Council of Ministers' Radio and TV Committee, of Sept. 4, 1962, CPA, fond 5, vol. 4818, Op. 33, case 207, 46–47.

46. Memorandum to the Central Committee from A. Egorov and A. Yakovlev, of the Central Committee's Department of Propaganda to the Union Republics, Sept. 26, 1962, CPA, fond 5, vol. 4818, Op. 33, case 207, 48.

47. Botho Kirsch, "Deutsche Welle's Russian Service, 1962–1985," in *Western Broadcasting over the Iron Curtain*, ed. K. R. M. Short (London: Croom Helm, 1986), 158–71, 159, and Juergen Reiss, "Deutschlandfunk: Broadcasting to East Germany and Eastern Europe," in *Western Broadcasting over the Iron Curtain*, ed K. R. M. Short (London: Croom Helm, 1986), 172–75, 172–84.

48. Helmut S. Ruppert, deputy head of the German Program, DW, interviewed by the author, Cologne, July 7, 1994.

49. Botho Kirsch, head of the East European desk, DW, interviewed by the author, Cologne, July 7, 1994.

50. Dieter Weirich, director-general of DW, interviewed by the author, Cologne, July 7, 1994.

51. Michail Antonow, head of the Bulgarian desk, DW, interviewed by the author, Cologne, July 7, 1994.

8. Clearer Airwaves (1963–1968)

1. Lisann, *Broadcasting*, 13–17, and Maurice Latey, "The End of Communist Jamming," *Ariel*, Aug. 1964, 17.

2. Note by Gregory Macdonald, head of the BBC Central European service, to James Monahan, controller, European services, Mar. 30, 1960, WAC E2/669/1.

3. Hearing before the Committee on Foreign Relations, U.S. Senate, 92d Cong., 1st sess., on S.18 and S.1936, May 24, 1971 (Washington, D.C.: USGPO, 1971), 47.

4. Lisann, *Broadcasting*, 154.

5. T. Kenzhebayev, "Timeliness Is the Sister of Success," *Sovetskoye Radio i Televideniye*, Mar. 1963, 8, quoted in Lisann, *Broadcasting*, 12.

6. M. Barmankulov, a dean of journalism, in "Battle on the Air," *Prostor*, Alma Ata, Aug. 1968, 110–14, quoted in Lisann, *Broadcasting*, 33.

7. A. Raphokin, a deputy chairman of the State Committee, in "Radio, Man and

His World," *Sovetskoye Radio i Televideniye,* May 1968, 5–7, quoted in Lisann, *Broadcasting,* 33.

8. Gayle Durham Hollander, "Recent Developments in Soviet Radio and Television Reporting," *Public Opinion Quarterly* 31, no. 3 (1967): 359–65, quoted in Lisann, *Broadcasting,* 34.

9. "Anti-Sovietism—One of the Main Trends in the Ideology of Modern Imperialism," *Kommunist* (unsigned) 10 (July 1965): 64–67, quoted in Lisann, *Broadcasting,* 36–37.

10. Quoted by David Nicholas in "Learn, Baby, Learn," *Times,* London, July 14, 1992.

11. Gabriel Partos, *The World that Came in from the Cold: Perspectives from East and West on the Cold War* (London: RIIA and BBC, 1993), 86.

12. Memorandum by N. Mesyatsev, July 2, 1965, CPA, fond 5, vol. 4,829, Op. 33, case 227, 49–50.

13. Memorandum by A. Yakovlev and P. Moskovski to the Central Committee, Mar. 9, 1966, CPA, fond 5, vol. 4,823, Op. 33, case 227, 51.

14. Memorandum to the Central Committee Propaganda Department from V. Semichastny, Dec. 31, 1965, CPA, fond 5, vol. 5,823, Op. 33, case 227, 209–10.

15. Ibid.

16. *Times,* London, Dec. 10, 1994.

17. William Taubman, *The View from Lenin Hills* (London: Hamish Hamilton, 1968), 78, 160.

18. Lisann, *Broadcasting,* 68.

19. Vladimir Osipov, "The Keys of the BBC," *Zhurnalist,* May 1968, 56–59, quoted in Lisann, *Broadcasting,* 68–69.

20. Lisann, *Broadcasting,* 67, 89–91.

21. I. Dzhus, "Around the Sharp Questions," *Pravda,* Jan. 26, 1967, quoted in Lisann, *Broadcasting,* 77.

22. Lisann, *Broadcasting,* 154–55.

23. Ellen Mickiewicz, *Media and the Russian Public* (New York: Praeger, 1981), 139.

24. Robert Evans, formerly Reuters chief representative, Moscow, interviewed by the author, Feb. 27, 1991.

25. Ludmilla Alexeyeva and Paul Goldberg, *The Thaw Generation: Coming of Age in the Post-Stalin Era* (Boston: Little, Brown, 1990), 130.

26. Ludmilla Alexeyeva, *Soviet Dissent: Contemporary Movements for National Religious and Human Rights* (Middletown, Conn.: Wesleyan Univ. Press, 1985), 277.

27. Andrei Amalrik, *Notes of a Revolutionary,* trans. Guy Daniels (New York: Alfred A. Knopf, 1982), 52.

28. Alexeyeva and Goldberg, *Thaw Generation,* 139.

29. Ibid., 182.

30. Lisann, *Broadcasting,* 91.

31. Nicholas Bethell, *Spies and Other Secrets: Memoirs of the Second Cold War* (London: Viking, 1994), 103.

32. Joshua Rubenstein, *Soviet Dissidents: Their Struggle for Human Rights* (London: Wildwood House, 1980), 72.

33. Alexeyeva, *Soviet Dissent,* 285–87.

34. Ibid., 318.

35. Vladimir Bukovsky, *To Build a Castle: My Life as a Dissenter,* trans. Michael Scammell (London: Andre Deutsch, 1978), 31–32.

36. Ibid., 210.

37. Ibid., 268–69.

38. Amalrik, *Notes*, 206.

39. Ibid., 251.

40. Ibid., 192.

41. Quoted by Valery Chalidze, *To Defend These Rights: Human Rights and the Soviet Union*, trans. Guy Daniels (London: Collins and Harvill Press, 1975), 68.

42. M. P. Mikhailov, and V. V. Nazarov, *Ideologicheskya diversiya-vooruzheniye imperializma* (Ideological diversion is the armament of imperialism) (Moscow: 1969), quoted in Chalidze, *Rights*, 69.

43. Jean Huteau and Bernard Ullmann, *AFP: Une histoire de l'Agence France-Presse, 1944–1990* (AFP: A history of Agence France-Presse, 1944–1990) (Paris: Robert Laffont, 1992), 406.

44. Amalrik, *Notes*, 283.

45. Donald Shanor, "The New Voice of Radio Free Europe" (research paper, preliminary, Columbia School of Journalism, Feb. 1968), 168–205.

46. Brian Crozier, *Free Agent: The Unseen War 1941–1991* (London: Harper Collins, 1993), 75.

47. CBS transcript, "CBS News Special Report," "In the Pay of the CIA: An American Dilemma," Mickelson Archive.

48. *New York Times*, Apr. 27, 1966.

49. Executive Sessions of the Senate Foreign Relations Committee (historical series), vol. 18, 89th Cong., 2d sess., 1966, 388. Made public Feb. 1993.

50. Erik Barnouw, *The Image Empire: A History of Broadcasting in the United States*, 3 vols. (New York: Oxford Univ. Press, 1966–70), iii, 107.

51. Lisann, *Broadcasting*, 25.

52. David Taylor, interviewed by the author, Munich, June 19, 1990.

53. Report (to accompany S. 18) Senate Committee on Foreign Relations, July 30, 1971, 10 (included in the speech of Senator Case [N.J.] delivered on Jan. 25, 1971), quoted in Mickelson, *America's Other Voice*, 125.

54. Meyer, *Facing Reality*, 133.

55. Sorenson, *Word War*, 240.

56. Ibid., 241–45.

57. Ibid., 246–47.

58. *New York Times*, June 1, 1967, quoted in D. R. Browne, *International*, 105.

59. *New York Times*, Apr. 10, 1969, quoted in D. R. Browne, *International*, 105.

60. Review of Sorenson, *Word War*, quoted in John W. Henderson, *The United States Information Agency* (New York: Praeger, 1969), 170.

61. James Monahan, controller of the BBC European services, "Broadcasting to Europe," 18.

62. Maurice Latey, head of the BBC's East European service, "Broadcasting to the USSR and Eastern Europe" (BBC lunch-time lecture, Nov. 11, 1964), 9–11.

63. Mansell, *Truth*, 245.

64. Latey, "Broadcasting," 12–15.

65. BBC, "European service," 21.

66. BIB Annual Report, 1989, 41–52, RFE/RL.

67. Holt, *Radio Free Europe*, 123.

68. Ibid., 123–37.

69. Ibid., 131.

70. Ibid., 133.

71. Ibid., 137.

72. USIA Report, "The Impact of Western Broadcasts in the Soviet Bloc," Mar. 1959, i, NARA.

73. USIA, sponsored survey, "The Attitudes, Opinions and Sources of Information Bearing upon the Hungarian Uprising of 1956," 1957, NARA.

74. USIA sponsored report, "Recent Information on Western Radio Listening in Poland During 1962," Jan. 28, 1963, NARA.

75. USIA, Mar. 1959 report, 1–11.

76. Note by Gregory Macdonald, assistant head of the BBC East European service, "Listening to Foreign Broadcasts in the USSR," Dec. 18, 1958, WAC E1/1971/1.

77. USIA, Mar. 1959 report, 24.

78. Ibid., 32–34.

79. Lisann, *Broadcasting*, 4–5.

80. USIA report, "Recent Information on the Voice of America Behind the Iron Curtain," Feb. 28, 1958, Declassified Dec. 21, 1992, NARA.

81. Report by Max Rallis, RL Munich, Jan. 14, 1970, Lodeesen Papers, Georgetown Univ. Library, Washington, D.C.

9. Czechoslovak Invasion and After (1968–1979)

1. Briggs, *History of Broadcasting* 5: 690–91.

2. Y. Nozhin, "The Law of Precedence," *Sovetskoye Radio i Televideniye*, May 1969, 34–37, quoted in Lisann, *Broadcasting*, 103.

3. Lisann, *Broadcasting*, 101–2.

4. Ralph Walter, in a letter to the author, Mar. 23, 1995.

5. Richard Davy, ed., *European Détente: A Reappraisal* (London: RIIA, 1992), 19.

6. John Barron, *KGB Today: The Hidden Hand* (London: Hodder and Stoughton; New York: Reader's Digest Press, 1983), 146–47, quoted in Crozier, *Free Agent*, 125.

7. Alexeyeva, *Soviet Dissent*, 335–36.

8. U.S. Department of State, 1975: 117–118, quoted in Abshire, *New Dimension*.

9. *New York Times*, Oct. 8, 1975, quoted in Abshire, *New Dimension*, 15.

10. Abshire, *New Dimension*, 15.

11. Martin Gilbert, *Shcharansky: Hero of Our Time* (London: Penguin, 1987), 235.

12. Bethell, *Spies*, 91.

13. Quoted in Robert G. Kaiser, *Russia: The People and the Power* (New York: Atheneum, 1976), 187.

14. Heil, *Voice Past*, 109.

15. Lendvai, *Bureaucracy of Truth*, 218–19.

16. Abshire, *New Dimension*, 15.

17. Richard Helms, former director, CIA, interviewed by the author, Washington, D.C., Sept. 28, 1993.

18. Cord Meyer, interviewed by the author by telephone, Washington, D.C., Oct. 4, 1993.

19. Quoted in Mickelson, *America's Other Voice*, 130.

20. J. William Fulbright, *The Arrogance of Power* (New York: Random House, 1966), 3, 246.

21. Richard Helms, interviewed by the author, Washington, D.C., Sept. 28, 1993.

22. *Congressional Record*, 92d Cong., 2d. sess., 1972, vol. 118, no. 21.

23. Ibid.

24. Mickelson, *America's Other Voice*, 129–38.

25. Statement by President Nixon, May 10, 1972, *The Right to Know,* Report of the Presidential Study Commission on International Radio Broadcasting (Washington, D.C.,: USGPO, 1973), app. A-3.

26. Mansell, *Broadcasting to the World.*

27. Letter of appointment to the commission chair, Aug. 9, 1972, U.S. Presidential Commission on International Broadcasting, *Right to Know,* app. A-1.

28. U.S. Presidential Commission on International Broadcasting, *Right to Know,* 2.

29. Ibid., 55.

30. Interview with American newsmen, *New York Times,* Apr. 2, 1972, quoted in U.S. Presidential Commission on International Broadcasting, *Right to Know,* ii.

31. Andrei D. Sakharov's book, *Progress, Coexistence and Intellectual Freedom,* quoted in U.S. Presidential Commission on International Broadcasting, *Right to Know,* 7.

32. U.S. Presidential Commission on International Broadcasting, *Right to Know,* 11, quoting J. William Fulbright, *Prospects for the West* (Cambridge, 1963), 20–21.

33. U.S. Presidential Commission on International Broadcasting, *Right to Know,* 3–4.

34. Ibid., 38.

35. Ibid., 4–5.

36. BIB annual report, 1979, 32, RFE/RL.

37. *New York Times,* July 24, 1970, and July 23, 1970, quoted in Laurien Alexandre, *The Voice of America: From Détente to the Reagan Doctrine* (Norwood, N.J.: Ablex Publishing, 1988), 24.

38. Frank Shakespeare, "Who's Winning the Propaganda War?" *U.S. News and World Report,* May 1, 1972, quoted in Alexandre, *Voice of America,* 26.

39. "Capitol Briefs," *Human Events,* Mar. 2, 1974, quoted in Alexandre, *Voice of America,* 27.

40. James Keogh's response to Representative Robert L. F. Sykes, Mar. 5, 1974, quoted by Heil in *Voice Past,* 105.

41. Heil, *Voice Past,* 107–8.

42. Whitley to Cape, Apr. 6, 1970, quoted in Mansell, *Truth,* 257.

43. Fraenkel, *BBC,* 155.

44. Record by Charles Curran of his meeting with Goronwy Roberts, minister of state, Foreign Office, Feb. 7, 1968, WAC E2/651/1.

45. Anthony Howard, *New Statesman,* Aug. 5, 1977, quoted in Mansell, *Truth,* 258.

46. *Economist,* Aug. 6, 1977, quoted in Mansell, *Truth,* 258.

47. Crozier, *Free Agent,* 120.

48. *Guardian,* Jan. 27, 1978.

49. Mary Seton-Watson, formerly head of the BBC Russian service, interviewed by the author, London, Aug. 8, 1991.

50. Mansell, *Truth,* 259–60.

51. Tusa, *Conversations,* 59–60.

52. Quoted in Robert M. Gates, *From the Shadows: The Ultimate Insider's Story of Five Presidents and How They Won the Cold War* (New York: Simon and Schuster, 1996), 95.

53. Artyom Panfilov, *Radiovoyna: Istoriya i sovremennost', Ocherki o vneshnepoliticheskoy radiopropagande fashistskoy Germanii, SShA, Anglii i FRG* (Radio wars: History and the contemporary world. Studies of foreign radio propaganda of fascist Germany, the U.S., England, and the Federal German Republic) (Moscow: Iskusstvo, 1984), 129–30.

54. David Wedgwood Benn, summary and analysis of "The BBC: History, Apparatus, Methods of Radio Propaganda" by Vladimir Artyomov and Vladimir Semyonov (Moscow 1979), *Historical Journal of Film, Radio and Television,* 4, no. 1, (1984) 73–89.

55. Ibid., 76, quoting from p. 134 of the book.

56. Georgi Markov, *The Truth that Killed* (London: Weidenfeld and Nicolson, 1983), 225.

57. Annabel Markov, Introduction, Markov, *Truth that Killed*, xii.

58. Maggi O'Sullivan, "Death on Waterloo Bridge," *London Portrait*, May 1990, 123–125.

59. Annabel Markov, Introduction, Markov, *Truth that Killed*, xiii.

60. *International Herald Tribune*, July 30, 1990.

61. *Evening Standard*, Feb. 3, 1990.

62. *Independent*, Feb. 22, 1991.

63. *Independent*, Nov. 15, 1991.

64. Oleg Kalugin with Fen Montaigne, *Spymaster: My 32 Years of Intelligence and Espionage Against the West* (London: Smith Gryphon, 1994), 178–79.

65. Kalugin, *Spymaster*, 180–83.

66. Richard H. Cummings, "Bulgaria: Code Name 'Piccadilly'—The Murder of Georgi Markov," *Intelligence*, no. 28, Internet, Jan. 8, 1996.

67. Peter Fraenkel, interviewed by the author, London, Mar. 9, 1994.

68. Cummings, "Bulgaria."

10. Solidarity (1979–1989)

1. Article in *La Stampa*, Mar. 3, 1992, quoted in Michael Bordeaux, "The Role of Religion in the Fall of Soviet Communism," Centre for Policy Studies, the Hugh Seton-Watson Memorial Lecture, London, Apr. 1992.

2. Cabasés, "Radio Vaticano," 1,223.

3. Radek Sikorski, *Spectator*, Sept. 10, 1994.

4. Report of an internal CIA review panel released as part of Senate Intelligence Committee hearings quoted in the *New York Times*, Oct. 2, 1991.

5. Adam Michnik, *Letters from Prison, and Other Essays*, trans. Maya Latynski (Berkeley and Los Angeles: Univ. of California Press, 1985), 162.

6. David Willey, *God's Politician: John Paul at the Vatican* (London: Faber and Faber, 1992), 7.

7. Father Lech Rynkiewicz, director of promotion and development, Vatican Radio, interviewed by the author, Rome, July 4, 1996.

8. Father Robert A. White, Gregorian Univ., Rome, interviewed by the author, Rome, July 2, 1996.

9. Jerzy Urban, Polish government spokesman, interviewed by Frederick Kempe in Warsaw and published in the *Wall Street Journal*, Aug. 14, 1984.

10. Michnik, *Letters*, 17–18.

11. Eva Hoffman, *Exit into History: A Journey Through Eastern Europe* (London: Heinemann, 1993), 39.

12. International Press Institute (IPI) report, Apr. 1994, 6.

13. Andrzej Swidlicki, *Political Trials in Poland 1981–1986* (Beckenham, Kent: Croom Helm, 1988), 106, 266.

14. *Time*, Feb. 24, 1992.

15. *Times*, London, Jan. 25, 1992.

16. John Tusa, *A World in Your Ear: Reflections on Changes* (London: Broadside Books, 1992), 19.

17. Roger Boyes, *The Naked President: A Political Life of Lech Walesa* (London: Secker and Warburg, 1994), 113.

18. Anthony T. Salvia, "Poland's Walesa Addresses RFE/RL Fund Conference," *Shortwaves,* Nov. 1989, 1.

19. Jacques Semelin, "Communication et Résistance: Les Radios occidentales comme vecteur d'ouverture à l'est" (Communication and resistance: Western radios as the vector for the opening to the east) (Paris: Réseaux no. 53, CNET, June 1992), 9–24.

20. Paul Lendvai, *Financial Times,* Nov. 20, 1980.

21. *Wall Street Journal,* June 12, 1981.

22. Michnik, *Letters,* 103.

23. Message to the Polish Section, RFE, May 3, 1992, BIB 1993 annual report, 5, RFE/RL.

24. BIB 1990 annual report, 4, RFE/RL.

25. Timothy Garton Ash, "Poland after Solidarity" quoting Bronislaw Geremek in a review of Geremek's book, *The Year 1989: Bronislaw Geremek Relates, Jacek Zakowski Asks, New York Review of Books,* June 13, 1991.

26. Georgui Vatchnadze interviewed by the author and Robert Evans, Reuters chief correspondent in Moscow, Moscow, June 10, 1991.

27. CIA, "USSR, and Eastern Europe Review," Sept. 11, 1980, declassified after FOIA request, Oct. 1994.

28. Vitaly Korotich, editor of *Ogonyok,* interviewed by the author and Robert Evans, Moscow, June 11, 1991.

29. Leonid Kravchenko, head of Soviet television, interviewed by the author and Robert Evans, Moscow, June 12, 1991.

30. Botho Kirsch, interviewed by the author, Cologne, July 7, 1994.

31. Jonathan Eyal, "Recent Developments in the Jamming of Western Radio Stations Broadcasting to the USSR and Eastern Europe," Radio Liberty research report, Nov. 7, 1986, RFE/RL.

32. *Komsomol'skaya pravda,* May 20, 1981, quoted in Sergei Voronitsyn, "Latest Soviet Efforts to Counter the Influence of Foreign Radio Broadcasts," Radio Liberty research report, July 5, 1982, RFE/RL.

33. *Komsomol'skaya pravda,* Mar. 11, 1982, quoted in Voronitsyn, "Latest Soviet Efforts."

34. *Trud,* Apr. 10, 1982, quoted in Voronitsyn, "Latest Soviet Efforts."

35. *Sotsialisticheskaya industriya,* Apr. 9, 1982, quoted in Voronitsyn, "Latest Soviet Efforts."

36. *Izvestia,* July 10, 1984, quoted in Arnold Beichman, "The Story of Radio Free Europe," the *National Review,* Nov. 2, 1984, and carried on the RFE B-Wire, Oct. 22, 1984.

37. *New York Times,* Aug. 25, 1987.

38. BIB annual report 1988, 23, RFE/RL.

39. *New York Times,* Aug. 25, 1987.

40. Ibid.

41. Hedrick Smith, *The New Russians* (London: Hutchinson, 1990), 26.

42. Russian journalists, interviewed by the author and Robert Evans, June 11, 1991.

43. R. Eugene Parta, "SAAOR at RFE/RL," in *Western Broadcasting over the Iron Curtain,* ed. K. R. M. Short, 227–44 (London: Croom Helm, 1986), 230.

44. CIA report, "Impact of Western Radio Broadcasts in the Soviet Union," distributed May 5, 1986, released in Oct. 1994 after FOIA request.

45. Hélène Carrère d'Encausse, *The End of the Soviet Empire: The Triumph of the Nations,* trans. Franklin Philips (New York: Basic Books, 1992), xii.

46. Bethell, *Spies,* 37.

47. Kaiser, *Russia,* 247.

48. BIB annual report 1984, 11, RFE/RL.

49. *Sunday Times,* London, May 19, 1991.

50. International Civil Aviation Organization (ICAO), "Report of the Completion of the Fact-Finding Investigation Regarding the Shooting Down of Korean Air Lines Boeing 747 (Flight KE 007) on 31 August 1983," May 28, 1993, author's collection.

51. Kaiser, *Russia,* 244.

52. Elena Bonner, interviewed by the author, Montreal, Sept. 9, 1992.

53. Carrère d'Encausse, *Soviet Empire,* 15.

54. Kaiser, *Russia,* 262.

55. Pavel Litvinov, *The Demonstration in Pushkin Square,* trans. Manya Harari (London: Harvill Press, 1969), 9.

56. Karl Marx, "Debates on Freedom of the Press and Publication of Proceedings of the Assembly of the States," in Karl Marx and Frederick Engels, *Collected Works,* vol. 1, *Karl Marx: 1835–43* (New York: International Publishers, 1975), 167–68, quoted in Hedrick Smith, *New Russians,* 95.

57. Kaiser, *Russia,* 224–25.

58. Remnick, *Lenin's Tomb,* 520.

59. *Sunday Times,* London, Jan. 5, 1986.

60. Vitali Vitaliev, *Dateline Freedom* (London: Hutchinson, 1991), 65–66.

61. Julia Wishnevsky, "Western Radio Stations and Soviet Law," Radio Liberty research report, Jan. 16, 1985, RFE/RL.

62. *Sunday Times,* London, Nov. 3, 1985.

63. Scott Shane, *Dismantling Utopia: How Information Ended the Soviet Union* (Chicago: Ivan R. Dee, 1994), 40.

64. "Truth Is in the Air," *Economist,* June 6, 1987, 17–19.

65. Henry Hamman and Stuart Parrott, *Mayday at Chernobyl* (London: New English Library, 1987), 14–16.

66. Piers Paul Read, *Ablaze: The Story of Chernobyl* (London: Martin Secker and Warburg, 1993), 245.

67. *Independent,* Aug. 21, 1991.

68. Hedrick Smith, *New Russians,* 99.

69. James E. Oberg, *Uncovering Soviet Disasters: Exploring the Limits of Glasnost* (London: Robert Hale, 1988), 253.

70. Grigori Medvedev, *The Truth about Chernobyl,* trans. Evelyn Rossiter (London: I. B. Tauris, 1989), 20.

71. Ibid.

72. Charlton, *Eagle,* 133.

73. Marquis de Custine, *Empire of the Czar: A Journey Through Eternal Russia* (1839; reprint, New York: Doubleday, 1989), 268–69.

74. Kingsley Amis, *Memoirs* (London: Hutchinson, 1991), 239.

75. George Bailey, "The Perception Mongers: Reflections on Soviet Propaganda," Occasional Paper 44, Institute for European Defence and Strategic Studies (London, 1990), 25–26.

76. David Wedgwood Benn, *From Glasnost to Freedom of Speech: Russian Openness and International Relations* (London: RIIA, 1992), 29–30.

77. Henrikas Yushkiavitshus, interviewed by the author, Paris, Sept. 29, 1995.

78. CIA cable, Jan. 1988, Declassified Documents ND 1887, 1989.

79. BIB annual report 1989, 1, RFE/RL.

80. Yushkiavitshus, interview.

81. Mickelson, *America's Other Voice*, 5–8.

82. Note by Glenn Ferguson, president of RFE/RL to RFE/RL staff, Feb. 22, 1981, RFE/RL.

83. Mickelson, *America's Other Voice*, 8.

84. BIB annual report 1982, 1, RFE/RL.

85. Mickelson, *America's Other Voice*, 9.

86. *Primetime Live*, Jan. 3, 1991, show no. 175.

87. Ibid.

88. David Yallop, *To the Ends of the Earth: The Hunt for the Jackal* (London: Jonathan Cape, 1993), 435.

89. "Ex-Radio Employee Given Jail Term for Plans to Bomb RFE/RL," *Shortwaves*, Sept.–Oct. 1993, 2–4.

90. Letter of November 1991 from Kalman Georgyi, Hungarian state prosecutor, to RFE/RL, quoted in story by RFE/RL, "Carlos and the RFE connection," Aug. 18, 1994.

91. "Ex-KGB General Addresses RFE/RL Staffers in Munich," *Shortwaves*, Aug.–Sept. 1991, 8.

92. Kalugin, *Spymaster*, 194–96.

93. *Shortwaves*, Sept.–Oct. 1993, 2–4.

94. William Marsh of RFE/RL, interviewed by the author, Munich, June 11, 1993.

95. *Sunday Times*, London, Nov. 3, 1985.

96. William A. Buell, "RFE/RL in the Mid 1980s," in *Western Broadcasting over the Iron Curtain*, ed. K. R. M. Short, 69–97 (London: Croom Helm, 1986), 72.

97. Richard M. Nixon, *The Real War* (New York: Warner Books, 1980), 310.

98. Quoted in BIB annual report 1983, 5, RFE/RL.

99. BIB annual report 1983, 25, RFE/RL.

100. BIB annual report 1984, 1, RFE/RL.

101. George Urban, former director, RFE, interviewed by the author, Brighton, England, Mar. 22, 1991.

102. Ralph Walter, former director, RFE, interviewed by the author, Munich, June 7, 1993.

103. Trip report, "Oversight of Operations of Radio Free Europe/Radio Liberty, Inc.," Mar. 8, 1985, author's collection.

104. "VOA Modernization: Slow Going," *Broadcasting*, Oct. 24, 1988, 60.

105. Edward Mainland, Mark Pomar, and Kurt Carlson, "The Voice Present and Future: VOA, the USSR and Communist Europe," in *Broadcasting over the Iron Curtain*, ed. K. R. M. Short (London: Croom Helm, 1986), 113–36, 136.

106. Based on figures provided to author by VOA, Oct. 28, 1992.

107. Mainland, Pomar, and Carlson, "Present and Future," 124.

108. Heil, *Voice Past*, 110.

109. *Foreign Affairs*, May 1980, quoted in Heil, *Voice Past*, 108.

110. Mainland, Pomar, and Carlson, "Present and Future," 125.

111. Alexandre, *Voice of America*, 103.

112. U.S. National Security Council, NSSD 45, July 15, 1982, 90447 Secret, partially declassified, Dec. 20, 1991, NARA. Facsimile reproduced in Christopher Simpson, *National Security Directives of the Reagan and Bush Administrations: The Declassified History of U.S. Political and Military Policy, 1981–1991.* (Boulder: Westview Press, 1995), 155.

113. U.S. National Security Council, NSDD 77, Jan. 14, 1983, NARA, facsimile reproduced in Simpson, *Directives*, 265.

114. President Reagan, *Los Angeles Times*, Sept. 11, 1983, quoted in Alexandre, *Voice of America*, 118.

115. "Wick Legacy: Making a Difference," *Broadcasting*, Nov. 7, 1988, 43–44.

116. *ABC World News Tonight*, June 17, 1993, transcript no. 3120.

117. Peter Schweizer, *Victory: The Reagan Administration's Secret Strategy That Hastened the Collapse of the Soviet Union* (New York: Atlantic Monthly Press, 1994), 89, interview with Wick.

118. Schweizer, *Victory*, 121.

119. RFE/RL executive, interviewed by the author.

120. Quoted in Fred Coleman, *The Decline and Fall of the Soviet Empire: Forty Years That Shook the World, from Stalin to Yeltsin* (New York: St. Martin's Press, 1996), 63.

121. *Washington Post*, May 19, 1996.

122. Quoted in Timothy W. Ryback, *Rock Around the Bloc: A History of Rock Music in Eastern Europe and the Soviet Union* (New York: Oxford Univ. Press, 1990), 86.

123. *New York Times*, Oct. 7, 1988.

124. *Los Angeles Times*, Mar. 1, 1988.

125. Alvin A. Snyder, *Warriors of Disinformation: American Propaganda, Soviet Lies and the Winning of the Cold War, an Insider's Account* (New York: Arcade Publishing, 1995), 91.

126. *BBC Annual Report and Handbook 1981*, 49.

127. *BBC Annual Report and Handbook 1983*, 50.

128. *BBC Annual Report and Handbook 1981*, 47.

129. *BBC Annual Report and Handbook 1983*, 51.

130. *BBC Annual Report and Handbook 1981*, 49.

131. *Tiesa*, Nov. 17, 18, 1983, quoted in Fraenkel, *BBC*, 145.

132. Georgui Vatchnadze, *Antenny napravlenny na Vostok. Formy i metody imperialisticheskoy radiopropagandy na strany sotsializma* (The aerials are directed against the East. The forms and methods of imperialist radiopropaganda against socialist countries.), 2d ed. (Moscow: Politizdat, 1977), quoted in Fraenkel, *BBC*, 146.

133. *Pravda*, Sept. 23, 1980, quoted in Fraenkel, *BBC*, 146.

134. *Literary Gazette*, 1986, quoted in Tusa, *A World*, 65–66.

135. Quoted in Fraenkel, *BBC*, 147.

136. *BBC Annual Report and Handbook 1981*, 49.

137. *BBC Annual Report and Handbook 1983*, 51.

138. Quoted in Tusa, *A World*, from 1971, 75.

139. Peter Fraenkel, interviewed by the author, Mar. 9, 1994.

140. *BBC Annual Report and Handbook 1982*, 48.

141. *BBC Annual Report and Handbook 1987*, 115.

11. Revolutions (1989)

1. Timothy Garton Ash, *We The People: The Revolution of '89 Witnessed in Warsaw, Budapest, Berlin and Prague* (Cambridge: Granta Books, 1990), 17.

2. Robert Gillette, of RFE, interviewed by the author, Munich, June 8, 1993.

3. *New York Times*, Nov. 12, 1989.

4. Mark Frankland, *The Patriot's Revolution: How East Europe Won its Freedom* (London: Sinclair Stevenson, 1990), 111.

5. Alajos Chrudinak, editor-in-chief, Foreign Politics and Documentary Films Department, Hungarian Television, interviewed by the author, Budapest, Jan. 18, 1990.

6. Ibid.

7. George Schoepflin, "The End of Communism in Eastern Europe," *International Affairs* 66, no. 1 (Jan. 1990): 8.

8. Dieter Buhl, "Window to the West. How Television from the Federal Republic Influenced Events in East Germany," discussion paper D-5, Joan Shorenstein Barone Center on the Press, Politics, and Public Policy, Harvard Univ., John F. Kennedy School of Government, 1990, 2.

9. Bernard Gwertzman and Michael T. Kaufman, *The Collapse of Communism* (New York: Times Books, 1990), 217.

10. Kurt R. Hesse, "Western Media in the GDR," quoted in Buhl, "Window to the West," 3.

11. *Observer*, Dec. 10, 1989.

12. *Times*, London, May 30, 1990; *International Herald Tribune*, July 18, 1990; John Simpson, *Despatches from the Barricades: An Eye-Witness Account of the Revolutions that Shook the World 1989–90* (London: Hutchinson, 1990), 170.

13. Quoted in John Simpson, "How the KGB freed Europe," *Spectator*, Nov. 5, 1994, 11–12.

14. Summary by Jan Lopatka, Reuters, Prague, in a report to the author, Nov. 29, 1995.

15. Reuter report, Prague, May 2, 1995, Reuter Archives.

16. Michel Castex, *Un mensonge gros comme le siècle: Roumanie, histoire d'une manipulation* (A lie as big as the century: Romania, history of manipulation) (Paris: Albin Michel, 1990), 127–34.

17. *New York Times*, Dec. 23, 1989.

18. *Washington Post*, Dec. 28, 1989.

19. Antoine Spire of France Culture, quoted in Reporters sans Frontières, *Roumanie: Qui a menti?* (Romania: Who lied?) (Montpellier: Les Editions Reporters sans Frontières), 129.

20. Castex, *Mensonge*, 68.

21. *Financial Times*, Dec. 27, 1989.

22. *Daily Telegraph*, Dec. 13, 1994.

23. *International Herald Tribune*, Aug. 2, 1990.

24. Associated Press (AP) story from Bucharest, Dec. 29, 1989.

25. Quoted in the *Washington Post*, Dec. 29, 1989.

26. *New York Times*, Dec. 28, 1989.

27. *Washington Post*, Dec. 29, 1989.

28. Gillette, interview.

29. Tamas Palos, director general of MTI, the Hungarian News Agency, interviewed by the author, Budapest, Jan. 18, 1990.

30. *New York Times*, Nov. 14, 1989.

31. *Sunday Correspondent*, Jan. 21, 1990.

32. *Ogonyok*, Dec. 1989, quoted in *Spectator*, Dec. 30, 1989.

33. Gwertzman, *Collapse of Communism*, 225.

34. Ibid., 268.

35. Theodore Draper, *New York Review of Books*, Jan. 14, 1993.

36. Paul Eddy and Sara Walden, *Daily Telegraph*, Jan. 11, 1992.

37. Mickelson, *America's Other Voice*, 209.

38. RFE/RL sponsored survey of Romania, Mar.–Apr. 1990 with a sample of 1,495 nationals more than fifteen years old, RFE/RL.

39. "The Romanian Revolution and the Role of Radio in Bucharest, A Postal Questionnaire Impression," EEAOR report no. 793, July 1990, RFE/RL.

40. "Research on Audience to VOA and Other International Broadcasters in Eastern Europe," VOA paper, Sept. 1976, NARA, Declassified Feb. 11, 1993.

41. RFE/RL sponsored survey, 1990, base 1,611 nationals more than eighteen years old, but 40 percent were not asked these particular questions. RFE/RL.

42. EEAOR, "RFE and the New Czechslovak Media Environment: A Focus Group Study among Czechoslovaks, Feb. 1990," report no. 792, June 1990,

43. "The BBC in Poland, Results of a National Survey Conducted in February/ March 1989," International Broadcasting and Audience Research for the BBC, WAC.

44. "The BBC in Hungary, Results of a National Survey Conducted in June 1989," International Broadcasting and Audience Research for the BBC, WAC.

45. Tamas Szecsko, general secretary, International Association for Mass Communication Research, Budapest, interviewed by the author, Budapest, May 15, 1992.

46. "The BBC in the German Democratic Republic, Summer 1989, A Study of East German Travellers Visiting the Federal Republic of Germany and West Berlin," International Broadcasting and Audience Research for the BBC, WAC.

12. Epilogue: Gorbachev Listens to the Voices

1. Quoted in Shane, *Dismantling Utopia,* 266.

2. To Allen Weinstein, president of The Center for Democracy, Aug. 9, 1991, quoted in *Washington Post,* Aug. 10, 1991.

3. *Intermedia,* Nov.–Dec. 1991, quoting Media and Opinion Research, RFE/RL Research Institute.

4. "Russians Avid Consumers of Domestic Media," USIA Research memorandum, Apr. 8, 1992. USIA.

5. Iain Elliott, "Three Days in August: On-the-Spot Impressions," in *Russia at the Barricades: Eyewitness Accounts of the August 1991 Coup,* ed. Victoria E. Bonnell, Ann Cooper, and Gregory Freidin (Armonk, N.Y.: M. E. Sharpe, 1994), 289–300, 289.

6. *New York Times* interview with Sergei Medvedev, Sept. 25, 1991, Bill Keller, "Getting the News on 'Vremia'," in *Russia at the Barricades: Eyewitness Accounts of the August 1991 Coup,* ed. Victoria E. Bonnell, Ann Cooper, and Gregory Freidin (Armonk, New York: M. E. Sharpe, 1994), 301–7.

7. *Financial Times,* Aug. 22, 1991.

8. Quoted in Elliott, *Three Days,* 299.

9. *Times,* London, Aug. 23, 1991.

10. Transcript of press conference, Aug. 22, 1991, as broadcast and translated by CNN and transcribed by Reuters, *New York Times,* Aug. 23, 1991.

11. Mikhail Gorbachev, *The August Coup: The Truth and the Lessons* (London: Harper Collins, 1991), 27.

12. Quoted in *Times,* London, Aug. 23, 1991.

BIBLIOGRAPHY

Archives

Archives of the Central Committee of the Communist Party of the Soviet Union. (CPA), Moscow.

Archives of the Party and Mass Organizations of the former GDR (SAPMO-BArch), Berlin.

BBC, Written Archives Centre (WAC), Caversham Park, Reading, England.

Churchill College Archives, Cambridge, England. Cadogan Papers.

Department of State Archives, Washington, D.C.

Dwight D. Eisenhower Presidential Library (DDEL), Abilene, Kans. C. D. Jackson Papers.

Georgetown Univ. Library, Special Collections, Washington, D.C. Lodeesen and Kelley Papers.

Harry S. Truman Library (HSTL), Independence, Mo.

Hoover Institution on War, Revolution and Peace, Stanford Univ., Palo Alto, Calif. Mickelson Papers and copies of some Altschul Papers from the Lehman Collection, Columbia Univ. Library, New York, N.Y.

Lyndon B. Johnson Library, Austin, Texas.

Museum of Television and Radio, New York, N.Y.

National Archives (NARA), Washington, D.C.

National Security Archive, Washington, D.C.

Public Record Office (PRO), Kew, Surrey, England.

Radio Free Europe/Radio Liberty (RFE/RL) Archives, Munich. In mid-1995 administrative and current news archives moved with RFE/RL to Prague and old news archives to the Center for the Study of Post-War Communism, Budapest.

Reuters Archives, London.

U.S. Information Agency Archives (USIA), Washington, D.C.

Books

A Chronicle of Current Events: Journal of the Human Rights Movement in the USSR. London: Amnesty International Publications, 1971–79.

Abshire, David M. *International Broadcasting: A New Dimension in Western Diplomacy.* Beverly Hills, Calif.: Sage Publications, 1976.

Agee, Philip. *Inside the Company: CIA Diary.* New York: Stonehill, 1975.

Agee, Philip, and Louis Wolf. *Dirty Work: The CIA in Western Europe.* Secaucus, N.J.: Lyle Stuart, 1978.

Aldrich, Richard, ed. *British Intelligence Strategy and the Cold War, 1945–51.* London: Routledge, 1992.

Alexandre, Laurien. *The Voice of America: From Detente to the Reagan Doctrine.* Norwood, N.J.: Ablex Publishing, 1988.

Alexeyeva, Ludmilla. *Soviet Dissent: Contemporary Movements for National Religious and Human Rights.* Middletown, Conn.: Wesleyan Univ. Press, 1985.

————. *U.S. Broadcasting to the Soviet Union.* New York: U.S. Helsinki Watch Committee, c. 1986.

Alexeyeva, Ludmilla, and Paul Goldberg. *The Thaw Generation: Coming of Age in the Post-Stalin Era.* Boston: Little, Brown, 1990.

Almond, Mark. *The Rise and Fall of Nicolae and Elena Ceausescu.* London: Chapmans, 1992.

Amalrik, Andrei. *Notes of a Revolutionary.* Translated by Guy Daniels. New York: Alfred A. Knopf, 1982.

Amis, Kingsley. *Memoirs.* London: Hutchinson, 1991.

Andrew, Christopher, and Oleg Gordievsky. *KGB: The Inside Story.* London: Hodder and Stoughton, 1990.

Armstrong, David, and Erik Goldstein, eds. *The End of the Cold War.* London: Frank Cass, 1990.

Artyomov, Vladimir, and Vladimir Semyonov. *Bi-Bi-Si: Istoriya, Apparat, Metody radiopropagandy* (The BBC: History, apparatus, methods of propaganda). Moscow: Iskusstvo, 1979.

Ascherson, Neal. *The Polish August: The Self-Limiting Revolution.* New York: Viking Press, 1981.

Ash, Timothy Garton. *In Europe's Name: Germany and the Divided Continent.* New York: Random House, 1993.

————. *The Polish Revolution: Solidarity.* New York: Charles Scribner's, 1984.

————. *The Uses of Adversity: Essays on the Fate of Central Europe.* Cambridge: Granta Books, 1989.

————. *We The People: The Revolution of '89 Witnessed in Warsaw, Budapest, Berlin and Prague.* Cambridge: Granta Books, 1990.

Aster, Howard, ed. *Challenges for International Broadcasting.* Oakville, Ontario: Mosaic Press, 1991.

Bailey, George. *The Making of Andrei Sakharov.* London: Penguin Books, 1989.

Bain, L. B. *The Reluctant Satellites: An Eyewitness Report on East Europe and the Hungarian Revolution.* New York: Macmillan, 1960.

Barghoorn, Frederick C. *Soviet Foreign Propaganda.* Princeton, N.J.: Princeton Univ. Press, 1964.

Barnouw, Erik. *The Image Empire: A History of Broadcasting in the United States.* 3 vols. New York: Oxford Univ. Press, 1966–70.

Barrett, E. W. *Truth is Our Weapon.* New York: Funk and Wagnalls, 1953.

Barron, John. *KGB Today: The Hidden Hand.* London: Hodder and Stoughton; New York: Reader's Digest Press, 1983.

Bauer, R. A., A. Inkeles, and C. Kluckhohn. *How the Soviet System Works: Cultural, Psychological and Social Themes.* Cambridge, Mass.: Harvard Univ. Press, 1956.

Bea, Fernando. *Qui la Radio Vaticana . . . Mezzo secolo della Radio del Papa* (This is Vatican Radio: Half a century of the Pope's radio). Vatican City: Ufficio Propaganda e Sviluppo, 1981.

Becker, Jorg, and Tamas Szecsko, eds. *Europe Speaks to Europe: International Information Flows Between Eastern and Western Europe.* Oxford: Pergamon Press, 1989.

Behr, Edward. *"Kiss the Hand You Cannot Bite": The Rise and Fall of the Ceausescus.* London: Hamish Hamilton, 1991.

Benhalla, Fouad. *La Guerre radiophonique* (Radio war). Paris: Collection de la Revue Politique et Parlementaire, (RPP), 1983.

Beschloss, Michael R., and Strobe Talbot. *At the Highest Levels: The Inside Story of the End of the Cold War.* London: Little, Brown, 1993.

Bethell, Nicholas. *The Great Betrayal: The Untold Story of Kim Philby's Biggest Coup.* London: Hodder and Stoughton, 1984.

————. *Spies and Other Secrets: Memoirs of the Second Cold War.* London: Viking Press, 1994.

Billington, James H. *Russia Transformed: Breakthrough to Hope: Moscow, August 1991.* New York: Free Press, 1992.

Bittman, Ladislav. *The Deception Game: Czechoslovak Intelligence in Soviet Political Warfare.* Syracuse, N.Y.: Syracuse Univ. Research Corporation, 1972.

————. *The KGB and Soviet Disinformation: An Insider's View.* Washington, D.C.: Pergamon Brassey's, 1985.

Black, J. B. *Organising the Propaganda Instrument: The British Experience.* The Hague: Martinus Nijhoff, 1975.

Blum, William. *The CIA: A Forgotten History.* London: Zed Books, 1986.

Bogart, Leo. *Premises for Propaganda: The United States Information Agency's Operating Assumptions in the Cold War.* New York: Free Press, 1976.

Bonner, Elena. *Alone Together.* Translated by Alexander Cook. New York: Alfred A. Knopf, 1986.

Boyes, Roger. *The Naked President: A Political Life of Lech Walesa.* London: Secker and Warburg, 1994.

Brands, H. W. *The Devil We Knew: Americans and the Cold War.* New York: Oxford Univ. Press, 1993.

Briggs, Asa. *The BBC: The First Fifty Years.* Oxford: Oxford Univ. Press, 1985.

————. *The Collected Essays.* Vol. 3, *Serious Pursuits: Communications and Education.* Hemel Hempstead, England: Harvester Wheatsheaf, 1991.

————. *The History of Broadcasting in the United Kingdom.* 5 vols. Oxford: Oxford Univ. Press, 1961–95.

Brinton, William N., and Alan Rinzler, eds. *Without Force or Lies: Voices from the Revolution in Central Europe in 1989–90.* San Francisco, Calif.: Mercury House, 1990.

British Broadcasting Corporation. *Nation to Nation*. London, 1991.

————. *World Radio and Television Receivers*. London, Annual.

Brown, A. C. *The Last Hero: Wild Bill Donovan*. New York: Times Books, 1982.

Browne, D. R. *International Radio Broadcasting: The Limits of the Limitless Medium*. New York: Praeger, 1982.

Browne, J. F. *Surge to Freedom: The End of Communist Rule in Eastern Europe*. London: Adamantine Press, 1951.

Brunnquell, Frédéric. *Fréquence monde: Du poste colonial à RFI* (World frequency: From colonial radio to RFI). Paris: Hachette, 1992.

Brzezinski, Zbigniew. *The Grand Failure: The Birth and Death of Communism in the Twentieth Century*. New York: Macdonald, 1989.

Buell, William A. "RFE/RL in the Mid 1980s." In *Western Broadcasting Over the Iron Curtain*, edited by K. R. M. Short, 69–97. London: Croom Helm, 1986.

Bukovsky, Vladimir. *To Build a Castle: My Life as a Dissenter*. Translated by Michael Scammell. London: Andre Deutsch, 1978.

Buzek, Antony. *How the Communist Press Works*. London: Pall Mall Press, 1964.

Caroll, Wallace. *Persuade or Perish*. Boston: Houghton Mifflin, 1948.

Carrère d'Encausse, Hélène. *The End of the Soviet Empire: The Triumph of the Nations*. Translated by Franklin Philips. New York: Basic Books, 1992.

Castex, Michel. *Un mensonge gros comme le siècle: Roumanie, histoire d'une manipulation*. (A lie as big as the century: Romania, history of manipulation) Paris: Albin Michel, 1990.

Chalidze, Valery. *To Defend These Rights: Human Rights and the Soviet Union*. Translated by Guy Daniels. London: Collins and Harvill Press, 1975.

Charlton, Michael. *The Eagle and the Small Birds: Crisis in the Soviet Empire: From Yalta to Solidarity*. London: BBC, 1984.

————. *Footsteps from the Finland Station: Five Landmarks in the Collapse of Communism*. St. Albans, England: Claridge Press, 1992.

Childs, H. L., and J. B. Whitton, eds. *Propaganda by Shortwave*. Princeton, N.J.: Princeton Univ. Press, 1942.

Codding, G. A. *Broadcasting Without Barriers*. Paris: UNESCO, 1959.

Colby, William, and Peter Forbath. *Honorable Men: My Life in the CIA*. New York: Simon and Schuster, 1978.

Colby, William, with James McCargar. *Lost Victory: A Firsthand Account of America's Sixteen Year Involvement in Vietnam*. Chicago: Contemporary Books, 1989.

Cole, J. A. *Lord Haw-Haw: The Full Story of James Joyce*. London: Faber and Faber, 1964.

Cole, Robert. *Propaganda in Twentieth Century War and Politics: An Annotated Bibliography*. Lanham, Md.: Scarecrow, 1996.

Coleman, Fred. *The Decline and Fall of the Soviet Empire: Forty Years That Shook the World, from Stalin to Yeltsin*. New York: St. Martin's, 1996.

Coleman, Peter. *The Liberal Conspiracy: The Congress for Cultural Freedom and the Struggle for the Mind of Postwar Europe*. New York: Free Press, 1989.

Conquest, Robert. *The Great Terror: A Reassessment.* London: Hutchinson, 1990.

—————. *The Harvest of Sorrow: Soviet Collectivization and the Terror-Famine.* London: Hutchinson, 1986.

—————. *Stalin and the Kirov Murder.* London: Hutchinson, 1989.

—————. *Stalin: Breaker of Nations.* London: Weidenfeld and Nicolson, 1991.

—————. *Tyrants and Typewriters: Communiqués in the Struggle for Truth.* London: Hutchinson, 1989.

Cooper, Kent. *The Right to Know: An Exposition of the Evils of News Suppression and Propaganda.* New York: Farrar, Straus, and Cudahy, 1956.

Critchlow, James. *Radio Hole-in-the-Head/Radio Liberty: An Insider's Story of Cold War Broadcasting.* Washington, D.C.: American Univ. Press, 1995.

Crozier, Brian. *Free Agent: The Unseen War 1941–1991.* London: Harper Collins, 1993.

—————. *The Rebels: A Study of Post-War Insurrections.* London: Chatto and Windus, 1960.

Curran, Charles. *A Seamless Robe: Broadcasting Philosophy and Practice.* London: Collins, 1979.

Curry, Jane Leftwich, trans. and ed. *The Black Book of Polish Censorship.* New York: Random House, 1984.

Custine, Marquis de. *Empire of the Czar: A Journey Through Eternal Russia.* 1839. Reprint. New York: Doubleday, 1989.

Darling, Arthur B. *The Central Intelligence Agency: An Instrument of Government, to 1950.* University Park, Pa.: Penn State Univ. Press, 1990.

Daugherty, William E., and Morris Janowitz, eds. *A Psychological Warfare Casebook.* Baltimore, Md.: Johns Hopkins Press, 1958.

Davies, Norman. *God's Playground: A History of Poland.* 2 vols. 1981. Reprint with corrections. Oxford: Oxford Univ. Press, 1991.

Davy, Richard, ed. *European Détente: A Reappraisal.* London: RIIA, 1992.

Delmer, Sefton. *Black Boomerang.* London: Secker and Warburg, 1962.

Dennis, Everette E., George Gerbner, and Yassen N. Zassoursky, eds. *Beyond the Cold War: Soviet and American Media Images.* Newbury Park, Calif.: Sage Publications, 1991.

Dewhirst, Martin, and Robert Farrell, eds. *The Soviet Censorship.* Metuchen, N.J.: Scarecrow Press, 1973.

Dizard, Wilson. *The Strategy of Truth, the Story of the USIS.* Washington, D.C.: Public Affairs Press, 1965.

Djilas, Milovan. *Conversations with Stalin.* Translated by Michael B. Petrovich. Harmondsworth, England: Penguin Books, 1962.

—————. *The New Class: An Analysis of the Communist System.* London: Thames and Hudson, 1957.

Dukes, Paul. *A History of Russia: Medieval, Modern, Contemporary.* 1974. 2d ed. London: Macmillan, 1990.

Dulles, A. *The Craft of Intelligence.* Westport, Conn.: Greenwood Press, 1963.

Ebon, Martin. *The Soviet Propaganda Machine.* New York: McGraw-Hill, 1987.

Echikson, William. *Lighting the Night: Revolution in Eastern Europe*. London: Sidgwick and Jackson, 1990.

Eck, Hélène, ed. *La Guerre des ondes: Histoire des radios de langue française pendant la Deuxième Guerre Mondiale* (The war of the airwaves: History of French-language radios during the Second World War). Paris: Armand Colin, 1985.

Edelheit, Abraham J., and Hershel Edelheit. *The Rise and Fall of the Soviet Union: A Selected Bibliography of Sources in English*. Westport, Conn.: Greenwood Press, 1992.

Efimov, Boris. *Razyashchim udarom* (A shattering blow). Moscow: Plakat, 1985.

Eisenhower, Dwight D. *The White House Years: Waging Peace, 1956–1961*. New York: Doubleday, 1965.

Elder, Robert E. *The Information Machine: The USIA and American Foreign Policy*. Syracuse, N.Y.: Syracuse Univ. Press, 1968.

Elliott, Iain, "Three Days in August: On-the-Spot Impressions." In *Russia at the Barricades: Eyewitness Accounts of the August 1991 Coup*, edited by Victoria E. Bonnell, Ann Cooper, and Gregory Freidin, 289–300. Armonk, N.Y.: M. E. Sharpe, 1994.

Ellul, J. *Propaganda: The Formation of Men's Attitudes*. Translated by Konrad Kellen and Jean Lerner. New York: Alfred A. Knopf, 1965.

Emery, W. B. *National and International Systems of Broadcasting: Their History, Operation and Control*. East Lansing: Michigan State Univ. Press, 1969.

Felix, Christopher [James McCargar]. *The Spy and His Masters: A Short Course in the Secret War*. London: Secker and Warburg, 1963.

Fitzgerald, Merni Ingrassia. *The Voice of America*. New York: Dodd, Mead, 1987.

Foley, John P. *The Jeffersonian Cyclopedia*. New York: Funk and Wagnalls, 1900.

Fraenkel, Peter. "The BBC External Services: Broadcasting to the USSR and Eastern Europe." In *Western Broadcasting over the Iron Curtain*, edited by K. R. M. Short, 139–57. London: Croom Helm, 1986.

Frankland, Mark. *The Patriot's Revolution: How East Europe Won Its Freedom*. London: Sinclair Stevenson, 1990.

Fraser, L. *Propaganda*. London: Oxford Univ. Press, 1957.

Frederick, Howard, H. *Cuban-American Radio Wars: Ideology in International Communications*. Norwood, N.J.: Ablex Publishing, 1986.

Free Europe Committee. *The Story of the World Freedom Bell*. Minneapolis, Minn.: Nate L. Crabtree, 1951.

Fulbright, J. William. *The Arrogance of Power*. New York: Random House, 1966.

———. *The Price of Empire*. New York: Pantheon Books, 1989.

———. *Prospects for the West*. Cambridge, 1963.

Gaddis, John Lewis. *The Long Peace: Inquiries into the History of the Cold War*. New York: Oxford Univ. Press, 1987.

———. *Russia, The Soviet Union and the United States: an Interpretive History*. 2d ed. New York: McGraw-Hill, 1990.

———. *The United States and the End of the Cold War*. Oxford: Oxford Univ. Press, 1992.

Galambos, Louis, ed. *The Papers of Dwight D. Eisenhower*. Baltimore, Md.: Johns Hopkins Univ. Press, 1989.

Galantière, Lewis. *America and the Mind of Europe*. London: Hamilton, 1951.

Gates, Robert M. *From the Shadows: The Ultimate Insider's Story of Five Presidents and How They Won the Cold War*. New York: Simon and Schuster, 1996.

Gilbert, Martin. *Shcharansky: Hero of Our Time*. London: Penguin Books, 1987.

Gorbachev, Mikhail. *The August Coup: The Truth and the Lessons*. London: Harper Collins, 1991.

————. *Memoirs*. Translated by Georges Peronansky and Tatjana Varsavsky. New York: Doubleday, 1996.

————. *Perestroika*. London: Fontana/Collins, 1987.

Green, Fitzhugh. *American Propaganda Abroad: From Benjamin Franklin to Ronald Reagan*. New York: Hippocrene Books, 1988.

Greene, Sir Hugh. *The Third Floor Front: A View of Broadcasting in the Sixties*. London: Bodley Head, 1969.

Grisewood, Harman. *One Thing at a Time*. London: Hutchinson, 1968.

Grose, Peter. *Gentleman Spy: The Life of Allen Dulles*. New York: Houghton Mifflin, 1994.

Gwertzman, Bernard, and Michael T. Kaufman. *The Collapse of Communism*. New York: Times Books, 1990.

Haines, Gerald K. *A Reference Guide to Department of State Special Files*. Westport, Conn.: Greenwood Press, 1985.

Hale, J. A. *Radio Power: Propaganda and International Broadcasting*. London: Paul Elek, 1975.

Hall, James. *Radio Canada*. East Lansing: Michigan State Univ. Press (forthcoming).

Hamman, Henry, and Stuart Parrott. *Mayday at Chernobyl*. London: New English Library, 1987.

Havel, Vaclav. *Living in Truth*. Edited by Jan Vladislav. London: Faber and Faber, 1989.

————. *Disturbing the Peace*. Translated by Paul Wilson. London: Faber and Faber, 1990.

Hawkes, Nigel, ed. *Tearing Down the Curtain: The People's Revolution in Europe by a Team from the* Observer. London: Hodder and Stoughton, 1990.

Head, Sydney W. *World Broadcasting Systems: A Comparative Analysis*. Belmont, Calif.: Wadsworth, 1985.

Heil, Alan. "The Voice Past: The VOA, the USSR and Communist Europe." In *Western Broadcasting over the Iron Curtain*, edited by K. R. M. Short, 98–112. London: Croom Helm, 1986.

Held, Joseph, ed. *The Columbia History of Eastern Europe in the Twentieth Century*. New York: Columbia Univ. Press, 1992.

Henderson, John W. *The United States Information Agency*. New York: Praeger, 1969.

Hennessy, Peter. *Never Again: Britain 1945–1951*. London: Jonathan Cape, 1992.

Hixson, Walter L. *Parting the Curtain: Propaganda, Culture, and the Cold War, 1945–1961*. New York: St. Martin's, 1997.

Hoffman, Eva. *Exit into History: A Journey Through Eastern Europe*. London: Heinemann, 1993.

Hollander, Gayle Durham. *Soviet Political Indoctrination: Developments in Mass Media and Propaganda since Stalin*. New York: Praeger, 1972.

Hollander, Paul. *Political Pilgrims: Travels of Western Intellectuals to the Soviet Union, China and Cuba*. New York: Harper Colophon Books, 1981.

Holt, Robert T. *Radio Free Europe*. Minneapolis: Univ. of Minnesota Press, 1958.

Hope, Christopher. *Moscow! Moscow!* London: Heinemann, 1990.

Houseman, J. *Front and Center*. New York: Simon and Schuster, 1979.

Huteau, Jean, and Bernard Ullmann. *AFP: Une histoire de l'Agence France-Presse, 1944–1990* (A history of Agence France-Presse, 1944–1990). Paris: Robert Laffont, 1992.

Inkeles, Alex. *Public Opinion in Soviet Russia: A Study in Mass Persuasion*. Cambridge, Mass.: Harvard Univ. Press, 1967.

Irwin, Will. *Propaganda and the News, or What Makes You Think So*. 1936. Reprint. Westport, Conn.: Greenwood, 1970.

Jacquard, Roland. *La Guerre du mensonge: Histoire secrète de la désinformation* (The war of the lie: The secret history of disinformation). Paris: Plon, 1986.

Jansen, Sue Curry. *Censorship: The Knot that Binds Power and Knowledge*. Oxford: Oxford Univ. Press, 1988.

Jeffreys-Jones, Rhodri. *The CIA and American Democracy*. New Haven, Conn.: Yale Univ. Press, 1989.

Jones, Tony, ed. *Passport to World Band Radio*. Penn's Park, Pa.: International Broadcast Services, Annual.

Jowett, Garth S., and Victoria O'Donnell. *Propaganda and Persuasion*. Newbury Park, Calif.: Sage Publications, 1992.

Kaiser, Robert G. *Russia: The People and the Power*. New York: Atheneum, 1976.

Kalugin, Oleg, with Fen Montaigne. *Spymaster: My 32 Years of Intelligence and Espionage Against the West*. London: Smith Gryphon, 1994.

Kee, Robert. *Munich: The Eleventh Hour*. London: Hamish Hamilton, 1988.

Keller, Bill. "Getting the News on 'Vremia': Interview with Sergei Medvedev." In *Russia at the Barricades: Eyewitness Accounts of the August 1991 Coup*, edited by Victoria E. Bonnell, Ann Cooper, and Gregory Freidin, 301–7. Armonk, N.Y.: M. E. Sharpe, 1994.

Kendrick, Alexander. *Prime Time: The Life of Edward R. Murrow*. Boston: Little, Brown, 1969.

Kenez, Peter. *The Birth of the Propaganda State: Soviet Methods of Mass Mobilization 1917–1929*. Cambridge: Cambridge Univ. Press, 1985.

Kennan, George F. *Memoirs 1925–1950 and 1950–1963*. Boston: Little, Brown, 1967–72.

———. *Russia and the West under Lenin and Stalin*. Boston: Little, Brown, 1960.

Khruschchev, Nikita. *Khrushchev Remembers: The Glasnost Tapes*. Translated and edited by Jerrold L. Schecter with Vyacheslav V. Luchkov. New York: Little, Brown, 1990.

Kirsch, Botho. "Deutsche Welle's Russian Service, 1962–1985." In *Western Broadcasting over the Iron Curtain,* edited by K. R. M. Short, 158–71. London: Croom Helm, 1986.

———. "Der Kampf um die Freie Meinung," (The struggle for freedom of thought), in *Auftrag Deutschland, Nach der Einheit: Unser Land der Welt vermitteln,* edited by Dieter Weirich, 161–80. Mainz: v Hase und Koehler Verlag, 1993.

Kline, R. *Secrets, Spies and Scholars.* Washington, D.C.: Acropolis Books, 1976.

Koch, Stephen. *Double Lives: Spies and Writers in the Secret Soviet War of Ideas Against the West.* New York: Free Press, 1994.

Korotich, Vitaly, and Cathy Porter, eds. *The Best of Ogonyok.* London: Heinemann, 1990.

Kovrig, Bennett. *Of Walls and Bridges: The United States and Europe.* New York: New York Univ. Press, 1991.

Kuron, Jacek. *Maintenant ou jamais* (Now or never). Translated by Marie Bouvard. Paris: Fayard, 1993.

Kuznetsov, Edward. *Prison Diaries.* Translated by Howard Spier. Briarcliff Manor, N.Y.: Stein and Day, 1975.

Laqueur, Walter. *Europe since Hitler: The Rebirth of Europe.* London: Penguin Books, 1982.

Lasky, Melvin J., ed. *The Hungarian Revolution: The Story of the October Uprising.* London: Congress for Cultural Freedom and Martin Secker, 1957.

Lean, E. Tangye. *Voices in the Darkness: The Story of the European Radio War.* London: Secker and Warburg, 1943.

Lefeber, Walter. *America, Russia, and the Cold War, 1945–1984.* New York: Newbery Awards Records, 5th ed., 1985.

Leigh, David. *The Frontiers of Secrecy: Closed Government in Britain.* London: Junction Books, 1980.

Lendvai, Paul. *The Bureaucracy of Truth: How Communist Governments Manage the News.* London: Burnett Books, 1981.

Lenin, V. I. *Collected Works.* London: Lawrence and Wishart, 1960–.

———. *Polnoe sobranie sochinenii* (Completed works). Moscow: Izdatel'stvo Politicheskoi literatury, 1958–.

Leonhard, Wolfgang. *Child of the Revolution.* Translated by C. M. Woodhouse. London: Collins, 1957.

Levering, Ralph B. *The Cold War, 1945–72.* Arlington Heights, Ill.: Harland Davidson, 1982.

Lindahl, Rutger. *Broadcasting Across Borders.* Lund: CWK Gleerup, 1978.

Lippmann, Walter. *Public Opinion.* New York: Harcourt Brace, 1922.

Lisann, M. *Broadcasting to the Soviet Union: International Politics and Radio.* New York: Praeger, 1975.

Litvinov, Pavel. *The Demonstration in Pushkin Square.* Translated by Manya Harari. London: Harvill Press, 1969.

———. *The Trial of the Four: A Collection of Materials on the Cases of Galanskov, Ginzburg, Dobrovolsky and Lashkova, 1967–68.* Compiled, with commentary by Pavel Litvinov, English text edited and annotated by Peter Reddaway. Translated by Janis Sapiets, Hilary Sternberg, and Daniel Weissbort. London: Longman, 1972.

Lucas, W. Scott. *Divided We Stand: Britain, the U.S. and the Suez Crisis*. London: Hodder and Stoughton, 1991.

Lucas, W. Scott., and C. J. Morris. "A Very British Crusade: The Information Research Department and the Beginning of the Cold War." In *Intelligence Strategy and the Cold War*, edited by Richard Aldrich, 85–110. London: Routledge, 1992.

Macaulay, T. B. *History of England from the Accession of James II*. 1848. Reprint. London: Everyman, 1906.

McCavitt, W. E. *Radio and Television: A Selected Annotated Bibliography*. Metchuen, N.J.: Scarecrow Press, 1978.

McLuhan, Marshall. *Understanding Media: The Extensions of Man*. London: Routledge and Kegan Paul, 1964.

MacMahon, Arthur W. *Memorandum on the Postwar International Program of the United States*. Washington, D.C.: USGPO, 1945.

McNair, Brian. *Glasnost, Perestroika and the Soviet Media*. London: Routledge, 1991.

Mainland, Edward, Mark Pomar, and Kurt Carlson. "The Voice Present and Future: VOA, the USSR and Communist Europe." In *Broadcasting over the Iron Curtain*, edited by K. R. M. Short, 113–36. London: Croom Helm, 1986.

Mansell, Gerard. *Let Truth Be Told: 50 Years of BBC External Broadcasting*. London: Weidenfeld and Nicolson, 1982.

Marchenko, Anatoly. *My Testimony*. Translated by Michael Scammell. London: Pall Mall Press, 1969.

Marchetti, Victor, and John D. Marks. *The CIA and the Cult of Intelligence*. New York: Dell, 1974.

Marett, Robert, H. K. *Through the Back Door: An Inside View of Britain's Overseas Information Services*. Oxford: Pergamon, 1982.

Markov, Georgi. *The Truth that Killed*. London: Weidenfeld and Nicolson, 1983.

Mastny, Voitech. *The Helsinki Process and the Reintegration of Europe 1986–1991*. New York: New York Univ. Press, 1992.

Matelski, Marilyn J. *Vatican Radio: Propagation by the Airwaves*. Westport, Conn.: Praeger, 1995.

Mattelart, Tristan. *Le cheval de Troie audiovisuel: Le rideau de fer à l'épreuve des radios et des télévisions transfrontières* (The audiovisual Trojan Horse: The iron curtain put to the test by transborder radio and television). Grenoble: Presses universitaires de Grenoble, 1995.

Mayhew, Christopher. *Time to Explain: An Autobiography*. London: Hutchinson, 1987.

Medveded, Roy. *On Soviet Dissent. Interviews with Piero Ostellino*. Translated by William A. Packer and George Saunders. London: Constable, 1980.

Medveded, Roy, ed. *Samizdat Register 1: Voices of the Socialist Opposition in the Soviet Union*. London: Merlin Press, 1977.

Medvedev, Grigori. *The Truth about Chernobyl.* Translated by Evelyn Rossiter. London: I. B. Tauris, 1989.

Meyer, Cord. *Facing Reality: From World Federalism to the CIA.* New York: Harper and Row, 1980.

Meyerhoff, Arthur E. *The Strategy of Persuasion: The Use of Advertising Skills in Fighting the Cold War.* New York: Coward-McCann, 1965.

Michener, J. *The Bridge at Andau.* London: Fawcett, 1985.

Michie, A. A. *Voices Through the Iron Curtain: The Radio Free Europe Story.* New York: Dodd, Mead, 1963.

Michnik, Adam. *Letters from Prison, and Other Essays.* Translated by Maya Latynski. Berkeley and Los Angeles: Univ. of California Press, 1985.

Mickelson, Sig. *America's Other Voice: The Story of Radio Free Europe and Radio Liberty.* New York: Praeger, 1983.

Mickiewicz, Ellen. *Media and the Russian Public.* New York: Praeger, 1981.

————. *Split Signals: Television and Politics in the Soviet Union.* Oxford: Oxford Univ. Press, 1988.

Mikhailov, M. P., and V. V. Nazarov. *Ideologicheskya diversiya-vooruzheniye imperializma* (Ideological diversion is the armament of imperialism). Moscow, 1969.

Montague, Ludwell Lee. *General Walter Bedell Smith as Director of Central Intelligence. October 1950–February 1953.* University Park, Pa.: State Univ. Press, 1992.

Mosley, Leonard. *Dulles: A Biography of Eleanor Allen and John Foster Dulles and Their Family Network.* New York: Dial Press/James Wade, 1978.

Mytton, Graham, ed. *Global Audiences: Research for Worldwide Broadcasting 1993.* London: John Libbey, 1993.

New York Times interview with Sergei Medvedev, "Getting the News on 'Vremia'," Sept. 25, 1991. In *Russia at the Barricades: Eyewitness Accounts of the August 1991 Coup,* edited by Victoria E. Bonnell, Ann Cooper, and Gregory Freidin, 301–7. Armonk, N.Y.: M. E. Sharpe, 1994.

Nixon, Richard M. *The Real War.* New York: Warner Books, 1980.

Oberg, James E. *Uncovering Soviet Disasters: Exploring the Limits of Glasnost.* London: Robert Hale, 1988.

O'Neill, Michael J. *The Roar of the Crowd: How Television and People Power Are Changing the World.* New York: Times Books, 1993.

Orwell, George. *Nineteen Eighty-Four.* London: Martin Secker and Warburg, 1949.

Pacepa, Ion. *Red Horizons: Inside the Romanian Secret Service: The Memoirs of Ceausescu's Spy Chief.* London: Heinemann, 1988.

Panfilov, Artyom. *Radio SShA v psikhologicheskoy voyne* (U.S. radio in the psychological war). Moscow: Mezhdunarodnye otnosheniya, 1967.

————. *Radiovoyna: Istoriya i sovremennost', Ocherki o vneshnepoliticheskoy radiopropagande fashistskoy Germanii, SShA, Anglii i FRG* (Radio wars: History and the contemporary world. Studies of foreign radio propaganda of fascist Germany, the U.S., England, and the Federal German Republic). Moscow: Iskusstvo, 1984.

Panfilov, Artyom, and Yuri Karchevsky. *Subversion by Radio: Radio Free Europe and Radio Liberty.* Moscow: Novosti Press Agency Publishing House, 1974.

Parrot, Jacques. *La Guerre des ondes* (War of the airwaves). Paris: Plon, c. 1987.

Partner, Peter. *Arab Voices: The BBC Arabic Service, 1938–1988.* London: BBC, 1988.

Parta, R. Eugene. "SAAOR at RFE/RL." In *Western Broadcasting Over the Iron Curtain,* edited by K. R. M. Short, 227–44. London: Croom Helm, 1986.

Partos, Gabriel. *The World that Came in from the Cold: Perspectives from East and West on the Cold War.* London: RIIA and BBC, 1993.

Paulu, Burton. *Radio and Television Broadcasting in Eastern Europe.* Minneapolis: Univ. of Minnesota Press, 1974.

Peake, Hayden B. *The Reader's Guide to Intelligence Periodicals.* Washington, D.C.: NIBC Press.

Peterson, H. C. *Propaganda for War.* Norman: Univ. of Oklahoma Press, 1939.

Philby, Kim. *My Silent War.* London: MacGibbon and Kee, 1968.

Picaper, Jean-Paul. *Le Pont invisible: Ces radios et télévisions que l'est veut réduire au silence* (The invisible bridge: The radio and television that the east wants to silence). Paris: Plon, 1986.

Pirsein, R. *Voice of America: A History of the International Broadcasting Activities of the United States Government 1940–1962.* New York: Arno Press, 1979.

Powers, Thomas. *The Man Who Kept the Secrets: Richard Helms and the CIA.* London: Weidenfeld and Nicolson, 1979.

Pozner, Vladimir. *Eyewitness: A Personal Account of the Unraveling of the Soviet Union.* London: Hodder and Stoughton, 1992.

Pravda, Alex, ed. *The End of the Outer Empire: Soviet-East European Relations in Transition, 1985–90.* London: RIIA, Sage Publications, 1992.

Prins, Gwyn, ed. *Spring in Winter: The 1989 Revolutions.* Manchester, England: Manchester Univ. Press, 1990.

Radio Free Europe Research. *The Strikes in Poland, August 1980.* Munich: Radio Free Europe Research, Oct. 1980.

Ranelagh, John. *The Agency: The Rise and Decline of the CIA.* London: Weidenfeld and Nicolson, 1986.

———. *CIA, A History.* London: BBC Books, 1992.

Ransom, H. H. *The Intelligence Establishment.* Cambridge, Mass.: Harvard Univ. Press, 1958.

Ratesh, Nestor. *Romania: The Entangled Revolution.* New York: Praeger, 1991.

Rawnsley, Gary D. *Radio Diplomacy and Propaganda: The BBC and VOA in International Politics, 1956–64.* London: Macmillan, 1996.

Read, Donald. *The Power of News: The History of Reuters.* Oxford: Oxford Univ. Press, 1992.

Read, Piers Paul. *Ablaze: The Story of Chernobyl.* London: Martin Secker and Warburg, 1993.

Reddaway, Peter, ed. *Uncensored Russia: The Human Rights Movement in the Soviet Union.* London: Jonathan Cape, 1972.

Reed, John. *Ten Days that Shook the World*. New York: Boni and Liveright, 1919. Reprint. London: Penguin, 1977.

Reiss, Juergen. "Deutschlandfunk: Broadcasting to East Germany and Eastern Europe." In *Western Broadcasting over the Iron Curtain*, edited by K. R. M. Short, 172–84. London: Croom Helm, 1986.

Reith, J. C. W. *Into the Wind*. London: Hodder and Stoughton, 1949.

Remnick, David. *Lenin's Tomb, the Last Days of the Soviet Empire*. London: Viking Press, 1993.

Renner, Hans. *A History of Czechoslovakia since 1945*. London: Routledge, 1989.

Reporters sans Frontières. *Roumanie: Qui a menti?* (Romania: Who lied?) Montpellier: Les Editions Reporters sans Frontières, 1990.

Richardson, Charles. *From Churchill's Secret Circle to the BBC: The Biography of Lieutenant General Sir Ian Jacob*. London: Brasseys, 1991.

Ro'i, Yaacov. *The Struggle for Soviet Jewish Emigration 1948–1967*. Cambridge: Cambridge Univ. Press, 1991.

Roberts, Frank. *Dealing with Dictators: The Destruction and Revival of Europe 1930–1970*. London: Weidenfeld and Nicolson, 1991.

Rolo, Charles, J. *Radio Goes to War: The Fourth Front*. New York: G. P. Putnam's Sons, 1940.

Rose, Clive. *The Soviet Propaganda Network: A Directory of Organisations Serving Soviet Foreign Policy*. London: Pinter Publishers, 1988.

Rosenblum, Mort. *Who Stole the News? Why We Can't Keep Up with What Happens in the World and What We Can Do about It*. New York: John Wiley, 1993.

Rositzke, Harry. *The CIA's Secret Operations: Espionage, Counter-Espionage and Covert Action*. New York: Reader's Digest Press, 1977.

Rothberg, Abraham. *The Heirs of Stalin: Dissidence and the Soviet Regime, 1953–1970*. Ithaca, N.Y.: Cornell Univ. Press, 1972.

Rubenstein, Joshua. *Soviet Dissidents: Their Struggle for Human Rights*. London: Wildwood House, 1980.

Rubin, Ronald I. *The Objectives of the U.S. Information Agency: Controversies and Analysis*. New York: Praeger, 1968.

Ruzhnikov, Vsevolod. *Tak nachinalos': Istorikoteoreticheskyy ocherk Sovetskogo radioveshchaniya 1917–1928* (This was how it began: A history of the first ten years of Soviet radio, 1917–1928). Moscow: Iskusstvo, 1987.

Ryback, Timothy W. *Rock Around the Bloc: A History of Rock Music in Eastern Europe and the Soviet Union*. New York: Oxford Univ. Press, 1990.

Saerchinger, César. *Voice of Europe*. London: Victor Gollancz, 1938.

Sakharov, Andrei. *Memoirs*. Translated by Richard Lourie. New York: Alfred A. Knopf, 1990.

Schoepflin, George, ed. *Censorship and Political Communication: Examples from Eastern Europe*. London: Frances Pinter, 1983.

Schubiger, Claude. *La Guerre des ondes* (War of the airwaves). Lausanne: Librairie Payot, 1941.

Schweizer, Peter. *Victory: The Reagan Administration's Secret Strategy that Hastened the Collapse of the Soviet Union.* New York: Atlantic Monthly Press, 1994.

Seale, Patrick, and Maureen McConville. *Philby: The Long Road to Moscow.* New York: Simon and Schuster, 1973.

Selbourne, David. *Death of the Dark Hero: Eastern Europe 1987–90.* London: Jonathan Cape, 1990.

Semelin, Jacques. *La liberté au bout des ondes: Du coup de Prague à la chute du mur de Berlin* (Freedom via the airwaves: From the Prague coup to the fall of the Berlin wall). Paris: Belfond, 1997.

Seton-Watson, Mary. *Scenes from Soviet Life.* London: BBC Publications, 1986.

Shakespeare, Frank. "International Broadcasting and U.S. Political Realities." In *Western Broadcasting Over the Iron Curtain,* edited by K. R. M. Short, 57–68. London: Croom Helm, 1986.

Shane, Scott. *Dismantling Utopia: How Information Ended the Soviet Union.* Chicago: Ivan R. Dee, 1994.

Shanor, Donald R. *Behind the Lines: The War Against Soviet Censorship.* New York: St. Martin's Press, 1985.

Shelden, Michael. *Orwell.* London: Heinemann, 1991.

Shevardnadze, Eduard. *The Future Belongs to Freedom.* Translated by Catherine A. Fitzpatrick. London: Sinclair-Stevenson, 1991.

Shulman, Holly Cowan. *The Voice of America: Propaganda and Democracy, 1941–1945.* Madison: Univ. of Wisconsin Press, 1990.

Shultz, Richard H., and Roy Godson. *Dezinformatsia: Active Measures in Soviet Strategy.* Washington, D.C.: Pergamon-Brasseys, 1984.

Siegel, Arthur. *Radio Canada International: History and Development.* Oakville, Ontario: Mosaic Press, 1996.

Siepmann, C. A. *Radio, Television and Society.* Oxford: Oxford Univ. Press, 1950.

Silvey, Robert. *Who's Listening? The Story of BBC Audience Research.* London: George Allen and Unwin, 1974.

Simpson, Christopher. *National Security Directives of the Reagan and Bush Administrations: The Declassified History of U.S. Political and Military Policy, 1981–1991.* Boulder, Colo.: Westview Press, 1995.

―――. *Science of Coercion: Communication Research and Psychological Warfare, 1945–1960.* Oxford: Oxford Univ. Press, 1994.

Simpson, John. *Despatches from the Barricades: An Eye-Witness Account of the Revolutions that Shook the World 1989–90.* London: Hutchinson, 1990.

Sinyavsky, Andrey. *A Voice from the Chorus.* Translated by Kyril Fitzlyon and Max Hayward. London: Collins and Harvill Press, 1976.

Skilling, H. Gordon. *Samizdat and an Independent Society in Central and Eastern Europe.* London: Macmillan, 1989.

Smith, B. L., H. D. Lasswell, and R. Casey. *Propaganda, Communications and Public Opinion: A Comprehensive Reference Guide.* Princeton, N.J.: Princeton Univ. Press, 1946.

Smith, Hedrick. *The New Russians.* London: Hutchinson, 1990.

Smith, Jean E. *Lucius D. Clay: An American Life.* New York: Henry Holt, 1990.

Smith, Joseph. *The Cold War 1945–65.* Oxford: Basil Blackwell, 1989.

Smith, Paul A., Jr. *On Political War.* Washington, D.C.: National Defense Univ. Press, USGPO, 1990.

Smith, Walter Bedell. *Moscow Mission 1946–49.* London: Heinemann, 1950.

Snyder, Alvin A. *Warriers of Disinformation: American Propaganda, Soviet Lies and the Winning of the Cold War, an Insider's Account.* New York: Arcade Publishing, 1995.

Soley, Lawrence C. *Radio Warfare: OSS and CIA Subversive Propaganda.* New York: Praeger, 1989.

Soley, Lawrence C., and John S. Nichols. *Clandestine Radio Broadcasting: A Study of Revolutionary and Counter-Revolutionary Electronic Communication.* New York: Praeger, 1987.

Solzhenitsyn, Aleksandr. *Rebuilding Russia.* Translated by Alexis Klimoff. London: Harvill, 1991.

Sorenson, Thomas C. *The Word War: The Story of American Propaganda.* New York: Harper and Row, 1968.

Stone, Norman, and Eduard Strouhal. *Czechoslovakia: Crossroads and Crises, 1918–88.* London: Macmillan, 1989.

Sun Tzu. *The Art of War.* N.d. Translated by Samuel B. Griffith. Oxford: Oxford Univ. Press, 1963.

Sweeney, John. *The Life and Evil Times of Nicolae Ceausescu.* London: Hutchinson, 1991.

Swidlicki, Andrzej. *Political Trials in Poland 1981–1986.* Beckenham, Kent: Croom Helm, 1988.

Taubman, William. *The View from Lenin Hills.* London: Hamish Hamilton, 1968.

Taylor, Philip M. *Munitions of the Mind, War Propaganda from the Ancient World to the Nuclear Age.* London: Patrick Stephens, 1990.

Thayer, C. *Diplomat.* New York: Harper and Bros., 1979.

Thom, Francoise. *Newspeak: The Language of Soviet Communism.* London: Claridge Press, 1989.

Thomas, Evan. *The Very Best Men: The Early Years of the CIA.* New York: Simon and Schuster, 1995.

Thomas, Hugh. *Armed Truce: The Beginnings of the Cold War, 1945–46.* London: Hamish Hamilton, 1986.

Tismaneanu, Vladmir, ed. *In Search of Civil Society: Independent Peace Movements in the Soviet Bloc.* New York: Routledge, 1990.

Trethowan, Ian. *Split Screen.* London: Hamish Hamilton, 1984.

Troy, Thomas F. *Donovan and the CIA: A History of the Establishment of the CIA.* Frederick, Md.: Aletheia Books, 1975.

Tuch, Hans N. *Communicating with the World: U.S. Public Diplomacy Overseas.* New York: St. Martin's Press, 1990.

Tunstall, Jeremy. *The Media Are American: Anglo-American Media in the World.* New York: Columbia Univ. Press, 1977.

Tusa, John. *Conversations with the World.* London: BBC, 1990.

————. *A World in Your Ear: Reflections on Changes.* London: Broadside Books, 1992.

Tyson, James L. *Target America: The Influence of Communist Propaganda on U.S. Media.* Chicago: Regnery Gateway, 1981.

————. *U.S. International Broadcasting and National Security.* New York: Ramapo Press, 1983.

U.S. Department of State. *Foreign Relations of the United States* [hereafter *FRUS*]: 1950 I. Washington, D.C.: USGPO, 1997.

————. *FRUS*: 1955–57, 25. Washington, D.C., USGPO, 1976.

Urban, George. *End of Empire: The Demise of the Soviet Union.* Washington, D.C.: American Univ. Press, 1993.

————. *The Nineteen Days: A Broadcaster's Account of the Hungarian Revolution.* London: Heinemann, 1957.

————. ed. *Can the Soviet System Survive Reform?* London: Pinter, 1989.

————. ed. *Talking to Eastern Europe.* London: Eyre and Spottiswoode, 1964.

Vali, Ferenc A. *Rift and Revolt in Hungary: Nationalism Versus Communism.* Cambridge, Mass.: Harvard Univ. Press, 1961.

Vatchnadze, Georgui. *Antenny napravlenny na Vostok. Formy i metody imperialisticheskoy radiopropagandy na strany sotsializma* (The aerials are directed against the east. The forms and methods of imperialist radiopropaganda against socialist countries). 2d ed. Moscow: Politizdat, 1977.

————. *Les Médias sous Gorbatchev.* (The Media under Gorbachev). La Garenne-Colombes: Editions de l'Espace Européen, 1991.

Vitaliev, Vitali. *Dateline Freedom.* London: Hutchinson, 1991.

Walker, Andrew. *A Skyful of Freedom: 60 Years of the BBC World Service.* London: Broadside Books, 1992.

Wallis, Roger, and Stanley Baran. *The Known World of Broadcast News.* London: Routledge, 1990.

Ward, Frank, and Helen Koshits. "Radio Canada International and Broadcasting over the Iron Curtain." In *Western Broadcasting over the Iron Curtain,* edited by K. R. M. Short, 27–56. London: Croom Helm, 1986.

Warner, Geoffrey. "The Study of Cold War Origins." In *The End of the Cold War,* edited by David Armstrong and Erik Goldstein, 13–26. London: Frank Cass, 1990.

Wasburn, Philo C. *Broadcasting Propaganda: International Radio Broadcasting and the Construction of Political Reality.* Westport, Conn.: Praeger, 1992.

Wedgwood Benn, David. *From Glasnost to Freedom of Speech: Russian Openness and International Relations.* London: RIIA, 1992.

————. *Persuasion and Soviet Politics.* Oxford: Basil Blackwell, 1989.

West, N. *GCHQ: The Secret Wireless War, 1900–86.* London: Weidenfeld and Nicolson, 1986.

West, W. J. *The Larger Evils: Nineteen Eighty-Four: The Truth Behind the Satire.* Edinburgh: Canongate Press, 1982.

Wettig, G. *Broadcasting and Détente: Eastern Policies and the Implication for East-West Relations.* London: C. Hurst, 1977.

Whitton, John B. *Propaganda and the Cold War: A Princeton University Symposium.* Washington, D.C.: Public Affairs Press, 1963.

Willey, David. *God's Politician: John Paul at the Vatican.* London: Faber and Faber, 1992.

Wise, D., and T. Ross. *The Espionage Establishment.* London: Jonathan Cape, 1968.

Wood, James. *History of International Broadcasting.* London: Peter Peregrinus in association with the Science Museum, 1992.

Wood, Robert. *A World in Your Ear: The Broadcasting of an Era 1923–1964.* London: Macmillan, 1979.

Yakir, Pyotr. *A Childhood in Prison.* London: Macmillan, 1972.

Yakovlev, Nikolai. *CIA Target: The USSR.* Translated by Vic Schneierson and Dimitry Belyavsky. Moscow: Progress Publishers, 1984.

Yallop, David. *To the Ends of the Earth: The Hunt for the Jackal.* London: Jonathan Cape, 1993.

Yaroshenko, Vladimir. "Broadcasting in Russia." In *Broadcasting Around the World,* edited by W. E. McCavitt, 52–75. Blue Ridge Summit, Pa.: Tab Books, 1981.

———. *Chernyy efir: Podryvnaya propaganda v sisteme burzhuaznogo vneshnepoliticheskogo radioveshchaniya* (The black radio waves: Subversive propaganda in the bourgeois foreign-political radio system). Moscow: Iskusstvo, 1986.

Yergin, Daniel. *Shattered Peace: The Origins of the Cold War and the National Security State.* London: Andre Deutsch, 1978.

Young, John W. *Cold War Europe, 1945–1989: A Political History.* London: Edward Arnold, 1991.

Zeman, Z. A. B. *Nazi Propaganda.* London: Oxford Univ. Press, 1964.

Articles, Pamphlets, Scripts, Speeches and Papers

Adler, Kenneth Paul, Morris Janowitz, and Douglas Waples. "Competitive Broadcasting to Germany." A content analysis research report by the Committee on Communication, Univ. of Chicago, July 1950.

Ash, Timothy Garton. "Poland after Solidarity," quoting Bronislaw Geremek in a review of Geremek's book, *The Year 1989: Bronislaw Geremek Relates, Jacek Zakowski Asks, New York Review of Books,* June 13, 1991.

Bailey, George. "The Perception Mongers: Reflections on Soviet Propaganda." Occasional Paper 44, Institute for European Defence and Strategic Studies. London, 1990.

Beachcroft, T. O. "Calling All Nations." BBC pamphlet, n.d.

Beichman, Arnold. "The Story of Radio Free Europe," *National Review,* Nov. 2, 1984.

Bordeaux, Michael. "The Role of Religion in the Fall of Communism." Centre for Policy Studies, The Hugh Seton-Watson Memorial Lecture, London, Apr. 1992.

British Broadcasting Corporation. "British Broadcasting, A Bibliography." Pamphlet. 1958. Supplement, 1958–60.

————. "CIA: Berlin Cowboys." TV Program. June 24, 1992.

————. "The European Service of the BBC, 1938–1959." Pamphlet. Sept. 1959.

————. "Through the Iron Curtain: The BBC and the Cold War on the Air." *London Calling*. Supplement, Oct. 9, 1952.

Borra, Ranjan. "The Problem of Jamming in International Broadcasting." *Journal of Broadcasting* 11, no. 4 (Fall 1967).

Broadcasting. "VOA Modernization: Slow Going," Oct. 24, 1988, 61.

————. "Wick Legacy: Making a Difference," Nov. 7, 1988, 43–44.

Browne, Donald R. "The Voice of America: Policies and Problems." *Journalism Monographs of the Association for Education in Journalism* (AEJ), no. 43. Feb. 1976.

Buhl, Dieter. "Window to the West. How Television from the Federal Republic Influenced Events in East Germany." Discussion Paper D-5 of the Joan Shorenstein Barone Center on the Press, Politics, and Public Policy. Harvard Univ., John F. Kennedy School of Government, 1990.

Bumpus, B., and B. Skelt. "Seventy Years of International Broadcasting," *Communication and Society*, no. 14. Paris: UNESCO, 1985.

Cabasés, Félix Juan. "El servicio publico eclesial de Radio Vaticano (1967–1992)" (The ecclesiastical public service of Vatican Radio, 1967–92). Ph.D. diss., Basque Univ. 1994.

Columbia University, Bureau of Applied Social Research. "Listening to the Voice of America and Other Foreign Broadcasts" in Poland, Czechoslovakia, Hungary, Romania, and Bulgaria, plus a comparative report (6 reports total). New York: Columbia Univ., Oct. 1953, Jan. 1954.

Cummings, Richard H. "Bulgaria: Code Name 'Piccadilly'—The Murder of Georgi Markov." *Intelligence*, no. 28. Internet, no pagination, Jan. 8, 1996.

Draper, Theodore. "A New History of the Velvet Revolution." *New York Review of Books*, Jan. 14, 1993, 14–20.

Economist. "Think Small," Aug. 6, 1977.

————. "Truth Is in the Air," June 6, 1987.

Eyal, Jonathan. "Recent Developments in the Jamming of Western Radio Stations Broadcasting to the USSR and Eastern Europe." *Radio Liberty Research Report*, Nov. 7, 1986.

Foreign and Commonwealth Office (FCO) Library and Records Department Historians. "IRD, Origins and Establishment of the Foreign Office Information Research Department, 1946–48." London: FCO, Aug. 1995.

Free Europe Committee. "The Revolt in Hungary: A Documentary Chronology of Events Based Exclusively on Internal Broadcasts by Central and Provincial Radios Oct. 23, 1956–Nov. 4, 1956." New York, n.d.

Guback, Thomas H., and Steven P. Hill. "The Beginnings of Soviet Broadcasting and the Role of V. I. Lenin." *Journalism Monographs of the AEJ*, no. 26, Dec. 1972.

Haley, William. "Broadcasting as an International Force." Speech, Univ. of Nottingham, Dec. 1, 1950.

Harries, Owen. "The Cold War and the Intellectuals." *Commentary* 92, no. 4 (Oct. 1991): 13–20.

Hollander, Gayle Durham. "Recent Developments in Soviet Radio and Television Reporting. *Public Opinion Quarterly* 31, no. 3 (1967): 359–69.

Human Events, "Capital Briefs," Mar. 2, 1974.

Institute of Communications Research, "Comparison of the English Language Services of the Voice of America, the British Broadcasting Corporation, Radio Moscow, from Broadcasts during December 1953. *Urbana*, Univ. of Illinois, July 1954.

J. A. [pseud.] "Radio in the Cold War." *World Today* 10, no. 6 (June 1954): 245–54.

Kruh, Louis. "Stimson, The Black Chamber and the 'Gentleman's Mail' Quote." *Cryptologia* 12, no. 2 (Apr. 1988): 65–80.

Latey, Maurice. "Broadcasting to the USSR and Eastern Europe." BBC lunch-time lecture, Nov. 11, 1964.

———. "The End of Communist Jamming." *Ariel*, Aug. 1964.

Leich, John Foster. "Great Expectations: The National Councils in Exile, 1950–60." Paper, Dec. 1, 1988. Author's collection.

Lippmann, Walter. "Why the Voice of America Should Be Abolished." *Readers Digest*, Aug. 1953, 41–43.

Lodeesen, Jon. "Radio Liberty (Munich): Foundations for a History." *Historical Journal of Film, Radio and Television* 6, no. 2 (1986): 197–210.

Mansell, Gerard. "Broadcasting to the World: Forty Years of the BBC External Services." Pamphlet. Jan. 1973.

Marchio, James David. "Rhetoric and Reality: The Eisenhower Administration and Unrest in Eastern Europe, 1953–1959." Ph.D. diss., American Univ., 1990.

Marx, Karl. "Debates on Freedom of the Press and Publication of Proceedings of the Assembly of the States." In Karl Marx and Frederick Engels, *Collected Works*, vol. 1, *Karl Marx: 1835–43*, 167–68. New York: International Publishers, 1975.

Monahan, James. "Broadcasting to Europe." BBC lunch-time lecture, Oct. 9, 1963.

Muggeridge, Douglas. "The New War of the Airwaves." BBC Pamphlet. Speech. Apr. 14, 1983.

Mytton, Graham, and Carol Forrester. "Audiences for International Radio Broadcasts." *European Journal of Communication* 3, no. 4 (Dec. 1988): 457–81.

Nicolson, Harold. "The British Council, 1934–1955." In *Twenty-first Anniversary Report of the British Council*. London: The British Council, 1955.

Ostermann, Christian F. "The United States, The East German Uprising of 1953, and the Limits of Rollback." Working paper, no. 11, Cold War International History Project, Woodrow Wilson International Center for Scholars, Washington, D.C., Dec. 1994.

O'Sullivan, Maggi. "Death on the Waterloo Bridge." *London Portrait* (May 1990): 123–25.

Radio France Internationale. "Radio France International 1931–92: Aux vents de l'histoire." (Radio France Internationale 1931–92: On the winds of history). Paris: Apr. 1993.

Rodnick, David. "Through the Iron Curtain." Supplement to *London Calling*, Aug. 28, 1952.

Rogers, Rosemarie S. "The Soviet Audience: How It Uses the Mass Media." Ph.D. diss., Massachusetts Institute of Technology, 1967.

Salvia, Anthony T. "Poland's Walesa Addresses RFE/RL Fund Conference." *Shortwaves*, Nov. 1989, 1.

Schoepflin, George. "The End of Communism in Eastern Europe." *International Affairs* 66, no. 1 (Jan. 1990): 3–16.

Semelin, Jacques. "Communication et Résistance: Les radios occidentales comme vecteur d'ouverture à l'est." (Communication and resistance: Western radios as the vector for the opening to the east). Paris: Réseaux no 53, CNET, 9–24, June 1992.

Shakespeare, Frank. "A Study of the Western Media Strategies towards Eastern Europe and Their Implications for Europe's Future." Paper, Harvard Univ., June 1988.

———. "Who's Winning the Propaganda War?" *U.S. News and World Report*, May 1, 1972.

Shanor, Donald. "The New Voice of Radio Free Europe." Research Paper. Preliminary. Columbia School of Journalism. Feb. 1968.

Simpson, John. "How the KGB Freed Europe." *Spectator*, Nov. 5, 1994, 11–12.

Smith, Lyn. "Covert British Propaganda: The Information Research Department: 1947–77." *Millennium: Journal of International Studies*. 9, no. 1 (1980): 67–83.

Trethowan, Sir Ian. "The BBC and International Broadcasting." Lecture, London, Feb. 2, 1981.

U.S. Information Agency. "Four Decades of Broadcasting, RIAS Berlin, 1946–1986." Bonn, 1986.

Voronitsyn, Sergei. "Latest Soviet Efforts to Counter the Influence of Foreign Radio Broadcasts." *Radio Liberty Research Report*, July 5, 1982.

Wedgwood Benn, David. Summary and analysis of "The BBC: History, Apparatus, Methods of Radio Propaganda" by Vladimir Artyomov and Vladimir Semyonov (Moscow, 1979). *Historical Journal of Film, Radio, and Television* 4, no. 1 (1984), 73–89.

Public Reports

Board for International Broadcasting (BIB), *annual reports* RFE/RL.

British Broadcasting Corporation (BBC), *annual reports/handbooks*, WAC.

U.K. BBC Licence and Agreement Cmd. 6975 (1946); 8579 (1952); 2236 (1963); 4095 (1969); 8233 (1981).

U.K. *Hansard Parliamentary Debates*, London, 1945–.

U.K. National Audit Office. "Management of the BBC World Services," Report by the Comptroller and Auditor General. London: HMSO, June 2, 1992.

U.K. Select Committee on Estimates, 1951–52.

U.K. Summary of the Report of the Independent Committee of Enquiry into the Overseas Information Services, Cmd. 9138 (1954).

U.K. White Paper on Broadcasting, Cmd. 6852 (1946).

U.S. Congress, *Congressional Record*, Washington, D.C., 1945–.

U.S. Congress, House of Representatives Fourteenth Immediate Report. "Investigation of the State Department Voice of America Broadcasts." House Report No. 2350, 80th Congress, 2d. sess. Washington, D.C.: USGPO, 1948.

U.S. Congress, House of Representatives, Subcommittee of the Committee on Appropriations. Hearings on Department of State appropriations for 1952, 82d Congress, 1st sess.

U.S. Congress, Senate, Committee on Foreign Relations, Hearings on S.18 and S.1936, May 24, 1971. 92d Cong. 1st sess.

U.S. Congress, Senate, Committee on Foreign Relations. "U.S. Information Service in Europe, Implementation by the Department of State (as of 1/49) of the Recommendations Contained in the Reports of the Committee of Foreign Relations (Smith-Mundt Congressional Group), January 1948." Feb. 1949.

U.S. Congress, Senate, Executive Sessions of Foreign Relations Committee. Vol. 18, 89th Cong., 2d sess., 1966.

U.S. Congress, Senate, Foreign Relations Subcommittee, Hearings on S. Res. 243, A Resolution Favoring an Expanded International Information and Education Program. 81st Cong., 2d sess., July 5, 6, 7, 1950.

U.S. Congress, Senate, Report No. 811 to accompany H. R. 3342. "Promoting the Better Understanding of the United States among the Peoples of the World and to Strengthen Cooperative International Relations." 80th Cong., 2d sess. Washington, D.C.: USGPO, Jan. 7, 1948.

U.S. Congress, Senate, Select Committee to Study Government Operations with Respect to Intelligence Activities, Supp. Staff Reports Book 4, 94th Cong., 2d sess., Apr. 23, 1976.

U.S. Congressional Research Service. "Radio Free Europe—A Survey and Analysis," by James R. Price, Mar. 22, 1972.

U.S. Congressional Research Service. "Radio Liberty— A Study of its Origins, Structure, Policy, Programming and Effectiveness," by Joseph G. Whelan, Mar. 22, 1972.

U.S. Presidential Study Commission on International Broadcasting (Eisenhower Commission). *The Right to Know.* Washington, D.C.: USGPO 1973.

Voice of America (VOA), *Annual Reports*, USIA.

Interviews

Antonow, Michail. By author. Cologne, Germany. July 7, 1994.

Bonner, Elena. By author. Montreal, Canada. Sept. 9, 1992.

Borgomeo, Pasquale. By author. Washington, D.C. Nov. 6, 1990. Rome, Italy. July 5, 1996.

Braden, Thomas. By Sig Mickelson by telephone. Tape recording. May 6, 1982.

Cabasés, Félix Juan. By author. Rome, Italy. July 3, 1996.

Chrudinak, Alajos. By author. Budapest, Hungary. Jan. 18, 1990.

Evans, Robert. By author. London, England. Feb. 27, 1991.

Fraenkel, Peter. By author. London, England. Mar. 9, 1994.

Gillette, Robert. By author. Munich, Germany. June 8, 1993.

Goodpaster, Andrew J. By Thomas Soapes. Oct. 11, 1977.

Griffith, William. By author. Munich, Germany. June 8, 1993.

Hargreaves, Terry. By author. Montreal, Canada. Sept. 9, 1992.

Helms, Richard. By author. Washington, D.C. Sept. 28, 1993.

Johnson, Peter. By author. London, England. May 6, 1996.

Kirsch, Botho. By author. Cologne, Germany. July 7, 1994.

Korotich, Vitalay. By author and Robert Evans. Moscow, Russia. June 11, 1991.

Kravchenko, Leonid. By author and Robert Evans. Tape recording. Moscow, Russia. June 11, 1991.

Mansell, Gerard. By author. London, England, May 17, 1995.

Marsh, William W. By author. Munich, Germany. June 11, 1993.

Mater, Gene. By author. Washington, D.C. Oct. 17, 1990.

Mayhew, Christopher. By author. London, England. Feb. 4, 1994.

McCargar, James. By author. Washington, D.C. Oct. 18, 1990.

Meyer, Cord. By author. Washington, D.C. Oct. 7, 1992. By telephone Oct. 4, 1993.

Miall, Leonard. By author. London, England. Feb. 16, 1993.

Mink, Andras. By Duncan Shiels. Budapest, Hungary. Nov. 22, 1996.

Nowak, Jan. By author. Washington, D.C. Oct. 19, 1990. Budapest, Hungary. Sept. 29, 1996.

Palos, Tamas. By author. Budapest, Hungary. Jan. 18, 1990.

Ruzhnikov, Vsevolod N. By author and Robert Evans. Tape recording. Moscow, Russia. June 13, 1991.

Ruppert, Helmut S. By author. Cologne, Germany. July 7, 1994.

Rynkiewicz, Lech. By author. Rome, Italy. July 4, 1996.

Seton-Watson, Mary. By author. London, England. Aug. 8, 1991.

Szecsko, Tamas. By author. Budapest, Hungary. May 15, 1992.

Taylor, David. By author. Munich, Germany. June 19, 1990.

Urban, George. By author. Brighton, England. Mar. 22, 1991.

Vatchnadze, Georgiu. By author and Robert Evans. Tape recording. Moscow, Russia. June 10, 1991.

Walter, Ralph. By author. Munich, Germany. June 21, 1990.

Washburn, Abbott. By author. Washington, D.C. Nov. 2, 1992.

Washburn, Wanda (née Allender). By author. Washington, D.C. Nov. 2, 1992.

Wedgwood Benn, David. By author. London, England. Jan. 15, 1996.

Weirich, Dieter. By author. Cologne, Germany. July 7, 1994.

Wheeler, Charles. By author. London, England. May 2, 1996.

White, Robert A. By author. Rome, Italy. July 6, 1996.

Wittner, Maria. By author and Duncan Shiels. Budapest, Hungary. Sept. 28, 1996.

Yushkiavitshus, Henrikas. Paris, France. Sept. 29, 1995.

ACKNOWLEDGMENTS

THIS BOOK would not have been possible without the help of those listed below:

Alison Adams, Secretary.

Richard Aldrich, Editor of *British Intelligence Strategy and the Cold War.*

Mohsin Ali, Former Diplomatic Editor, Reuters.

Rolf Anger, Head, Europe Programme, DW.

Michail Antonow, Head, Bulgarian Programme, DW.

Martin Bachstein, Broadcast Analysis Department, RFE/RL.

Peter Bale, Chief Correspondent, Reuters, Romania.

Susanne Bangha, Head, Czech and Slovak Programmes, DW.

Sandor Barcs, former General Director of the Hungarian News Agency, MTI, former President of Hungarian Radio.

Peter Baumgartner, former Deputy Director, Public Affairs, RFE/RL.

Myron Belkind, Managing Director, AP Ltd.

Richard G. Bird, former Public Affairs Specialist, RFE/RL.

Elena Bonner, author of *Alone Together* and widow of Academician Sakharov.

Ludmilla Bonushkina, Researcher, Moscow.

Pasquale Borgomeo, Director-General, Vatican Radio.

Lord Asa Briggs, author of *The History of Broadcasting in the United Kingdom.*

Michal Broniatowski, former Reuter Correspondent, Warsaw.

Anthony Cave Brown, author of *The Last Hero, Wild Bill Donovan.*

Donald R. Browne, author of *International Radio Broadcasting.*

Malcolm Byrne, Director of Analysis, the National Security Archive, Washington, D.C.

Félix Juan Cabasés, Gregorian University, Rome.

Richard W. Carlson, former Director, VOA.

David Chipp, former Editor-in-Chief, the Press Association.

Alajos Chrudinak, Editor-in-Chief, Foreign Policy and Documentary Films Department, Hungarian Television.

Mario Corti, Deputy Director, Information Resources Department, RFE/RL.

Richard H. Cummings, former Director of Security, RFE/RL.

Sapiyat Dakhshukova, Interpreter, Moscow University.

Sherwood Demitz, VOA, Washington, D.C.

Wilson P. Dizard, author of *The Strategy of Truth.*

Gerd R. von Doemming, former Chief, Eurasian Division, VOA.

Helmut Drueck, Intendant, RIAS Berlin.

Yermolina Dzhana, Interpreter, Moscow University.

Kim Andrew Elliott, Audience Research Officer, VOA.

Frank Ellis, Lecturer, Department of Russian and Slavonic Studies, University of Leeds.

Jon Elliston, Researcher, Washington, D.C.

Robert Elphick, former Chief Correspondent, Reuters, Moscow.

Robert Evans, former Chief Representative, Soviet Union, Reuters.

Dariusz Fikus, Editor-in-Chief, *Rzeczpospolita*, Warsaw.

Peter Fraenkel, former Controller, European Services, BBC External Services.

John Fruehwirth, editor, Syracuse University Press.

Gregory Garland, Board for International Broadcasting.

Michael Gartner, former President, NBC News.

Patricia Gate-Lynch, Director of Public Affairs, RFE/RL, Washington, D.C.

Ilona Gazdag, Reuters, Budapest.

David G. Gibson, Media Research Specialist, USIA.

Robert Gillette, Director, RFE.

Bruce Gregory, Staff Director, United States Advisory Commission on Public Diplomacy.

William Griffith, former Political Adviser, RFE.

Julian Hale, author of *Radio Power.*

James Hall, Professor, Radio, Television, Film, University of Southern Mississippi.

Terry Hargreaves, Executive Director, Radio Canada International.

Andras B. Hegedus, Institute for the History of the 1956 Hungarian Revolution, Budapest.

Alan Heil, Deputy Chief of Programming, VOA.

Richard Helms, former Director of the CIA.

Paul Henze, former Deputy Political Adviser, RFE.

Peter Herrmann, Deputy Director, Media and Opinion Research Department, RFE/RL.

James Hershberg, Coordinator Cold War History Project, The Woodrow Wilson Center, Washington, D.C.

Paul Holmes, Senior Correspondent, Reuters, Italy.

John Howkins, former Executive Director, International Institute of Communications.

Karol Jakubowicz, Chairman of the Supervisory Board, Polish Television.

Peter Johnson, former BBC Correspondent.

Ross Johnson, former Director, RL.

Damian Kalbarczyk, Deputy Editor, *Respublica*, Warsaw.

Jacquie Kavanagh, Written Archivist, BBC.

Stephen Kettle, former Prague Correspondent, Reuters.

Botho Kirsch, former Head, East European Programmes, DW.

Kevin Klose, President, RFE/RL.

Tom C. Korologos, Chairman, United States Advisory Commission on Public Diplomacy.

Vitaly Korotich, former Editor, *Ogonyok.*

William H. Kratch, Director, New York Programming Center, RFE/RL.

Leonid Kravchenko, former Chairman, All-Union State Television and Radio Broadcasting Company, Moscow.

Jan Krcmar, former Prague Correspondent, Reuters.

Istvan Kulcsar, Diplomatic Correspondent, Hungarian Radio.

André Larquie, Président-Directeur Général, Radio France Internationale.

Paul Lendvai, author of *The Bureaucracy of Truth.*

David Lewis, former Senior Budapest Correspondent, Reuters.

Jon Lodeesen, former Head of Russian Service, RFE/RL.

Jan Lopatka, Reporter, Reuters, Prague.

Dasha Lotareva, Researcher, Moscow.

W. Scott Lucas, author of *Divided We Stand.*

James McCargar, former European Director, Political Programs, Free Europe Committee.

Colin McIntyre, former Chief Correspondent, Austria and Eastern Europe, Reuters.

Eileen Mahoney, Professor, National Center for Communication Studies, George Washington University.

Martin Manning, Archivist, USIA.

Gerard Mansell, former Managing Director, External Services, BBC, and author of *Let Truth Be Told.*

Michael R. Marchetti, Vice-president of Finance, Treasurer, and Comptroller, RFE/RL, Washington, D.C.

William W. Marsh, former President, RFE/RL.

Gene Mater, former News Director, RFE.

Corinne Mauzac, Reuters, Moscow.

Lord Mayhew, former Parliamentary Under Secretary of State for Foreign Affairs.

Cord Meyer, former CIA executive in charge of RFE and RL and author of *Facing Reality.*

Leonard Miall, former Chief Washington Correspondent, BBC, and Member of the British Political Warfare Mission to U.S.

Sig Mickelson, former President, RFE/RL and author of *America's Other Voice.*

Andras Mink, Research Fellow, Open Society Archives, Budapest.

David Morton, Head of Russian and Ukrainian Services, BBC World Service.

Graham Mytton, Head, Audience Research & Correspondence, BBC World Service.

Lyle Nelson, Thomas More Storke Professor of Communication Emeritus, Stanford University.

Eva Neumann-Wehrke, Marketing Assistant, DW.

Mitya New, Chief Correspondent, Reuters, Hungary.

Juhani Niinisto, Head, External Broadcasting, Finnish Broadcasting Company.

Jan Nowak, former Head of Polish Service, RFE.

Walter Nutz, former Head, Media Research, DW.

Joseph D. O'Connell, Director, Office of External Affairs, VOA.

Elzbieta Olechowska, Manager, Europe Service, Radio Canada International.

Daniel Ollivier, Director of Development and Communication, Radio France Internationale.

Michael J. O'Neill, author of *The Roar of the Crowd*.

John Owston, Librarian, World Service, BBC.

Michael Palmer, Professor, Department of Sciences and Techniques of Expression and Communication, Sorbonne Nouvelle, Paris.

Tamas Palos, Chief Editor, *Frenczy Europress* Budapest and former Head of the Hungarian News Agency, MTI.

Peter J. Parish, Director, Institute of United States Studies, Institute of Historical Research, University of London.

Stuart Parrott, former London Bureau Chief, RFE/RL.

Eugene R. Parta, Director, Media & Opinion Research Department, RFE/RL.

Hayden B. Peake, Adjunct Professor of History and Intelligence Studies, Defense Intelligence College, Washington, D.C.

Gene Pell, former President, RFE/RL.

Mark Pomar, former Executive Director, Board for International Broadcasting.

A. Russell Poole, former Vice-President, Management, RFE/RL.

Philip Pullella, Reuters Vatican Correspondent.

Alexander Putko, former Commentator, Radio Moscow.

John Ranelagh, author of *The Agency, The Rise and Decline of the CIA*.

Donald Read, author of *Reuters, The Power of News*.

Iwanna I. Rebet, Chief Librarian, RFE/RL.

Norman Reddaway, former Head of International Research Department, Foreign Office.

Robert Redlich, former Director, Public Affairs, RFE/RL.

James V. Risser, Director, John S. Knight Fellowships, Department of Communication, Stanford University.

Tibor Ritter, First Deputy President, Hungarian Radio and Deputy Head of Party Agitation and Propaganda Department 1970–86.

Guy Robert, Chef du Service de l'Auditoire et de la Prospective, Radio France Internationale.

Frank Roberts, former British Ambassador, Moscow.

Marjorie Robertson, Researcher, Washington D.C.

Helmut S. Ruppert, Deputy Head, German Programme, DW.

Vsevolod N. Ruzhnikov, Lecturer in the History of Soviet Radio, Moscow University.

Lech Rynkiewicz, Director of Promotion and Development, Vatican Radio.

Dennis Savage, Researcher, London.

Karol Sawicki, Director, News Programming, TV/Radio, Warsaw.

Nicholas B. Scheetz, Manuscripts Librarian, Georgetown University.

Patrick Seale, coauthor of *Philby*.

Mary Seton-Watson, former Head of Russian Service, External Services, BBC.

Duncan Shiels, Reuter Correspondent, Budapest.

K.R.M. Short, Editor of *Western Broadcasting Over the Iron Curtain*.

Terry B. Shroeder, former Director, Public Affairs, RFE/RL.

Holly Cowan Shulman, author of *The Voice of America, Propaganda and Democracy, 1941–1945.*

Marcia Slonim, former Russian dissident and World Service, BBC, Moscow.

Pat Spencer, Researcher, London.

David Stamp, Chief Correspondent, Czech and Slovak Republics, Reuters.

David Storey, former Chief Correspondent, Austria and Eastern Europe, Reuters.

Tamas Szecsko, General Secretary, International Association for Mass Communication Research, Budapest.

Andrew Tarnowski, former Senior Warsaw Correspondent, Reuters.

John E. Taylor, Military Reference Branch, National Archives, Washington, D.C.

David Taylor, Research Department, RFE/RL.

Justine Taylor, former Archivist, Reuter History Project.

Michael Tracey, author of *A Variety of Lives, A Biography of Sir Hugh Greene.*

Karl-Heinz Treiss, former Head, Monitoring Service, DW.

John Tusa, former Managing Director, World Service, BBC, and author of *Conversations with the World.*

Chase Untermeyer, former Director, VOA.

George Urban, former Director, RFE and author of *The Nineteen Days.*

Emil Varadi, Correspondent, Reuters, Budapest.

Georgui Vatchnadze, author of *The Aerials are Directed Against the East.*

Peter Voth, Researcher, Washington, D.C.

Ralph Walter, former Director, RFE.

Wesley K. Wark, Professor, Department of History, University of Toronto.

Abbott Washburn, former Director, Crusade for Freedom and former Deputy Director, USIA.

Wanda Washburn, former secretary to Director, Crusade for Freedom.

David Wedgwood Benn, former head of Yugoslav Section, BBC World Service.

Sidney Weiland, former Diplomatic Editor, Reuters.

Dieter Weirich, Director-General, DW.

Charles Wheeler, BBC Correspondent.

Robert A. White, the Center for Interdisciplinary Study of Communications, Gregorian University, Rome.

Graham Williams, Editor, Continental Europe, Reuters.

Mark Wood, Editor-in-Chief, Reuters.

Henrikas Yushkiavitshus, former Vice-Chairman, USSR State Television and Radio Committee.

Yassen N. Zassoursky, Dean, Faculty of Journalism, Moscow University and co-editor of *Beyond the Cold War.*

INDEX

ABC, 171, 176–77

Abshire, David M., 144, 148

Acheson, Dean, 40, 59

Acquired immunodeficiency syndrome (AIDS), 166

Adamovich, Oleg, 195

Adenauer, Konrad, 47, 73

Afghanistan, 163, 166

Agence France Presse (AFP), 109

Aims: of BBC, 13, 131; of Free Europe Committee Inc., 39; of RFE, 44–45; of RL, 58; of VOA, 35

Albania: audience research about, 133; BBC service to, 61, 132; RFE service to, 49; Vatican Radio service to, 107; VOA service to, 59

Alexeyeva, Ludmilla, 122–23

Allen, George V., 35, 37, 93, 94, 101, 102

Allender, Wanda, 48–49

Allgemeiner Deutscher Nachricht- endienst (ADN), 186–87

Alliluyeva, Svetlana, 106

Altschul, Frank, 24, 39, 41, 44, 49–50, 51, 53–54, 55

Amalrik, Andrei, 123, 125, 152

Ambler, Dennis, 33–34

American Committee for Liberation from Bolshevism (AMCOMLIB), 126

American Committee for the Freedom of the Peoples of the USSR (AMCOMLIB), 56–58, 126

American Council on Private International Communications (ACPIC), 143

American Society of Newspaper Editors (ASNE), 17

Andropov, Yuri, 72, 167

Antiradio measures 6–7. *See also* Jamming

Antisemitism, 52, 53

Antonow, Michail, 115

Arbatov, Georgiy, 139

Arbeitsgemeinschaft der oeffentlich- rechtlichen Rundfunkanstalten der Bundesrepublik Deutschland (ARD), 114, 183

Armenia, 57–58, 59; Vatican Radio service to, 107

Arrogance of Power, The (Fulbright), 142

Artyomov, Vladimir, 179; and Vladimir Semyonov, 152–53

Assassination, xii, 99, 153–56

Associated Press (AP), 17, 18, 109, 187

Attacks on staff of Western radios, 170–172. *See also* Assassination

Attlee, Clement, 14, 26, 27

Audience research: into Albanian audience, 133; at Brussels World Fair, 135; by BBC, 191–92; into Bulgarian audience, 63, 66, 133, 190; into Czechoslovak audience, 63, 132–34, 190–91; into East European audience, 62–66, 167, 190–92; into East German audience, 63, 133, 184, 192; into Hungarian audience, 63, 78–79, 132–34, 190, 192; by Hungary, 192; into impact of broadcasts, 65, 78–79, 132, 136; into Latvian audience, 63; and listener- ship, 132–36; and mail, 133, 191; by Poland, 192; into Polish audience, 63, 132–34, 190–92; by RFE, 78–79, 132–33, 190–91; by RL, 132, 135, 193–94; into Romanian audience, 63, 66, 133, 190–91; into Soviet audience, 62, 63, 134–36, 163–64, 193–94; by Soviet Union, 122; by USIA, 62–66, 78–79, 133–36, 194; by VOA, 191

Aurora, 1

United States Voice of America
(VOA) (cont.)
Smith-Mundt Act, 35; and Soviet
1991 coup, 193, 195–96; Soviet
attacks on, 119, 121, 178; and Soviet
Union services, 59, 84, 98, 149, 163–
64, 175, 178; staff of, 59, 101, 175;
Tatar service of, 59, 84; and
television, 178; and tone of
broadcasts after beginnings of
détente, 93–94, 101, 103, 175; and
tone of broadcasts in early cold war,
16–17, 36–37, 59, 84–85, 129–30;
transmitters of, 60, 175; tributes to,
191; and truth, 6, 38; Turkestani
service of, 59, 84; Ukrainian service
of, 59, 175; and United States
Information and Educational
Exchange Act of 1948 P.L.402 (see
above Smith-Mundt Act); and USIA
conflicts, 103, 129; Uzbek service of,
175; WORLDNET, 178
Urban, George, 173–74
Urban, Jerzy, 158
U.S. News and World Report, 18
Uzbekistan, 175

Vasarhelyi, Miklos, 190
Vatchnadze, Georgui, 160, 161
Vatican Radio, 107–9; Albanian service
of, 107; Armenian service of, 107;
Bulgarian service of, 107;
Byelorussian service of, 107;
Czechoslovakia services of, 107, 108;
German service of, 107; Hungarian
service of, 107; inauguration of, 3;
and Jesuits, 3; Latvian service of,
107; Lithuanian service of, 107;
Polish service of, 107, 157; and
propaganda, 107; Romanian service
of, 107; Russian service of, 107;
Slovak service of, 107; Ukrainian
service of, 107, 109; Yugoslavia
services of, 107
View from the Lenin Hills, The (Taubman),
121
Vlasov, General, 57

Voice of America. See United States Voice
of America (VOA)
Vremya, 194
Vyshinsky, Andrei, 25–26

Walentynowicz, Anna, 159
Walesa, Lech, 159, 160, 181
Wallace, Mike, 128
Walter, Ralph, 100, 174
Warner, Christopher, 28
Washburn, Abbott, 47
Washington Post: on CIA funding of
anticommunist programs, 127–
29; on Romanian Revolution,
187, 189
Weirich, Dieter, 115
Western Radios: attacks on staff of,
98–99; 113, 170–72 (see also
Assassination); comparative
popularity of, 66; and consumer
goods, xiv, 189; and counselling
restraint, xiv, 70–71; and cultural
links, 189; and dissidents, 122–26,
188; manipulation of, 184–88; and
music, 65; and music, popular, xiv;
programming of, xiv, 36–37, 119–20;
Soviet attacks on, 121; transcripts of,
161; and truth, xiii; 121, 131, 152–53.
See also specific Radio
Western way of life, xiii, xiv
West European Advisory Committee of
RFE (WEAC), 145
West Germany. See Germany, Federal
Republic of
Wheeler, Charles, 33, 34
Whitley, Oliver, 150–51
Wick, Charles Z., 176–77
Wiles, Peter, 104–5
Wisner, Frank G., 42, 52, 56, 80
Wittner, Maria, 82–83
WORLDNET, 178
World War II, 6–9

Yakolev, Alexandr, 168
Yakovlev, Yegor, 161–62, 170
Yallop, David, 171